VISUAL QUICKPRO GUIDE

FLASH CS4 PROFESSIONAL ADVANCED

FOR WINDOWS AND MACINTOSH

Russell Chun

 Peachpit Press

Visual QuickPro Guide

Flash CS4 Professional Advanced for Windows and Macintosh
Russell Chun

Peachpit Press
1249 Eighth Street
Berkeley, CA 94710
510/524-2178
510/524-2221 (fax)

Find us on the Web at: www.peachpit.com
To report errors, please send a note to: errata@peachpit.com
Peachpit Press is a division of Pearson Education.

Editor: Rebecca Gulick
Copy Editor: Anne Marie Walker
Proofreader: Liz Welch
Production Coordinator: Myrna Vladic
Compositor: Jerry Ballew
Indexer: Valerie Haynes Perry
Technical Reviewer: H. Paul Robertson
Cover Design: Peachpit Press

Notice of Rights

Notice of Liability

Trademarks

ISBN 13: 978-0-321-57350-6
ISBN 10: 0-321-57350-1

9 8 7 6 5 4 3 2 1

Printed and bound in the United States of America

Thank you

Bringing this book to you, as always, took the efforts of a team, to which I owe my gratitude. I want to thank my editor, Anne Marie Walker, project editor, Rebecca Gulick, production coordinator, Myrna Vladic, and compositor, Jerry Ballew. I would like to especially thank Paul Robertson, whose keen insight and detailed technical review were invaluable.

Finally, I want to thank readers like you. When I first discovered Flash, it fired up my imagination and challenged me to see how I could use the technology to deliver richer and more immersive content. I hope this book helps to inspire you to use Flash in the same way.

—*Russell Chun*

TABLE OF CONTENTS

Introduction

Adobe Flash CS4 Professional is one of the hottest technologies on the Web today. Leading corporate Web sites use its streamlined graphics to communicate their brands, major motion picture studios promote theatrical releases with Flash movies, and online news and educational sites provide rich user experiences with Flash interactivity.

As a vector-based animation and authoring application, Flash is ideal for creating high-impact, low-bandwidth Web sites incorporating animation, text, video, sound, and database integration. With robust support for complex interactivity and server-side communication, Flash is increasingly the solution for developing Internet applications as well. From designer to programmer, Flash has become the tool of choice for delivering dynamic content across various browsers and platforms.

As the popularity of Flash increases, so does the demand for designers and developers who know how to tap its power. This book is designed to help you meet that challenge. Learn how to build complex animations; integrate sophisticated interfaces and navigation schemes; and dynamically control graphics, video, sound, and text. Experiment with the techniques discussed in this book to create the compelling media that Flash makes possible. It's not an exaggeration to say that Flash is revolutionizing the Web. This book will help you be a part of that revolution—so boot up your computer and get started.

Who Should Use This Book

This book is for designers, animators, and developers who want to take their Flash skills to the next level. You've already mastered the basics of tweening and are ready to move on to more complex tasks, such as importing video, masking, controlling dynamic sound, or detecting collisions between graphics on the Stage. You may be familiar with Flash CS3, but you are eager to explore the new animation features in CS4—the completely revamped motion tween model, inverse kinematics, and the support for 3D. You may not be a hard-core programmer, but you're ready to learn how ActionScript can control vector and bitmap graphics, sounds, and text. You want to integrate interactivity with your animations to create more responsive environments, to create complex user interface elements like pull-down menus, and to learn how Flash communicates with outside applications such as Web browsers. If this description fits, then this book is right for you.

This book explores the advanced aspects of Flash CS4 Professional and some of the key new features, so you should already be comfortable with the basic tools and commands for creating simple Flash movies. You should know how to create and modify shapes and text with the drawing tools and be able to create symbols. You should also know how to create a very simple motion tween in the new CS4 way and know how to work with shape tweens. You should know your way around the Flash interface: how to move from the Stage to symbol editing mode to the Timeline and how to manipulate layers and frames. You should also be familiar with importing and using bitmaps and sounds, and assigning basic actions to frames for navigation. To get up to speed, review the tutorials that come with the software, or pick up a copy of *Flash CS4 Professional for Windows and Macintosh: Visual QuickStart Guide* by Katherine Ulrich (Peachpit, 2008).

Goals of This Book

The aim of this book is to demonstrate the advanced features of Flash CS4 Professional through a logical approach, emphasizing how techniques are applied. You'll learn how techniques build on each other and how groups of techniques can be combined to solve a particular problem. Each example you work through puts another skill under your belt; by the end of this book, you'll be able to create sophisticated interactive Flash projects.

For example, creating a pull-down menu illustrates how simple elements—invisible buttons, event handlers, button-tracking options, and movie clips—come together to make more complex behaviors. Examples illustrate the practical application of techniques, and additional tips explain how to apply these techniques in other contexts.

How to use this book

The concepts in this book build on each other: The material at the end is more complex than that at the beginning. If you're familiar with some of the material, you can skip around to the subjects that interest you, but you'll find it most useful to learn the techniques in the order in which they appear.

As with other books in the Visual QuickPro Guide series, tasks are presented for you to do as you read about them, so that you can see how a technique is applied. Follow the step-by-step instructions, look at the figures, and try the tasks on your computer. You'll learn more by doing and by taking an active role in experimenting with these exercises. Many of the completed tasks are provided as FLA and SWF files on the companion Web site: Go to www.peachpit.com/flashcs4visualquickpro to download the sample files and study how they were made.

When code is presented, it is set apart in a different font. When a line of code is meant to be typed on a single line but is forced onto a second line in this book, you'll see a small arrow like this ($\rightarrow$) indicating the continuation of the code.

Tips follow the tasks to give you hints about how to use a shortcut, warnings about common mistakes, and suggestions about how techniques can be extended.

Occasionally, you'll see sidebars in gray boxes. Sidebars discuss related matters that aren't directly task oriented. They include interesting and useful concepts that can help you better understand how Flash works.

What's in this book

This book is organized into four parts:

◆ **Part I: Approaching Advanced Animation**

   This part covers advanced techniques for graphics and animation, including the new motion tween model and the Motion Editor, inverse kinematics, support for positioning objects in 3D space, and strategies for shape tweening, masking, and using digital video.

◆ **Part II: Interactivity**

   This part introduces ActionScript 3.0, the scripting language Flash uses to add interactivity to a movie. You'll learn the ways in which Flash can respond to input from the viewer and how you can create complex navigation schemes with multiple Timelines. You'll also see how Flash communicates with external files and applications such as Web browsers.

◆ **Part III: Transforming Graphics and Sound**

   This part demonstrates how to dynamically control the basic elements of any

Flash movie—its graphics and sound—through ActionScript.

◆ **Part IV: Working with Information**

   The last part focuses on how to retrieve, store, modify, and test information to create complex Flash environments that can respond to changing conditions.

◆ **Appendix: Keyboard Key Codes**

   The appendix gives you quick access to the key code values and matching keyboard constants for the keys on your keyboard.

What's on the companion Web site

Accompanying this book is a Web site at www.peachpit.com/flashcs4visualquickpro that contains nearly all the Flash source files for the tasks. You can download the files and see how each task was created, study the ActionScript, and use the ActionScript to do further experimentation. Sample media such as audio and video files are provided for your use. You'll also find a list of Web links to sites that are devoted to Flash and that showcase the latest Flash techniques and provide tutorials, articles, and advice.

Additional resources

Use the Web to your advantage. There is a thriving, active, international community of Flash developers; within it, you can share your frustrations, seek help, and show off your latest Flash masterpiece. Free forums and a significant number of Flash-related blogs exist for all levels of Flash users. Begin your search for Flash resources with the list of Web sites on the companion Web site and by choosing Help > Flash Help in the Flash application, which provides access to an online searchable ActionScript language reference and Flash manual.

GOALS OF THIS BOOK

What's New in Flash CS4 Professional

Whether you're a beginner or an advanced user, a designer or a programmer, a number of new features in Flash CS4 Professional will appeal to you. The following are just a few of the capabilities that make Flash CS4 Professional even more powerful, flexible, and easy to use.

New animation capabilities

Motion tweening will never be the same. Completely overhauled, animation is now object-based, which means tweens are applied to objects on the Stage rather than to keyframes on the Timeline. The new motion tween model provides direct manipulation of the path of an object's motion, independent control over every attribute of the object, and a powerful new panel, the Motion Editor, to visualize and manage each tween. You can now position and animate objects in real 3D space. Flash CS4 supports motion in the x, y, and z axes, which is bound to have you dizzy with possibilities, if not from the motion itself! Flash CS4 also introduces a new way to animate called inverse kinematics, which makes animating objects with joints quick and easy.

Support for state-of-the-art video

Adobe Video Encoder is now Adobe Media Encoder with support for the latest H.264 video codec. Use Adobe Video Encoder to manage all your media files and to correctly format videos to present them in stunning, true high-definition. The latest Flash player recognizes both the FLV video format and the latest F4V video format.

Expanded interactivity

ActionScript 3.0 has improved with powerful new language elements added that help you build richer and more interactive applications. Additional elements include classes that support the new motion tween model and inverse kinematics animation, and new properties that control an object's position and orientation in 3D space. There are new methods for drawing, new methods to dynamically generate sound, new methods that allow you to save and load files directly on a user's computer, and a whole slew of other language enhancements that expand the programming toolkit.

Part I: Approaching Advanced Animation

BUILDING COMPLEXITY

The key to creating complex animations in Flash is to build them from simpler parts. You should think of your Flash project as being a collection of simpler motions, just as the movement of a runner is essentially a collection of rotating limbs. Isolating individual components of a much larger, complicated motion allows you to treat each component with the most appropriate technique, simplifies the tweening, and gives you better control with more refined results.

To animate a runner, for example, you would first consider how to simplify the animation into separate motions. Animating the entire sequence at the same time would be impossible, because the many elements making up the motion change in different ways as they move. The rotation of her legs and arms can be created with different poses using inverse kinematics, a powerful new feature of Flash CS4. Her hair could be a shape tween that lets you show its flow, swing, and slight bouncing effect as she runs. And her entire body can move across the Stage as a motion tween.

Learning to combine different techniques and break animation into simpler parts not only solves difficult animation problems but also forces you to use multiple layers and think in smaller, independent components. By doing so, you set up the animation so that it's easy to manage now and revise later.

This chapter describes some advanced approaches to basic animation techniques such as motion tweening, shape tweening, and masking, and a few of the new features in Flash CS4 such as inverse kinematics and 3D.

Motion Tweening Strategies

Motion tweening lets you interpolate any of the instance properties of a symbol, such as its location, size, rotation, color, and transparency, as well as any filters that have been applied to the symbol instance. Because of its versatility, motion tweening can be applied to a variety of animation tasks, making it the foundation of most Flash projects. Because motion tweening deals with instance properties, it's a good idea to think of the technique in terms of instance tweening. Regardless of whether actual motion across the Stage is involved, changing instance properties through time requires motion tweening. Thinking of it as instance tweening will help you distinguish when and where to use motion tweening as opposed to shape tweening, inverse kinematics, or frame-by-frame animation.

The motion tween model

Flash CS4 Professional introduces a powerful new way to create motion tweens. If you are a long-time Flash user, it may take a little getting used to, but you'll be surprised at how much easier and flexible it is to apply motion tweens to symbol instances.

You should already know how to create a basic tween in Flash CS4. This book will help you move forward and understand tweening's more advanced features. Some key differences between the new motion tween model in Flash CS4 and the classic tween model in previous versions:

◆ Motion tweens are now object based, so tweens are applied directly to objects instead of keyframes. The target object of a motion tween can easily be swapped with a different instance.

◆ Motion tweens are separated on a special layer called a tween layer in a tween span. The tween span can be selected as a single object and moved, expanded and contracted to change its duration, or copied and pasted. Flash does not allow any drawing or other objects placed within a tween span.

◆ You have independent control over each property of the instance (position, scale, color effect, filter) and can change property values over time with curves in a new panel called the Motion Editor.

◆ The path of the motion is no longer on a separate guide layer but is part of the motion tween. The path can be directly manipulated with Bezier precision or freely scaled, skewed, rotated, or even replaced.

Figure 1.1 Right-click (Windows) or Ctrl-click (Mac) directly on the object you want to animate, and choose Create Motion Tween.

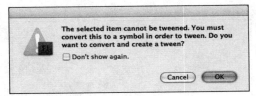

Figure 1.2 Motion tweens require that the object be either a symbol or text.

Figure 1.3 A Tween layer is reserved for motion tweening.

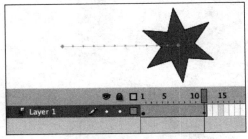

Figure 1.4 This instance of a star moves from left to right in a motion tween. The black triangle in the last frame of the tween span represents a keyframe for the new position.

To create a motion tween:

1. Right-click (Windows) or Ctrl-click (Mac) on an object on the Stage, and choose Create Motion Tween from the context menu that appears (**Figure 1.1**).

   Flash may ask to convert the selected object into a symbol for it to be tweened. Click OK (**Figure 1.2**).

   Flash automatically converts your selection to a symbol, which is saved in your Library. Flash also puts the symbol instance in a separate Tween layer and adds one second of frames so you can begin to animate the instance. Tween layers are distinguished by a special icon in front of the layer name, and the frames are tinted blue (**Figure 1.3**). Tween layers are reserved for motion tweens, and hence, no drawing is allowed on a Tween layer.

2. Move the playhead to a desired end point on the Tween layer.

3. Move the instance to a different position on the Stage.

   Flash smoothly animates the change in positions (**Figure 1.4**).

✔ Tip

■ If you are more comfortable working with the older way of animating, you can do so by relying on the Classic Tween option. Select the first keyframe containing your instance, and then choose Insert > Classic Tween. However, the new features, such as the Motion Editor, are not available for classic tweens.

Editing the path of the motion

The path that an instance moves during a motion tween is graphically shown as a stroke on the Stage. Dots along the path indicate the instance's position at each frame (**Figure 1.5**). You can directly manipulate the path with a variety of tools, including the Selection tool, the Subselection tool, the Delete Anchor Point tool, the Convert Anchor Point tool, or the Free Transform tool.

To change the location of the path:

1. Click on the motion path with the Selection tool.

   The motion path becomes highlighted indicating that the whole path is selected.

2. Click and drag the motion path to a new location on the Stage (**Figure 1.6**).

   The motion path is moved. The motion tween proceeds from its new location.

   or

   Select the motion path and change the X and Y values in the Property inspector under Path (**Figure 1.7**).

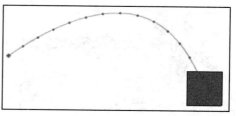

Figure 1.5 The curved line on the Stage represents the path of motion of an object. The dots on the line represent the location of the object at each frame during the tween span.

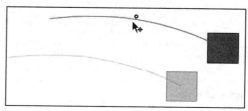

Figure 1.6 Move the path to move the location of the motion tween.

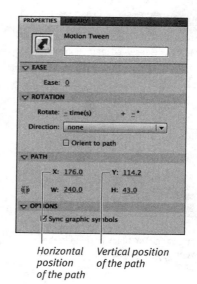

Horizontal position of the path

Vertical position of the path

Figure 1.7 Change the X and Y values in the Property inspector to change the location of the motion tween.

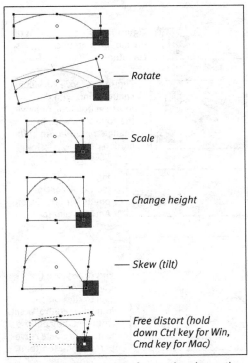

— Rotate

— Scale

— Change height

— Skew (tilt)

— Free distort (hold down Ctrl key for Win, Cmd key for Mac)

Figure 1.8 Use the Free Transform tool to change the shape of the path.

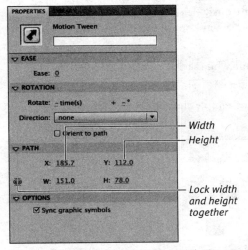

— Width
— Height

— Lock width and height together

Figure 1.9 Change the W and H values in the Property inspector to change the width and height of the motion path. Click the Lock button to maintain the width and height proportions.

To change the shape of the path:

1. Select the Free Transform tool and click on the motion path on the Stage.

   The Free Transform control points appear around the motion path.

2. Drag the Free Transform control points to change the overall shape of the motion path. The position of your mouse pointer on various control points determines the type of transformation (**Figure 1.8**):

   On corner points. Changes the overall width and height of the path. Hold down the Shift key to constrain the proportions.

   Near corner points. Rotates the path.

   Side points. Changes either the width or the height of the path.

   Sides. Skews (tilts) the path.

   or

   Select the motion path and change the W and H values in the Property inspector under Path (**Figure 1.9**).

   The W and H values change the width and the height of the motion path.

✔ Tip

- When using the Free Transform tool, you can move the white circle, which represents the center point around which all transformations are made. Double-click the white circle to reset its position.

MOTION TWEENING STRATEGIES

To change the curvature of the path:

◆ Choose the Selection tool and drag a portion of the motion path to change its curvature (**Figure 1.10**).

or

Choose the Subselection tool and move the individual control points to new positions, or drag the control handles to change the curvature (**Figure 1.11**).

or

Choose the Delete Anchor Point tool and click on a control point on the motion path.

The control point and its associated curve are deleted (**Figure 1.12**).

or

Choose the Convert Anchor Point tool and click on a control point on the motion path and drag out the control handles.

The control handles change the curvature of the path at that point (**Figure 1.13**).

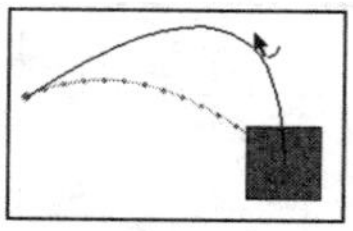

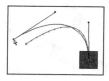

Figure 1.10 Drag a segment of the motion path to change its curvature.

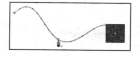

Figure 1.11 Move individual control points with the Subselection tool, or move the control handles to change the curvature of the motion path.

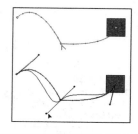

Figure 1.12 Delete individual control points with the Delete Anchor Point tool.

Figure 1.13 Use the Convert Anchor Point tool to click on an individual control point (top) and drag out the handles to create curves at that point (bottom).

Multiple Motion Paths

If you are designing multiple motion tweens with intersecting motion paths, it is often helpful to see all the motion paths for all the tweens simultaneously. Select a tween on the Timeline or its motion path on the Stage, and from the Property inspector options menu, choose Always Show Motion Paths (**Figure 1.14**).

Flash displays all the motion paths so you can edit one while seeing its relationship to the others (**Figure 1.15**).

If you only want to see a subset of all the motion paths, simply click on the Hide Layer options in the layers that you want to hide.

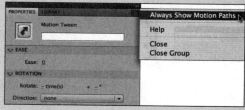

Figure 1.14 Choose Always Show Motion Paths from the Property inspector options menu to display motion paths for all your layers.

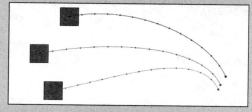

Figure 1.15 These three motion tweens are on separate layers, but their motion paths are displayed simultaneously.

To delete the path:

◆ Select the path and press the Delete key on the keyboard.

The path is deleted (but the tween still exists), and the object of the motion tween remains stationary.

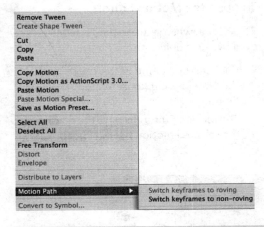

To reverse the path:

◆ Right-click (Windows) or Ctrl-click (Mac) the motion path and choose Motion Path > Reverse Path (**Figure 1.16**).

The path remains the same; however, the target object begins at the end point and travels in the reverse direction.

To copy and paste a motion path:

1. Select a stroke on a different layer or a motion path from another tween, and copy the stroke (Edit > Copy).

2. Select the motion path and paste the stroke (Edit > Paste in Center).

The copied stroke replaces the motion path.

Figure 1.16 Use Reverse Path to change the direction of a motion tween.

Roving and Nonroving Keyframes

Flash automatically adjusts the positions of property keyframes so that the speed of the motion is consistent throughout a tween. As you edit the motion path, the property keyframes adjust so the object moves the same distance in each frame (**Figure 1.17**). This way of automatically adjusting keyframes is known as *roving keyframes*.

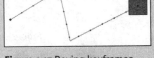

Figure 1.17 Roving keyframes automatically distribute the object's position along its path equally.

However, you may not want your motion to be consistent throughout the path. You can change the tween to *non-roving keyframes* by right-clicking (Windows) or Ctrl-clicking (Mac) the motion path and choosing Motion Path > Switch keyframes to non-roving (**Figure 1.18**). Flash will fix the positions of the keyframes in the tween span so that any further edits to the path will increase or decrease the speed of the object in particular segments of the tween (**Figure 1.19**).

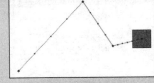

Figure 1.19 With non-roving keyframes, this object moves along different segments on its path at different speeds.

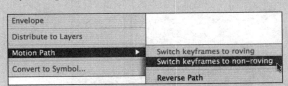

Figure 1.18 Roving keyframes is the default setting. Choose non-roving keyframes to prevent Flash from automatically distributing the object's position.

MOTION TWEENING STRATEGIES

Using the Motion Editor

Keyframes are specific to each property of an instance. For example, a single motion tween can have keyframes for position and different keyframes for alpha. Managing these *property keyframes* may seem daunting, but fortunately you can use the Motion Editor (Window > Motion Editor) to visualize and keep track of all your different property keyframes.

The Motion Editor provides a graphical representation of the changing values for all the properties of an instance in a motion tween. For example, if an object moves from left to right on the Stage, the Motion Editor shows the change in the X-position values as a line on a graph (**Figure 1.20**). Learning to read

and understand the Motion Editor is essential for creating more sophisticated, advanced animations.

You can add any number of keyframes along the graph for any of the properties and change their values.

To open the Motion Editor:

1. Select a tween span on the Timeline or a tweened object on the Stage.

2. Click on the Motion Editor tab behind the Timeline, or choose Window > Motion Editor.

   The Motion Editor displays the graphs for the selected motion tween (**Figure 1.21**).

Figure 1.20 The Motion Editor shows the X position of this object changing from frame 1 to frame 16.

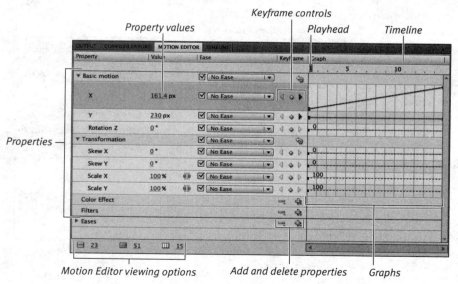

Figure 1.21 The Motion Editor displays the properties of the instance on the left and their changing values on the right.

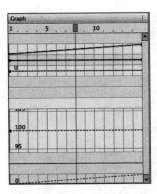

Figure 1.22 The graph portion of the Motion Editor has a vertical red playhead, just as the Timeline does.

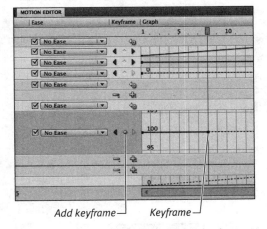

Add keyframe ⎯ Keyframe ⎯

Figure 1.23 Click on the diamond to add a keyframe to the currently selected property. Here, a keyframe for Alpha (transparency) has been inserted at frame 8.

To add a property keyframe:

1. Move the playhead to the desired frame on the Timeline (**Figure 1.22**).

2. Click the diamond icon next to the selected property.

   A keyframe at that point in time, indicated by a black square, is inserted for the property (**Figure 1.23**).

   or

   Right-click (Windows) or Ctrl-click (Mac) on any point along the graph and choose Add Keyframe (**Figure 1.24**).

   A keyframe at that point in time, indicated by a black square, is inserted for the property.

   or

   Ctrl-click (Windows) or Cmd-click (Mac) on any point along the graph (**Figure 1.25**).

   A keyframe at that point in time, indicated by a black square, is inserted for the property.

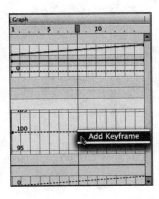

Figure 1.24 Add a keyframe directly from the context menu (right-click for Windows, Ctrl-click for Mac).

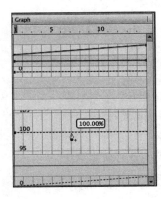

Figure 1.25 Add a keyframe by holding down the Ctrl key (Windows) or Cmd key (Mac) and clicking on the graph.

MOTION TWEENING STRATEGIES

11

To change the value of a property keyframe:

◆ Drag the keyframe up or down to its new value.

The value for the property keyframe changes (**Figure 1.26**).

or

Drag the playhead to the selected keyframe and change the value under the Value column.

The value for the property keyframe changes (**Figure 1.27**).

✔ Tips

■ Change the value of multiple keyframes at once by holding down the Shift key and selecting multiple keyframes and then dragging the multiple keyframes to new values. The line segment or segments between the selected keyframes will move together.

■ Move quickly between keyframes by clicking on the left-facing or the right-facing arrowhead. The adjacent keyframes will be selected.

To remove a property keyframe:

◆ Right-click (Windows) or Ctrl-click (Mac) on any keyframe and choose Remove Keyframe.

The selected keyframe is removed (**Figure 1.28**).

or

Select a keyframe and click on the yellow diamond icon.

The selected keyframe is removed.

or

Ctrl-click (Windows) or Cmd-click (Mac) on any keyframe.

The selected keyframe is removed.

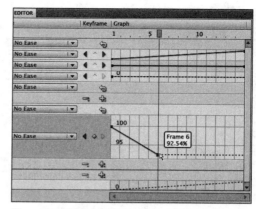

Figure 1.26 The keyframe at frame 6 for the Alpha property has been dragged down to about 92.5%. The resulting tween will show the object fade slightly from frame 1 to frame 6.

Figure 1.27 Change the value for any keyframe directly with numerical precision. The value column for the Alpha property at this keyframe shows 92.5429%.

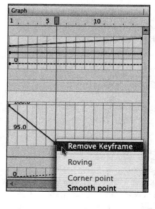

Figure 1.28 Choose Remove Keyframe to delete a keyframe along the graph.

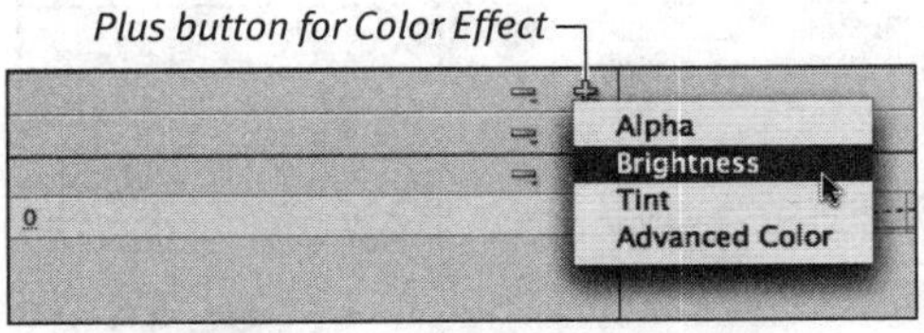

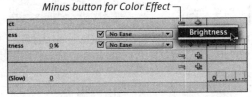

Figure 1.29 In this example, the Brightness property is being added to the Motion Editor.

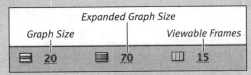

Figure 1.30 In this example, the Brightness property is being deleted from the Motion Editor.

To reset the value of a property keyframe:

◆ Click the Reset Values button in the upper-right corner of the property category.

The property returns to its initial value.

To add a property:

◆ Click the Plus button next to the Property category (Color Effect, Filters, or Eases) and select the desired property (**Figure 1.29**).

The selected property is added to the Motion Editor.

To remove a property:

◆ Click the Minus button next to the Property category (Color Effect, Filters, or Eases) and select the property to remove (**Figure 1.30**).

The selected property is removed from the Motion Editor.

MOTION TWEENING STRATEGIES

Motion Editor Display Options

There are many options you can set in the Motion Editor to help you be more comfortable accessing its information.

You can move the horizontal splitter bar that separates the Motion Editor with the Stage to increase the height of the panel. You can also expand or collapse any of the property categories by clicking on the small triangles next to the property category names. When you select a specific property, the graph expands to show more of that property.

At the bottom left of the Motion Editor, three buttons change the viewing area of the properties and their graphs (**Figure 1.31**). The Graph Size button changes the height of the rows of unselected properties. The Expanded Graph Size button changes the height of the row of the selected property. The Viewable Frames button changes the number of frames that are viewable along the Timeline.

Figure 1.31 Change the viewing options for the Motion Editor to best suit your working environment.

Easing in the Motion Editor

You can also change the curvature of the graph at any keyframe of all the properties except for the X, Y, and Z. Changing the curvature affects how fast or slow the values change. A straight line represents a linear change—an equal amount of change happens throughout the tween. A curved line represents a nonlinear change known as an *ease*.

Easing shows how fast or slow the change in values happens. You could have your tween start slowly and end quickly (*ease-in*), or your tween could start quickly and gradually slow down (*ease-out*). Easing is a way to add a sense of acceleration and deceleration, which can give weight and naturalness to an otherwise mechanical animation.

Flash also provides a number of preset eases that you can apply to any property, including the X, Y, and Z (**Figure 1.32**).

Using the preset eases is an easy way of making complex motions without explicitly defining keyframes. For example, you can quickly create bounces or shudders in a motion tween by simply applying a custom ease that moves back and forth between the values of a property keyframe.

To create a smooth curve:

◆ Right-click (Windows) or Ctrl-click (Mac) a property keyframe (except for X, Y, or Z), and choose Smooth point, Smooth left, or Smooth right (**Figure 1.33**).

   Smooth point. Control handles appear from both sides of the keyframe, which you can move to change the curvature of the graph.

   Smooth left. A control handle appears from the left side of the keyframe, which you can move to change the curvature of the graph to the left of the keyframe.

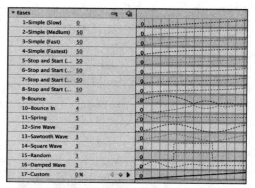

Figure 1.32 The Preset eases available in the Motion Editor.

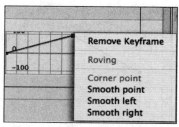

Figure 1.33 Choose one of the Smooth options to change the curvature of the graph at any keyframe (except for the X, Y, or Z properties).

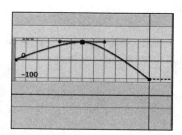

Figure 1.34 The handles affect the curvature of the graph at the keyframe.

MOTION TWEENING STRATEGIES

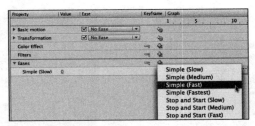

Figure 1.35 Choose a preset ease from the Plus button next to the Ease category.

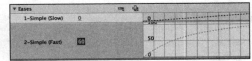

Figure 1.36 The Strength value of a preset ease changes its curvature.

Figure 1.37 Apply the preset ease to a property. Here, the preset ease is applied to the Basic Motion category, so the X, Y, and Z changes of the object will be affected by the ease.

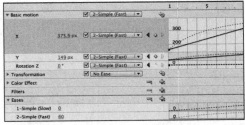

Figure 1.38 The curved dotted line superimposed over the X graph shows how the preset ease affects the X property.

Smooth right. A control handle appears from the right side of the keyframe, which you can move to change the curvature of the graph to the right of the keyframe.

or

Alt-click (Windows) or Option-click (Mac) a property keyframe (except for X, Y, or Z), and drag out the control handles to change the curvature of the graph (**Figure 1.34**).

To remove a curve:

◆ Right-click (Windows) or Ctrl-click (Mac) a property keyframe (except for X, Y, or Z), and choose Corner point.

The control handles disappear from the keyframe, and the graph on both sides of the keyframe becomes a straight line.

To apply a preset ease:

1. Click the Plus button on the Eases category and choose a preset ease.

   The selected preset ease appears in the Motion Editor (**Figure 1.35**).

2. Select the preset ease and change its value.

   The value of the preset ease determines the strength and direction of the ease. You can visually see the effect in the graph (**Figure 1.36**).

3. Choose the ease in the Ease pull-down menu next to the property you want it to affect (**Figure 1.37**).

   The preset ease is applied to the property. The ease curve is superimposed on the graph to show how it affects the property values over time (**Figure 1.38**).

Continues on next page

MOTION TWEENING STRATEGIES

✔ Tips

■ You can also apply ease-in and ease-out effects from the Property inspector. In the Timeline (not the Motion Editor), select the motion tween. In the Property inspector, enter a value for the ease between -100 (ease-in) and 100 (ease-out). Eases applied via the Property inspector, however, will be applied globally to all the properties throughout the entire motion tween. With the Motion Editor, you have precise control over individual properties and eases between keyframes.

■ For classic tweens, you can edit the easing profile from the Property inspector. Select the Edit easing button to access the Custom Ease-in/Ease-out editor.

Interpreting the Ease Curves

The ease curves indicate how a property value changes over time. The *x*-axis of the graph represents time, and the *y*-axis represents the property value. If the change is uniform—that is, the value changes an equal amount at every frame—the graph is a straight line. If there is an upward sloping curve at the beginning and a flattening out at the end (**Figure 1.39**), that means that there is a greater change in the *y*-axis (the property value) for the frames at the beginning and a smaller change in the *y*-axis for the frames at the end. The result is a rapid acceleration of the property at the start and a gradual slow-down at the end.

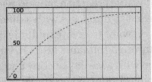

Figure 1.39 A graph showing an ease-out.

The curve doesn't always have to travel in one direction only, and the curve doesn't have to end at the last property value. In fact, interesting effects can be achieved if the curve moves back and forth between property values. For example, the curve of the Spring ease (**Figure 1.40**) moves rapidly from the beginning property value to the ending property value in the first few frames, and then moves back and forth until finally settling at a point a little more than halfway between the beginning and end values. If this ease is applied to a motion tween of position, the result would be a springing action back and forth between two points on the Stage until the object rests about halfway between.

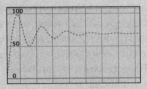

Figure 1.40 The Spring ease rapidly moves from the beginning value (0) to the end value (100) and swings back and forth until settling somewhere in the middle.

The value of the ease curves determines their strength and direction. The curvature becomes more pronounced in both directions, and the result on the ease becomes more noticeable. For other ease curves, the value determines the frequency, or the number of waves or bumps in the curve (**Figure 1.41**).

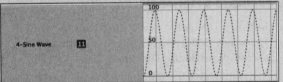

Figure 1.41 This Sine Wave ease has 11 peaks and valleys.

For total control, you can choose Custom from the Ease menu (**Figure 1.42**). The Custom ease lets you create your own curve and apply it to any of the properties.

Simple (Slow)
Simple (Medium)
Simple (Fast)
Simple (Fastest)
Stop and Start (Slow)
Stop and Start (Medium)
Stop and Start (Fast)
Stop and Start (Fastest)
Bounce
Bounce In
Spring
Sine Wave
Sawtooth Wave
Square Wave
Random
Damped Wave
Custom

Figure 1.42 Choose the bottom option from the preset Ease menu for a custom graph.

MOTION TWEENING STRATEGIES

Duplicating motion

If you've created a motion tween that you want to duplicate with a different object, or you want to create multiple objects going through the same motion, you can easily do so with a variety of copy and paste and swapping options. For example, imagine that you've created a transition for the first slide of a photo slide show. Now you want to duplicate that transition with the next ten slides. You can select the motion tween of the first slide and copy all the characteristics of that tween—its rotation, scaling, position, color, or filter changes. Then you can apply the characteristics of that tween to the subsequent slides.

Copying and pasting motion and swapping out the tweened object make it easy to create complex animations with repetitive motion such as a photo slide show or perhaps a group of fluttering leaves.

To duplicate a motion tween:

◆ Hold down the Alt key (Windows) or the Option key (Mac) and drag a tween span to a new layer on the Timeline.

Flash duplicates the motion tween (**Figure 1.43**).

or

1. In the Timeline, right-click (Windows) or Ctrl-click (Mac) on a tween span and choose Copy Frames (**Figure 1.44**).

The selected tween span is copied.

2. Right-click (Windows) or Ctrl-click (Mac) on a destination frame and choose Paste Frames (**Figure 1.45**).

The copied tween is duplicated in the new location.

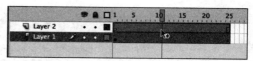

Figure 1.43 This tween span from Layer 1 is copied and pasted into Layer 2.

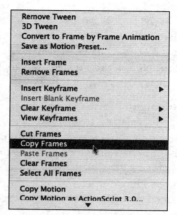

Figure 1.44 Use Copy Frames to copy a tween span.

Figure 1.45 Use Paste Frames to paste a copied tween span.

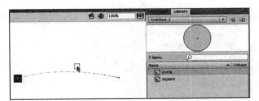

Figure 1.46 The existing tween uses the square movie clip. Drag another instance from the Library onto the tween to swap instances.

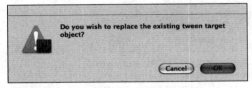

Figure 1.47 Click OK to accept the Flash dialog warning box.

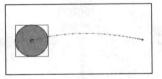

Figure 1.48 The original tween with the square movie clip is replaced with the circle movie clip.

Figure 1.49 Choose Swap Symbol to replace the target of a tween with another instance.

To swap the target object of a tween:

1. Drag a new symbol from the Library and drop it on an existing tweened object on the Stage (**Figure 1.46**).

   A warning dialog box appears asking whether you want to replace the tweened object (**Figure 1.47**).

2. In the dialog box, click OK.

   Flash replaces the existing object with the one you dragged out of the Library (**Figure 1.48**).

   or

1. Right-click (Windows) or Ctrl-click (Mac) on the tweened object and choose Swap Symbol (**Figure 1.49**).

   The Swap Symbol dialog box appears (**Figure 1.50**).

2. In the dialog box, select your replacement symbol and click OK.

   Flash swaps the symbols, aligning their registration points.

Figure 1.50 Choose a different symbol to swap for the original.

MOTION TWEENING STRATEGIES

To copy motion and apply it to another object:

1. In the Timeline, right-click (Windows) or Ctrl-click (Mac) on a tween span and choose Copy Motion (**Figure 1.51**).

   The selected motion of the tween span is copied.

2. On the Stage or on the Timeline, right-click (Windows) or Ctrl-click (Mac) a different symbol instance and choose Paste Motion from the context menu (**Figure 1.52**).

   Flash duplicates the motion of the first tween and applies it to the second symbol instance (**Figure 1.53**).

✔ Tip

- Paste Motion Special (not discussed here) is for classic tweening.

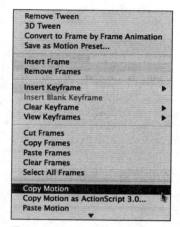

Figure 1.51 Choose Copy Motion to copy just the motion but not the target of the tween associated with the motion.

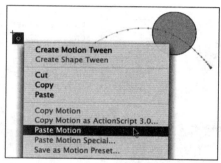

Figure 1.52 Choose Paste Motion to apply the copied motion to a different instance.

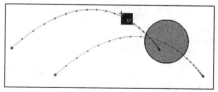

Figure 1.53 The copied motion from the tween with the circle is pasted and applied to the square.

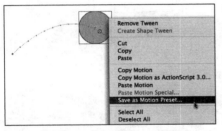

Figure 1.54 The Motion Presets panel contains premade tweens and lets you save tweens that you create.

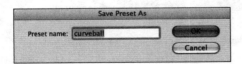

Figure 1.55 Choose Save as Motion Preset to keep frequently used tweens.

Figure 1.56 This tween will be saved in the Motion Presets panel as curveball.

Figure 1.57 The tween called curveball can be applied to other instances.

Saving tweens as motion presets

If you want to save your motion tweens, perhaps to apply them in future projects or to share them with other developers, you can do so in the Motion Presets panel. The Motion Presets panel (Window > Motion Presets) is much like a library of favorite or useful tweens. The Motion Presets panel comes loaded with many basic tweens that you can use (**Figure 1.54**).

You can also save your own tweens and share them with others. Using the Motion Presets panel will save you time and effort.

To save a tween as a motion preset:

1. Right-click (Windows) or Ctrl-click (Mac) on a tween span in the Timeline or on a tweened object on the Stage and choose Save as Motion Preset (**Figure 1.55**).

   The Save Preset As dialog box appears.

2. Enter a name to identify your tween and click OK (**Figure 1.56**).

   Your tween is saved in the Custom Presets folder in the Motion Presets panel and is available to be applied to other objects (**Figure 1.57**).

   or

1. Select a tween span on the Timeline or a tweened object on the Stage.

Continues on next page

MOTION TWEENING STRATEGIES

2. In the Motion Presets panel, click the Save Selection as Preset button. Alternatively, choose Save from the Motion Presets options menu (**Figure 1.58**).

Your tween is saved in the Custom Presets folder in the Motion Presets panel and is available to be applied to other objects.

To apply a motion preset:

1. Select a symbol instance on the Stage.

2. In the Motion Presets panel, select a motion preset and click the Apply button (**Figure 1.59**). Alternatively, right-click (Windows) or Ctrl-click (Mac) the motion preset and choose Apply at current location.

The motion preset is applied to your instance. The current position of the instance on the Stage is used as the initial position of the tween (**Figure 1.60**).

✔ Tip

■ If you want the selected symbol instance to be the ending position of the motion preset, choose End at Current Location from the Motion Presets panel options pull-down menu.

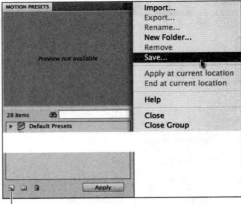

— Save Selection as Preset button

Figure 1.58 You can also save a tween from the Motion Presets options menu (top) or from the Save Selection as Preset button (bottom).

Figure 1.59 Choose a preset and a preview of the tween appears in the top window.

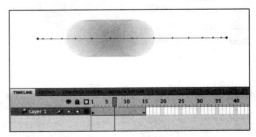

Figure 1.60 The preset tween is applied to your own instance.

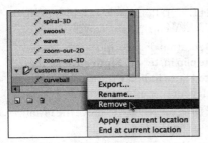

Figure 1.61 Choose Remove to delete a tween from the Motion Presets panel.

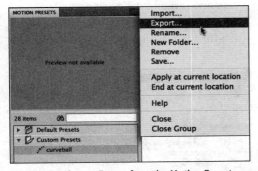

Figure 1.62 Choose Export from the Motion Presets options menu to save a tween to an external file.

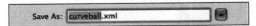

Figure 1.63 This tween is saved as the XML document curveball.xml.

To delete a motion preset:

◆ Select the motion preset and click the Trash icon. Alternatively, right-click (Windows) or Ctrl-click (Mac) on the motion preset and choose Remove (**Figure 1.61**).

A dialog appears asking you to confirm your choice. When you click Delete, Flash deletes the motion preset from the Motion Presets panel.

To organize your motion presets:

◆ Double-click the name of your motion preset to rename it. Or, right-click (Windows) or Ctrl-click (Mac) and choose Rename.

◆ Click the New Folder icon to create a new folder to organize your motion presets.

◆ Double-click the name of your folder. Or, right-click (Windows) or Ctrl-click (Mac) on the folder and choose Rename.

◆ Drag your motion presets and drop them on the highlighted folders to move them into different folders.

✔ Tip

■ You cannot rename, move, or delete the motion presets that are provided in the Default Presets folder.

To export a motion preset:

1. Select a motion preset.

2. In the Motion Presets panel options menu, choose Export. Or, right-click (Windows) or Ctrl-click (Mac) the motion preset and choose Export (**Figure 1.62**).

   The Save As dialog box appears.

3. Provide a name for the motion preset file. Click OK or Save (**Figure 1.63**).

   The file will be saved as an XML file, which you can share with fellow animators or developers.

To import a motion preset:

1. In the Motion Presets panel options menu, choose Import (**Figure 1.64**).

   The Open dialog box appears.

2. Choose the XML file of the motion preset. Click Open.

   The motion preset is imported into the Motion Presets panel.

Animating in 3D

Flash CS4 supports true 3D motion. Animating in 3D presents the thrill (but complication) of a third (z) axis for depth in addition to the horizontal (x) and vertical (y) axes. You can move or rotate any movie clip instance (or dynamically created instance of the *DisplayObject* class, discussed in Chapter 7, "Controlling and Displaying Graphics") in three dimensions with full control over the amount of perspective distortion and the location of the vanishing point.

Use the 3D Rotation tool to rotate an object along any of its three axes and the 3D Translation tool to move an object along any of its three axes.

For example, create a *Star Wars*-style opening scrolling text screen by rotating the text along its x-axis to tilt it, and then translating it along the y and z-axes to have it disappear in the horizon. Create confetti that realistically tumble in 3D, or develop games with cards that flip as they are dealt. Only your imagination is the limit.

To rotate an object in 3D space:

1. Begin with a movie clip instance on the Stage.

2. Select the 3D Rotation tool and click on your movie clip instance on the Stage.

   A 3D rotation display appears on your movie clip instance (**Figure 1.65**). The colored lines indicate the axes along which your instance can move.

   Red. Drag the red line to move the instance around the x-axis.

   Green. Drag the green line to move the instance around the y-axis.

   Blue. Drag the blue circle to move the instance around the z-axis.

   Orange. Drag the orange circle to move the instance freely around all three axes.

Figure 1.64 Choose Import from the Motion Presets options to import a tween that has been saved in an XML document.

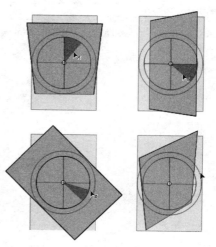

Figure 1.65 Use the 3D Rotation tool to rotate a movie clip instance in 3D space. This rectangle can be rotated along the x-, y-, or z-axis, or freely along any three of the axes.

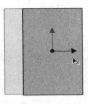

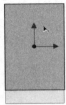

Figure 1.66 Use the 3D Translation tool to move a movie clip instance in 3D space. This rectangle can be moved along the x- (horizontal), y- (vertical), or z- (in and out) axis.

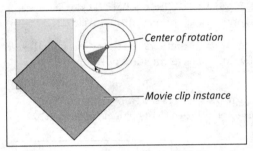

Center of rotation

Movie clip instance

Figure 1.67 The 3D display is moved off of the movie clip instance, changing its center of rotation.

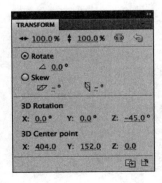

Figure 1.68 The Transform panel shows the values for the 3D rotation and 3D center point, which you can change.

To move an object in 3D space:

1. Begin with a movie clip instance on the Stage.

2. Select the 3D Translation tool and click on your movie clip instance on the Stage.

   A 3D translation display appears on your movie clip instance (**Figure 1.66**). The colored lines indicate the axes along which your instance can move.

   Red. Drag the red line to move the instance along the x-axis.

   Green. Drag the green line to move the instance along the y-axis.

   Blue. Drag the blue circle to move the instance along the z-axis.

To change the center point of 3D rotation:

◆ Move the white circle of the 3D display.

   Subsequent 3D rotations will move the instance relative to the new center point (**Figure 1.67**).

To reset the center point of 3D rotation:

◆ Double-click the white circle of the 3D display.

   The 3D center point is restored.

✔ Tips

■ You can also rotate a movie clip instance in 3D or change its center point in the Transform panel (Window > Transform) (**Figure 1.68**).

Continues on next page

MOTION TWEENING STRATEGIES

- You can also rotate or move multiple objects in 3D. Use the Shift key to select additional instances. Double-clicking the center point of the 3D display for multiple selections will place the center point between all the selected instances (**Figure 1.69**).

- You can turn on or off the 3D display that appears over your objects in the General Preferences dialog box (Flash > Preferences).

- You cannot Edit in Place an instance that has been rotated or moved in 3D space. You must edit the instance in symbol editing mode.

- 3D objects are not supported in mask layers.

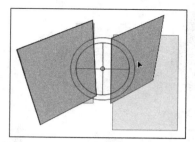

Figure 1.69 These two rectangles are rotated together in 3D space using the single 3D display, which has been centered between both instances.

Global vs. Local Transformations

When you choose the 3D Rotation or 3D Translation tool, you need to be aware of the Global Transform option at the bottom of the Tools panel (**Figure 1.70**). The Global Transform option toggles between a global option (button depressed) and a local option (button raised).

Moving an object with the global option on makes the transformations relative to the global (Stage) coordinate system. The 3D display shows the three axes in constant position, no matter how the object is rotated or moved (**Figure 1.71**).

However, moving an object with the global option turned off makes the transformations relative to itself. The 3D display shows the three axes oriented relative to the object (**Figure 1.72**).

Global Transform option

Figure 1.70 The Global Transform option is at the bottom of the Tools panel.

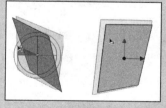

Figure 1.71 With the Global Transform option on, the 3D rotation and 3D translation displays are always perpendicular to the Stage and remain constant.

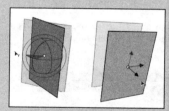

Figure 1.72 With the Global Transform option off, the 3D rotation and 3D translation displays are oriented to the object, not to the Stage. Notice that the 3D Rotation tool (left) shows a globe with the three axes relative to the rectangle, and the 3D Translation tool (right) shows the z-axis pointing out from the rectangle, not from the Stage.

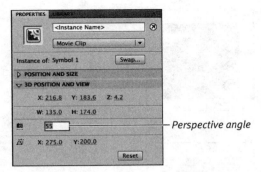

Figure 1.73 Change the Perspective angle in the Property inspector.

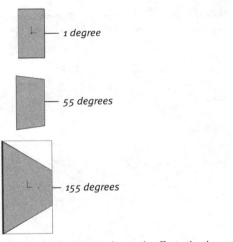

Figure 1.74 The perspective angle affects the degree of distortion of objects in perspective and how quickly parallel lines recede in the distance.

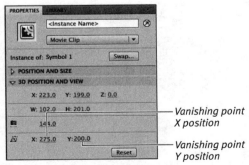

Figure 1.75 Change the vanishing point in the Property inspector.

To change the perspective:

1. Select a 3D object on the Stage.

2. In the Property inspector, change the value of the perspective angle (**Figure 1.73**).

   The default perspective angle is 55 degrees, which is similar to a normal camera. You can change the value from 1 to 180 degrees, which determines the amount of distortion due to perspective rendering (**Figure 1.74**). The greater the angle, the more severe the objects appear to recede in the distance.

To change the vanishing point:

1. Select a 3D object on the Stage.

2. In the Property inspector, change the value of the X and Y vanishing point positions (**Figure 1.75**).

   The default position of the vanishing point is in the middle of the Stage. The vanishing point represents the point on the horizon at which parallel lines disappear, just like the tracks of a railroad (**Figure 1.76**).

✔ Tip

- Changing the perspective angle or the vanishing point changes the settings for all the 3D objects on the Stage.

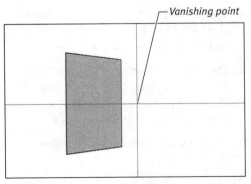

Figure 1.76 The vanishing point is represented by a horizontal and vertical line.

MOTION TWEENING STRATEGIES

Modeling in 3D

Flash CS4 supports 3D space but not actual 3D modeling. The objects remain flat with no real depth—a movie clip rotated 90 degrees and viewed on its edge essentially disappears.

However, with a little patience you can combine several flat objects and move and rotate them in 3D space to create 3D objects on your own! For example, combining six squares rotated at right angles from each other makes a cube. Converting the six squares to a movie clip symbol allows you to move and rotate the whole cube in 3D space on the Stage.

To create a 3D cube:

1. Select the Rectangle tool and, while holding down the Shift key, draw a rectangle on the Stage.

2. In the Property inspector, make the width and height 100 pixels each, make the fill color 50% transparent, and align the square in the middle of the Stage (**Figure 1.77**).

3. Select the rectangle and choose Modify > Convert to Symbol (F8).

   In the dialog box that appears, choose Movie Clip for Type and set the registration at the center point. Click OK.

   The rectangle is converted to a movie clip symbol (**Figure 1.78**).

4. Choose Edit > Copy (Ctrl-C for Windows, Cmd-C for Mac).

   The movie clip instance is copied.

5. Choose Edit > Paste in Place (Shift-Ctrl-V for Windows, Shift-Cmd-V for Mac).

   Flash pastes the instance in the exact location from where you copied it.

6. Open the Transform panel (Window > Transform).

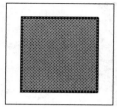

Figure 1.77 Create a square with a semitransparent fill in the middle of the Stage.

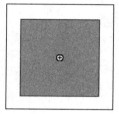

Figure 1.78 Convert the square into a movie clip.

First square

Second square (seen on edge)

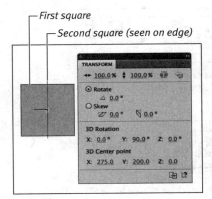

Figure 1.79 Rotate the second instance 90 degrees

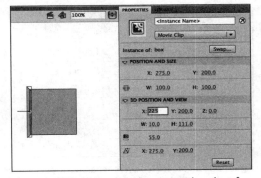

Figure 1.80 Move the second square to the edge of the first square.

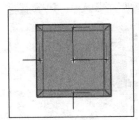

Figure 1.81 The six squares rotated and moved into place create a cube.

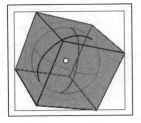

Figure 1.82 Use the 3D Rotation tool or the 3D Translation tool to move or tween your 3D cube.

7. In the Transform panel, enter 90 for the 3D Rotation along the *y*-axis.

The rectangle rotates so you see it on its edge (**Figure 1.79**).

8. In the Property inspector, change the X position value under 3D Position and View so that the second rectangle's edge aligns with the first rectangle.

The X position value should be 50 pixels less than its previous position (**Figure 1.80**). You now have two squares that form a T.

9. In the Property inspector, change the Z position value under 3D Position and View so that the second square is 50 pixels less than its current value.

The square moves toward you. You now have two rectangles that form an L.

10. Continue copying and pasting in place the rectangles, and rotating and moving them using the Transform panel and the Property inspector. For the "top" and "bottom" sides of the cube, you need to rotate them on the *y*-axis rather than the *x*-axis. For the front edge, you only need to move it along the *z*-axis.

You should end up with a total of six rectangles at 90 degrees from each other with their edges aligned. The rectangles facing each other should be 100 pixels apart (**Figure 1.81**).

11. Select all six movie clip instances.

12. Choose Modify > Convert to Symbol (F8).

In the dialog box that appears, choose Movie Clip for Type and set the registration at the center point. Click OK.

The flat rectangles that have been moved and rotated in 3D space are converted to a single movie clip symbol of a cube. You can then use the 3D Rotation or Translation tool to move the cube as a whole (**Figure 1.82**).

MOTION TWEENING STRATEGIES

Animating titles

Frequently, splash screens on Flash Web sites feature animated titles and other text-related materials that twirl, tumble, and spin until they all come into place as a complete design. Several techniques can help you accomplish these kinds of effects quickly and easily. The Break Apart command, when applied to a block of static text, breaks the text into its component characters while keeping them as live, editable text. This command lets you painlessly create separate text fields for the letters that make up a word or title. You can then use the Distribute to Layers command to isolate each of those characters on its own layer, ready for motion tweening.

When you begin applying motion tweens to your individual letters or words, it's useful to think and work backward from the final design. Establish the end keyframes containing the final positions of all your characters, for example. Then, in the first keyframes, you can change the characters' positions and apply as many transformations as you like, knowing that the final resting spots are secured.

To animate the letters of a title:

1. Select the Text tool, and make sure Static Text is selected in the Property inspector.

2. On the Stage, type a title you want to animate (**Figure 1.83**).

3. Choose Modify > Break Apart (Ctrl-B for Windows, Cmd-B for Mac).

   Flash replaces the static text title with individual static text letters (**Figure 1.84**).

4. Choose Modify > Timeline > Distribute to Layers (Ctrl-Shift-D for Windows, Cmd-Shift-D for Mac).

   Each selected item on the Stage is placed in its own layer below the existing layer. In this case, the newly created layers are named with the individual letters automatically (**Figure 1.85**).

Figure 1.83 Create static text on the Stage with the Text tool.

Figure 1.84 Breaking apart a block of static text results in static text of the individual letters.

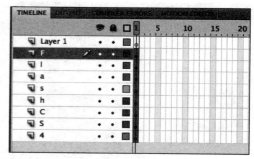

Figure 1.85 Distribute to Layers separates the selected items in their own layers.

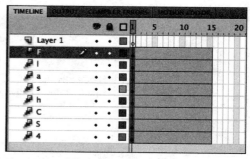

Figure 1.86 Each letter has its own tween.

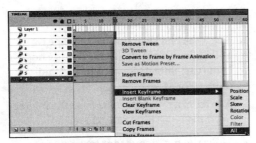

Figure 1.87 Insert a keyframe at the last frame in all the tween spans.

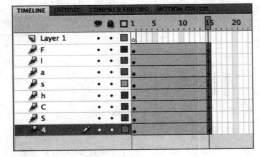

Figure 1.88 The last keyframe fixes the final position for all the letters.

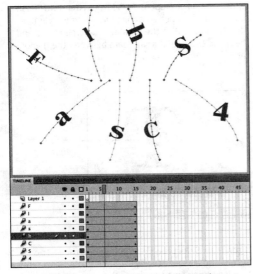

Figure 1.89 The letters tumble and fall into place at the last keyframe.

5. While all the individual letters are selected, choose Insert > Motion Tween, or right-click (Windows) or Ctrl-click (Mac) on the selected letters and choose Create Motion Tween from the context menu.

   Flash creates a tween span for each letter in each layer and adds one second's worth of frames on the Timeline (**Figure 1.86**).

6. Hold down the Ctrl key (Windows) or the Cmd key (Mac) and select the last frames of all the layers.

7. Right-click (Windows) or Ctrl-click (Mac) on the selected frames and choose Insert Keyframe > All (**Figure 1.87**).

   A keyframe for all properties is inserted in the last frame for all the selected layers (**Figure 1.88**).

8. In the first keyframe of each layer, rearrange and transform the letters according to your creative urges.

   Flash animates all these text elements coming together as a complete title (**Figure 1.89**).

✔ Tip

- You won't be able to animate the Color Effect properties (Tint, Alpha, Brightness) of your letters unless you convert each of them into a symbol. If you want to animate a Color Effect property, select each letter and choose Modify > Convert to Symbol.

MOTION TWEENING STRATEGIES

Shape Tweening Strategies

Shape tweening is a technique for interpolating amorphous changes that can't be accomplished with instance transformations such as rotation, scale, and skew. Fill, stroke, gradient, and alpha are all shape attributes that can be shape tweened. While motion tweening is based on a new object model, shape tweening still relies on a keyframe model where you establish a beginning keyframe and an end keyframe with a shape tween applied to the frames in between.

Flash applies a shape tween by using what it considers to be the most efficient, direct route. This method sometimes has unpredictable results, creating overlapping shapes or seemingly random holes that appear and merge (**Figure 1.90**). These undesirable effects usually are the result of keyframes containing shapes that are too complex to tween at the same time.

Simplifying a complicated shape tween into more basic parts and separating those parts in layers results in a more successful interpolation. Shape hints give you a way to tell Flash what point on the first shape corresponds to what point on the second shape. Sometimes, adding intermediate keyframes helps a complicated tween by providing a transition state and making the tween go through many more manageable stages.

Using shape hints

Shape hints force Flash to map points on the first shape to corresponding points on the second shape. By placing multiple shape hints, you can control more precisely the way your shapes will tween.

To add a shape hint:

1. Select the first keyframe of the shape tween, and choose Modify > Shape > Add Shape Hint (Ctrl-Shift-H for Windows, Cmd-Shift-H for Mac).

   A letter in a red circle appears in the middle of your shape (**Figure 1.91**).

2. Move the first shape hint to a point on your shape.

   Make sure that the Snap to Objects modifier for the Selection tool is turned on to snap your selections to vertices and edges.

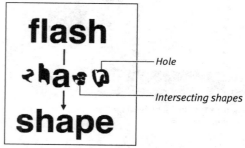

Figure 1.90 An attempt to shape tween the word "flash" to the word "shape" all at once in a single layer has poor results. Notice the breakups between the s and the p and the hole that appears between the h and the e.

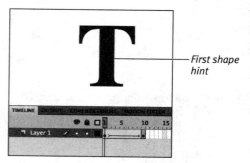

Figure 1.91 Select the first keyframe of the shape tween, and choose Modify > Shape > Add Shape Hint. The first shape hint appears in the center of the Stage.

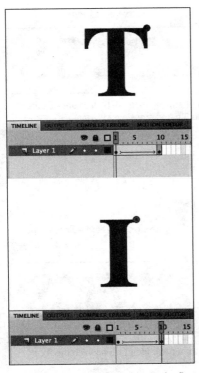

Figure 1.92 The first shape hint in the first keyframe (top) and its match in the last keyframe (bottom).

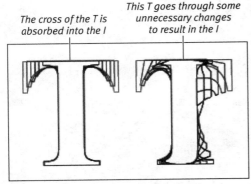

The cross of the T is absorbed into the I

This T goes through some unnecessary changes to result in the I

Figure 1.93 Changing from a T to an I with shape hints (left) and without shape hints (right).

3. Select the last keyframe of the shape tween, and move the matching circled letter to a corresponding point on the end shape.

This shape hint turns green and the first shape hint turns yellow, signifying that both have been moved into place correctly (**Figure 1.92**).

4. Continue adding shape hints, up to a maximum of 26, to refine the shape tween (**Figure 1.93**).

To delete a shape hint:

◆ Drag the shape hint off the Stage.

The matching shape hint in the other keyframe is deleted automatically.

To remove all shape hints:

◆ While on the first keyframe of a shape tween, choose Modify > Shape > Remove All Hints.

✔ Tips

■ Place shape hints in order either clockwise or counterclockwise. Flash more easily understands a sequential placement than one that jumps around.

■ Shape hints need to be placed on an edge or a corner of the shape. If you place a shape hint in the fill or outside the shape, the original and corresponding shape hints will remain red, and Flash will ignore them.

■ To view your animation without the shape hints, choose View > Show Shape Hints (Ctrl-Alt-H for Windows, Cmd-Option-H for Mac). Flash deselects the Show Shape Hints option, and the shape hints are hidden.

■ If you move your entire shape tween by using Edit Multiple Frames, you'll have to reposition all your shape hints. Unfortunately, you can't move all the shape hints at the same time.

Using intermediate keyframes

Adding intermediate keyframes can help a complicated tween by providing a transition state that creates smaller changes that are more manageable. Think about this process in terms of motion tweening. Imagine that you want to create the motion of a ball starting from the top left of the Stage, moving to the top right, then to the bottom left, and finally to the bottom right. You can't create just two position keyframes—one with the ball at the top-left corner of the Stage and one with the ball in the bottom-right corner—and expect Flash to tween the zigzag motion. You need to establish the intermediate position so that Flash can create the motion in stages. The same is true with shape tweening. You can better handle one dramatic change between two shapes by using simpler, intermediate keyframes.

To create an intermediate keyframe:

1. Study how an existing shape tween fails to produce satisfactory results when tweening the letter *Z* to the letter *S* (**Figure 1.94**).

2. Insert a keyframe (F6) at an intermediate point within the tween.

3. In the newly created keyframe, edit the shape to provide a kind of stepping stone for the final shape (**Figure 1.95**).

   The shape tween has smaller changes to go through with smoother results (**Figure 1.96**).

Intersecting shapes

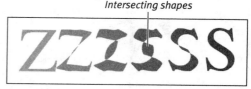

Figure 1.94 Changing a Z to an S all at once causes the shape to flip and cross over itself.

Figure 1.95 An intermediate shape.

Figure 1.96 The Z makes an easy transition to the intermediate shape (middle) from which the S can tween smoothly.

Using layers to simplify shape changes

Shape tweening lets you create very complex shape tweens on a single layer, but doing so can produce unpredictable results. Use layers to separate complex shapes and create multiple but simpler shape tweens.

Figure 1.97 A hole appears at the outline of the first shape when a shape tween is applied to change an F to a D.

Figure 1.98 The hole and the solid shapes are separated on two layers.

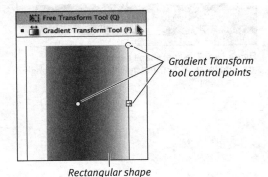

Gradient Transform tool control points

Rectangular shape

Figure 1.99 Use the Gradient Transform tool from the Toolbox to change the way a gradient fill is applied to a shape.

When a shape tween is applied to change the letter *F* to the letter *D,* for example, the hole in the last shape appears at the edges of the first shape (**Figure 1.97**). Separating the hole in the *D* and treating it as a white shape allows you to control when and how it appears. Insert a new layer, and create a second tween for the hole. The compound tween gives you better, more refined results (**Figure 1.98**).

Using shape tweens for gradient transitions

It helps to think about shape tweening as a technique that does more than just *morphing*, or interpolating one amorphous contour to another. After all, shape tweening can be used on any of the attributes of a shape, such as line weight; stroke color, including its alpha or gradient; and fill color, including its alpha or gradient. You can create interesting effects just by shape tweening color gradients. For example, changing the way a gradient is applied to a particular fill using the Gradient Transform tool can be an easy way to move a gradient across the Stage; combined with changing contours, it can produce atmospheric animations like clouds or puffs of smoke.

To create a gradient transition with shape tweening:

1. Select the Rectangle tool, and draw a large rectangle on the Stage.

2. Fill the shape with a radial or linear gradient.

3. Select the Gradient Transform tool by clicking and holding down the Free Transform tool and selecting the second option. Click the rectangle on the Stage.

   The control handles for the Gradient Transform tool appear for the gradient (**Figure 1.99**).

Continues on next page

4. For this task, move the center point handle of the gradient to the left side of your rectangle.

5. Create a new keyframe later on the Timeline.

6. Select the last keyframe, and click the rectangle with the Gradient Transform tool.

The control handles for the Gradient Transform tool appear for the gradient in the last keyframe.

7. Move the center point handle of the gradient to the far right side of the rectangle, and change the rotation, scale, or angle of the gradient as you desire.

Your two keyframes contain the same rectangular shape, but the gradient fills are applied differently (**Figure 1.100**).

8. Select the first keyframe and choose Insert > Shape Tween (or right-click [Windows], Ctrl-click [Mac] on the first keyframe and choose Create Shape Tween).

Flash tweens the transformation of the gradient fills from the first keyframe to the last keyframe. The actual contour of the rectangle remains constant.

9. Delete the outlines of the rectangle.

The gradient moves from left to right (**Figure 1.101**).

✔ Tip

■ You can't shape tween between different kinds of gradients; that is, you can't shape tween from a radial gradient to a linear gradient, or vice versa.

Rotation handle of Gradient Transform tool

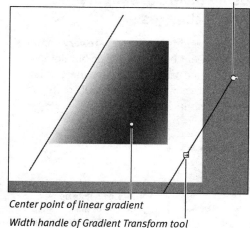

Center point of linear gradient

Width handle of Gradient Transform tool

Figure 1.100 In the last keyframe, use the Gradient Transform tool to change the way the linear gradient fills the rectangle. Here, the linear gradient is moved to the far right side, tilted, and made narrower.

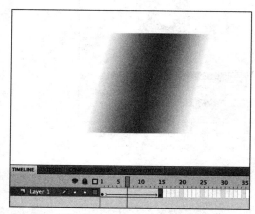

Figure 1.101 The final shape tween makes the gradient twist, widen, and move across the rectangle.

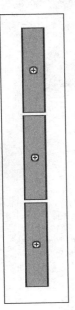

Figure 1.102 Three movie clip instances are placed on the Stage, arranged end to end.

Using Inverse Kinematics

When you want to animate an object that has multiple parts connected with joints, such as a walking person, Flash CS4 makes it easy to do so with a new feature called inverse kinematics. *Inverse kinematics* is a mathematical way to calculate the different angles of a jointed object to achieve a certain configuration. You can pose your object in a beginning keyframe, and then set a different pose at a later keyframe. Flash will use inverse kinematics to figure out the different angles for all the joints to get from the first pose to the next pose.

Inverse kinematics makes animating easy because you don't have to worry about animating each segment of an object or limb of a character. You just focus on the overall poses.

There are really two ways of using inverse kinematics: the first way is to join together several movie clip instances, and the second way is to define individual segments inside a single shape.

Inverse kinematics with movie clips

The first step when using inverse kinematics is to define the *bones* of your object. You use the Bone tool to do that. The Bone tool tells Flash how a series of movie clip instances are connected to each other. The set of connected movie clips is known as the *armature*, and each of the movie clips is known as a *node*.

To create an armature:

1. Position several movie clip instances on the Stage in roughly the layout in which you want them to be linked (**Figure 1.102**).

2. Select the Bone tool in the Tools panel.

Continues on next page

3. Click on the top of the first movie clip and drag the Bone tool to the top of the second movie clip (**Figure 1.103**).

Your first bone is defined. Flash shows the bone as a skinny triangle with a round joint at its origin and a round joint at its tip. Each bone is defined from the base of the first instance to the base of the second. For example, to build an arm, you would click on the shoulder side of the upper arm and drag it to the elbow side of the lower arm.

Flash creates a new layer for your armature called *a pose layer*, a special layer that supports inverse kinematics. Motion tweens, shape tweens, and drawing are not allowed in pose layers.

4. Continue adding nodes to the armature by clicking on the tip of the first bone and dragging it to the base of the next object (**Figure 1.104**).

✔ Tips

■ To add additional nodes to an armature, you must place the movie clips you want to add in a different layer. Then use the Bone tool to link the existing armature in the pose layer to the movie clips in the other layer. Flash will add the movie clips as additional nodes.

■ If you want your bones to connect to the registration points of your objects, you can select the Snap to Objects option at the bottom of the Tools panel.

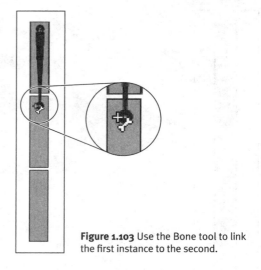

Figure 1.103 Use the Bone tool to link the first instance to the second.

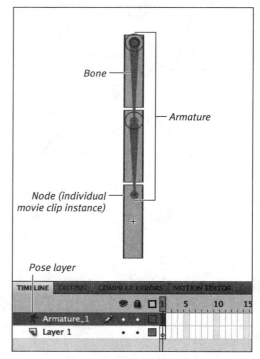

Figure 1.104 The Bone tool links these three instances together in an armature. The armature is separated on its own layer in the Timeline.

USING INVERSE KINEMATICS

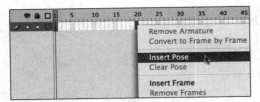

Figure 1.105 A new pose will be inserted in frame 20.

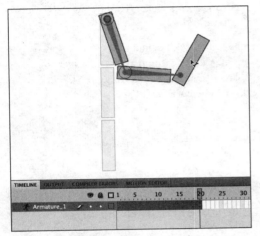

Figure 1.106 In the second pose, move the armature to a new position. The connections make it easy to animate the entire object at once.

To insert a pose:

1. Select a later frame on the Timeline and right-click (Windows) or Ctrl-click (Mac) and choose Insert Pose.

A new pose is created, which is very much like a new keyframe for the armature (**Figure 1.105**).

2. In the second pose, move the armature into another position.

Flash automatically animates the armature from the first pose to the second (**Figure 1.106**).

✔ Tip

■ To isolate the rotation of an individual node, hold down the Shift key as you pose the armature. This will make making minor adjustments to the armature easier and more exact.

To delete a pose:

◆ Right-click (Windows) or Ctrl-click (Mac) on a pose on the Timeline and choose Clear Pose.

The selected pose on the Timeline is removed.

To move a pose on the Timeline:

◆ Ctrl-click (Windows) or Cmd-click (Mac) to select a pose, and then drag it to a different position along the Timeline.

The selected pose moves to a different position on the Timeline.

To edit an armature:

◆ Use the Free Transform tool to scale, rotate, or move individual nodes.

◆ Hold down the Alt key (Windows) or the Option key (Mac) to drag a node to a new position.

◆ Select a bone and press the Delete key to remove a bone and all the bones connected to it down the chain.

USING INVERSE KINEMATICS

Armature Hierarchy

The first bone of an armature is referred to as the parent, and the bone that is linked to it is called the child. A bone can have more than one child attached to it, as well. For example, an armature of a person would have a pelvis connected to two thighs, which in turn are attached to two lower legs of their own. The pelvis is the parent, each thigh is a child, and the thighs are siblings to each other. As your armature becomes more complicated, you can use the Property inspector to navigate up and down the hierarchy using these relationships.

When you select a bone in an armature, the top of the Property inspector displays a series of arrows (**Figure 1.107**).

You can click the arrows to move through the hierarchy and quickly select and view the properties of each node. If the parent bone is selected, you can click the down arrow to select the child. If a child bone is selected, you can click the up arrow to select its parent, or click the down arrow to select its own child, if it has one. The sideways arrows navigate between sibling nodes.

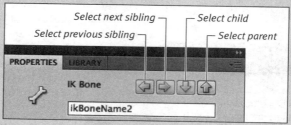

Figure 1.107 Navigate through the armature hierarchy with the arrows in the Property inspector.

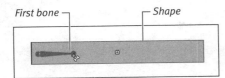

Figure 1.108 Use the Bone tool to create an armature inside a single shape.

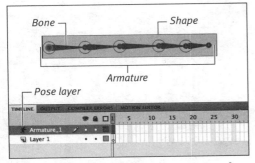

Figure 1.109 The Bone tool creates an armature of five segments inside this rectangular shape. The armature is separated on its own layer in the Timeline.

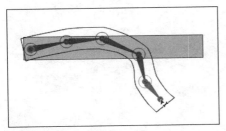

Figure 1.110 In new poses, you can select any bone and change the shape around it.

Inverse kinematics with shapes

Another way you can use inverse kinematics is to define several bones inside a single shape. By providing an internal armature to a shape, you can control how the contours of the shape move and bend, somewhat like shape tweening. Use inverse kinematics with shapes to create the undulating motion of a snake or the flexing of someone's biceps.

To create an armature inside a shape:

1. Create a single shape on the Stage. The shape can be drawn in either Drawing mode or Object Drawing mode.

2. Select the Bone tool in the Tools panel.

3. Click inside the shape and drag the Bone tool a little ways inside the shape (**Figure 1.108**).

   Your first bone is defined.

   Flash puts your armature in a *pose layer*, a special layer that supports inverse kinematics. Motion tweens, shape tweens, and drawing are not allowed in pose layers.

4. Click on the narrow end of the first bone and drag out the next bone a little farther inside the shape.

5. Continue adding bones until the armature extends throughout the shape (**Figure 1.109**).

   Using the Selection tool, you can click and drag any of the bones to create a pose and the shape will deform to match the internal armature (**Figure 1.110**). Animating an armature inside a shape is the same process as animating an armature of separate movie clips (see the previous tasks in this chapter, "To insert a pose," "To delete a pose," and "To move a pose on the Timeline").

To edit the shape around an armature:

◆ Use the Paintbucket tool to change the fill color of the shape.

◆ Use the Inkbottle tool to change the stroke color and stroke height of the shape.

◆ Use the Subselection tool to change the contours of the shape.

◆ Use the Add Anchor Point tool to add new points on the contour of the shape.

◆ Use the Delete Anchor Point tool to delete points on the contour of the shape.

◆ Hold down the Alt key (Windows) or the Option key (Mac) and drag the entire shape with its armature to a new position on the Stage.

To edit the bones of the armature:

◆ Use the Subselection tool to move the base or the tips of the bones into new positions within the shape. You can only do this with the initial armature in the first pose.

◆ Select a bone with the Selection tool and press the Delete key to remove a bone and all the bones connected to it down the chain.

Refining Shape Behavior with the Bind tool

The organic control of a shape by its armature is a result of a mapping between control points along the shape and its bones. Hence, where the bones rotate, the shape follows.

You can edit the connections between the bones and their control points with the Bind tool, which is hidden under the Bone tool. The Bind tool displays which control points are connected to which bones and lets you break those connections and make new ones.

When you choose the Bind tool and select a bone, all the connected control points on the shape are highlighted in yellow (**Figure 1.111**).

If you want to redefine which control points are connected to the selected bone, you can do the following:

◆ Shift-click to add additional existing control points to the bone.

◆ Ctrl-click (Windows) or Cmd-click (Mac) to remove control points from the bone.

◆ Drag a connection line between the bone and the control point.

You can also click on any control point on the shape. The selected control point is highlighted in red, and all the connected bones are highlighted in yellow (**Figure 1.112**).

If you want to redefine which bones are connected to the selected control point, you can do the following:

◆ Shift-click to add additional bones to the control point.

◆ Ctrl-click (Windows) or Cmd-click (Mac) to remove bones from the control point.

◆ Drag a connection line between the control point and the bone.

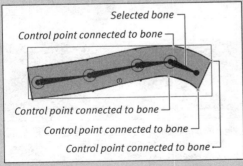

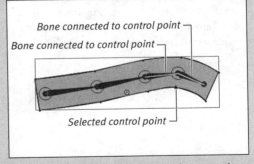

Figure 1.111 The Bind tool defines the connections between a bone and its control points on the shape.

Figure 1.112 The Bind tool also shows the connections between a particular control point on the shape and its associated bone or bones.

USING INVERSE KINEMATICS

Options for joint rotation and translation

When you build your armature, the various joints freely rotate, which may not be particularly realistic. Many armatures in real life are constrained to certain angles of rotation. For example, you can rotate your lower leg to be parallel with your thigh, but you can't rotate it past the knee (at least I hope you can't!). When working with armatures, whether they are in a shape or part of a series of linked movie clips, you can choose to constrain the rotation of the joints, or even constrain the translation (side-to-side or up-and-down movement) of the joints.

To constrain the rotation of joints:

1. Click on a bone to select it.

2. In the Property inspector, select the Constrain check box under Joint:Rotation (**Figure 1.113**).

   The joint for the selected bone is constrained.

3. Change the values for Min and Max to set the minimum and maximum degrees of rotation for the selected joint.

   The allowable range of rotation appears on the joint on the Stage (**Figure 1.114**). The Min and Max values are relative to the current position of the bone.

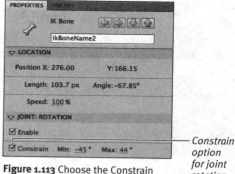

Constrain option for joint rotation

Figure 1.113 Choose the Constrain option in the Property inspector to limit the rotation of any joint.

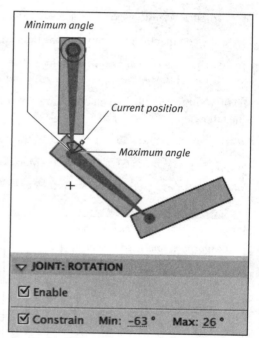

Figure 1.114 The middle node is constrained from its current position from 63 degrees counterclockwise to 26 degrees clockwise.

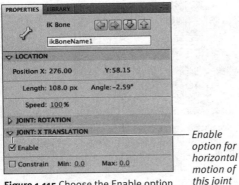

Figure 1.115 Choose the Enable option for Joint: X Translation or Joint: Y Translation in the Property inspector to enable movement of the joint.

Enable option for horizontal motion of this joint

To enable joint translation:

1. Click on a bone to select it.

2. In the Property inspector, select the Enable check box under Joint:X Translation and/or Joint:Y Translation (**Figure 1.115**).

   The joint for the selected bone can now freely move around on the Stage.

3. Select the Constrain check box and change the values for Min and Max to set the minimum and maximum amount of movement for the selected joint.

   The allowable range of motion appears on the joint on the Stage (**Figure 1.116**). The Min and Max values are relative to the current position of the bone.

✔ Tip

- If you enable joint translation, it's a good idea to also disable joint rotation to prevent wild joint movements. An armature with both joint translation and rotation is difficult to control.

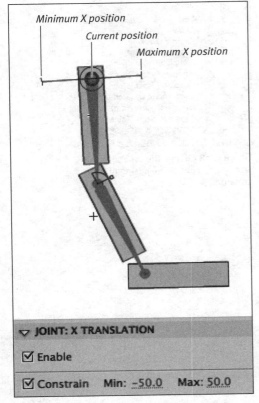

Figure 1.116 The top node can move left and right, indicated by the horizontal line. It is constrained from its current position to 50 pixels to the left and 50 pixels to the right.

Changing joint speed

Joint speed refers to the stickiness, or stiffness, of a joint. A joint with a low value for joint speed will be sluggish. A joint with a high value for joint speed will be more responsive. You can set the joint speed value for any selected joint in the Property inspector.

The joint speed is apparent when you drag the very end of an armature. If there are slow joints higher up on the armature chain, those particular joints will be less responsive and will rotate to a lesser degree than the others. Changing joint speed will help you pose your armatures more realistically, but it does not affect the actual animation.

To change joint speed:

◆ Select a bone and, in the Property inspector, change the value of Speed (**Figure 1.117**).

The Speed values can range from 0% (frozen) to 200% (very responsive). The normal value is 100%.

Controlling armature easing

Armatures do not have access to the Motion Editor and its sophisticated controls for eases. However, there are a few standard eases available from the Property inspector. Easing can make your armatures move with a sense of gravity due to acceleration or deceleration of their motion.

To control easing:

◆ Select a pose layer and, in the Property inspector, choose the Type of ease and change the value of the Strength (**Figure 1.118**). The Type indicates the kind of easing, and the Strength determines the direction and severity of the ease.

Ease-in. To start gradually and quickly come to a stop, set the Type to any of the Simple options and set the Strength to a *negative* number.

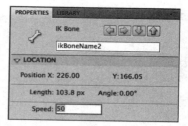

Figure 1.117 A Speed value of 50 makes this joint a little more sluggish than normal.

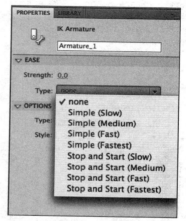

Figure 1.118 Change the Type and Strength to control the easing of your armature.

Figure 1.119 Choose Runtime in the Property inspector to enable interactive control of your armature. Choose Authortime to set multiple poses along the Timeline for Flash to animate.

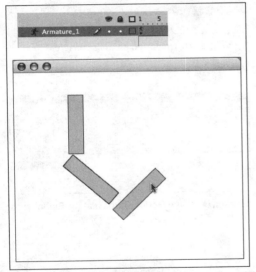

Figure 1.120 The Runtime option is only allowed when your armature has a single pose. In the Test Movie environment, viewers can move your armature interactively.

Ease-out. To start quickly and gradually come to a stop, set the Type to any of the Simple options and set the Strength to a *positive* number.

Ease-in and Ease-out. To start gradually, speed up in the middle, and then gradually come to a stop, set the Type to any of the Stop and Start options and set the Strength to a *negative* number.

Ease-out and Ease-in. To start quickly, slow down in the middle, and then end quickly, set the Type to any of the Stop and Start options and set the Strength to a *positive* number. This setting creates an unusual motion, which you probably won't use very much.

Runtime and authortime armatures

Authortime armatures are those that you pose along the Timeline and play as straightforward animations. Runtime armatures are interactive and allow the user to move your armature. You can make any of your armatures—whether they are made with a series of movie clips or made with a shape—into an authortime or a runtime armature. Runtime armatures, however, are restricted to armatures that only have a single pose.

To make a runtime armature:

◆ Select a pose layer and, in the Property inspector, choose Runtime under the Options section (**Figure 1.119**).

A tiny armature icon appears in the pose layer to indicate the Runtime option. When you test your movie (Control > Test Movie), you can interact with the armature (**Figure 1.120**).

Creating Special Effects

Because Flash's drawing tools are vector based, you normally wouldn't think of incorporating special effects, such as a motion blur or color blending, which are associated with bitmap applications like Adobe Photoshop or After Effects. But using filters and blends, those special effects can be created directly in Flash. This technique can give your Flash movies more depth and richness by going beyond the simple flat shapes and gradients of vector drawings.

The following tasks demonstrate a blur effect using filters and a color blending effect using blends.

A *blur* is an effect that occurs when the camera is out of focus. Blurs are particularly effective for transitions; you can animate a blurry image coming into sharp focus.

To create a blur-to-focus effect:

1. In Flash, create the image you want to blur using the drawing tools or by importing an image to the Stage. In this example, we use a photo.

2. Right-click (Windows) or Ctrl-click (Mac) on the image and choose Create Motion Tween.

   Flash asks whether you want to convert the selection to a movie clip symbol to begin motion tweening. Click OK.

   Flash converts the selection to a movie clip symbol and adds one second's worth of frames to the newly created tween span on the Timeline (**Figure 1.121**).

   In Flash, filters can only be applied to a movie clip symbol, a button symbol, or text.

3. Open the Motion Editor (Window > Motion Editor).

4. Move the red playhead to the first frame of the tween.

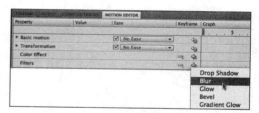

Figure 1.121 This imported photo is converted to a movie clip symbol and motion tweened.

Figure 1.122 In the Motion Editor, add the Blur filter to the Filters category.

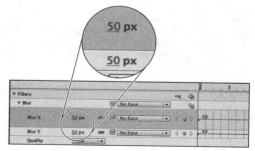

Figure 1.123 Increase the value of the Blur filter to 50 pixels.

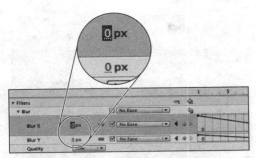

Figure 1.124 In the last frame of the motion tween, decrease the value of the Blur filter to 0 pixels. The downward sloping graph shows the gradual transition.

Figure 1.125 The resulting tween of the Blur filter makes an effective transition.

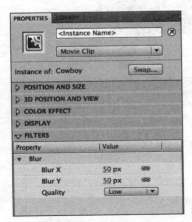

Figure 1.126 The various filters are also available from the Property inspector.

5. Click the Plus button next to Filters and choose Blur (**Figure 1.122**).

   The Blur filter is added to the list of properties.

6. Make sure the Link icon is selected so the Blur X and Blur Y change together. Increase the values of Blur X and Blur Y to the desired blurriness (**Figure 1.123**).

   Blur X indicates how much blurring should be applied to the object in the horizontal (*x*-axis). Blur Y does the same for vertical (*y*-axis) blur. Because these are independent values, you can create a blur in just one direction if you choose to unlink the properties.

7. Move the red playhead to the last frame of the tween.

8. Change the value of Blur X and Blur Y to 0 (**Figure 1.124**).

   Flash animates your image's change from blurred to focused (**Figure 1.125**).

✔ Tips

- You can also access and apply the various filters from the Filters section of the Property inspector. Choose your tweened object and, in the Property inspector, click the Add Filter button and choose Blur (**Figure 1.126**).

- The Quality property controls how smooth the blur will be. A higher quality blur will be smoother and closer to what you might get using a Blur filter in Photoshop, but it also makes the Flash Player work harder, so it could slow down the playback of your movie.

- You can use any filter in this manner to create a transition. Experiment with the numerous filters to suit your movie.

- A movie clip instance can have more than one filter applied to it.

CREATING SPECIAL EFFECTS

To blend colors from one object on another:

1. Create or import an image in a new layer.

2. Create a new layer above the first, and then create or import an image in this top layer.

   In this example, static text is placed in the top layer, and a photo is imported in the bottom layer (**Figure 1.127**).

3. Select the text in the top layer and choose Modify > Convert to Symbol (F8). Choose movie clip as the type of symbol.

   Flash converts your selection into a movie clip symbol. Blend effects from the Property inspector can only be applied to movie clip and button instances.

4. Select the movie clip instance on the Stage. In the Property inspector, choose a Blending mode from the pull-down menu (**Figure 1.128**).

   Flash blends the colors of the movie clip instance with all the images in the layers below it. The different Blending modes determine how the colors interact. Some Blending modes darken the colors, whereas others lighten or even reverse them. The best way to understand the Blending modes is to experiment! (For more detailed information about color Blending modes and how you can control them purely with ActionScript, see the section "Blending Colors" in Chapter 7.)

✔ Tips

- A movie clip instance can only have one blending effect.

- Blending effects cannot be motion tweened.

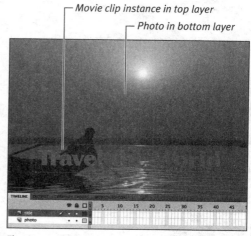

Movie clip instance in top layer

Photo in bottom layer

Figure 1.127 The text is a movie clip instance in a layer above the photo.

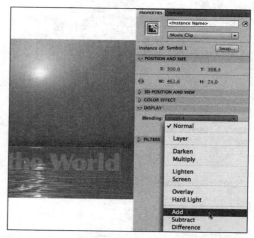

Figure 1.128 Choosing a Blending mode in the Property inspector makes colors of the movie clip instance blend in different ways with the image below it.

Using Masks

Masking is a simple way to reveal portions of a layer or the layers below it. This technique requires making one layer a mask layer and the layers below it the mask*ed* layers.

By adding tweening to the mask layer, the masked layers, or both, you can go beyond simple, static peepholes and create masks that move, change shape, and reveal moving images. Use animated masks to achieve such complex effects as moving spotlights, magnifying lenses that enlarge underlying pictures, or "x-ray" types of interactions that show more detail within the mask area. Animated masks are also useful for creating cinematic transitions such as wipes, in which the first scene is covered as a second scene is revealed; and iris effects, in which the first scene collapses in a shrinking circle, leaving a second scene on the screen.

You can add even more complexity to animated masks by inserting normal layers above and below them. A shape filled with an alpha gradient, for example, can make the hard edges of a mask fade out slowly for a subtle spotlight.

In the mask layer, Flash sees all fills as opaque shapes, even if you use a transparent solid or gradient. As a result, all masks have hard edges. To create a softer edge, place a gradient with a transparent center either under or over the mask to hide the edges.

Using movie clips in mask layers provides more possibilities, including multiple masks and even dynamically generated masks that respond to the user. Because dynamic masks rely on ActionScript, however, they'll be covered in detail later (in Chapter 7) after you've learned more about Flash's scripting language.

To tween the mask layer:

1. In Layer 1, create a background image or import a bitmap.

2. Insert a new layer above the first layer.

3. Select the top layer, and choose Modify > Timeline > Layer Properties.

   or

   Double-click the layer icon in the top layer. The Layer Properties dialog box appears.

4. Select Layer Type: Mask.

5. Select the bottom layer, and choose Modify > Timeline > Layer Properties.

6. Select Layer Type: Masked.

   The top layer becomes the mask layer, and the bottom layer becomes the masked layer (the layer that is affected by the mask) (**Figure 1.129**).

7. Create a tween in the mask layer (the top layer) and insert sufficient frames in the masked layer (the bottom layer) to match (**Figure 1.130**).

   You can create a motion tween, a classic tween, or a shape tween in the mask layer.

8. Lock both layers to see the effects of your animated mask on the image in the masked layer (**Figure 1.131**).

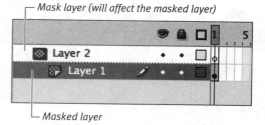

Mask layer (will affect the masked layer)

Masked layer

Figure 1.129 Layer 2 is the mask layer, and Layer 1 is the masked layer.

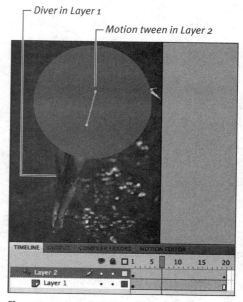

Diver in Layer 1

Motion tween in Layer 2

Figure 1.130 A motion tween of a growing, moving circle is on the mask layer. The diver image is on the masked layer.

Figure 1.131 The motion tween uncovers the image of the diver. Only the part of the photo that is under the mask is revealed.

Figure 1.132 The moving spotlight in the mask layer (spotlight) uncovers the stained-glass image in the masked layer (bitmap). A duplicate darker image resides in the bottom, normal layer (dark bitmap).

✔ Tips

■ Use two images that vary slightly, one in the masked layer and one in a normal layer under the masked layer. This technique makes the animated mask act as a kind of filter that exposes the underlying image. For example, add a bright image in the masked layer and a dark version of the same image in a normal layer under the masked layer. The mask creates a spotlight effect on the image (**Figure 1.132**).

■ Explore other duplicate image combinations, such as a sharp image and a blurry image, a grayscale image and a color image, or an offset image (**Figure 1.133**).

■ Place a tween of an expanding box in the mask layer that covers the Stage to simulate cinematic wipes between images (**Figure 1.134**).

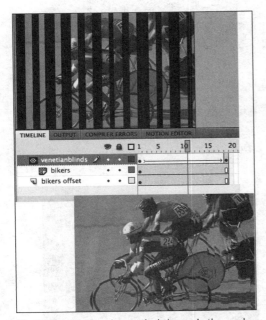

Figure 1.133 The moving vertical shapes in the mask layer (venetianblinds) uncover the image of bicyclists in the masked layer (bikers). A duplicate image in the bottom normal layer (bikers offset) is shifted slightly to create the rippling effect.

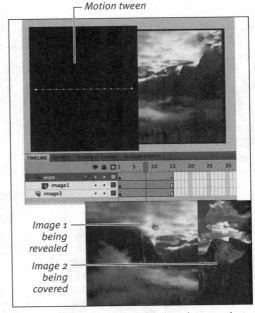

Figure 1.134 The mask layer contains a large motion tween that covers the entire Stage. This technique creates a cinematic wipe between an image in the masked layer (image 1) and an image in the bottom, normal layer (image 2).

To tween the masked layer:

1. Beginning with two layers, modify the top to be the mask layer and the bottom to be the masked layer.

2. Draw a filled shape or shapes in the mask layer (the top layer) (**Figure 1.135**).

   This area becomes the area through which you see your animation on the masked layer.

3. Create a shape tween or a motion tween in masked layers (the bottom layers) that pass under the shapes in the mask layer. You can have as many masked layers as you want under a single mask layer (**Figure 1.136**).

4. Lock both layers to see the effects of your animated masked layers as they show up behind your mask layer (**Figure 1.137**).

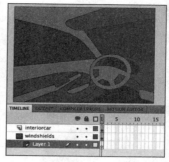

Figure 1.135 The windshield shapes are in the mask layer called windshields. The drawing of the car interior is in a normal layer above the windshields layer.

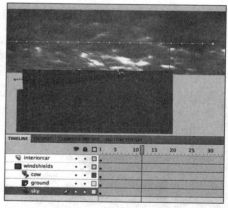

Figure 1.136 Several motion tweens in masked layers (cow and sky) move under the windshield shapes in the mask layer.

Figure 1.137 The images of the cow, ground, and sky show under the mask, creating the illusion of the car's forward motion.

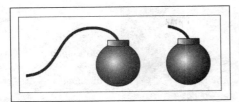

Figure 1.138 The fuse of a bomb shortens.

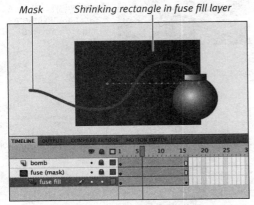

Mask   Shrinking rectangle in fuse fill layer

Figure 1.139 The bomb's fuse is a thin shape in the mask layer. The rectangle is a motion tween in the masked layer that shrinks, making the fuse appear to be shortening.

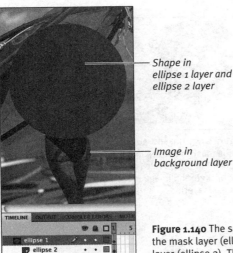

Shape in ellipse 1 layer and ellipse 2 layer

Image in background layer

Figure 1.140 The same ellipse appears in both the mask layer (ellipse 1) and the top masked layer (ellipse 2). The image of the windsurfer is in the bottom masked layer (background).

✔ **Tip**

■ This approach is a useful alternative to using shape tweens to animate borders or similar types of objects that grow, shrink, or fill in. Imagine animating a fuse that shortens to reach a bomb (**Figure 1.138**). Create a mask of the fuse, and animate the masked layer to become smaller slowly, making it look like the fuse is shortening (**Figure 1.139**). Other examples that could benefit from this technique include trees growing, pipes or blood vessels flowing with liquid, text that appears as it's filled with color, or drawing a pathway on a map. Just remember that Flash doesn't recognize strokes in the mask layer; if you want to create thin lines in the mask layer, use fills only.

To create a soft-edged mask:

1. Create a mask layer and a masked layer.

2. Place or draw a background image in the masked layer (the bottom layer).

3. Draw an ellipse in the mask layer (the top layer).

4. Copy the ellipse.

5. Insert a new layer between the mask layer and the masked layer.

   Your new layer will become a masked layer.

6. Choose Edit > Paste in Place (Ctrl-Shift-V for Windows, Cmd-Shift-V for Mac).

   An ellipse appears in the new masked layer, right under the ellipse in the top mask layer (**Figure 1.140**).

Continues on next page

USING MASKS

7. Fill the pasted ellipse with a radial gradient, defined with a transparent center to an opaque perimeter, in the same color as the Stage (**Figure 1.141**).

8. Lock all three layers to see the effects of the mask (**Figure 1.142**).

The mask layer lets you see through an elliptical area. The top masked layer hides the edges of the ellipse by creating a gradual fade toward the center. The bottom masked layer holds the contents of your background image (**Figure 1.143**).

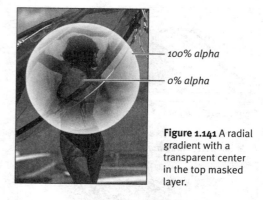

100% alpha

0% alpha

Figure 1.141 A radial gradient with a transparent center in the top masked layer.

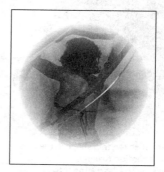

Figure 1.142 The resulting soft-edged mask.

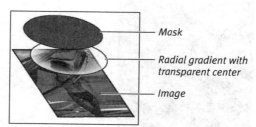

Mask

Radial gradient with transparent center

Image

Figure 1.143 The soft-edged mask is the combination of the mask in the top layer (mask layer), a radial gradient in the middle layer (top masked layer), and the background image in the bottom layer (bottom masked layer).

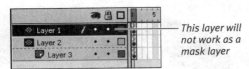

This layer will not work as a mask layer

Figure 1.144 Layer 1 and Layer 2 are both defined as mask layers, but only Layer 2 affects Layer 3 — the masked layer.

Figure 1.145 Two independent spotlights moving, each uncovering portions of the image.

Figure 1.146 Choose Movie Clip to create a new movie clip symbol.

Creating multiple masks

Although Flash allows multiple masked layers under a single mask layer, you can't have more than one mask layer affecting any number of masked layers (**Figure 1.144**). To create more than one mask, you must use movie clips. Why would you need multiple masks? Imagine creating an animation that has two spotlights moving independently on top of an image (**Figure 1.145**). Because the two moving spotlights are tweened, they have to be on separate layers. The solution is to incorporate the two moving spotlights into a movie clip and place the movie clip on the mask layer.

You'll learn much more about movie clips in Chapter 5, "Controlling Multiple Timelines." If you'd like, skip ahead to read about movie clips and return when you feel comfortable.

To create multiple masks:

1. Create a mask layer and a masked layer.

2. Place your image on the masked layer (the bottom layer).

3. Choose Insert > New Symbol (Ctrl-F8 for Windows, Cmd-F8 for Mac).
   The Create New Symbol dialog box appears.

4. Enter a descriptive name, and choose Movie Clip (**Figure 1.146**); then click OK.
   Flash creates a movie clip symbol, and you enter symbol editing mode for that symbol.

Continues on next page

USING MASKS

5. Create two motion tweens of spotlights moving in different directions on the Timeline of your movie clip symbol (**Figure 1.147**).

6. Return to the main Stage, and drag an instance of your movie clip symbol into the mask layer (the top layer) (**Figure 1.148**).

7. Choose Control > Test Movie to see the effects of the movie clip mask.

The two motion tweens inside the movie clip both mask the image on the masked layer.

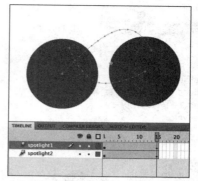

Figure 1.147 The two moving spotlights are motion tweens inside a movie clip.

✔ Tips

■ To see what your masks are uncovering, use a transparent fill or choose the View Layer as Outlines option in the Layer Properties dialog box (**Figure 1.149**).

■ To prevent the animation inside the movie clip from looping constantly, add a keyframe to its last frame and add a stop () action.

Figure 1.148 An instance of the movie clip is in the top (mask) layer, and the image of the bikers is in the bottom (masked) layer.

Outline of spotlight tweens

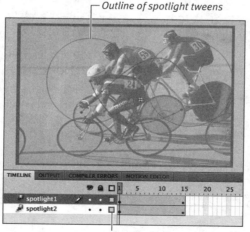

Show as Outlines option

Figure 1.149 Viewing your masks as outlines lets you see the image underneath. Choose the View Layer as Outlines option in the Layer Properties dialog box, or click the Show as Outlines icon in your layer.

Working with Video

2

Web sites are increasingly turning to Flash to deliver online video. Video sharing sites like YouTube and Google Video, news sites like the *New York Times*, and movie previews use Flash to play video for its image quality, compression, and wide compatibility and penetration. This chapter explores the exciting possibilities of integrating video in your Flash project. Flash makes working with video easy with the Import Video wizard, which takes you step by step through the process, and Adobe Media Encoder, a standalone application that converts your video to the proper format and gives you options for editing, cropping, resizing, and setting levels of compression.

There are two main ways to use video in Flash. One way is to embed video directly within your Flash movie, and the other is to keep video separate and download it to play through Flash. When you embed video into Flash, it's easy to integrate other Flash elements and interactivity. You can create truly interactive movies, for example, by adding buttons and hotspots, sounds, and vector graphics over the video. Playing external video, on the other hand, is better suited for longer video so your audience can watch as it downloads. For playback of external video, Flash provides ready-made player interfaces. You can also use video to create other unique effects—consider rotoscoping, a technique that uses video as a guide for your Flash animation. Use this effect to give hand-drawn, frame-by-frame animated sequences a live-motion feel.

Preparing Video for Flash

Whether you embed video into Flash or play back external video, you need to format your video correctly. The appropriate video format for Flash is Flash Video, which uses the extension .flv or the extension .f4v. F4V is the latest Flash Video format that supports the H.264 standard, a state-of-the-art video codec that delivers high quality with remarkably efficient compression. A codec stands for *c*ompression-*dec*ompression, and it is a method for the computer to compress a video file to save space, and then decompress it to play it back. FLV is the standard format for previous versions of Flash and uses the older codecs, Sorenson Spark or On2 VP6.

You have several ways to acquire digital video. You can shoot your own footage using a video camera and transfer it to your computer. Alternatively, you can use copyright-free video clips that are available on a CD or DVD, or the Web from commercial image stock houses. Any way you go, adding digital video is an exciting way to enrich a Flash Web site.

✔ Tip

- Flash can actually play back any video encoded in H.264, so your video file doesn't have to have the .f4v extension. For example, a video with a .mov extension encoded by QuickTime Pro with H.264 is compatible with Flash.

What Makes a Good Video?

We all know a good video when we see one. But how do you create and prepare digitized videos so they play well and look good within Flash? Knowing a little about the video compression that is built into Flash will help.

The various codecs compress video both spatially and temporally. *Spatial compression* happens within a single frame, much like JPEG compression on an image. *Temporal compression* happens between frames, so the only information that is stored is the differences between two frames. Therefore, videos that compress well contain localized motion or very little motion (such as a talking head), because the differences between frames are minimal. (In a talking-head video, only the mouth is moving.) For the same reasons, transitions, zooms, and fades don't compress or display well—stick with quick cuts if possible.

Here are a few other tips, not related to compression, for making a good embedded video:

- Keep the size small (360×270 is a good rule for videos with a 4:3 aspect ratio) and the length of the video short. Often, a few well-placed moments of video are enough to heighten the drama of your Flash movie.

- Maintain reasonable frame rates if you intend to embed video into Flash. Although video may run at about 30 frames per second (fps), use 12 to 15 fps.

- Shoot in digital. You'll get a cleaner image by using a digital source rather than filming in analog and then converting to digital.

Using Adobe Media Encoder

You can convert your video files into the proper FLV or F4V format using Adobe Media Encoder CS4, a stand-alone application that comes with Flash CS4. You can convert single files or multiple files (known as batch processing) to make your workflow easier.

Several popular formats for digital video are QuickTime (MOV), MPEG, AVI, and DV. Fortunately, Adobe Media Encoder supports all of them.

To add a video file to Adobe Media Encoder:

1. Launch Adobe Media Encoder, which comes installed with Adobe Flash CS4.

   The opening screen has a window that lists any current video files that have been added for processing. The window should be empty (**Figure 2.1**).

2. Choose File > Add or click the Add button on the right.

   A dialog box opens for you to select a video file.

3. Navigate to your video file and click OK (Mac) or Open (Windows).

   The selected video file is added to the display list and is ready for conversion to an FLV or F4V format (**Figure 2.2**).

✔ Tip

■ You can also add video files to Adobe Media Encoder by simply dragging your video file from your desktop and dropping it in the display list.

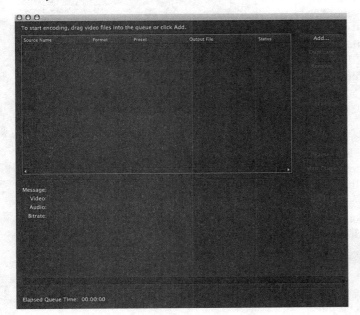

Figure 2.1 Adobe Media Encoder prepares videos in the correct format for Flash. The large central window is the display list, which lists the videos that you want to encode. The display list is currently empty.

Figure 2.2 This display list in Adobe Media Encoder contains one video that has been added.

To remove a video file from Adobe Media Encoder:

1. In the display list, select the video file.

2. Click the Remove button.

   A dialog box appears asking you to confirm whether you want to remove the selected video and its settings. Click Yes to remove the video file from the display list.

✔ Tip

- You can select multiple files for removal by holding down the Ctrl key (Windows) or Shift key (Mac) and selecting multiple video files in the display list.

To convert a video file to Flash Video:

1. In the display list, select the FLV/F4V option for Format (**Figure 2.3**).

2. Under the Preset options, choose your desired encoding profile (**Figure 2.4**).

   You can choose one of many of the standard preset options from the menu. The options determine the format (either the newer F4V or the older FLV) and the size of the video. The Web Medium option will convert your original video to 360 pixels wide by 272 pixels high, which is an average size to display video in a Web browser. In parentheses, Flash indicates the minimum Flash Player version required to play the selected video format.

   Choose Same as Source if your source video is already sized to the correct dimensions that you desire.

3. Click on the Output File.

   You can choose to save the converted file in a different location on your computer and choose a different filename. Your original video will not be deleted or altered in any way.

Figure 2.3 Choose FLV/F4V from the Format pull-down menu to select the encoding format.

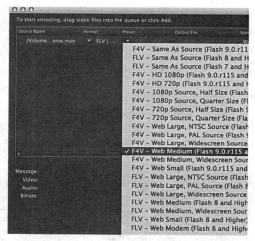

Figure 2.4 Choose your desired setting from the Preset pull-down menu. Choose F4V Web Medium or FLV Web Medium to convert your video into a Flash-compatible format at a medium size. Choose F4V Same As Source or FLV Same As Source if your video is already at your desired dimensions.

USING ADOBE MEDIA ENCODER

4. Click Start Queue.

Adobe Media Encoder begins the encoding process (**Figure 2.5**). The Media Encoder displays the settings for the encoded video, shows the progress, and shows a preview of the video. When the encoding process finishes, a green check in the display window indicates that the file has been converted successfully.

✔ Tips

■ If you have multiple video files to encode to F4V or FLV format, you can do so with Adobe Media Encoder all at once easily in a process known as batch processing. Each file can even have its own settings. Click the Add button to add additional videos to the display list. Choose a different format for each file, if desired. Click Start Queue to begin the batch processing.

■ You can change the status of individual files in the queue by selecting the file in the display list and choosing Edit > Reset Status or Edit > Skip Selection. Reset Status will remove the green check from a completed file so it can be encoded again, whereas Skip Selection will make Adobe Media Encoder skip that particular file in the batch processing.

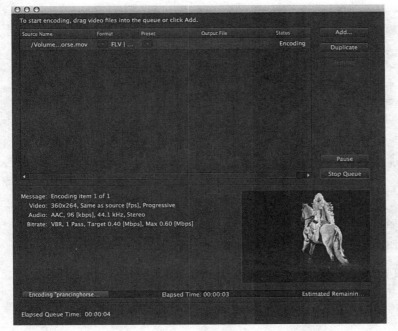

Figure 2.5 During the encoding process, Adobe Media Encoder shows the progress, the output specifications, and a preview of the video. The process may take seconds or several minutes, depending on the length and size of your video. This may be a good time to get yourself a cup of coffee.

Understanding Encoding Options

You can customize many settings in the conversion of your original video to the Flash Video format.

In some situations, you may want to crop the edges of a video to remove unsightly background or to display your video in an unconventional format. Or, you may decide to use just a portion of the video rather than all of it. Using Adobe Media Encoder, you can make the necessary adjustments to crop the video frame, resize the video, change the starting and ending points of the video, adjust the type of compression and the compression levels, or apply filters to the video.

Figure 2.6 Click the Preset selection to customize the encoding setting for that particular video.

Figure 2.7 Choose Edit > Export Settings to customize the encoding setting for that particular video.

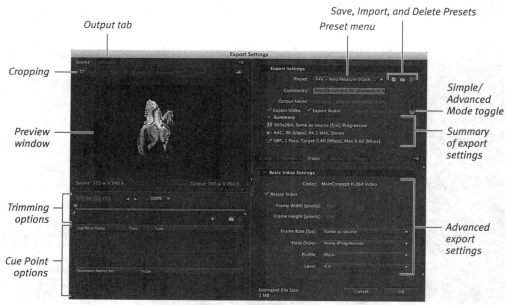

Figure 2.8 The Export Settings dialog box contains options for customizing cropping and resizing, trimming video length, adding cue points, and changing the video and audio compression levels.

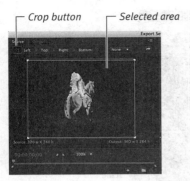

Crop button *Selected area*

Figure 2.9 Select the Crop button to select only a portion of your video. The white box with the four corner control points indicates the selected area.

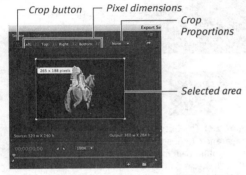

Crop button *Pixel dimensions* *Crop Proportions*

Selected area

Figure 2.10 Drag the sides or corners of the selection to cut unwanted material from the edges of the video. Enter numeric values in the Left, Top, Right, and Bottom fields for pixel-level precision. Constrain the crop with the Crop Proportions pull-down menu.

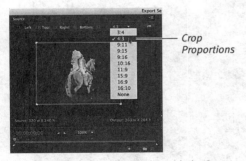

Crop Proportions

Figure 2.11 Constrain the selection with the Crop Proportions pull-down menu. A 4:3 proportion is the traditional aspect ratio for standard-definition video. A 16:9 proportion is the aspect ratio for high-definition video and cinematic presentations.

To display encoding options:

◆ Click on the Preset selection in the display window (**Figure 2.6**).

or

Choose Edit > Export Settings (**Figure 2.7**).

The Export Settings dialog box appears (**Figure 2.8**). A summary of the current output specifications are listed on the upper-right corner, cropping and trimming options are on the left, and advanced options for video and audio compression are on the bottom right.

To crop your video:

1. Click the Crop button at the upper-left corner of the Export Settings dialog box.

   The cropping box appears over the video preview window (**Figure 2.9**).

2. Drag the sides inward to crop from the top, bottom, left, or right.

   The grayed out portions outside the box will be discarded. Adobe Media Encoder displays the new dimensions next to your cursor. You can also use the Left, Top, Right, and Bottom settings above the preview window to enter exact pixel values (**Figure 2.10**).

3. If you want to keep the crop in a standard proportion, click the Crop Proportions menu and choose a desired ratio (**Figure 2.11**).

   The cropping box will be constrained to the selected proportions.

4. To see the effects of the crop, click the Output tab.

5. Change the Crop Setting pull-down menu to your desired output.

   Scale to Fit. Maintains the final output size but enlarges the final crop to fit the dimensions. Your video may lose quality if you enlarge beyond the resolution of the source.

   Continues on next page

Black Borders. Maintains the final output size and adds black to the areas that are cropped.

Change Output Size. Changes the final output size to the dimensions of the crop.

The preview window shows how your final video will appear (**Figure 2.12**).

6. Click OK to accept the crop settings.

   or

   Exit the Crop tool without accepting the crop settings by clicking the Crop button again under the Source tab.

To adjust the video length:

1. Click and drag the playhead (top marker) to scrub through your video to preview the footage. Place the playhead at the desired beginning point of your video.

   Time markers indicate the number of seconds that have elapsed (**Figure 2.13**).

2. Click the Set In Point icon.

   The In point moves to the current position of the playhead (**Figure 2.14**).

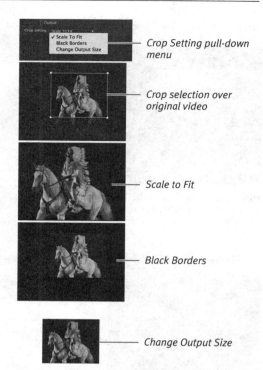

Crop Setting pull-down menu

Crop selection over original video

Scale to Fit

Black Borders

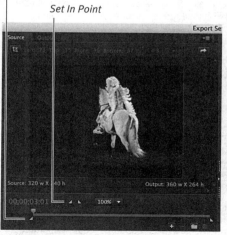

Change Output Size

Figure 2.12 The Output tab shows the final cropped appearance. Choose the options under the Crop Setting pull-down menu to determine the relationship between the crop and the output size.

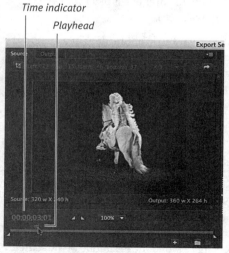

Time indicator

Playhead

Figure 2.13 Move the playhead to the point at which you want the video to begin.

In point marker

Set In Point

Figure 2.14 Click the Set In Point icon to mark the beginning of the video.

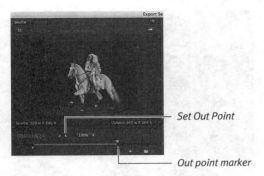

— Set Out Point

— Out point marker

Figure 2.15 Click the Set Out Point icon to mark the end of the video.

Advanced Mode/ Simple Mode icon

Video tab

Figure 2.16 Click the Video tab to resize your video.

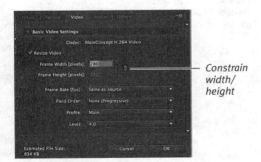

Constrain width/ height

Figure 2.17 The Resize video option lets you set how your video's size will be scaled. Click the Constrain button to keep the dimensions of your video proportional.

3. Drag the playhead to the desired ending point of your video.

4. Click the Set Out Point icon.

The Out point moves to the current position of the playhead (**Figure 2.15**).

5. You can also simply drag the In and Out markers to bracket the desired video segment.

6. Click OK to accept the new settings to trim the length of your video.

✔ Tips

■ When the playhead is selected, you can use the left or the right arrow keys on your keyboard to move back or ahead frame by frame for finer control.

■ You can double-click the time marker to enter an exact numerical value for the time.

To resize your video:

1. Click the Video tab on the right side of the screen under the Export Settings (**Figure 2.16**). If the Video tab is not visible, click the Advanced Mode/Simple Mode icon to show or hide the advanced export settings.

2. Select the Resize Video check box.

3. Change the values for Frame Width and Frame Height to change the dimensions of your video.

If you want to maintain the original aspect ratio of your video, click the Constrain box (**Figure 2.17**).

4. Click OK to accept the new resize settings.

UNDERSTANDING ENCODING OPTIONS

To select your own video compression settings:

1. Click the Format tab on the right side of the screen under the Export Settings. If the Video tab is not visible, click the Advanced Mode/Simple Mode icon to show or hide the advanced export settings.

2. Choose either the FLV format or the newer F4V format (**Figure 2.18**).

   Embedding video into Flash requires the FLV format. To download external video, you can use either the FLV or the F4V format.

3. Click the Video tab. Choose the video settings that will give the best trade-off between video file size and image quality for your movie. Depending on the format that you've chosen in step 2, you will be presented with different options:

   Codec. If you've selected the FLV format, the codec indicates which of the two available codecs will be used to compress your video. Choose the codec that best matches your file needs.

   Flash uses one of two codecs (*compression-decompression* schemes) to import and display video: either the On2 VP6 codec, which requires Flash Player 8 or later, or the Sorenson Spark codec, which requires Flash Player 7 or later. These codecs are *lossy*, meaning some (usually less important or less visible) video information is discarded to make the file smaller. The compressed movie appears similar to the original but not exactly the same (**Figure 2.19**).

   Encode Alpha Channel. If your video has an alpha channel (transparent background), select this option. Alpha channels are only supported in the FLV format with the On2 VP6 codec.

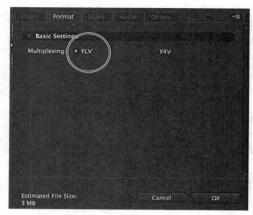

Figure 2.18 Choose FLV if you want to embed your video in Flash. Choose either FLV or F4V if you want to play back external video from Flash.

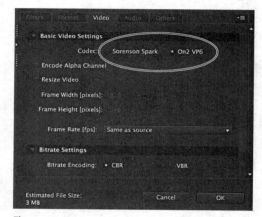

Figure 2.19 Sorenson Spark and On2 VP6 are the two different codecs available only for the FLV format. Sorenson Spark is compatible with Flash Player 7 or later, whereas On2 VP6 requires Flash Player 8 or later.

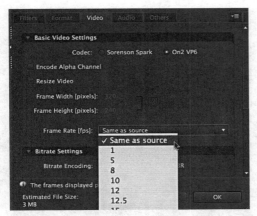

Figure 2.20 If you plan to embed video into Flash, you must set the frame rate of your video to be identical to the frame rate of your Flash movie. Choose "Same as source" only if you want to play back external video from Flash.

Figure 2.21 The Bitrate Settings determine the bandwidth required to download the video.

Resize Video. You can change the width and height or constrain the proportions for the new width and height. Refer to the task, "To resize your video," earlier.

Frame rate. Lets you choose whether to match the frame rate of your video to the frame rate of your Flash movie. For embedded video, you'll want to choose the same frame rate of your Flash movie. This choice ensures that an embedded video plays at its intended speed even if its frame rate is different than that of the Flash document. With the "Same as source" setting, a video shot at 30 frames per second (fps) and brought into a Flash movie running at 15 fps will last twice as long (and play twice as slowly) as the original source video. You should choose "Same as source" only when encoding for playback of external video (**Figure 2.20**).

Bitrate Settings. Determines the *bitrate*, which is the quality of video based on download speeds measured in kilobits per second (kbps). Flash may alter the quality of individual frames to keep the download at a consistent speed. Remember, the higher the kilobits per second of your chosen setting, the higher the quality of your video but the larger the file size. The higher the bitrate, the higher quality of the video (**Figure 2.21**).

Continues on next page

UNDERSTANDING ENCODING OPTIONS

Advanced Settings. Select the Set Key Frame Distance option to change the keyframe distance. The *keyframe distance* is how frequently complete frames of your video are stored. The frames between keyframes (known as *delta frames*) store only the data that differs between the delta frame and the preceding keyframe. A keyframe interval of 24, for example, stores the complete frame every twenty-fourth frame of your video. If your video contains the action of someone raising his hand between frames 17 and 18, only the portion of the image where the hand is being raised is stored in memory until frame 24 when the full frame is stored. The lower you set the keyframe interval, the more keyframes are stored and the larger the file. For video where the image doesn't change much (such as a talking head in front of a solid background), a higher keyframe interval works well. For video with lots of movement and changing images, a lower keyframe interval is necessary to keep the image clear (**Figure 2.22**).

4. Click OK to accept your custom video settings.

Figure 2.22 Adjust the Key Frame Distance option based on how often significant visual changes occur in your video. A higher Key Frame Distance setting means there are fewer keyframes, so less information is recorded.

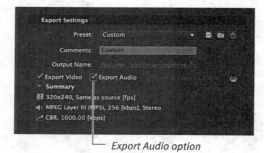

Export Audio option

Figure 2.23 Select the Export Audio check box if you want to keep audio in your video. Deselect the check box if you only want to export video.

To select your own audio compression settings:

1. Select the Export Audio option under Export Settings if you want audio exported with your video. Deselect the option if you just want to export video with no audio (**Figure 2.23**).

2. Click the Audio tab on the right side of the screen under the Export Settings. If the Audio tab is not visible, click the Advanced Mode/Simple Mode icon to show or hide the advanced export settings.

3. Choose the audio settings that will give the best trade-off between file size and audio quality for your movie. Depending on the format you've chosen (FLV or F4V), you will be presented with different audio options (**Figure 2.24**).

   Codec. AAC is a high-quality audio compression scheme for the F4V format. MP3 is the older audio compression scheme for the FLV format.

   Output Channels. Choose Mono for a single channel or Stereo for two channels (left and right).

   Frequency. The higher the frequency, the higher quality the sound. Select 44.1 kHz for CD-quality sound.

   Bitrate Settings. The higher the bitrate, the higher quality the sound.

4. Click OK to accept your custom audio settings.

Audio settings for FLV format   Audio settings for F4V format

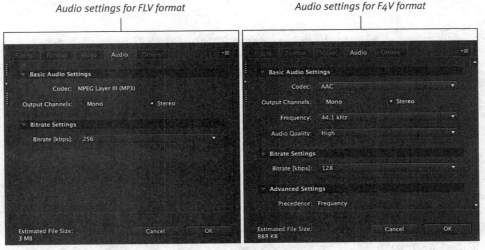

Figure 2.24 There are different audio settings, depending on if you've chosen the FLV format or the F4V format. Bitrate and Frequency determine the audio quality (the higher the number, the better the quality).

To save your custom encoding options:

1. In the Export Settings dialog box, click the Save Preset button (**Figure 2.25**).

2. In the dialog box that opens, provide a descriptive name for the video and audio options. Click OK (**Figure 2.26**).

3. Return to the queue of videos. You can apply your custom setting to additional videos by simply choosing it from the Preset pull-down menu (**Figure 2.27**).

Save Preset

Figure 2.25 You can save your custom Export Settings to apply to other videos.

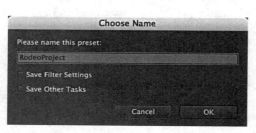

Figure 2.26 Provide a name for your custom setting.

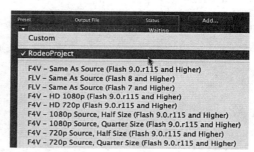

Figure 2.27 Your custom setting is available under the Preset pull-down menu.

Other Ways to Create Flash Video Files

You can create FLV and F4V files in a variety of ways. Using Adobe Media Encoder to encode the video as described in this chapter is the easiest, most basic method. There are also third-party applications, such as:

◆ On2 Flix (www.on2.com)   ◆ Sorenson Squeeze (www.sorensonmedia.com)

Alternatively, if you have QuickTime installed on your machine, you can use the Flash FLV QuickTime Export plug-in, which enables many video-editing applications to export the FLV format. You can use the professional video-editing tools in these applications to prepare your video and then export an FLV file directly from your application for use as streaming video in a Flash movie.

You can use the Flash FLV QuickTime Export plug-in from within these applications:

◆ Adobe After Effects   ◆ Apple Final Cut Pro

◆ Apple QuickTime Pro   ◆ Avid Xpress DV

QuickTime also supports the H.264 codec, which is the codec of the F4V format.

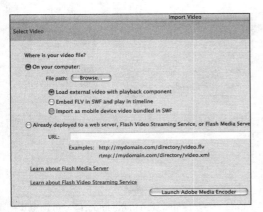

Figure 2.28 The Import Video wizard guides you through the process of integrating video with your Flash projects.

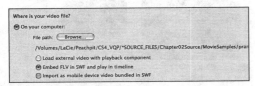

Figure 2.29 Choose "Embed FLV in SWF and play in timeline" to embed your video.

Figure 2.30 Adobe Media Encoder is easily accessible from the Import Video wizard.

Embedding Video into Flash

Everybody loves movies. So when you can add video to your Flash Web site, you'll likely create a richer and more compelling experience for your viewers.

You can embed an FLV file into Flash (but not F4V), and then add effects such as graphics, animation, masking, and interactivity; you can even apply motion tweens to your embedded video. Embedding video is the simplest way to add video and the only way to integrate video with other Flash elements on your Timeline. However, embedding video has several limitations. Embedded video is only good for short video because Flash cannot maintain audio synchronization beyond about two minutes. There is also a maximum length of 16,000 frames for embedded movies. Another drawback is the increase in file size of your Flash movie. Embedding video puts the video file inside your Flash document, so be aware of the longer download times for your audience and the more tedious testing and authoring sessions for you.

To embed a video in Flash:

1. From the File menu, choose Import > Import Video.

   The Import Video wizard appears (**Figure 2.28**).

2. Click the Browse button; in the dialog box that appears, select the FLV file you want to embed and click Open.

3. Back in the Import Video wizard, choose "Embed FLV in SWF and play in timeline"; click Next/Continue (**Figure 2.29**).

   If you have not yet converted your video to the FLV format, you can launch Adobe Media Encoder by clicking the button Launch Adobe Media Encoder (**Figure 2.30**).

Continues on next page

Continues on next page

EMBEDDING VIDEO INTO FLASH

4. The next screen of the Import Video wizard presents the Embedding options. Set the Symbol type to Embedded video; select the options "Place instance on stage," "Expand timeline if needed," and "Include audio" (**Figure 2.31**). Click Next/Continue.

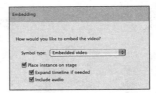

Figure 2.31 The Embedding step lets you choose settings for embedding your video.

5. The Import Video wizard proceeds to the final screen (**Figure 2.32**), summarizing your video embedding settings.

6. Click Finish.

Flash embeds the video in your document, putting a video symbol in your Library and an instance of the video on the Stage in the active layer (**Figure 2.33**).

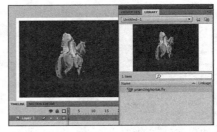

Figure 2.32 The final step in the Import Video wizard summarizes your settings.

✔ Tips

■ When embedding an FLV into Flash, remember to encode the FLV at the same frame rate as your Flash file. This is an important step to keep the frame rate of your video consistent with the frame rate of your Flash movie. This ensures your video plays at its intended speed.

Figure 2.33 The embedded video is placed on the Stage and Flash adds frames to the Timeline to accommodate the video. The video is stored in the Library.

■ Flash can't display the soundtrack of embedded FLVs, so if your original video file has sound, you won't hear it within the Flash authoring environment. When you publish your Flash movie or test it by choosing Control > Test Movie, the sound will be audible.

■ If you have more frames than are needed in a layer containing an embedded FLV, Flash displays the last frame of the video until the end of the Timeline. To make the end of the Timeline match up with the end of the video, select the excess frames and choose Edit > Timeline > Remove Frames.

Figure 2.34 For videos with an alpha channel (transparency), choose FLV for the format and On2 VP6 for the codec, and select the Encode Alpha Channel option (top). This allows you to embed video with transparent backgrounds (bottom) such as a weatherperson in front of a weather map.

- If you do not have sound, check your source video clip. Sometimes a QuickTime file uses an audio compression scheme that Flash doesn't recognize. You may have to export your video with a different audio compression from another application.

- If you have video with a transparent background (an alpha channel), you can import it into Flash and still preserve the transparency. In Adobe Media Encoder, click the Video tab and select the Encode Alpha Channel option (**Figure 2.34**). Alpha channels are only supported with the On2 VP6 video codec (Flash Player 8 and later).

To swap an embedded video:

1. Double-click the video icon or the preview window in your Library.

   or

   Click the video symbol in the Library; then, from the Library window's Options menu, choose Properties (**Figure 2.35**).

   The Video Properties dialog box appears showing the symbol name and the original video file's location (**Figure 2.36**).

2. Click Import.

3. Choose a new FLV file and click Open.

   Flash swaps the existing FLV video with the newly selected FLV.

4. Click OK.

   The new FLV replaces the old FLV in the Library and on any existing instances on the Stage (**Figure 2.37**).

Figure 2.35 Select the video in your Library and choose Properties from the Options menu.

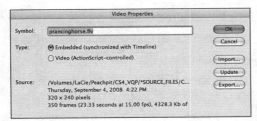

Figure 2.36 The Video Properties dialog box shows the name of the symbol and the location of the original video file, as well as the properties of the compressed video (dimensions, time, and size).

Figure 2.37 The newly selected video replaces the previous one in the Library.

EMBEDDING VIDEO INTO FLASH

Playback of External Video

So far, you've learned how to encode your videos and embed and play video in Flash. However, embedded video has a length restriction (16,000 frames, or approximately 8.5 minutes of 30 fps video). Also, embedded video begins to lose synchronization with its audio after about two minutes. Most important, embedded video significantly increases the file size of your Flash movie. You can bypass these problems by loading an external video file with a Flash playback component. This means that Flash dynamically loads video that is kept separate from the Flash file.

Playback of external video (formerly referred to as *progressive download*) requires that your video be in the FLV or F4V file format.

Flash provides a special component known as a *skin* to give you control over the playback of your external video. Chapter 6, "Managing External Communication," looks at more advanced ways to load and control external video using ActionScript.

It's important to remember that since the video resides outside your Flash movie, you cannot synchronize other Flash elements to your video. If you want to synchronize your video to other Flash elements, you should use embedded video. Refer to **Table 2.1** for a summary comparison of embedded video and external playback.

Table 2.1

Embed vs. External Playback		
	EMBED	EXTERNAL PLAYBACK
Video length	Under 2 min with audio, or 16,000 frames total	No restriction
Flash Player	Versions 6 and later	Versions 7 and later
Usage	Short, small (320 x 240) video clips that need to be synchronized to other Flash elements on the Timeline	Longer, larger (720 x 580) video clips that do not need to be synchronized to other Flash elements on the Timeline
Video frame rate	Must be the same frame rate as Flash	Can be at a different frame rate than Flash
File size	Increases because video is contained within SWF	No effect, but FLV/F4V must accompany your SWF (or your SWF must be given the correct path to find the FLV/F4V)
Interface	None	Ready-made interfaces, or "skins," are available to control the playback of the video. Flash player skins are small SWF files that are also kept external to your main Flash movie and must accompany your SWF.
Editability	Edit video and reimport into Flash	Edit video and convert to FLV/FV without opening Flash

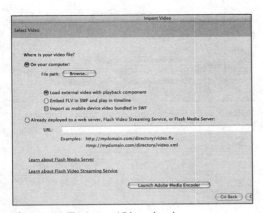

Figure 2.38 The Import Video wizard.

Figure 2.39 After you've selected your video file, choose the first option, "Load external video with playback component."

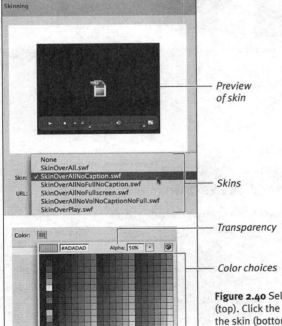

Preview of skin

Skins

Transparency

Color choices

Figure 2.40 Select a video player skin from the pull-down menu (top). Click the color chip to change the color and transparency of the skin (bottom). The preview window shows you how the controls will appear with your video.

To play back external video:

1. Choose File > Import > Import Video to open the Import Video wizard (**Figure 2.38**).

2. Use the Browse button to select the video file that you want and click Next/Continue. Your video *must* be an FLV or an F4V formatted video.

   If you have not yet converted your video to the FLV/F4V format, you can launch Adobe Media Encoder by clicking the Launch Adobe Media Encoder button.

3. Select "Load external video with playback component," and click Next/Continue (**Figure 2.39**).

4. On the Skinning screen, choose a player skin and a color for your video player from the menu, and click Next/Continue (**Figure 2.40**).

   The player skin provides a viewing window and playback controls for your video. From the pull-down menu, choose a skin that includes different playback controls and from the adjacent color chip choose a color (or a transparency level). In the preview window you can see how your skin will appear. Note that some skins add the controls over the video, and some add the controls under the video.

   Continues on next page

If you do not want any playback controls for your video, choose None from the top of the menu (**Figure 2.41**).

5. On the final screen, review the summary of settings, and then click Finish.

A video playback component appears on the Stage and in the Library (**Figure 2.42**). This component controls the playback of your external FLV/F4V file. Position the component anywhere on the Stage and at the keyframe at which you want the video to begin playing.

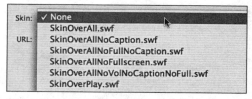

Figure 2.41 Choose the top option, None, to present your video without controls.

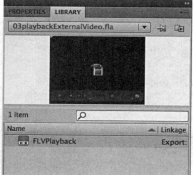

Figure 2.42 The video playback component is added to your Library and placed on the Stage. The black square represents your video.

Playback of External Video vs. Streaming

Playback of external video uses progressive streaming that allows the video to start playing as soon as video information reaches the Flash Player rather than wait to download the entire video file.

For long videos, you may want to use *true video streaming*, which lets viewers jump to any point in the video even if it hasn't downloaded yet. However, true video streaming requires a special video streaming server (like Flash Video Streaming Services or the Flash Media Server). These services are geared more toward sophisticated and commercial applications like video chats and live video streaming.

Figure 2.43 Your video is only visible when you publish your movie or select Control > Test Movie. The video playback component uses the skin that you chose as the interface and streams the video file.

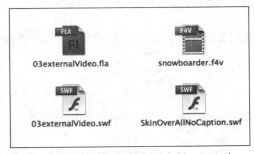

Figure 2.44 For playback of external video to work, your Flash movie (SWF) must be able to find and access the video file. If you are using a skin, the SWF file for the skin must also accompany your Flash movie. All three of these files (the Flash movie SWF, the FLV/F4V, and the skin SWF) are required to play.

6. To see your video, you must choose Control > Test Movie.

   Flash plays the external FLV/F4V file with the video playback component and the skin that you chose (**Figure 2.43**). The FLV/F4V file and a small SWF file for the player skin you selected is saved in the same folder as your Flash document and your SWF file (**Figure 2.44**).

✔ Tip

■ In addition to the predefined player skins, you can create a custom skin by either modifying parts of a predefined skin or creating your own skin from scratch. However, to do this, you need to write some custom ActionScript. For details, see the Flash ActionScript Help (Help > Flash Help).

Changing video playback options

You can change the way your video plays within Flash by changing the options in the video playback component. The video playback component is simply the player for the external video. By changing the options in the Parameters panel, you can change the "skin," or the appearance, of the player as well as other playback features.

To change the skin of the video playback component:

1. Click the video playback component on the Stage.

2. Select Window > Component Inspector (Shift-F7).

   The Component Inspector window appears (**Figure 2.45**).

3. Find the skin parameter (in the first column) and click the current value (in the second column). Click the magnifying glass icon (**Figure 2.46**).

   The Select Skin dialog box appears.

4. Choose a different skin and/or color for your player (**Figure 2.47**). Click OK.

   Once you test (Control > Test) or publish your Flash movie, the new skin will be saved in the same folder as your Flash document.

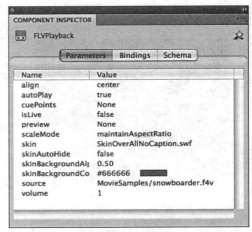

Figure 2.45 The Component Inspector lets you set options for your video player skin and other Flash components. The first column is the parameter, and the second column is the value for that parameter.

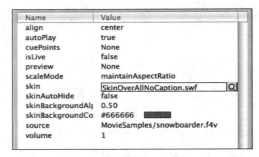

Figure 2.46 The "skin" parameter determines which playback interface to use.

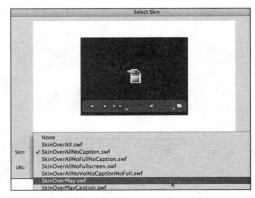

Figure 2.47 Set a new skin.

Skin transparency (0 to 1.0) ⎤   ⎡ *Skin color*

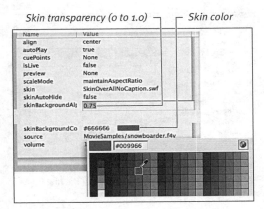

Figure 2.48 Set a new skin color and transparency directly in the Component Inspector.

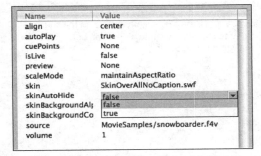

Figure 2.49 Set skinAutoHide to true or false to hide or show the interface. Be careful when hiding the interface because users won't necessarily know how to access the controls.

5. In the Parameters tab of the Component Inspector, find the parameters for skinBackgroundAlpha and skinBackgroundColor. Click the current value (in the second column) to change the transparency of the skin or the background color of the skin (**Figure 2.48**).

6. In the Parameters tab of the Component Inspector, find the parameter for skinAutoHide. Click the current value (in the second column) to change whether or not the interface is always visible (**Figure 2.49**).

▲ Set skinAutoHide to true to keep the interface hidden until the mouse pointer moves over the video.

▲ Set skinAutoHide to false to have the interface be visible all the time.

To change the playback of the external video:

1. Click the video playback component on the Stage.

2. Select Window > Component Inspector (Shift-F7) if the Component Inspector is not open.

   The Component Inspector window appears.

3. Find the autoPlay parameter (in the first column) and click the current value (in the second column) (**Figure 2.50**).

   ▲ Set autoPlay to true to have the video automatically begin playing.

   ▲ Set autoPlay to false to have the video paused at the first frame.

To change the path to the external video:

1. Click the video playback component on the Stage.

2. Open the Component Inspector (Window > Component Inspector, Shift-F7).

3. Find the source parameter (in the first column) and click the current value (in the second column). Click the magnifying glass icon.

   The Content Path dialog box appears (**Figure 2.51**).

4. Click the folder icon to browse to the new location of your FLV/F4V file.

   Flash changes the path to your video file in the Parameters panel so that the video playback component can find the file and play it.

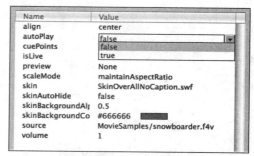

Figure 2.50 Set autoPlay to true or false to make the video play automatically or be paused at the first frame.

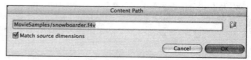

Figure 2.51 Click the magnifying icon in the source value to change the name or location of the file that the video player loads.

Figure 2.52 A video that is good for rotoscoping contains dramatic or interesting motion with a clear distinction between background and foreground.

A simple tracing of this gorilla was made with the Pencil tool set on the Smooth Pencil mode.

Lock the layer containing the video to prevent yourself from moving it accidentally.

Figure 2.53 Zoom in to the area you want to trace and use the imported video file as your guide.

Rotoscoping

Rotoscoping is a traditional animator's technique that involves tracing live-motion film to create animation. This process is named after an actual machine, the Rotoscope, which projected live-action film onto an animation board. There, an animator could easily trace the outline of an actor frame by frame to get natural motion that would be too difficult to animate by hand. In the early days, Disney animators often used rotoscoping to do studies, and feature movies and commercials rely on rotoscoping even today.

You can use Flash to import and display digitized videos of actors or moving objects, and then do the rotoscoping yourself.

To copy the motion of a video:

1. Embed an FLV video as described earlier in this chapter (**Figure 2.52**).

2. Lock the layer that contains the video.

3. Add a new layer above the layer that contains your video.

4. Begin tracing the actors or the action in the new layer in keyframe 1 with any of the drawing tools (**Figure 2.53**).

5. Add a blank keyframe by choosing Insert > Timeline > Blank Keyframe.

    An empty keyframe appears in the next frame.

6. Trace the actors or action in the empty keyframe you just created.

Continues on next page

ROTOSCOPING

7. Continue the process of adding blank keyframes and tracing until your sequence is complete (**Figure 2.54**).

8. Delete the layer that contains the imported video to see the final rotoscoped animation (**Figure 2.55**).

In this example, rotoscoping produces a very simple outline of the action, but you can trace any level of detail depending on the desired effect.

✔ Tips

■ To make it easier to see the video below your tracings, you can select the Show Layers As Outlines option in your active layer, or you can use a semitransparent color until you finish the entire sequence.

■ Use the Onion Skin buttons (**Figure 2.56**) to help you see your drawings in the previous keyframes.

■ Use the comma (,) and period (.) keys to move backward or forward on the Timeline in one-frame increments. This technique helps you go back and forth rapidly between frames to test the differences between your drawings, much like a traditional animator flips between two tracings.

Figure 2.54 Rotoscoping this gorilla results in a layer of keyframes with drawings that follow its gait.

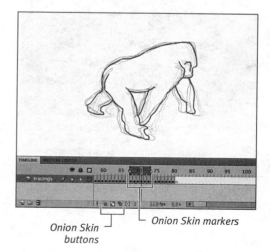

Onion Skin buttons

Onion Skin markers

Figure 2.56 Use the Onion Skin buttons below the Timeline to show multiple frames in front of or behind the current frame. Move the Onion Skin markers to show fewer or more frames. This Onion Skin shows five total frames: three frames behind and two frames ahead of the current frame 71.

Figure 2.55 When you play the finished rotoscoped animation, you'll see how natural the animation appears even if the tracings are very simple.

Part II: Interactivity

Getting a Handle on ActionScript

3

ActionScript is Flash's programming language for adding interactivity to your graphics and movies. You can use ActionScript to create anything from simple navigation within your Flash movie to complex interfaces that react to the location of the viewer's pointer, arcade-style games, and even full-blown e-commerce sites with dynamically updating data. In this chapter, you'll learn how to construct ActionScript to create effective Flash interaction. Think of the process as learning the grammar of a foreign language: First, you must learn how to put nouns and verbs together and integrate adjectives and prepositions; then you can expand your communication skills and have meaningful conversations by building your vocabulary. This chapter will give you a sound ActionScript foundation upon which you can build your Flash literacy.

If you're familiar with object-oriented programming languages such as Java, PHP, or JavaScript, you'll recognize the similarities in ActionScript. Although there are slight differences, the basic syntax and the handling of objects—reusable pieces of code—remain the same.

Even if you don't have any programming experience, you'll see in this chapter that Flash provides tools to help you write script. You'll learn about the logic of objects and how the Actions panel can give you hints during the scripting process.

What Is ActionScript 3.0?

Like any language, ActionScript evolves over time. Introduced in Flash CS3, ActionScript 3.0 is simply the latest version of the Flash programming language that lets you control graphics, animation, sound, and interactivity. However, ActionScript 3.0 represents a significant change (some may say revolutionary) from the previous versions because in many ways it is conceptually and architecturally different. Key differences from ActionScript 2.0 include:

- New ways of handling data that result in a much faster playback performance.

- A new model for detecting and responding to events (like a mouse click or a keyboard input).

- A display list, which manages the dynamic display of all kinds of graphics on the Stage.

- Low-level object control, so ActionScript can now control virtually every kind of Flash element.

- Less dependence on the movie clip symbol as the main actor in advanced Flash projects. ActionScript 3.0 now provides different objects that are more specific to the task rather than relying on the movie clip for a wide variety of purposes.

- Changes in the actual language, so users familiar with the previous versions of ActionScript will have to relearn commands (`getURL` is now `navigateToURL`, `_root` is now `root`, properties like `_x` changed to simply `x`).

Though dramatic, the changes in ActionScript 3.0 provide a clear advantage in performance and overall sophistication that advanced object-oriented programmers and developers of rich Internet applications will appreciate. But newcomers to ActionScript should begin their study with the basic building blocks—objects and classes.

Figure 3.1 Objects in the real world include things like a cow, a tree, and a person.

Human class

Adam   Betty   Zeke

Figure 3.2 Adam, Betty, and Zeke are three objects of the Human class. Flash doesn't have such a class, but this analogy is useful for understanding objects.

About Objects and Classes

At the heart of ActionScript are objects and classes. *Objects* are specific pieces of data—such as sound, graphics, text, and numeric values—that you create in Flash and use to control the movie. A date object, for example, retrieves information about the time and the date, and an array object manipulates data stored in a particular order.

All the objects you use and create belong to larger collective groups known as *classes*. Flash provides certain classes for you to use in your movie. These built-in classes handle a wide range of Flash elements such as data (`Array` class, `Math` class) and sound and video (`Sound` class, `Video` class).

Learning to code in ActionScript centers on understanding the capabilities of objects and their classes, and using them to interact with one another and with the viewer.

In the real world, you're familiar with objects such as a cow, a tree, and a person (**Figure 3.1**). Flash objects range from visible things, such as a movie clip of a spinning ball, to more abstract concepts, such as the date, pieces of data, or the handling of keyboard inputs. Whether concrete or abstract, however, Flash objects are versatile because after you create them, you can reuse them in different contexts.

Before you can use objects, you need to be able to identify them, and you do so by name just as you do in the real world. Say you have three people in front of you: Adam, Betty, and Zeke. All three are objects that can be distinguished by name. All three belong to the collective group known as *humans*. You can also say that Adam, Betty, and Zeke are all *instances* of the Human class (**Figure 3.2**). In ActionScript, *instances* and *objects* are synonymous, and the terms are used interchangeably in this book.

About Methods and Properties

Each object of a class (Zeke of the humans, for example) differs from the others in its class by more than just its name. Each person is different because of several defining characteristics, such as height, weight, gender, and hair color. In object-oriented programming, you say that objects and classes have properties. Height, weight, sex, and hair color are all properties of the Human class (**Figure 3.3**).

In Flash, each class has a predefined set of properties that lets you establish the uniqueness of the object. The Sound class has many properties, one of which is length, which measures the duration of a sound in milliseconds. The MovieClip class, on the other hand, has different properties, such as height, width, and rotation, which are measures of the dimensions and orientation of a particular movie clip object. By defining and changing the properties of objects, you control what each object is like and how each object appears, sounds, and behaves.

Objects also do things. Zeke can run, sleep, and talk. The things that objects can do are known as *methods*. Each class has its own set of methods. The MovieClip class, for example, has a gotoAndStop() method that sends the Flash playhead to a particular frame on its Timeline, and the Date class has a getDay() method that retrieves the day of the week. When an object does something by using a method, you say that the method is *called* or that the object *calls* the method.

Understanding the relationships between objects, classes, properties, and methods is important. Putting objects together so that the methods and properties of one influence the methods and properties of another is what drives Flash interactivity. The key to building your ActionScript vocabulary is learning the properties and methods of different classes.

Figure 3.3 Adam, Betty, and Zeke are human objects with different properties. Names and properties differentiate objects of the same class.

✔ Tip

- It helps to think of objects as nouns, properties as adjectives, and methods as verbs. Properties describe their objects, whereas methods are the actions that the objects perform.

Betty.weight=135   Zeke.weight=188

Figure 3.4 The hypothetical weight property describes Betty and Zeke. In Flash, many properties of objects can be both read and modified with ActionScript.

Symbols and Classes

Symbols aren't classes. Symbols aren't even objects. It's true that most types of symbols (like movie clips, buttons, bitmaps, and video) have an associated class, which is perhaps the source of some confusion. For the most part, symbols that appear in the Library aren't objects or classes because they don't have methods and properties that you can control with ActionScript.

Symbols are simply reusable assets, like blueprints, created in or imported to the Library. You create instances, or copies, of the symbols to use in your movie. When you place an instance of certain symbols, such as a button or a movie clip, on the Stage and give it a name, it becomes an instance of the corresponding class (SimpleButton or MovieClip) that you can manipulate using ActionScript.

Writing with Dot Syntax

As with other foreign languages, you must learn the rules of grammar to put words together. *Dot syntax* is the convention that ActionScript uses to put objects, properties, and methods together into statements. You connect objects, properties, and methods with dots (periods) to describe a particular object or process. Here are two examples:

```
Zeke.weight = 188

Betty.weight = 135
```

The first statement assigns the value 188 to the weight of Zeke. The second statement assigns the value 135 to the weight of Betty. The dot separates the object name (Zeke, Betty) from the property (weight) (**Figure 3.4**).

In this statement, the object Betty is linked to the object shirt:

```
Betty.shirt.color = "gray"
```

The object shirt, in turn, has the property color, which is assigned the value gray. Notice that with dot syntax you use multiple dots to maintain object hierarchy. When you have multiple objects linked in this fashion, it's often easier to read the statement backward. So you could read it as "Gray is the color of the shirt of Betty."

Continues on next page

WRITING WITH DOT SYNTAX

Now consider the following statement:

`Zeke.run()`

This statement causes Flash to call the method `run()` on the object Zeke, which causes him to do something. The parentheses after `run` signify that `run` is a method, not a property. You can think of this construction as noun-dot-verb (**Figure 3.5**). Methods often have *parameters* (sometimes called arguments) within the parentheses. These parameters affect how the method is executed.

For example, both of these statements will make the `Zeke` and `Adam` objects perform the `run()` method, but because each method contains a different parameter, the way the run is performed is different—Zeke runs fast, and Adam runs slowly:

`Zeke.run(fast)`

`Adam.run(slow)`

Each method has its own set of parameters that you must learn. Consider the basic Flash action `gotoAndPlay(20, "Scene1")`. The method `gotoAndPlay()` belongs to the `MovieClip` class. The parenthetical parameters, `(20, "Scene1")`, refer to the frame number and the scene, so calling this method makes the playhead of the object jump to Scene1, frame 20, and begin playing.

Mouse.hide()

Adam.run()

Figure 3.5 Dot syntax lets you make objects call methods. Just as the hypothetical method `run()` could make the Adam object begin to jog, the real Flash method `hide()`, when applied to the Mouse object, makes the pointer disappear.

More on Punctuation

Dot syntax allows you to construct meaningful processes and assignments with objects, properties, and methods. Additional punctuation symbols let you do more with these single statements.

The semicolon

To terminate individual ActionScript statements and start new ones, you use the semicolon (;). The semicolon functions as a period does in a sentence—it concludes one idea and lets another one begin. Here are two examples:

```
myMovieClip.stop();
```

```
myMovieClip.rotation = 45;
```

The semicolons separate the statements so that the object called myMovieClip stops playing, and then it is rotated 45 degrees. Each statement is executed in order from the top down, like a set of instructions or a cookbook recipe.

✔ Tip

■ Flash will still understand ActionScript statements even if you don't use semicolons to terminate each one. It's good practice, however, to include them in your scripts.

Curly braces

Curly braces ({}) are another kind of punctuation that ActionScript uses frequently. Curly braces group related blocks of ActionScript statements. When you assign actions to respond to an event, for example, those actions appear within curly braces in a statement called a *function*:

```
function doThisAfterButtonClick () {
        myMovieClip.stop();
        myMovieClip.rotation = 45;
}
```

In this case, both the stop action and the change in rotation are executed when this function is called. Notice how the curly braces are separated on different lines to make the related ActionScript statements easier to read.

Commas

Commas (,) separate the parameters of a method. A method can take many parameters. The gotoAndPlay( ) method, for example, can take two: a frame number and a scene name. With commas separating the parameters, the ActionScript code looks like this:

```
gotoAndPlay(20, "Scene 1");
```

Some methods may have three, four, or perhaps even ten parameters, but as long as you separate the parameters with commas, Flash knows how to handle the code.

Capitalization

ActionScript 3.0 is case sensitive. That is, it knows the difference between lowercase letters and uppercase letters, so you must be very careful and conscientious about capitalizations in all your code.

Colons

Colons (:) identify the type of object. When you first encounter Zeke, for example, you can identify him with the statement, Zeke:Human because Zeke is an instance of the Human class. Colons are important whenever new instances are introduced so that Flash knows what kind of data to associate with the object. You'll learn more about colons and the process of *strict typing* later in this chapter.

The Actions Panel

The Actions panel is a Flash dialog box that lets you access all the actions that control your Flash movie. The Actions panel provides Script Assist, a mode in which you are guided through the process of writing code by using a fill-in-the-blanks style to write commands. However, writing ActionScript code directly is far more efficient and in the long run the better way to learn because you won't spend your time hunting for a command buried deep within menus. This book will not show you how to write code with Script Assist.

However, don't worry that you'll be left alone in your code writing. As you write your own ActionScript, the Actions panel provides hints as you enter code and also automates some of the formatting. The Actions panel can also check for errors and give you access to the ActionScript Reference Guide.

To open the Actions panel:

◆ From the Window menu, choose Actions (F9 on Windows, Option-F9 on Mac).

or

Alt-double-click (Windows) or Option-double-click (Mac) a keyframe in the Timeline.

or

Right-click (Windows) or Ctrl-click (Mac) a keyframe in the Timeline and choose Actions at the bottom of the context menu.

or

Select a keyframe and click the Actions icon on the top-right corner of the Property inspector (**Figure 3.6**).

To undock the Actions panel:

◆ Grab the Actions panel by its tab and drag it out of its current location.

The Actions panel undocks with its panel set and becomes a free-floating window.

To redock the Actions panel:

1. Grab the Actions panel by its tab or top horizontal bar and drag it over the different panels on your desktop.

   The different panels will highlight, indicating that you can dock the Actions panel in that location.

2. Drop the Actions panel.

   The Actions panel docks with the highlighted panels.

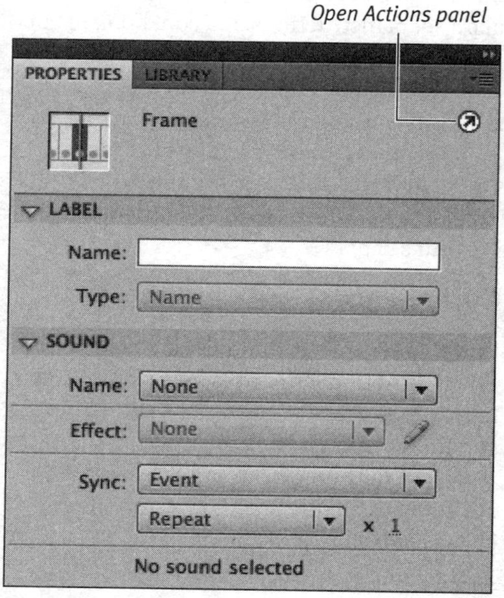

Figure 3.6 In the Property inspector, click the icon with the arrow to open the Actions panel.

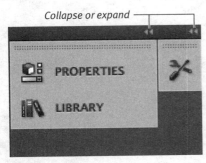

Collapse or expand

Figure 3.7 The Actions panel as well as the other panels can be viewed as icons or icons and text by clicking the double-headed arrow at the top-right corner.

✔ Tips

■ You can choose to view your Actions panel, as well as all your other panels, as icons and text, thus freeing up more of your screen. Choose the double-headed arrow icon at the top-right corner of the Actions panel to collapse or expand it (**Figure 3.7**).

■ The Actions panel can be minimized just like other windows by clicking on the top light-gray horizontal bar (**Figure 3.8**). Expand the panel by clicking on the light-gray horizontal bar again.

■ Resize the Actions panel by clicking and dragging the bottom-right corner.

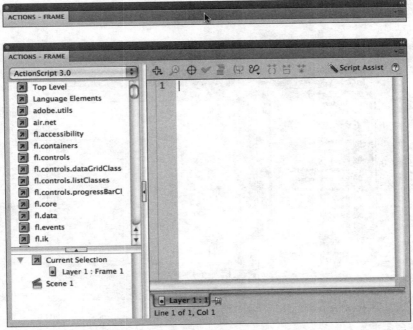

Figure 3.8 Clicking on the top light-gray horizontal bar can collapse the Actions panel (top). Clicking on it again restores it (bottom). You can also use the double-headed arrow icon on the top right to collapse the panel to icon mode.

Actions panel layout

The Actions panel features several sections and multiple ways to enter ActionScript statements (**Figure 3.9**). The Actions toolbox on the left side displays all the available commands, organized by *packages*, which are groups of related classes. At the bottom of the categories colored in yellow, an index lists all the ActionScript commands in alphabetical order. You can use the Script navigator in the lower-left portion of the Actions panel to navigate to different scripts within your Flash movie. In the right section, your completed script appears in the Script pane. This part of the Actions panel also offers additional functions when the panel is in the special Script Assist mode. At the top, a row of buttons and an options pop-up menu provide additional features.

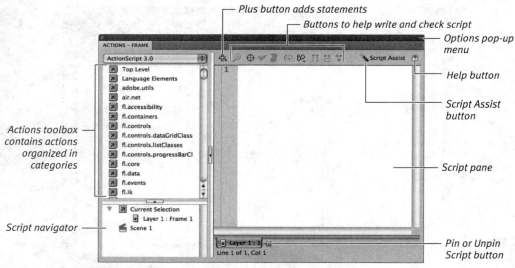

Figure 3.9 The Actions panel.

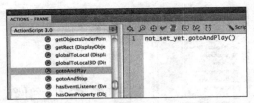

Figure 3.10 Add an action by choosing a statement from the Actions toolbox. Here, the action gotoAndPlay() has been added to the Script pane, and Flash indicates that there is still code missing before it.

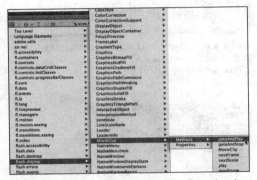

Figure 3.11 Add an action by choosing it from the plus button's pull-down menus.

Adding ActionScript

Now that you know where the Actions panel is located, how do you add ActionScript code? You must first select a keyframe on the Timeline in which you want to add ActionScript. This tells Flash when to carry out those instructions. Most often, ActionScript is put on the very first keyframe of your Flash movie.

Next, open the Actions panel and add code by directly typing in the Script pane or by choosing code from the categories or menus provided.

To add an action in the Script pane:

1. Select the keyframe on the Timeline where you want to assign an action.

2. In the Script pane of the Actions panel, begin typing the desired action.

   or

   Open a category from the left toolbox of the Actions panel and double-click the desired action or drag it into the Script pane.

   The action appears in the Script pane. The action may be incomplete, and Flash tells you what additional elements need to be provided to complete the statement (**Figure 3.10**).

   or

   Click the plus button above the Script pane and choose the action from the pull-down menus (**Figure 3.11**).

   The action appears in the Script pane.

✔ Tip

- While making your selection in the Actions toolbox, you can use the arrow keys, the Page Up and Page Down keys, or the Home and End keys to navigate through the list. Press Enter or the spacebar to open or close categories or to choose an action to put in the Script pane.

THE ACTIONS PANEL

To edit actions in the Script pane:

◆ Highlight the action, and then click and drag it to a new position in the Script pane.

or

Highlight the action and use Copy, Cut, or Paste from the keyboard (Ctrl-C, Ctrl-X, or Ctrl-V on Windows; Cmd-C, Cmd-X, or Cmd-V on the Mac) or from the context menu (right-click on Windows, Ctrl-click on the Mac). Don't use Copy, Cut, or Paste from the Edit menu because those commands only affect the objects on the Stage.

To remove an action from the Script pane:

◆ Highlight the action and use the Delete key to remove it from the Script pane.

To modify the Actions panel display:

◆ Drag or double-click the vertical splitter bar, or click the arrow button that divides the Actions toolbox and Script pane, to collapse or expand an area (**Figure 3.12**).

or

Drag or double-click the horizontal splitter bar, or click the arrow button that divides the Actions toolbox and Script navigator, to collapse or expand an area (**Figure 3.13**).

To show earlier versions of ActionScript:

◆ If you are authoring for earlier versions of the Flash Player and need to use commands from ActionScript 1.0 or 2.0, click the pull-down menu above the Actions toolbox and select a different version (**Figure 3.14**).

The categories in the Actions toolbox change to only show actions that you can use for that version.

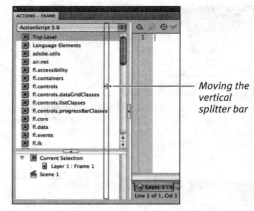

Moving the vertical splitter bar

Figure 3.12 Resize the Script pane by dragging or clicking the vertical splitter bar that separates it from the Actions toolbox.

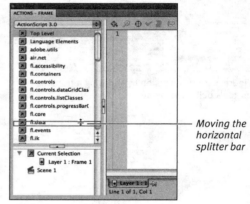

Moving the horizontal splitter bar

Figure 3.13 Resize the Actions toolbox by dragging or clicking the horizontal splitter bar that separates it from the Script navigator.

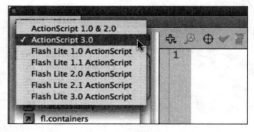

Figure 3.14 Choose an ActionScript version from the top pull-down menu.

Actions panel options

The Actions panel provides many features that can help you write reliable code quickly and easily. Chapter 12, "Managing Content and Troubleshooting," explains many other debugging tools in detail.

When you're writing ActionScript in the Script pane, you can use *code hints*, which appear as you type. Code hints recognize what kind of action you're typing and offer choices and prompts on how to complete it. Flash makes it easy to be an expert! You can also customize the format options so that your code looks just the way you want it for ease of reading and understanding.

Coding help is always available in the Actions panel. The Help button, for example, calls up the Help site on the Adobe Flash Web site and sends you directly to the description and usage of any action selected in the Actions toolbox in case you have trouble remembering what a particular action does or how it's used.

If you want to keep an ActionScript visible as you select other elements in your Flash movie, you can do so by pinning your script. *Pinning* makes your script "stick" in the Script pane until you unpin it. This technique is useful if you've forgotten the name of a text box or a movie clip and need to reference it in an ActionScript statement. You can pin your current script, and then go look for your text box or movie clip. Your script remains in place so that you can make the necessary edits.

Other Places for ActionScript

The Timeline isn't the only place you can put ActionScript. More advanced coders often will create their own ActionScript classes or extend the functionality of Flash's preexisting classes. In those cases, ActionScript is written in a separate text file (the filename is identical to the custom class name with the extension *.as* to indicate that it is ActionScript). The text file is saved in the same directory as the Flash file. When you create your own classes this way, you must use the `import` statement in the script to use the preexisting classes to build upon.

You can also put your ActionScript in an external text file and have Flash include it in the Timeline when you publish your SWF. Use the `include` statement on the Timeline at the point in which you want to insert the external script. Any changes to the script in the external text file, however, will require you to republish the SWF, because the code is not imported at runtime.

To use code hints:

1. Enter an action in the Script pane, and then type the opening parenthesis.

   Flash detects the action and anticipates that you will enter its parameters. A code hint appears to guide you (**Figure 3.15**). If an action has different contexts in which it can be used, the tooltip shows those options (**Figure 3.16**).

2. Enter the first parameter and then a comma.

   The bold in the code hint advances to highlight the next required parameter (**Figure 3.17**).

3. Continue entering the required parameters and type a closing parenthesis to finish the action.

   The code hint disappears (**Figure 3.18**).

   or

1. Enter an object target path and then a period or a colon.

   Flash anticipates that you will enter a method or property after a period or a data type after a colon. A menu-style code hint appears to guide you (**Figure 3.19**).

2. Choose the appropriate term from the menu.

   Flash fills in your choice, completing that part of your code (**Figure 3.20**).

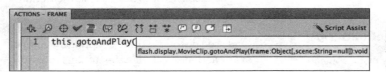

Figure 3.15 A code hint guides you as you enter ActionScript. The first required parameter for this action is the frame.

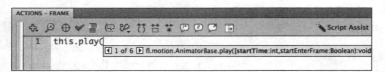

Figure 3.16 The action play() can be used in six different contexts. The code hint shows you which objects are involved in the six ways.

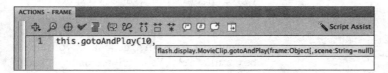

Figure 3.17 After you enter the first parameter (the frame), the code hint directs you to the next parameter. The next parameter for this action is the scene.

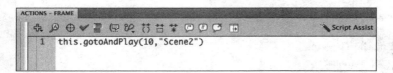

Figure 3.18 When you enter the closing parenthesis, the code hint disappears.

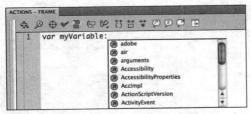

Figure 3.19 The code hint provides a scrolling list of actions appropriate for the preceding object. This list contains the possible data types.

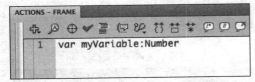

Figure 3.20 When you complete the statement, the code hint disappears.

— Show Code Hint button

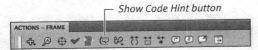

Figure 3.21 The Show Code Hint button is above the Script pane.

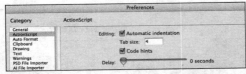

Figure 3.22 In the Preferences dialog box, you can change the time that it takes for code hints to appear or turn off that feature completely.

✔ Tips

■ There are two ways to trigger code hints for object methods and properties. Flash gives code hints for objects when you specify the data type of the object when you first define it. Learn more about defining and naming variables later in this chapter. In addition, you can trigger code hints by giving your object a name that ends with a recognizable suffix. Flash provides code hints for a button, for example, if the name of the button ends with _btn.

■ Dismiss a code hint by pressing the Esc key or clicking a different place in your script.

■ Navigate the menu-style code hints by using the arrow keys, the Page Up and Page Down keys, or the Home and End keys. You can also start typing, and the entry that begins with the letter you type will appear in the code hint. Press Enter or the key that will follow the method or property (for example, a space, comma, or parenthesis) to choose the selection.

■ You can call up code hints manually by pressing Ctrl-spacebar or by clicking the Show Code Hint button above the Script pane when your pointer is in a spot where code hints are appropriate (**Figure 3.21**).

■ Change the delay time for code hints to appear or turn off code hints by choosing Preferences from the Actions panel's Options menu. When the Preferences dialog box appears, change your preferences in the ActionScript options category (**Figure 3.22**).

THE ACTIONS PANEL

To set formatting options:

1. From the Actions panel's Options menu, choose Preferences.

The Flash Preferences dialog box appears.

2. Choose the Auto Format category.

3. Set the different formatting options and specify the way a typical block of code should appear (**Figure 3.23**); then click OK.

4. Choose Auto Format from the Actions panel's Options menu (Ctrl-Shift-F for Windows, Cmd-Shift-F for Mac), or click the Auto Format button above the Script pane (**Figure 3.24**).

Flash formats your script in the Script pane according to the preferences you set in the Auto Format category of the Flash Preferences dialog box (step 3).

To get information about an action:

◆ Select an ActionScript term in the Actions toolbox or in the Script pane, and then click the Help button above and to the right of the Script pane (**Figure 3.25**).

or

Right-click (Windows) or Ctrl-click (Mac) an action in the Actions toolbox or in the Script pane and select View Help from the context menu that appears.

Your browser opens the Help section of the Adobe Web site with information on the selected ActionScript term. The typical entry in the Help site contains information about usage and syntax, lists parameters and their availability in various Flash versions, and shows sample code.

To pin or unpin a script in the Script pane:

◆ With ActionScript visible in the Script pane, click the Pin Active Script button at the bottom of the Actions panel (**Figure 3.26**). To unpin the script, click the button again.

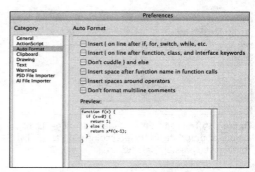

Figure 3.23 The Auto Format category in the Flash Preferences gives you a preview of how a typical block of code will look with the selections you make.

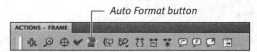

Figure 3.24 The Auto Format button is above the Script pane.

Figure 3.25 Make liberal use of the Help button to access ActionScript references.

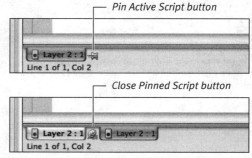

Figure 3.26 The Pin Active Script button (top) toggles to Close Pinned Script (bottom).

Editing ActionScript

When the code in the Script pane of the Actions panel becomes long and complex, you can check, edit, and manage it using the Options menu of the Actions panel. There are menu options for searching and replacing words, importing and exporting scripts, and printing your scripts, as well as for different ways to display your script, such as using word wrap (**Figure 3.27**).

You can use the Find and Replace functions in the Actions panel to quickly change variable names, properties, or even actions. For example, if you create a lengthy script involving the variable `redTeamStatus` but change your mind and want to change the variable name, you can replace all instances of `redTeamStatus` with `blueTeamStatus`. You can find all the occurrences of the property `height` and replace them with `width`, or you can locate all the occurrences of the action `gotoAndStop` and replace them with `gotoAndPlay`.

The Import Script and Export Script functions of the Actions panel let you work with external text editors.

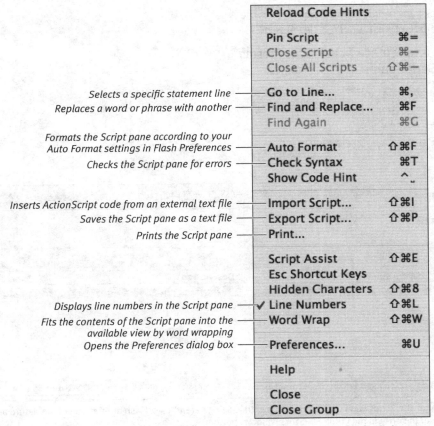

EDITING ACTIONSCRIPT

Figure 3.27 The Options menu of the Actions panel contains editing functions for the Script pane.

To check the syntax in the Script pane:

◆ In the Actions panel, choose Options > Check Syntax (Ctrl-T for Windows, Cmd-T for Mac).

   or

   Click the Check Syntax button above the Script pane (**Figure 3.28**).

   Flash checks the script in the Script pane for errors in syntax. If it finds an error, it displays a warning dialog box (**Figure 3.29**) and reports any errors in a Compiler Errors window, which tells you the location and description of the error (**Figure 3.30**).

✔ Tip

■ Check Syntax only reports the errors in the current Script pane, not for the entire movie.

To find and replace ActionScript terms in the Script pane:

1. In the Actions panel, choose Options > Find and Replace (Ctrl-F for Windows, Cmd-F for Mac).

   The Find and Replace dialog box appears.

Check Syntax button

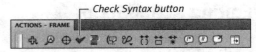

Figure 3.28 The Check Syntax button is the check mark icon above the Script pane.

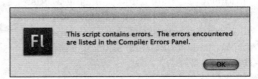

Figure 3.29 The error warning for a bad script.

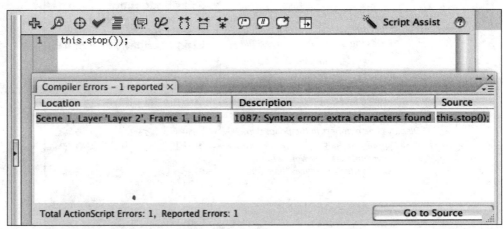

Figure 3.30 The Script pane (top) contains an extra closing parenthesis. Flash notifies you of the nature and location of the error in the Compiler Errors window (bottom).

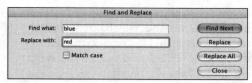

Figure 3.31 Every occurrence of blue will be replaced with red.

2. In the Find what field, enter a word or words that you want Flash to find. In the Replace with field, enter a word or words that you want the found words to be replaced with. Select the Match case check box to make Flash distinguish between uppercase and lowercase letters (**Figure 3.31**).

3. Click Replace to replace the first instance of the found word, or click Replace All to replace all instances of the found word.

✔ Tip

■ The Find and Replace dialog box replaces all the occurrences of a particular word or phrase only in the current Script pane of the Actions panel. To replace every occurrence of a certain word in the whole movie, you need to go to each script and repeat this process.

To import an ActionScript:

1. Select Options > Import Script (Ctrl-Shift-I for Windows, Cmd-Shift-I for Mac).

2. In the dialog box that appears, choose the text file that contains the ActionScript you want to import and click Open.

Flash inserts the ActionScript contained in the text file into the current Script pane at the insertion point.

To export an ActionScript:

1. Select Options > Export Script (Ctrl-Shift-P for Windows, Cmd-Shift-P for Mac).

2. Enter a destination filename and click Save.

Flash saves a text file that contains the entire contents of the current Script pane. The recommended extension for external ActionScript files is *.as*, as in myCode.as.

EDITING ACTIONSCRIPT

Using Objects

Now that you know what objects are and how to operate the Actions panel, you can begin to script with objects and call their methods or evaluate and assign new properties.

Flash provides existing classes (grouped in packages) that reside in the Actions toolbox. These Flash classes have methods and properties that control different elements of your Flash movie, such as graphics, sound, data, time, and mathematical calculations. You can also build your own classes or extend the functions of an existing class, a topic that is beyond the scope of this book.

Variables, data types, and strict typing

In ActionScript, like most programming languages, you access and manipulate objects using variables. *Variables* are containers that hold information. You can create, change the contents of, and discard variables at any time. In ActionScript 3.0, it's necessary to define the existence of a variable, which is known as *declaring* the variable, before you use it. To declare a variable, you use the ActionScript keyword var followed by the name of the variable, which is followed in turn by a colon and the type of information the variable will be used to store. The different kinds of information that variables can contain are known as *data types*.

Examples of typical types of variables are a user's score (Number data type), an Internet address (String data type), a date object (Date data type), and the on/off state of a toggle button (Boolean data type). In ActionScript 3.0, you specify the data type of your variable when you create it; Flash will allow only values of that data type to be stored in the variable. This is called *strict typing*. Strict data typing prevents you from accidentally assigning the wrong type of data to a variable, which can cause problems during the playback of your movie. Strict data typing involves adding a colon (:) and the data type after the name of your variable. For example, if you want to create a variable called myScore to hold a number, you write var myScore:Number.

Table 3.1 lists the most basic data types that variables can hold. However, a variable can be declared with any ActionScript class as its data type, including any of the built-in classes and classes you create yourself.

Table 3.1

Some Data Types

DATA TYPE	DESCRIPTION EXAMPLE	EXAMPLE
Number	A numeric value	var myTemp:Number = 98.6
int	An integer (whole number)	var myGolfScore:int = -4
uint	An unsigned integer (a non-negative whole number)	var myZipCode:uint = 11215
String	A sequence of characters, numbers, or symbols. A string is always contained within quotation marks.	var yourEmail:String ="johndoe@domain.com"
Boolean	A value of either true or false. The words aren't enclosed in quotation marks.	var buttonPressed:Boolean = true
Object	A generic object to which you can add properties or methods. Used in cases where a simple object is needed.	var myObj:Object = new Object()
Any of the Flash classes	An object type	var myMusic:Sound = new Sound()

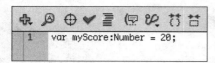

```
1    var myScore:Number = 20;
```

Figure 3.32 Variables can be initialized to hold different kinds of information. The word var indicates that myScore is a variable, the colon and word Number indicate that the variable can only hold numbers, and the equals sign assigns the numerical value 20 to the variable.

✔ **Tips**

- It's good practice to initialize your variables in the first frame of your Timeline. That way, you keep them all in the same place and can edit their initial values easily.

- When you assign a value that is one of the intrinsic data types (Number, String, Boolean) to a variable, even if you're assigning to one variable the value in another, Flash determines the value and puts it in your variable at that moment. If the property or the referenced variable subsequently changes, the value of your variable won't change unless you reassign it. Consider this example: var xPosition:Number = mouseX;. When you initialize the variable called xPosition in the first frame of your movie, it holds the *x*-coordinate of the pointer. As you move the pointer around the screen, the property mouseX changes but the variable xPosition does not. The variable xPosition still holds the original *x*-coordinate from when it was initialized.

Once you declare a variable, you *initialize* it, or put information into the variable for the first time. Initializing a variable in the Actions panel involves using the equals sign (=), which assigns a value to a variable. The name of the variable goes on the left side of the equals sign, and a value to be assigned goes on the right side. This point is crucial: the expression $a = b$ is *not* the same as $b = a$. So you can put a number in your myScore variable like this: myScore = 20. It's common to merge the declaration and initializing in a single line like so: var myScore:Number=20. When you initialize a variable at the same time you declare the variable, it's clear which part of the statement is the variable and which part is the new value.

To declare and initialize a variable:

1. Select the first frame of the Timeline and open the Actions panel.

2. In the Script pane, enter the keyword var.

3. Next, enter a descriptive name for your variable.

   Your variable name should follow certain rules. See the sidebar "The Rules of Naming" for more information.

4. Type a colon and then the data type of the variable.

5. Type the equals sign (=) and then the initial value that you want the variable to hold.

   The value on the right side of the equals sign is assigned to the variable on the left side (**Figure 3.32**).

USING OBJECTS

The Rules of Naming

Although you're free to make up descriptive names for your objects, you must adhere to the following simple rules. If you don't, Flash won't recognize your object's name and will likely give you an error:

◆ Don't use spaces or punctuation (such as slashes, dots, and parentheses), because these characters often have a special meaning to Flash.

◆ You can use letters, numbers, and underscore characters, but you must *not* begin the name with a number.

◆ You can't use certain words for variable names because they are reserved for special functions or for use as keywords in ActionScript. If you try to use them as variables, Flash will display an error message when you test your movie. The following is a partial list of these words:

as, break, case, catch, class, const, continue, default, delete, do, else, extends, false, finally, for, function, if, implements, import, in, instanceof, interface, internal, is, native, new, null, package, private, protected, public, return, super, switch, this, throw, to, true, try, typeof, use, var, void, while, with, each, get, set, namespace, include, dynamic, final, native, override, static

Those are the only three rules. Some additional general naming strategies, however, can make your scripts easier to understand, debug, and share:

◆ Variable names should describe the information that the variables hold. The variable names playerScore and spaceshipVelocity, for example, are appropriate and will cause fewer headaches than something like xyz or myVariable.

◆ Use a consistent naming practice. A common method is to use multiple words to describe an object and to capitalize the first letter of every word except the first. The names spinningSquare1, spinningSquare2, and leftPaddle, for example, are intuitive, descriptive, and easy to follow in a script. Remember that ActionScript 3.0 is case sensitive! Using a consistent naming practice will help you avoid mismatches between your object name and your ActionScript code due to capitalization.

◆ It sometimes helps to add suffixes to names to describe the object type. Using the standard suffix _mc for movie clips and _btn for buttons readily identifies the objects. Although strict typing makes Flash recognize all variable names and their associated data type for code hinting in the Actions panel, adding suffixes, especially to generic variable names, often makes the code more understandable.

```
var myArea:Number = myLength * myWidth;
var dogYears:Number = 7 * Age;
var myProgress:Number = currentFrame / totalFrames;
```

Figure 3.33 Some examples of expressions. The variable names are on the left side of the equals signs, and the expressions are on the right.

Expressions and strings

Using expressions and using strings are two important ways to describe and manipulate data. An *expression* is a statement that may include variables, properties, and objects, and must be resolved (figured out) before Flash can determine its value. Think of an expression as being an algebraic formula, like $a^2 + b^2$. The value of the expression has to be calculated before it can be used (**Figure 3.33**).

A *string*, on the other hand, is a statement that Flash uses *as is* and considers to be a collection of characters. The string "$a^2 + b^2$" is literally a sequence of seven characters (including the spaces around the plus sign but not the quotation marks). When you initialize a variable with a literal string value, you must enclose the characters in quotation marks.

Expressions and strings aren't mutually exclusive—that is, sometimes you can have an expression that includes strings! For example, the statement `"Current frame is "` + `currentframe` is an expression that puts together a string and the frame number of the main Timeline. You'll learn more about this kind of operation, called *concatenation*, in Chapter 11, "Manipulating Information."

✔ Tip

■ If quotation marks always surround a string, how do you include quotation marks in the actual string? You use the backslash (\) character before including a quotation mark. This technique is called *escaping* a character. The string `"The line \"Call me Shane\" is from a 1953 movie Western"` produces the following result: *The line "Call me Shane" is from a 1953 movie Western*. **Table 3.2** lists a few common escape sequences for special characters.

Table 3.2

Common Escape Sequences

SEQUENCE	CHARACTER
\b	Backspace
\r	New line
\t	Tab
\"	Quotation mark
\'	Single quotation mark
\\	Backslash

Creating objects

The first step to add interactivity with Flash objects is to create a new instance of a class. You do this by using the keyword new and then the name of the class and a pair of parentheses: new Human( ). This creates a new Human object. However, the new Human object needs a name. So you give the object a name by declaring a variable and assigning the new object to it.

```
var Zeke:Human = new Human( );
```

You've just created Zeke! The variable Zeke is strictly typed to hold a Human type object, and with the variable name, you can reference all the properties and methods of the Human class. The process is the same as creating an instance of, or *instantiating*, a symbol on the Stage, but here you do it purely with ActionScript.

Consider the following example:

```
var myData:Array = new Array( );
```

This statement makes a new Array instance called myData. The statement on the right side of the equals sign is called a *constructor*. Most classes have a constructor method, a special method that creates new instances of that class.

The following task demonstrates how to create an instance of the Date class, but the general technique works for instantiation of all objects.

To instantiate an object:

1. Select the first frame on the main Timeline and open the Actions panel.

2. In the Script pane, type var.

3. Enter a space and then a name for your new object.

4. ActionScript 3.0 requires strict typing, so enter a colon and then the object type. In this example, use Date.

5. Type an equals sign (=) and then the constructor, new Date( ).

   The full statement creates a new Date object with the name you entered. Your Date object is instantiated and ready to use (**Figure 3.34**).

Figure 3.34 The finished statement creates an object called myDate from the Date class.

Using Objects

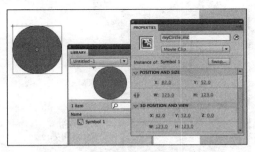

Figure 3.35 Instantiation of a movie clip symbol from the Library to the Stage involves naming it in the Property inspector.

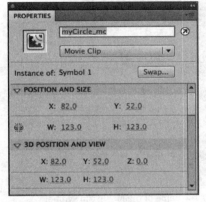

Figure 3.36 The Property inspector for a selected movie clip. The name of this movie clip object is myCircle_mc.

Creating instances on the Stage

A few types of ActionScript objects, such as movie clips, buttons, and text fields, are unique because you often create them visually by adding an instance from the Library (for button and movie clip symbols) or using the drawing tools (for text fields). Instantiation of these objects involves two steps: placing an instance on the Stage and naming that instance in the Property inspector. These two steps accomplish the same task that the constructor function performs for other Flash classes (**Figure 3.35**). The result is the same: A named object, or an instance, of a class is created. You can manipulate that object by calling its methods or evaluating its properties.

Later in the book, you'll learn how to create SimpleButton instances (Chapter 4), MovieClip instances (Chapter 7), and TextField instances (Chapter 10), and place them on the Stage using only code.

To name a movie clip instance or a button instance:

1. Create a movie clip symbol or a button symbol.

2. Drag an instance of the symbol from the Library to the Stage.

3. Select the instance.

4. At the top of the Property inspector, enter a unique name for your instance (**Figure 3.36**).

   Now you can use this name to refer to your movie clip instance or your button instance with ActionScript.

Continues on next page

✔ Tip

■ The name of your symbol (the one that appears in the Library) and the name you give it in the Property inspector are two different identifiers (**Figure 3.37**). The name that appears in the Library is a symbol property and basically is just an organizational reminder. The name in the Property inspector is more important because it's the actual name of the object and will be used in targeting paths. End your movie clip instance name with _mc and your button instances with _btn so that the Actions panel can identify the object type.

Calling methods

Often, the next step after creating a new object involves calling the object's methods. Recollect that you can call a method by using an object's name followed by a period and then the method with its parameters within parentheses. All the methods of a particular class can be found in the Methods category of that class category in the Actions toolbox.

When you call an object's method, the code in the Script pane will look something like this:

```
myShape.startDrag();
```

This statement calls the method startDrag() of the object called myShape, and as a result, the graphic called myShape will follow the mouse pointer.

Sometimes when you call an object's method, a value is returned. Essentially, the object does something and then comes back to you with an answer. In that case, it's useful to put that answer or result in another variable so you can store it and analyze it. Your ActionScript would look something like this:

```
var currentDate:Number = myDate.getDate();
```

This statement calls the method getDate() from the myDate object and puts the

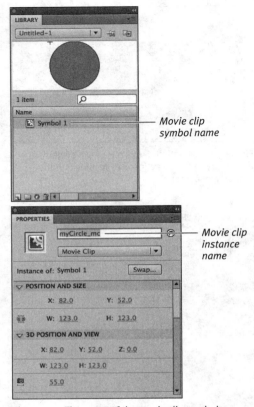

Movie clip symbol name

Movie clip instance name

Figure 3.37 The name of the movie clip symbol appears in the Library (Symbol 1), and the name of the movie clip instance appears in the Property inspector (myCircle_mc).

```
1  var myDate:Date= new Date();
2  myTextField_txt.text
```

Figure 3.38 The Date object called myDate retrieves the current date from your computer's internal clock, and the statement myTextField_txt.text refers to the contents of a text field.

```
1  var myDate:Date = new Date();
2  myTextField_txt.text=String(myDate.getDate());
```

Figure 3.39 Convert the results of the getDate() method to a string, and then assign it to the text property of a text field called myTextField_txt.

— Select Dynamic Text
— Enter instance name here

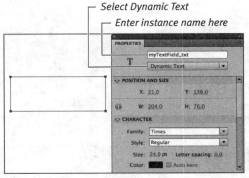

Figure 3.40 Your text field on the Stage should be set to Dynamic Text with myTextField_txt entered as the instance name.

information it retrieves into the variable called currentDate.

The following task continues the task "To instantiate an object" and calls a method of your newly created Date object. Later chapters introduce specific classes, provide more information about the Date class, and show you how to use methods to control your Flash movie.

In this example, Flash calls the getDate() method, which retrieves the current date. For the user to see the returned value, you must display it in a dynamic text field. You'll learn more about text fields in Chapter 10, "Controlling Text."

To call a method of an object:

1. Continuing with the task "To instantiate an object," open the Actions panel and start a new line of code.

2. Enter myTextField_txt and then a period (.), and choose "text" from the code hint menu that appears (**Figure 3.38**).

3. Enter an equals sign (=) followed by the statement, String(myDate.getDate());.

   The object myDate retrieves the date and is converted to text. The text will be displayed in the text field called myTextField_txt (**Figure 3.39**).

4. Select the Text tool and drag out an empty text field on the Stage.

5. In the Property inspector, choose Dynamic Text from the pull-down menu, and in the <Instance Name> field, enter myTextField_txt (**Figure 3.40**).

6. Test your movie by choosing Control > Test Movie.

   Flash instantiates a Date object (from the earlier task) and then calls the getDate() method. The returned value (the day of the month) is converted into text and put in the text field on the Stage.

Assigning properties

You can change the properties of objects simply by assigning new values on the right side of an equals (=) symbol. For example, this statement assigns the word *hello* to the `text` property of the object called `myTextField_txt`:

```
myTextField_txt.text = "hello";
```

Sometimes properties are read-only, which means they can't be changed, but you can still use them in expressions to test certain conditions.

To assign a value to a property:

1. In the Script pane, enter the object name and then a dot.

   The code hint pull-down menu appears, displaying a list of choices available to the particular object.

2. Select the desired property.

   The statement consisting of the object name, a dot, and the property appears.

3. Enter an equals (=) symbol and then a value.

   A new value is assigned to the property (**Figure 3.41**).

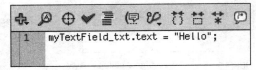

Figure 3.41 Assigning a value to a property. The string "Hello" is assigned to the `text` property of the text field called `myTextField`.

About Functions

If objects and classes are at the heart of ActionScript, functions must lie in the brain. Functions are the organizers of ActionScript. Functions group related ActionScript statements to perform a specific task. Often, you need to write code to do a certain thing over and over. Functions eliminate the tedium of manually duplicating the code by putting it in one place where you can call on it to do its job from anywhere, at any time, as many times as necessary. You'll see in Chapter 4, "Advanced Buttons and Event Handling," that functions are essential for building responses to events—creating true interactivity.

As you learned earlier in this chapter, the objects `Adam`, `Betty`, and `Zeke` can perform certain tasks called methods. If these objects were to put on a dinner party, they could organize themselves and do the following:

```
Adam.answerDoor();
Betty.serveDinner();
Zeke.chitChat();
```

But every Friday night when they have a dinner party, you'll have to write the same three lines of code—not very efficient if these objects plan to entertain often. Instead, you can write a function that groups the code in one spot:

```
function dinnerParty() {
    Adam.answerDoor();
    Betty.serveDinner();
    Zeke.chitChat();

}
```

Now, every Friday night you can invoke the function by name and write the code `dinnerParty()`. The three statements inside the function's curly braces will be executed.

Building functions

To create a function, start the line of code with the word `function`, then a space, and then give your function a name. The rules of naming functions are the same as those for variables. Add a pair of parentheses and curly braces. Your statement may look something like this:

```
function doExplosion() {
}
```

Add actions within the curly braces. Then, when you need the function, call it by name, like this: `doExplosion()`.

The following task builds a function that dynamically creates a text field, adds a bit of text, and displays it on the Stage. By consolidating all these statements, you can create this title with one call to a single function—and do so multiple times from different places in your movie. You'll learn more about text in Chapter 10, so focus more on how the function works.

To build and call a function:

1. Select the first keyframe of the main Timeline and open the Actions panel.

2. Enter the following code:

   ```
   function createTitle(){
   }
   ```

   The function called createTitle is created. Statements within the curly braces will be executed when the function is called.

3. Create a blank line in between the curly braces and enter the following code:

   ```
   var myText:TextField = new TextField();
   myText.text = "Welcome to Flash";
   this.addChild(myText);
   ```

   The first line within the function creates a new object from the TextField class. The second line assigns some text to its contents, and the last line displays it on the Stage.

4. On a new line outside the function, call the function by entering the following:

   ```
   createTitle();
   ```

   Test your movie by choosing Control > Test Movie (**Figure 3.42**).

✔ Tip

■ A function has a *scope*, meaning that it belongs to the timeline on which it's defined. If you call a function from a different timeline, you'll have to precede your call with the correct path. For example, myMovieClip_mc.createTitle() would call the function on the timeline of the movie clip called myMovieClip_mc. The actions from the function will still pertain to its own timeline.

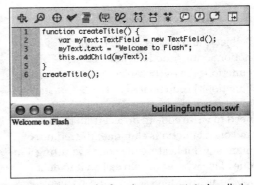

Figure 3.42 When the function createTitle is called, all the statements in between the function's curly braces are executed, and the piece of text is dynamically displayed (bottom).

Accepting parameters

When you define a function, you can tell it to perform a certain task based on parameters that you provide, or *pass*, to the function at the time you call on it. This arrangement makes functions more flexible because the work they do is tailored to particular contexts.

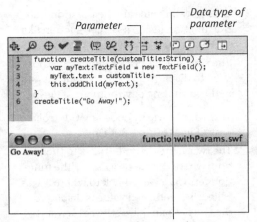

Parameter is used to customize text

Figure 3.43 This function requires a parameter, which is used to customize the text that is displayed (below).

To build a function that accepts parameters:

1. Continuing with the file you used in the preceding task, select the first keyframe and open the Actions panel.

2. With your pointer between the parentheses of the function statement, enter

   `customTitle:String`

   The variable `customTitle` is the parameter, and it is strictly typed to hold a string value.

3. Change the second line of the function body so that it reads

   `myText.text = customTitle;`

   The parameter is used in one or more of the function statements.

4. Change the call to the function with this:

   `createTitle ("Go Away!");`

5. Test your movie by choosing Control > Test Movie (**Figure 3.43**).

   The parameter that you provide in the initial call ("Go Away!") is passed to the function. The function uses that parameter to customize its set of actions. You can call the function many times with different parameters.

✔ Tip

■ Note that when you define a function's parameters, they should also be strictly typed. So after the parameter name, be sure to include a colon and the parameter's data type.

Returning a value

When you pass parameters to a function, you often want to know the results of a particular calculation. To make your function report a resulting calculation, use the `return` statement. The `return` statement, which you use within your function's body (between the curly braces), indicates that the value of an expression should be passed back when the function is called.

In the following task, you'll build a simple function that adds two numbers together and returns the result.

To build a function that returns a value:

1. Select the first keyframe of the main Timeline and open the Actions panel.

2. Enter the word `function`, then a space, and then enter a name for your function followed by open and closed parentheses.

3. Between the parentheses of the function, enter the following parameters:

   `a:Number, b:Number`

4. After the parentheses, add a colon, and then the data type `Number`.

5. Add an open and closed curly brace.

6. Between the curly braces for the function, enter the word `return`, followed by an expression to add the two parameters. The full function code should look like this:

   ```
   function simpleAdd(a:Number,
   → b:Number):Number {
      return (a + b);
   }
   ```

7. On a new line outside the function, call the function inside a `trace()` action like so: `trace(simpleAdd(3, 5));`

   The `trace()` action is a debugging tool used to display values in the Output panel in the authoring environment of Flash.

8. Test your movie by choosing Control > Test Movie (**Figure 3.44**).

   The two values (3 and 5) pass to the function, where they're processed. The function returns a value back to where it was called. The returned value is displayed in the Output panel. Use the `return` statement whenever you need to receive a value from a function.

✔ Tip

■ Note that the returned value of a function should also be strictly typed. After the closing parenthesis of the function, enter a colon and then the data type of the returned value. If the function doesn't return a value, you should use the keyword `void`.

```
function simpleAdd(a:Number, b:Number):Number {
    return (a + b);
}
trace(simpleAdd(3, 5));
```

```
OUTPUT
8
```

Figure 3.44 This function requires two parameters and returns a number. The `trace()` action displays the returned value in the Output panel in the authoring environment (below).

```
1   //
2   // Building an object example
3   // first instatiate a Date object
4   //
5   var myDate:Date = new Date();
6   //
7   // now get the date, convert to string
8   // and display in textfield
9   //
10  myTextField_txt.text=String(myDate.getDate());
```

Figure 3.45 Comments interspersed with ActionScript statements help make sense of the code.

Line comment button

Figure 3.46 The Line comment button lets you insert comments on a single line.

Using Comments

After you've built a strong vocabulary of Flash actions and are constructing complex statements in the Actions panel, you should include remarks in your scripts to remind you and your collaborators of the goals of the ActionScript. Comments help you keep things straight as you develop intricate interactivity and relationships among objects (**Figure 3.45**).

To create a line comment:

◆ Click the Line comment button at the top of the Script pane, and then enter your comments (**Figure 3.46**).

or

In the Script pane, manually type two slashes (//) followed by your comments.

Comments appear in a different color than the rest of the script, making them easy to locate.

To create a block comment:

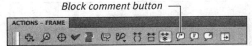

◆ Click the Block comment button at the top of the Script pane, and then enter your comments between the /* and the */ (**Figure 3.47**).

Figure 3.47 The Block comment button lets you insert multiline comments.

Block comments can span multiple lines as long as they lie between the slash-asterisk and the asterisk-slash.

or

In the Script pane, manually type a slash and an asterisk (/*) followed by your comments. Close your comment with an asterisk and slash (*/).

✔ Tips

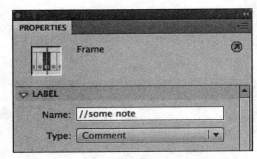

Figure 3.48 In the Property inspector, double slashes indicate a comment in a frame label.

■ Don't worry about creating too many comments. Comments aren't compiled with the rest of the script, so they won't bog down performance. Also, because they aren't included in the exported SWF file, they don't increase the final file size.

■ The slash convention for creating comments in ActionScript is the same for creating them in keyframes. When you choose Comment in the Label type pull-down menu in the Property inspector, the name in the <Frame Label> field automatically begins with two slashes (//). You can also enter two slashes manually to begin a frame comment (**Figure 3.48**).

Advanced Buttons and Event Handling

Creating graphics and animation in Flash is only half the story. The other half is interactivity, which involves giving the viewer control of those graphics and animation via buttons, the keyboard, and the mouse. Interactivity is essential for basic site navigation and interfaces on the Web, as well as for game development, online tutorials, or anything else that requires the viewer to make choices.

What makes a movie interactive? Interactivity is the back-and-forth communication between the user and the movie. In a Flash movie, the user might react to something that's going on by moving the pointer, clicking the mouse button, or pressing a key on the keyboard. That reaction may trigger a response from the Flash movie, which in turn prompts the user to do something else. The things that the user does—mouse movements, button clicks, or keyboard presses—are part of things that happen, called events. Events form the basis of interactivity. There are many kinds of events—some are user driven whereas others are not. You'll learn to make Flash listen for these events and respond to them. This whole process is known as event handling.

This chapter first introduces events, listeners, and functions used to respond to events. Next, it explores the simplest class for creating interactivity: the `SimpleButton` class. You'll learn how to extend its functionality by creating invisible buttons, animated buttons, and more complex buttons, such as a pull-down menu. You'll also learn about the classes and events that are involved in keyboard input and the context menu. Additionally, you'll learn an important event known as the `ENTER_FRAME` event, which you'll rely on to create continuously running actions. Understanding these classes and event handling is essential to creating Flash interactivity because these elements are the scaffold on which you'll hang virtually all your ActionScript.

Listening for Events

Events are things that happen that Flash can recognize and respond to. A mouse click is an event, as are mouse movements and keypresses on the keyboard. Events can also be things that the user doesn't initiate. The completion of a sound, for example, is an event. Anytime an event happens, an object of the Event class is created. When the mouse button is clicked, a MouseEvent object (a subclass of the Event class) is created. When a key on the keyboard is pressed, a KeyboardEvent object (another subclass of the Event class) is created. It may seem a little strange that an object represents an event, but remember Flash objects can be very abstract!

With all these events happening, you need a way to detect and respond to them. You detect an event by creating an event handler. An event handler simply tells Flash what to do when a specific kind of event happens. Creating an event handler is a two-part operation: first, you add a listener to detect the event and trigger a function, and second, you create the function that tells Flash how to respond. (It actually doesn't matter if you create the listener first or the function first. As long as they are both in the same block of code, the event handler will work.)

For example, if you want to listen for a mouse click on top of a particular button, you add an event listener to that object as follows:

```
myButton_btn.addEventListener
→ (MouseEvent.CLICK, reportClick);
```

The addEventListener() method takes two parameters. The first is the specific kind of event that you want to detect. All the event objects have properties (like MouseEvent.CLICK), which give more specificity to the event. The second parameter is the name of your function, which is triggered when the event is detected.

Next, add a function as the response to the event. Create the function with a parameter strictly typed to the MouseEvent object, like so:

```
function reportClick
→ (myevent:MouseEvent):void {

    // do something in response

}
```

In between the curly braces of the function, you add actions as the response. The word myevent in this example is the parameter name that you make up that refers to the event.

The actual object that receives the event (in this example, it is the button called myButton_btn) can be referenced in the function by using the property target. In the preceding example, the expression myevent.target references myButton_btn.

When you no longer need to listen for an event, you can delete the listener with the method removeEventListener(). The method takes two parameters, which are identical to the ones in the addEventListener() method.

Event Flow

Event handling is a little more involved than what is described here. When an event occurs and an `Event` object is created, the `Event` object systematically moves through other objects on the Flash Stage in a process known as the event flow. There are three parts to the event flow: a capture phase, a target phase, and a bubbling phase. Imagine that a mouse click happens on a button that is inside a movie clip on the Stage (**Figure 4.1**). The `MouseEvent` object is created, is dispatched from the Stage, and flows down to the movie clip and to the button inside the movie clip. That downward flow through those objects is the capture phase. The target phase involves the time the `MouseEvent` object is at the target (the button). Then the `MouseEvent` object proceeds to bubble, or flow, up the hierarchy to the main Stage (**Figure 4.2**). This round-trip flow is important because it lets you put a listener at any point along its path and still detect the event. In other words, the listener doesn't have to be tied to the object where the event occurs.

However, many events don't proceed through all three phases of the event flow. Some events, such as the `Event.ENTER_FRAME` object, are dispatched directly to the target object and don't participate in a capture or bubbling phase.

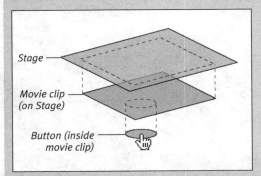

Figure 4.1 Events traverse the display list, which are the objects on the Stage. This example shows the main Stage with a movie clip on it. Inside the movie clip is a button, where a mouse click occurs.

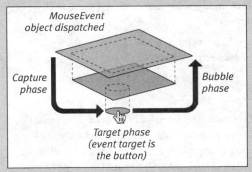

Figure 4.2 When a mouse click occurs on a target (shown here as the button), a MouseEvent is dispatched and travels from the Stage down to the event target, and then bubbles upward back to the Stage. Listeners are usually put on the event target, but it is not required. For example, a listener could be put on the movie clip, and it would detect events happening on the movie clip or on objects inside the movie clip.

Mouse Detection

Mouse events such as a button click, double-click, or simply moving the mouse are handled by the MouseEvent class. Since the mouse is one of the primary means through which a user interacts with a Flash movie, it's important to understand how to listen and respond to mouse events.

The simplest event is the button click, which happens when the user presses and then releases the mouse button. You can detect and respond to a button click by first attaching a listener to the main Stage (referred to as stage) and using the property MouseEvent.CLICK as follows:

```
stage.addEventListener(MouseEvent.CLICK,
→ reportClick);
```

Next, create a function with a MouseEvent parameter:

```
function reportClick
→ (myevent:MouseEvent):void {

    // do something in response

}
```

If you want to detect a click on a particular object, use the object's name instead of the word stage. Flash can listen for a mouse event on any object of the InteractiveObject class displayed on the Stage (button, text field, Loader, Sprite, movie clip, or the Stage).

Table 4.1 details the specific properties that describe the events of the MouseEvent object.

To detect a mouse click on the Stage:

1. Select the first frame of the main Timeline, and open the Actions panel.

2. Assign a listener to the main Stage with the following code:

```
stage.addEventListener (MouseEvent.
→ CLICK, reportClick);
```

When the MouseEvent.CLICK event is detected on the main Stage, the function called reportClick is triggered.

Table 4.1

MouseEvent Properties	
PROPERTY	DESCRIPTION
CLICK	Happens when the mouse button is clicked
DOUBLE_CLICK	Happens when the mouse button is clicked twice in rapid succession
MOUSE_MOVE	Happens when the mouse pointer moves
MOUSE_DOWN	Happens when the mouse button is pressed
MOUSE_UP	Happens when the mouse button is released
MOUSE_OVER	Happens when the mouse moves from a nontarget area over a target area
MOUSE_OUT	Happens when the mouse moves from a target area out of the target area
MOUSE_WHEEL	Happens when the mouse wheel is rotated

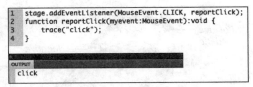

```
1  stage.addEventListener(MouseEvent.CLICK, reportClick);
2  function reportClick(myevent:MouseEvent):void {
3      trace("click");
4  }
```
```
OUTPUT
click
```

Figure 4.3 The event handler in the Actions panel (above) makes the Output panel display "click" in authoring mode whenever the mouse button is clicked (below).

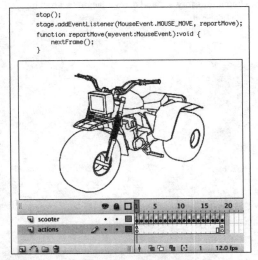

```
stop();
stage.addEventListener(MouseEvent.MOUSE_MOVE, reportMove);
function reportMove(myevent:MouseEvent):void {
    nextFrame();
}
```

Figure 4.4 This movie contains a frame-by-frame animation of a three-wheeler that rotates. Any time the mouse pointer moves, Flash advances to the next frame.

3. On the next available line, enter the following function:

   ```
   function reportClick
   → (myevent:MouseEvent):void {
       // do something in response
   }
   ```

   In between the curly braces, enter actions as a response.

4. Choose Control > Test Movie.

   Whenever you click the mouse button, Flash performs the actions listed within the reportClick function (**Figure 4.3**).

To detect a mouse movement on the Stage:

1. Select the first frame of the main Timeline, and open the Actions panel.

2. Assign a listener to the main Stage with the following code:

   ```
   stage.addEventListener
   → (MouseEvent.MOUSE_MOVE, reportMove);
   ```

   When the MouseEvent.MOUSE_MOVE event is detected on the main Stage, the function called reportMove is called.

3. On the next available line, enter the following function:

   ```
   function reportMove
   → (myevent:MouseEvent):void {
       // do something in response
   }
   ```

   In between the curly braces, enter actions as a response.

4. Choose Control > Test Movie.

   Whenever you move the mouse, Flash performs the actions listed within the reportMove function (**Figure 4.4**).

MOUSE DETECTION

The mouse wheel

The mouse wheel is a third button that is nestled between the left and right mouse buttons and spins forward or backward like a wheel. By listening for the `MouseEvent.MOUSE_WHEEL` event, you can respond to the mouse wheel motion and direction. For example, you can connect the forward or backward motion of the mouse wheel to the up or down scrolling of text or to the selection of items in a pull-down menu.

The `MOUSE_WHEEL` event has the property `delta`, which is a number that indicates how quickly and in what direction the user spins the mouse wheel. A positive (+) delta refers to a forward motion (away from the user) of the mouse wheel (**Figure 4.5**). A negative (–) delta refers to a backward motion (toward the user). The values of `delta` range from –3 to 3. You can use the `delta` property within the function of your event handler to respond according to the direction of the mouse wheel.

Although you can author the `MOUSE_WHEEL` event handler on either a Macintosh or Windows, the playback functionality is only available on Windows.

To detect mouse wheel motion:

1. Select the first frame of the main Timeline, and open the Actions panel.

2. Add the listener to the stage:
   ```
   stage.addEventListener
   → (MouseEvent.MOUSE_WHEEL,
   → moveRocket);
   ```

3. On the next available line, create the function that will respond to the `MouseEvent`. In between the curly braces of the function, incorporate the `delta` property of the `MouseEvent` object to reflect the forward or backward roll of the mouse wheel:
   ```
   function moveRocket
   → (myevent:MouseEvent):void{
     myRocket_mc.x += myevent.delta;
   }
   ```

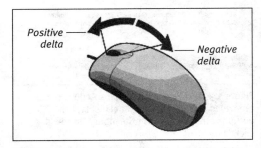

Figure 4.5 The mouse wheel returns a positive delta when it rolls forward and a negative delta when it rolls backward.

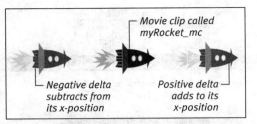

Figure 4.6 The movie clip on the Stage moves to the right if the delta property is positive and moves to the left if the delta property is negative.

```
stage.addEventListener(MouseEvent.MOUSE_WHEEL, moveRocket);
function moveRocket (myevent:MouseEvent):void{
    myRocket_mc.x+=myevent.delta;
}
```

Figure 4.7 The full code for responding to the mouse wheel on the Stage. When the mouse wheel rolls forward, the movie clip moves to the right. When the mouse wheels rolls backward, the movie clip moves to the left.

```
myRocket_mc.addEventListener(MouseEvent.MOUSE_WHEEL, moveRocket)
function moveRocket (myevent:MouseEvent):void{
    myRocket_mc.x+=myevent.delta;
}
```

Figure 4.8 To detect the mouse wheel event just on the target, add the listener to the target instead of the Stage.

Figure 4.9 The movie clip called myRocket_mc will change its x-position only when the user rolls the mouse wheel when it is over the movie clip.

In this event handler, the movement of the mouse wheel adds or subtracts from the horizontal position of the movie clip called myRocket_mc (**Figure 4.6**).

4. Choose Control > Test Movie on a Windows computer.

As you move the mouse wheel backward or forward, the movie clip on the Stage changes its position (**Figure 4.7**).

To target an object to respond to mouse wheel motion:

1. Continue with the previous task.

2. Select the first frame of the main Timeline, and open the Actions panel.

3. Change the addEventListener() method to target the movie clip myRocket_mc instead of the stage (**Figure 4.8**).

4. Choose Control > Test Movie on a Windows computer.

Now the listener only detects the MOUSE_WHEEL event over the movie clip instance. When you move the mouse wheel over the movie clip on the Stage, the movie clip changes its position (**Figure 4.9**).

✔ Tip

■ Multiline text fields (discussed in Chapter 10, "Controlling Text") automatically scroll in response to the mouse wheel. You can, however, disable the mouse wheel with the text field property mouseWheelEnabled. Set the mouseWheelEnabled property of any text field to false like this:

myTF_txt.mouseWheelEnabled = false;.

The text field called myTF_txt will no longer respond automatically to the mouse wheel.

The SimpleButton Class

In the previous section, you were able to listen for a mouse click on the Stage. But more often than not, you'll want to detect a mouse click when it happens on a specific object on the Stage, like a button, movie clip, or a text field. The SimpleButton class handles the visual objects that interact with the mouse pointer. Flash lets you define four special keyframes of a button symbol that describe how the button looks and responds to the mouse: the Up, Over, Down, and Hit states. The Up state shows what the button looks like when the pointer isn't over the button. Over shows what the button looks like when the pointer is over the button. Down shows what the button looks like when the pointer is over the button with the mouse button pressed. And Hit defines the actual active, or *hot*, area of the button (**Figure 4.10**).

It's important to realize that events can target many kinds of objects, not just buttons. Buttons just give you a convenient way to create graphics that provide visual feedback when the mouse is interacting with them.

To detect a mouse event on a button:

1. Create a button symbol (Insert > New Symbol), and drag an instance of the newly created button symbol from the Library on to the Stage.

2. Select the button instance, and enter a descriptive name in the Property inspector. Add the suffix _btn to the name. In this example, the button name is mybutton_btn (**Figure 4.11**).

   This name is the name of your button object; you'll use it to reference the button from ActionScript. This name is *not the same one that appears in your Library.*

3. Select the first frame of the main Timeline, and open the Actions panel.

Figure 4.10 The four keyframes of a button symbol.

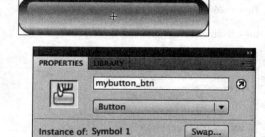

Figure 4.11 The button instance is named mybutton_btn in the Property inspector.

```
mybutton_btn.addEventListener(MouseEvent.CLICK, reportClick);
function reportClick(myevent:MouseEvent):void {
    stop();
}
```

Figure 4.12 The event handler consists of an event listener and a function. In this example, the movie will stop when the button is clicked.

Figure 4.13 When the mouse click occurs over this button, named `mybutton_btn`, the actions in the function are executed.

4. In the first line of the Script pane, assign a listener to your button. The target should be the name of your button, like so:

   `mybutton_btn.addEventListener`
   `(MouseEvent.CLICK, reportClick);`

   When the `MouseEvent.CLICK` event happens on the button, the function called `reportClick` is called.

5. On the next available line, enter the following function:

   `function reportClick`
   `→ (myevent:MouseEvent):void {`

   `// do something in response`

   `}`

   The function name `reportClick` and parameter name `myevent` can be any name of your own choosing as long as they conform to the standard naming practice. In between the curly braces, enter actions as a response (**Figure 4.12**).

6. Choose Control > Test Movie.

   Whenever you click the mouse button on the button instance, Flash performs the actions listed within the `reportClick` function (**Figure 4.13**).

✔ Tips

- As described in Chapter 3, "Getting a Handle on ActionScript," it's recommended that you end all instance names for buttons with _btn so that Flash can provide the appropriate code hints in the Script pane.

- When you create your event handler on the main Timeline, your button must be present on the Stage at the same time so Flash knows what object it references. If you create the event handler in keyframe 1, for example, but your button doesn't appear until keyframe 10, Flash will give you a compile error.

To select different mouse events:

1. Highlight the existing first parameter of the addEventListener() method, and press the Delete key.

2. Type in the name of a different event that should trigger the function (such as MouseEvent.DOUBLE_CLICK, MouseEvent. MOUSE_OVER, etc.) (**Figure 4.14**).

✔ Tips

■ You can add more than one listener to the same object. A MouseEvent.MOUSE_DOWN may trigger one event handler, whereas a MouseEvent.MOUSE_UP may trigger another, like so:

```
myobject.addEventListener
→ (MouseEvent.MOUSE_DOWN,
→ downFunction);
myobject.addEventListener
→ (MouseEvent.MOUSE_UP,
→ upFunction);
```

■ Don't confuse the MouseEvent.MOUSE_OVER button event with the Over keyframe of your button symbol. Both involve detecting when the pointer is over the hit area. But the Over state describes how your button looks when the mouse is over the hit area, whereas the MouseEvent.MOUSE_OVER event triggers the function for that event. The keyframes of a button symbol define how it looks, and the event handler defines what it does (**Figure 4.15**).

```
mybutton_btn.addEventListener(MouseEvent.MOUSE_OVER, reportClick);
function reportClick(myevent:MouseEvent):void {
    // do something
}
```

Figure 4.14 Change the MouseEvent properties to listen for different kinds of mouse events.

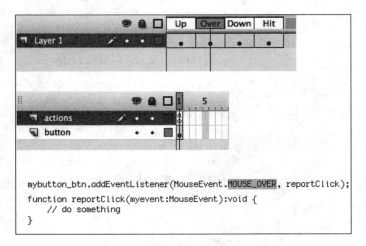

```
mybutton_btn.addEventListener(MouseEvent.MOUSE_OVER, reportClick);
function reportClick(myevent:MouseEvent):void {
    // do something
}
```

Figure 4.15 The keyframes of a button symbol (top) provide the visual feedback to mouse interaction, and the ActionScript code on the Timeline (bottom) tells Flash what to do when an event happens.

Mouse Events in ActionScript 2.0

So far, you've seen only one way to manage event handling, by creating a function and using the method `addEventListener()` to detect an event. However, if you're authoring under a previous ActionScript version, you should use the older way of handling mouse clicks. First, in the Property inspector, name the button or movie clip on the Stage. Then, in the Actions panel, target the button or movie clip and assign a function to the first keyframe on the Timeline, like so:

```
myButton_btn.onRelease=function(){
    // do a response
};
```

There is even an older technique for handling events that involves attaching the event handler code directly to a button instance by selecting the button before typing in the code. You use a special event handler syntax as in the following:

```
on (release) { //do a response }
```

It's best to avoid the third way of handling events because your code becomes scattered among individual buttons on the Stage. As your movie becomes more complex and you have more buttons to deal with, you'll find it difficult to isolate and revise button events. Putting the event handler on the main Timeline is standard practice and the recommended route.

Assigning event handlers directly to button instances is required, however, if you're creating a Flash document that will be published for Flash Player 4 or for Flash Lite 1.1 or earlier. (Flash Lite is the version of the Flash Player that is used on many portable devices such as cell phones.)

Invisible Buttons

You can exploit the flexibility of Flash button symbols by defining only particular states. If you leave empty keyframes in all states except for the Hit state, you create an invisible button (**Figure 4.16**). Invisible buttons are extremely useful for creating multiple generic hotspots to which you can assign actions. By placing invisible button instances on top of graphics, you essentially have the power to make any area on the Stage react to the mouse pointer. For example, you can place several invisible buttons over a map graphic to create hidden hotspots (**Figure 4.17**).

When you drag an instance of an invisible button onto the Stage, you see the hit area as a transparent blue shape, which allows you to place the button precisely. When you choose Control > Enable Simple Buttons (Ctrl-Alt-B for Windows, Cmd-Option-B for Mac), the button disappears to show you its playback appearance.

To create an invisible button:

1. Choose Insert > New Symbol (Ctrl-F8 for Windows, Cmd-F8 for Mac).

   The Create New Symbol dialog box appears.

2. Type the symbol name of your button, choose Button as the Type, and click OK.

   A new button symbol is created in the Library, and you enter symbol editing mode.

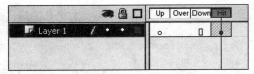

Figure 4.16 An invisible button symbol only has its Hit keyframe defined.

Two instances of the same invisible button symbol cover different spots on this map to make those areas interactive.

Figure 4.17 Two invisible button instances over a map.

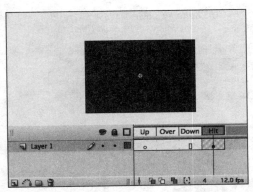

Figure 4.18 An invisible button symbol. The rectangle in the Hit keyframe defines the active area of the button.

Invisible button instance on the Stage

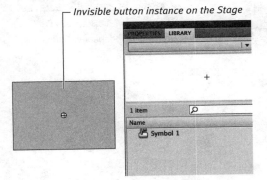

Figure 4.19 An invisible button, when placed from the Library on the Stage, will display a transparent blue area that is identical to its Hit keyframe.

3. Select the Hit keyframe.

4. Choose Insert > Timeline > Keyframe (F6). A new keyframe is created in the Hit state.

5. With the Hit keyframe selected, draw a generic shape that serves as the hotspot for your invisible button (**Figure 4.18**).

6. Return to the main Timeline.

7. Drag an instance of the symbol from the Library onto the Stage.

A transparent blue shape appears on the Stage, indicating the Hit state of your invisible button (**Figure 4.19**).

8. Move, scale, and rotate the invisible button instance to cover any graphic.

When you choose Control > Enable Simple Buttons, the transparent blue area disappears, but your pointer changes to a hand to indicate the presence of a button.

9. Give the button instance a name in the Property inspector and assign an event listener for it in the Actions panel as described in the previous tasks.

INVISIBLE BUTTONS

Animated Buttons and the Movie Clip Symbol

Animated buttons display an animation in any of the first three keyframes (Up, Over, and Down) of the button symbol. A button can spin when the pointer rolls over it, for example, because you have an animation of a spinning graphic in the Over state. How do you fit an animation into only one keyframe of the button symbol? Use a movie clip.

A movie clip is a special kind of symbol that allows you to have animations that run regardless of where they are or how many actual frames the instance occupies. This feature is possible because a movie clip's Timeline runs independently of any other Timeline, including other movie clip Timelines and the main movie Timeline in which the movie clip resides. This independence means that as long as you establish an instance on the Stage, a movie clip animation plays all its frames regardless of where it is. Placing a movie clip instance in a single keyframe of a button symbol makes the movie clip play whenever that particular keyframe is displayed. That is the basis of an animated button.

The butterfly movie clip instance resides in one frame of the main Timeline.

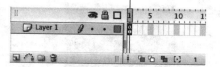

All ten frames of the movie clip symbol still play.

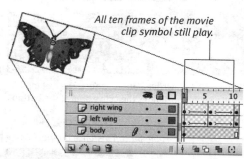

Figure 4.20 Movie clips have independent timelines.

Comparing a Movie Clip Instance with a Graphic Instance

How does a movie clip instance differ from a graphic instance? If you create the same animation in both a movie clip symbol and a graphic symbol and then place both instances on the Stage, the differences become clear. The graphic instance shows its animation in the authoring environment, displaying however many frames are available in the main Timeline. If the graphic symbol contains an animation lasting ten frames and the instance occupies four frames of the main Timeline, you see only four frames of the animation. Movie clips, on the other hand, don't work in the Flash authoring environment. You need to export the movie as a SWF file to see any movie clip animation or functionality. When you export the movie (you can do so by choosing Control > Test Movie), Flash plays the movie clip instance continuously regardless of the number of frames the instance occupies and even when the movie has stopped.

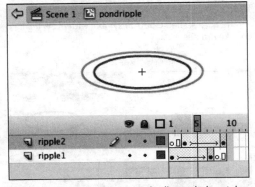

Figure 4.21 Create a new movie clip symbol by naming it and selecting the Movie Clip Type.

Figure 4.22 The pondRipple movie clip symbol contains two shape tweens of an oval getting bigger and gradually fading.

Movie clip instance
(on Stage)

Movie clip symbol
(in Library)

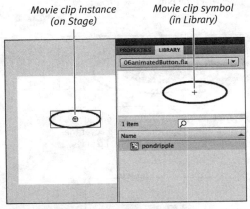

Figure 4.23 Bring an instance of a movie clip symbol onto the Stage by dragging it from the Library.

An animation of a butterfly flapping its wings, for example, may take ten frames in a movie clip symbol. Placing an instance of that movie clip on the Stage in a movie that has only one frame still lets you see the butterfly flapping its wings (**Figure 4.20**). This functionality is useful for cyclical animations that play no matter what else may be going on in the current timeline. Blinking eyes, for example, can be a movie clip placed on a character's face. No matter what the character does—whether it's moving or static in the current timeline—the eyes blink continuously.

To create a movie clip:

1. Choose Insert > New Symbol.

   The Create New Symbol dialog box appears.

2. Type a descriptive name for your movie clip symbol, choose Movie Clip as the Type, and click OK (**Figure 4.21**).

   You now enter symbol editing mode.

3. Create the graphics and animation on the movie clip timeline (**Figure 4.22**).

   Notice how the navigation bar above the Timeline tells you that you're currently editing a symbol.

4. Return to the main Stage.

   Your movie clip is stored in the Library as a symbol, available for you to bring onto the Stage as an instance (**Figure 4.23**).

✔ Tip

■ New instances of movie clips begin playing automatically from the first frame, as do instances in different scenes.

To create an animated button:

1. Create a movie clip symbol that contains an animation, as described in the preceding task.

2. Create a button symbol, and define the four keyframes for the Up, Over, Down, and Hit states (**Figure 4.24**).

3. In symbol editing mode, select either the Up, Over, or Down state for your button, depending on when you would like to see the animation.

4. Drag your movie clip symbol from the Library to the Stage (**Figure 4.25**).

   The movie clip instance is inside the button symbol.

5. Return to the main movie Timeline, and drag an instance of your button symbol to the Stage.

6. Choose Control > Test Movie.

   Your button instance plays the movie clip animation continuously as your pointer interacts with the button (**Figure 4.26**).

✔ Tips

■ Stop the continuous cycling of your movie clip by placing a stop() action in the last keyframe of your movie clip symbol. Because movie clips have independent timelines, they respond to frame actions. Graphic symbols don't respond to any frame actions.

■ To better organize animated buttons, it's useful to create a new layer in the timeline of your button symbol and reserve it specifically for the animation (**Figure 4.27**).

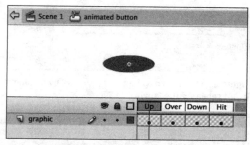

Figure 4.24 A simple button symbol with ovals in all four keyframes.

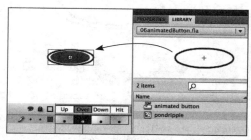

Figure 4.25 The Over state of the button symbol. Place an instance of the pondRipple movie clip in this keyframe to play the pond-ripple animation whenever the pointer moves over the button.

Figure 4.26 The completed animated button. When the pointer passes over the button, the pondRipple movie clip plays.

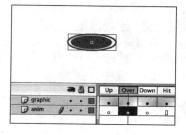

Figure 4.27 A new layer in the button symbol timeline helps organize the animation.

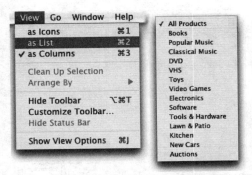

Figure 4.28 Typical pull-down menus: a Mac OS system menu (left) and a Web menu (right).

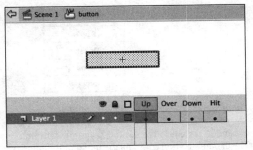

Figure 4.29 A generic button with the four keyframes defined.

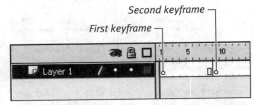

Figure 4.30 The pull-down menu movie clip timeline contains two keyframes: one at frame 1 and another at frame 9.

Complex Buttons

You can use a combination of invisible buttons, animated buttons, and movie clips to create objects with complex behaviors such as pull-down menus. The pull-down (or pop-up) menu is a kind of button that is common in operating systems and Web interfaces, and is useful for presenting several choices under a single heading. The functionality consists of a single button that expands to show more buttons and collapses when a selection has been made (**Figure 4.28**).

To build your own pull-down menu, the basic strategy is to nest symbols inside of each other. A simple way is to place buttons inside a movie clip. The buttons specify which frames within the movie clip timeline to play. Whether the menu is expanded or collapsed is determined within the movie clip. Placing an instance of this movie clip on the Stage allows you to access either the expanded or collapsed state independently of what's happening in your main movie.

To create a simple pull-down menu:

1. Create a button symbol that will be used for the top menu button as well as the choices in the expanded list.

2. Add a filled rectangle to the Up, Over, Down, and Hit keyframes (**Figure 4.29**).

3. Create a new movie clip symbol.

   Enter symbol editing mode for the movie clip.

4. Insert a new keyframe at a later point in the movie clip Timeline.

   You now have two keyframes inside your movie clip symbol. The first one will contain the collapsed state of your menu, and the second one will contain its expanded state (**Figure 4.30**).

Continues on next page

5. Drag one instance of your button symbol into the first keyframe, and add text over the instance to describe the button.

This is the collapsed state of your menu.

6. Drag several instances of your button symbol into the second keyframe, align them with one another, and add text over these instances to describe the buttons.

This is the expanded state of your menu.

7. Add a new layer, and place frame labels to mark the collapsed and expanded keyframes (**Figure 4.31**).

In the Frame Label field of the Property inspector, enter collapsed for the first keyframe and expanded for the second keyframe.

The frame labels let you see clearly the collapsed and expanded states of your movie clip, and let you use the gotoAndStop() action with frame labels instead of frame numbers.

8. Select the button instance in the first keyframe, and give it an instance name.

9. Add a new layer; select the first keyframe in that layer, and open the Actions panel.

10. In the first line of the Script pane, add the action stop().

Without this stop() in the first frame of your movie clip, the menu would open and close repeatedly because of the automatic cycling of movie clips. The stop() action ensures that the movie clip stays on frame 1 until you click the menu button (**Figure 4.32**).

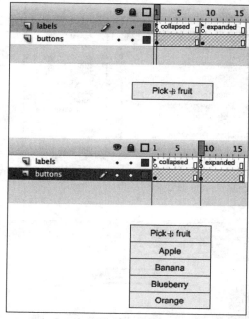

Figure 4.31 The two states of your pull-down menu. The collapsed state is in the first keyframe (top); the expanded state is in the second keyframe (bottom). The expanded state contains the initial button plus four button instances that represent the menu choices.

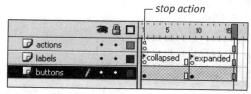

Figure 4.32 The movie clip timeline for the pull-down menu. A stop action is assigned to the first frame in the top layer.

```
stop();
pick_btn.addEventListener(MouseEvent.CLICK, expandmenu);
function expandmenu(myevent:MouseEvent):void {
    gotoAndStop("expanded");
}
```

Figure 4.33 The stop action plus the event handler for the button in the first keyframe. When this button is clicked, Flash goes to the expanded keyframe.

New keyframe with actions for buttons that show up here ⌐

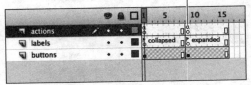

Figure 4.34 When buttons appear on a later frame (frame number 9), add a new keyframe at the same frame number with event handler code for those buttons.

11. On the next line of the Script pane, add an event listener for the button that is on the first keyframe of your movie clip:

    ```
    pick_btn.addEventListener
    → (MouseEvent.CLICK, expandmenu);
    ```

    This listener listens for a mouse click on the button called `pick_btn` (**Figure 4.33**).

12. On the next available line of the Script pane, add a function that goes to the expanded keyframe of the movie clip, like so:

    ```
    function
    → expandmenu(myevent:MouseEvent):
    → void {
        this.gotoAndStop("expanded");
    }
    ```

    When this function is called, the current timeline is targeted (with the keyword `this`) and the playhead goes to the frame labeled `expanded`. Make sure that the frame label is within quotation marks.

13. Select the first button instance on the last keyframe, and give it an instance name.

14. In the layer with your ActionScript, select the frame above the `expanded` keyframe, and add a new keyframe.

    In this keyframe, you'll add the code for the buttons in the expanded menu.

    You have to put more code here because you can't add event handler code to buttons until they're present on the Stage. Otherwise, Flash won't find the button instances and can't reference them from the code (**Figure 4.34**).

    Continues on next page

COMPLEX BUTTONS

15. With your new keyframe selected, open the Actions panel and add an event listener for the first button in the expanded keyframe:

```
pick2_btn.addEventListener
→ (MouseEvent.CLICK, collapsemenu);
```

This listener listens for a mouse click on the button called `pick2_btn`.

16. Next, add a function that goes back to the `collapsed` keyframe, like so:

```
function collapsemenu(myevent:Mouse
→ Event):void {
    this.gotoAndStop("collapsed");
}
```

17. Assign instance names to each of the remaining button instances on this keyframe, and repeat step 15 to add event handler code for each of them (**Figure 4.35**).

18. Return to the main movie Timeline, and place an instance of your movie clip on the Stage.

19. Choose Control > Test Movie to see how your pull-down menu works.

When you click the first button, the buttons for your choices appear because you direct the playhead to go to the `expanded` keyframe on the movie clip timeline. When you click one of the buttons in the expanded state, the buttons disappear, returning you to the `collapsed` keyframe of the movie clip timeline. All this happens independently of the main movie Timeline, where the movie clip instance resides (**Figure 4.36**).

At this point, you've created a complex button that behaves like a pull-down menu but doesn't actually do anything (except modify itself). In Chapter 5, "Controlling Multiple Timelines," you'll learn how to make timelines communicate with one another, which enables you to create complex navigation systems.

```
pick2_btn.addEventListener(MouseEvent.CLICK, collapsemenu);
apple_btn.addEventListener(MouseEvent.CLICK, collapsemenu);
banana_btn.addEventListener(MouseEvent.CLICK, collapsemenu);
blueberry_btn.addEventListener(MouseEvent.CLICK, collapsemenu);
orange_btn.addEventListener(MouseEvent.CLICK, collapsemenu);
function collapsemenu (myevent:MouseEvent):void{
    gotoAndStop("collapsed");
}
```

Figure 4.35 The ActionScript for the buttons in the expanded keyframe sends the Flash playhead to the frame labeled `collapsed` and stops there.

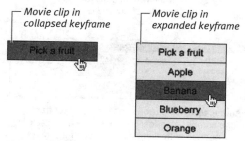

Figure 4.36 The two states of the pull-down menu work independently of the main Timeline.

✔ Tips

■ Use edit commands such as Copy and Paste to create similar blocks of code such as event handlers for several buttons. Once you paste in a copy of the code, don't forget to change the name of the targets and functions to which the event handler is assigned.

■ When you understand the concept behind the simple pull-down menu, you can create menus that are more sophisticated by adding animation to the transition between the collapsed state and the expanded state. Instead of having the expanded state suddenly pop up, for example, you can create a tween that makes the buttons scroll down gently. Change the body of the function on the first keyframe of your movie clip to `gotoAndPlay()` instead of `gotoAndStop()` to see the tweens.

Figure 4.37 The button-tracking options in the Property inspector.

Button-tracking Options

You can define a button instance in the Property inspector in one of two ways: "Track as Button" or "Track as Menu Item" (**Figure 4.37**). These two tracking options determine whether button instances can receive a button event even after the event has started on a different button instance. The "Track as Menu Item" option allows this to happen; the "Track as Button" option doesn't. The default option, "Track as Button," is the typical behavior for buttons; it causes one button event to affect one button instance. More complex cases, such as pull-down menus, require multiple button instances working together.

Imagine that you click and hold down the menu button to see the pop-up choices, drag your pointer to your selection, and then release the mouse button. You need Flash to recognize the MouseEvent.MOUSE_UP event in the expanded menu even though the MouseEvent.MOUSE_DOWN event occurred in the collapsed menu for a different button instance (in fact, in a different frame altogether). Choosing "Track as Menu Item" allows these buttons to receive these events and gives you more flexibility to work with combinations of buttons and events.

In the second task, you refine the pull-down menu with the MouseEvent.MOUSE_OVER event so that the menu collapses if the user's pointer wanders off the menu. This technique is important to keep pull-down menus expanded only when your viewer is making a choice from the menu.

To set "Track as Menu Item" for a pull-down menu:

1. Continue with the pull-down menu, as described in the preceding task.

2. Go to symbol editing mode for the movie clip.

3. Select the keyframe on frame 1 containing the event handler for the button instance, and change the mouse event to `MouseEvent.MOUSE_DOWN` (**Figure 4.38**).

4. Select the keyframe containing the ActionScript for the expanded section. Replace all the `MouseEvent.CLICK` events with `MouseEvent.MOUSE_UP` (**Figure 4.39**).

5. Select each button instance in the expanded keyframe.

6. In the Property inspector, choose "Track as Menu Item" (**Figure 4.40**).

   The button instances in the expanded menu will now trigger a `MouseEvent.MOUSE_UP` event even if the `MouseEvent.MOUSE_DOWN` event occurs on a different instance.

7. Return to the main Timeline, and test your movie.

   You now click and hold down the mouse button to keep the menu open, and then release the mouse button when you've made your selection.

✔ Tip

■ When you set "Track as Menu Item" for this pull-down menu, the expanded button instances display their Down state as you move your pointer over them. This display occurs because your mouse button is, in fact, pressed, but that event occurred earlier on a different instance.

```
stop();
pick_btn.addEventListener(MouseEvent.MOUSE_DOWN, expandmenu);
function expandmenu(myevent:MouseEvent):void {
    gotoAndStop("expanded");
}
```

Figure 4.38 The collapsed-menu button listens for the `MOUSE_DOWN` event.

```
pick_btn2.addEventListener(MouseEvent.MOUSE_UP, collapsemenu);
apple_btn.addEventListener(MouseEvent.MOUSE_UP, collapsemenu);
banana_btn.addEventListener(MouseEvent.MOUSE_UP, collapsemenu);
blueberry_btn.addEventListener(MouseEvent.MOUSE_UP, collapsemenu);
orange_btn.addEventListener(MouseEvent.MOUSE_UP, collapsemenu);
function collapsemenu (myevent:MouseEvent):void{
    gotoAndStop("collapsed");
}
```

Figure 4.39 The expanded-menu buttons listen for the `MOUSE_UP` event.

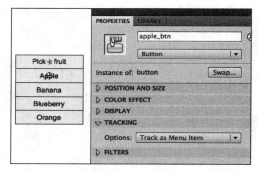

Figure 4.40 You need to change the setting to "Track as Menu Item" for each button instance in the expanded section of the timeline.

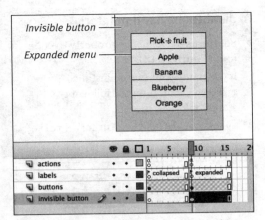

Figure 4.41 When the pointer leaves one of the buttons in the expanded state of the menu, it rolls over the invisible button that sits in the bottom layer.

```
pick2_btn.addEventListener(MouseEvent.MOUSE_UP, collapsemenu);
apple_btn.addEventListener(MouseEvent.MOUSE_UP, collapsemenu);
banana_btn.addEventListener(MouseEvent.MOUSE_UP, collapsemenu);
blueberry_btn.addEventListener(MouseEvent.MOUSE_UP, collapsemenu);
orange_btn.addEventListener(MouseEvent.MOUSE_UP, collapsemenu);
invisible_btn.addEventListener(MouseEvent.MOUSE_OVER, collapsemenu);
function collapsemenu(myevent:MouseEvent):void {
    gotoAndStop("collapsed");
}
```

Figure 4.42 The MOUSE_OVER event is detected on the invisible button, making the playhead jump to the keyframe labeled collapsed.

To set a MOUSE_OVER event to collapse the menu:

1. Continuing with the pull-down menu constructed in the preceding task, go to symbol editing mode for the movie clip.

2. Add a new layer under the existing layers.

3. In the new layer, create an invisible button, and place an instance in a new keyframe corresponding to the expanded keyframe.

   Your invisible button instance should be slightly larger than the expanded menu (**Figure 4.41**).

4. Select the invisible button instance.

5. In the Property inspector, give the invisible button an instance name.

6. Select the keyframe containing the event handler actions for your expanded menu buttons. In the Actions panel, assign a listener for your invisible button to detect a MouseEvent.MOUSE_OVER event (**Figure 4.42**):

   ```
   invisible_btn.addEventListener
   → (MouseEvent.MOUSE_OVER,
   → collapsemenu);
   ```

7. Return to the main Timeline, and test your movie.

   The invisible button instance under the expanded menu detects whether the pointer leaves any of the other button instances. If it does, Flash sends the movie clip back to frame 1 and collapses the menu.

BUTTON-TRACKING OPTIONS

Changing Button Behavior

Because the buttons you create are objects of the `SimpleButton` class and objects of the larger class `InteractiveObject`, you can control their properties by using dot syntax. Many button properties control the way a button looks (such as its width, height, and rotation) as well as the way the button behaves (such as its button tracking). In Chapter 7, "Controlling and Displaying Graphics," you will explore the ways to manipulate graphics, including buttons. Here, you will learn to change properties that affect a button's behavior.

To disable a button:

◆ Set the `mouseEnabled` property to code font.

If you name your button instance `mybutton_btn`, enter the following statement:

`mybutton_btn.mouseEnabled = false;`

Your button will no longer interact with the mouse pointer and will no longer display its `Over` or `Down` keyframes. In addition, mouse events won't be captured on this button.

To remove an event listener:

◆ Use the `removeEventListener()` method with its two parameters set identical to the ones used in the `addEventListener()` method.

If you name your button instance `mybutton_btn`, enter the following statement:

`mybutton_btn.removeEventListener`
`→ (MouseEvent.CLICK, myfunction);`

Although your button will still interact with the mouse pointer, the listener will no longer detect a mouse click and call on the function called `myfunction`.

To disable the hand pointer:

◆ Set the `useHandCursor` property to code font (**Figure 4.43**).

If you name your button instance `mybutton_btn`, enter the following statement:

`mybutton_btn.useHandCursor = false;`

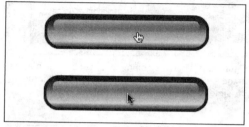

Figure 4.43 When the normal hand pointer (above) is disabled, only the arrow pointer will show up (below).

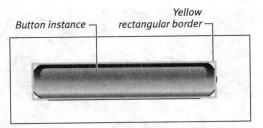

Figure 4.44 When you use the Tab key, buttons show their focus with a yellow rectangular border in their Over state.

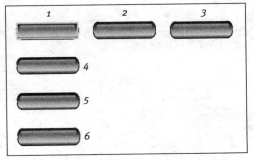

Figure 4.45 The automatic order of button focusing with the Tab key is by position. The numbers show the order in which the buttons will receive focus.

Changing button focus with the Tab key

The button focus is a way of selecting a button with the Tab key. When a Flash movie plays within a browser, you can press the Tab key and navigate between buttons, text fields, and movie clips. The currently focused button displays its Over state with a yellow rectangular border (**Figure 4.44**). Pressing the Enter key (or Return key on the Mac) is equivalent to clicking the focused button. Several properties of the InteractiveObject class (of which the SimpleButton is a subclass)—focusRect, tabEnabled, and tabIndex—deal with controlling the button focus. The property focusRect determines whether the yellow rectangular border is visible. If focusRect is set to false, a focused button displays its Over state but doesn't display the yellow rectangular highlight. The property tabEnabled, if set to false, disables a button's capability to receive focus from the Tab key.

The order in which a button, movie clip, or text field receives its focus is determined by its position on the Stage. Objects focus from left to right and then from top to bottom. So, if you have a row of buttons at the top of your movie and a column of buttons on the left side below it, the Tab key will focus each of the buttons in the top row first and then focus on each of the buttons in the column (**Figure 4.45**). After the last button receives the focus, the tab order begins again from the top row.

You can set your own tab order with the property tabIndex. Assign a number to the tabIndex for each button instance, and Flash will organize the tab order using the tabIndex in ascending order. Take control of the tab order to create more helpful forms, allowing the user to use the Tab and Enter keys to fill out multiple text fields and click multiple buttons.

To hide the yellow rectangular highlight over focused buttons:

◆ Set the focusRect property to false.

If you name your button instance mybutton_btn, for example, use the statement mybutton_btn.focusRect = false;

To disable focusing with the Tab key:

◆ Set the tabEnabled property to false.

If you name your button instance mybutton_btn, for example, use the statement mybutton_btn.tabEnabled = false;

To change the tab order of button focus:

1. Give each button instance a name in the Property inspector.

2. Select the first frame of the main Timeline, and open the Actions panel.

3. In the Script pane, enter your first button's instance name followed by a dot.

4. Type tabIndex after the dot.

5. For the value, you must indicate where in the tab order this object should be when the user presses the Tab key. Enter an equals symbol (=) and then a value (**Figure 4.46**).

This button instance will be in the tab order in the specified index.

6. Repeat steps 3–5 for each of your button instances. Continue to assign numbers in sequence to the tabIndex property of each button instance (**Figure 4.47**).

7. Choose File > Publish Preview > Default to view your movie in a browser.

When you press the Tab key, Flash follows the tabIndex in ascending order for button focusing (**Figure 4.48**).

✔ Tip

■ Some browsers intercept keypresses, so you may have to click the Flash movie in your browser window before you can use the Tab key to focus on buttons.

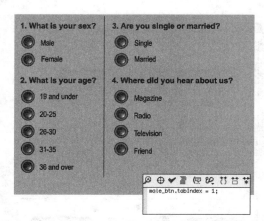

Figure 4.46 The button called male_btn will receive the first focus with the Tab key.

```
male_btn.tabIndex = 1;
female_btn.tabIndex = 2;
age19_btn.tabIndex = 3;
age20_btn.tabIndex = 4;
age26_btn.tabIndex = 5;
age31_btn.tabIndex = 6;
age36_btn.tabIndex = 7;
single_btn.tabIndex = 8;
married_btn.tabIndex = 9;
magazine_btn.tabIndex = 10;
radio_btn.tabIndex = 11;
television_btn.tabIndex = 12;
friend_btn.tabIndex = 13;
```

Figure 4.47 This block of code assigns the tabIndex properties for 13 different buttons.

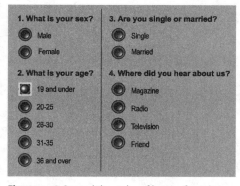

Figure 4.48 Control the order of button focusing to provide easier tab navigation through forms and questionnaires. This movie focuses buttons in columns to follow the question numbers rather than relying on Flash's automatic ordering.

Creating Buttons Dynamically

If you want to create a button dynamically—that is, during runtime while your Flash movie is playing—you can do so with the constructor `new SimpleButton()`. Creating buttons on the fly allows you to respond to your user and a changing environment. Rather than relying on buttons that have been created in advance, you can capture graphics that a user might draw or upload, and use them as buttons. After creating a new button from the `SimpleButton` class, you define its four keyframes, the `Up`, `Over`, `Down`, and `Hit` states, by assigning other objects to the properties `upState`, `overState`, `downState`, and `hitTestState`.

The `upState`, `overState`, `downState`, and `hitTestState` properties can take any kind of display object such as a loaded JPEG image, a movie clip, text field, or a dynamically drawn shape or sprite. In Chapter 7, you'll learn to create and manage the graphics on the Stage. In this example task, you'll create four shapes dynamically with the `new Shape()` constructor, and then assign those shapes to the keyframes of a newly created button.

To create a button dynamically:

1. Select the first frame of the Timeline, and open the Actions panel.

2. In the Script pane, enter the following code that creates a new `Shape` object and then draws a filled circle:

```
var myup:Shape = new Shape();
myup.graphics.beginFill(0xff4000);
myup.graphics.drawCircle(100,100,10);
```

The new `Shape` object called `myup` is created. The `beginFill()` method defines the color of the fill, and the `drawCircle()` method defines its location and size.

Continues on next page

CREATING BUTTONS DYNAMICALLY

3. Create three more new shapes with different colors in the same manner (**Figure 4.49**). These four shapes will be assigned to the four keyframes of the new button.

4. In the next line, instantiate a new button from the `SimpleButton` class, like so:

```
var mybutton:SimpleButton=new
→ SimpleButton();
```

5. Next, assign the four shapes to the properties of your new button as in the following code:

```
mybutton.upState=myup;

mybutton.overState=myover;

mybutton.downState=mydown;

mybutton.hitTestState=myhit;
```

6. To see the new button on the Stage, you must add it to the `stage` to be displayed with the following code:

```
stage.addChild(mybutton);
```

To see any dynamically generated graphic, you always need to use the method `addChild()`. The full ActionScript code can be seen in **Figure 4.50**.

7. Test your movie by choosing Control > Test Movie (**Figure 4.51**).

```
var myup:Shape = new Shape();
myup.graphics.beginFill(0xff4000);
myup.graphics.drawCircle(100,100,10);

var mydown:Shape = new Shape();
mydown.graphics.beginFill(0x004000);
mydown.graphics.drawCircle(100,100,10);

var myover:Shape = new Shape();
myover.graphics.beginFill(0xf34283);
myover.graphics.drawCircle(100,100,10);

var myhit:Shape = new Shape();
myhit.graphics.beginFill(0xf34004);
myhit.graphics.drawCircle(100,100,10);
```

Figure 4.49 Four circles are created dynamically. Each circle is an object of the Shape class.

```
var myup:Shape = new Shape();
myup.graphics.beginFill(0xff400);
myup.graphics.drawCircle(100,100,10);

var mydown:Shape = new Shape();
mydown.graphics.beginFill(0x004000);
mydown.graphics.drawCircle(100,100,10);

var myover:Shape = new Shape();
myover.graphics.beginFill(0xf34283);
myover.graphics.drawCircle(100,100,10);

var myhit:Shape = new Shape();
myhit.graphics.beginFill(0xf34004);
myhit.graphics.drawCircle(100,100,10);

var mybutton:SimpleButton=new SimpleButton();

mybutton.upState=myup;
mybutton.overState=myover;
mybutton.downState=mydown;
mybutton.hitTestState=myhit;

stage.addChild(mybutton);
```

Figure 4.50 A button is created dynamically, and the four shapes are assigned to the button's upState, overState, downState, and hitTestState (highlighted lines).

Figure 4.51 The circle shape appears on the Stage and behaves as a button.

Keyboard Detection

The keyboard is just as important an interface device as the mouse, and Flash lets you detect events occurring from keystrokes, both the downward keypress and the upward key release. This ability opens the possibility of having navigation based on the keyboard (using the arrow keys or the number keys, for example) or having keyboard shortcuts that duplicate mouse-based navigation schemes. Flash even lets you control live text that the viewer types in empty text fields in a movie; these text fields merit a separate discussion in Chapter 10, "Controlling Text." This section focuses on single or combination keystrokes with modifiers (like the Ctrl or Shift key) that trigger a response.

Just as a `MouseEvent` object is created when the user does something with the mouse, a `KeyboardEvent` object (another subclass of the Event class) is created when the keyboard is used.

You can detect and respond to the `KeyboardEvent` object by first attaching a listener to the main Stage (or another object like a text field) using the `addEventListener` method as follows:

```
stage.addEventListener
→ (KeyboardEvent.KEY_DOWN, detectText);
```

Next, create a function with a `KeyboardEvent` parameter:

```
function detectText
→ (myevent:KeyboardEvent):void {
    // do something in response
}
```

Table 4.2 details the specific properties that describe the events of the `KeyboardEvent` object.

Table 4.2

KeyboardEvent Properties	
PROPERTY	DESCRIPTION
KEY_UP	Happens when a key is released
KEY_DOWN	Happens when a key is pressed

Key-code values

The `KeyboardEvent` object is dispatched whenever any key on the keyboard is pressed. But to determine which particular key has been pressed, you have to use key-code values. Key-code values are specific numbers associated with each key (see Appendix A, "Keyboard Key Codes"). You use these codes to construct a conditional statement to determine a match. The key code for the spacebar, for example, is 32. So to see if the `KeyboardEvent` object's `keyCode` matches 32, you write the following:

```
if (myevent.keyCode==32){
    // spacebar was pressed
}
```

In this example, `myevent` is the name of the `KeyboardEvent` object and `keyCode` is a property whose value is the key code of the key that was pressed. This conditional statement checks if the key code of the key that was pressed matches the code for the spacebar.

Fortunately, you don't have to use clumsy numeric key codes all the time. The most common keys are conveniently assigned as properties of another class, the `Keyboard` class. These properties are constants that you can use in place of the key codes. The statement `Keyboard.SPACE`, for example, is the number 32. Appendix A also lists all the matching `Keyboard` constants for the key codes.

Two properties of the `KeyboardEvent` object, `shiftKey` and `ctrlKey`, can be used to test whether the Shift or the Ctrl key is being held down. These properties are either `true` or `false`.

To detect a keypress:

1. Select the first keyframe in the Timeline, and open the Actions panel.

2. In the Script pane, add a listener to the Stage with the addEventListener method, as follows:

```
stage.addEventListener
→ (KeyboardEvent.KEY_DOWN,
→ detectText);
```

When this listener detects a keypress, it triggers the function called detectText.

3. On the next available line, write a function with the KeyboardEvent object as a parameter, like so:

```
function detectText(myevent:Keyboard
→ Event):void {
    myarrow_mc.x+=5;
}
```

In between the curly braces of the function, put actions you want as a response. In this example, any keypress makes a movie clip called myarrow_mc move 5 pixels to the right.

4. Choose File > Publish Preview > Default to test your movie (**Figure 4.52**).

To detect a specific keypress:

1. Continue with the file you created in the previous task.

2. Select the first frame of the Timeline, and open the Actions panel.

3. Select the code in between the curly braces of the function and replace it with a conditional statement like this:

```
if (myevent.keyCode==Keyboard.RIGHT){
    myarrow_mc.x+=5;
}
```

The double equals symbol (==) checks the equivalence of the items on either side. If they are equivalent, the actions within the curly braces of the if statement are executed.

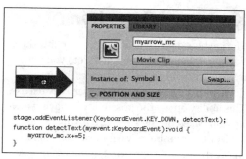

```
stage.addEventListener(KeyboardEvent.KEY_DOWN, detectText);
function detectText(myevent:KeyboardEvent):void {
    myarrow_mc.x+=5;
}
```

Figure 4.52 When the ActionScript code (below) detects a keypress, it moves the movie clip called myarrow_mc (above) to the right.

Keyboard Events in ActionScript 2.0

If you are authoring for Flash Player 8 and must use ActionScript 2.0, you need to resort to the older way of handling keyboard input. In the previous version of ActionScript, you also create listeners, but they are constructed from the generic Object class. The syntax and methods for detecting a particular keypress look like this:

```
var myListener:Object = new Object();
myListener.onKeyDown = function() {
    if (Key.isDown(Key.SPACE)) {
        //Spacebar pressed
    }
};
Key.addListener(myListener);
```

In this example, the isDown() method returns a true value if its parameter is the keycode of the key that was pressed. So you can enter a keycode for its parameter or use a constant (Key.SPACE). The last line is needed to register the listener to the Key class.

4. Choose File > Publish Preview > Default.

When you press a key, Flash dispatches a KeyboardEvent object and Flash calls the function. Within the function, Flash checks to see if the key that was pressed matches the right-arrow key. If so, the actions are carried out. In this example, a movie clip called myarrow_mc is moved 5 pixels to the right (**Figure 4.53**).

To detect keystroke combinations:

1. Continue with the file you created in the previous task.

2. Select the first frame of the timeline and open the Actions panel.

3. Change the code in between the parentheses of the if statement so that the statement reads

```
if (myevent.keyCode==Keyboard.RIGHT
→ && myevent.shiftKey==true){
    myarrow_mc.x+=5;
}
```

The logical *and operator (*&&*)* joins two statements so that both must be true for the entire statement to be true.

4. Choose File > Publish Preview > Default.

The if statement will perform the action within its curly braces only if both the right-arrow key and the Shift key are pressed together (**Figure 4.54**).

✔ Tips

■ The property ctrlKey maps to the Ctrl key on Windows and the Command (or Apple) key on the Macintosh.

■ In the Flash testing mode (Control > Test Movie), some keypresses may be interpreted as shortcut commands for the Flash tools, so use Choose File > Publish Preview > Default to test in the browser.

```
stage.addEventListener(KeyboardEvent.KEY_DOWN, detectText);
function detectText(myevent:KeyboardEvent):void {
    if (myevent.keyCode==Keyboard.RIGHT) {
        myarrow_mc.x+=5;
    }
}
```

Figure 4.53 If the right-arrow key is pressed, Flash moves the movie clip to the right.

```
stage.addEventListener(KeyboardEvent.KEY_DOWN, detectText);
function detectText(myevent:KeyboardEvent):void {
    if (myevent.keyCode==Keyboard.RIGHT && myevent.shiftKey==true) {
        myarrow_mc.x+=5;
    }
}
```

Figure 4.54 If the right-arrow key and the Shift key are both pressed, Flash moves the movie clip to the right. The operator && connects two statements, requiring both to be true.

The Contextual Menu

In the playback of any Flash movie, a contextual menu appears when you right-click (Windows) or Ctrl-click (Mac) on the movie. There are different types of contextual menus, including a standard menu that appears over any part of the Stage and an edit menu that appears over text fields (**Figure 4.55**). You can customize, to a certain extent, the items that appear in the standard and edit menus through the ContextMenu class. You can disable certain items or create your own custom items with the related ContextMenuItem class. You can even make different contextual menus appear over different objects like buttons, movie clips, or text fields.

Manipulating the contextual menu first requires that you instantiate a new object of the ContextMenu class, like so:

```
var myMenu:ContextMenu = new
→ ContextMenu();
```

After you have a new ContextMenu object, you can call its methods or set its properties to customize the items that appear. All the default menu items are properties of the object builtInItems. Setting each property to true or false enables or disables that particular item in the menu. For example, the following statement disables the print item in the ContextMenu object called myMenu:

```
myMenu.builtInItems.print = false;
```

See **Table 4.3** for the builtInItems properties of the ContextMenu class.

Finally, you must associate your ContextMenu object with the contextMenu property of another object, such as the main Stage, a text field, or a specific movie clip, like so:

```
myObject_mc.contextMenu = myMenu;
```

If you associate your ContextMenu object with a specific button or movie clip, your custom

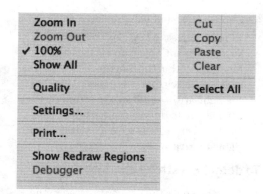

Figure 4.55 The standard contextual menu (left), and the edit contextual menu that appears over selectable text fields (right).

Table 4.3

builtInItems Properties		
PROPERTY	VALUE	Menu Items
forwardAndBack	true or false	Forward, Back
save	true or false	Save
zoom	true or false	Zoom in, Zoom out, 100%, Show all
quality	true or false	Quality
play	true or false	Play
loop	true or false	Loop
rewind	true or false	Rewind
print	true or false	Print

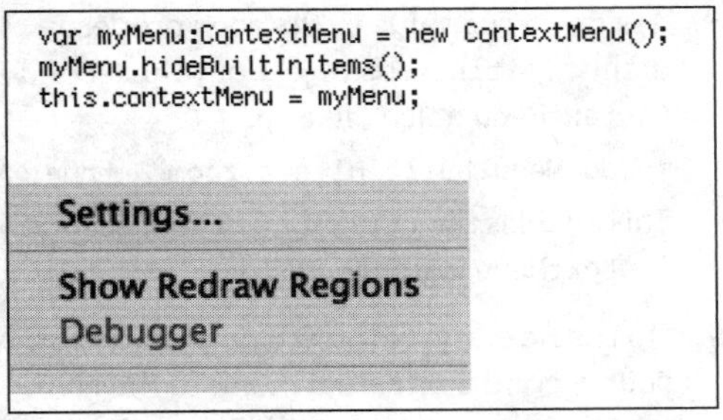

```
var myMenu:ContextMenu = new ContextMenu();
myMenu.hideBuiltInItems();
this.contextMenu = myMenu;
```

Settings...

Show Redraw Regions
Debugger

Figure 4.56 By using the `hideBuiltInItems()` method, you disable all built-in (default) items of the contextual menu. The final code (top) hides all the default items except for the Settings and Debugger items (bottom). The Show Redraw Regions item appears only in debugger versions of the Flash Player and won't appear for regular users.

contextual menu will appear when the user activates the contextual menu while the mouse pointer is over that object. For example, a map can have the Zoom item in its contextual menu enabled, whereas other objects may have the Zoom item in their contextual menu disabled.

To disable the contextual menu:

1. Select the first frame of the main Timeline, and open the Actions panel.

2. On the first line of the Script pane, instantiate a new `ContextMenu` object:

   `var myMenu:ContextMenu=new` → `ContextMenu();`

   A new `ContextMenu` object is named and created.

3. On the next line of the Script pane, call the `hideBuiltInItems()` method of your `ContextMenu` object, like so:

   `myMenu.hideBuiltInItems();`

   This method sets all the properties of the `builtInItems` object of `myMenu` to false, which hides the items of the contextual menu.

4. On the third line of the Script pane, assign your `ContextMenu` object to the `contextMenu` property of the Stage as follows:

   `this.contextMenu = myMenu;`

   The `ContextMenu` object now becomes associated with the main Timeline, so the default items of the main Timeline's contextual menu are hidden. The only items that remain are Settings, Show Redraw Regions, and Debugger (**Figure 4.56**).

To associate custom contextual menus with different objects:

1. Continue with the preceding task. Starting on the next available line in the Script pane, declare another ContextMenu object and instantiate the object using the constructor function, new ContextMenu().

   A second ContextMenu object is named (in this example, called myZoomMenu) and created (**Figure 4.57**).

2. Add a call to the hideBuiltInItems() method for your new ContextMenu instance.

   The items of your second ContextMenu object, like the first, are disabled.

3. Assign a true value to the zoom property of the builtInItems object of your second ContextMenu object, like so:

   myZoomMenu.builtInItems.zoom = true;

   This enables the Zoom item in your second ContextMenu instance.

4. On the next line of the Script pane, assign your second contextual menu to the contextMenu property of an object on the Stage, like so:

   map_mc.contextMenu = myZoomMenu;

   In this example, the completed statement associates the second ContextMenu object with the movie clip instance called map_mc (**Figure 4.58**).

```
var myMenu:ContextMenu = new ContextMenu();
myMenu.hideBuiltInItems();
this.contextMenu = myMenu;

var myZoomMenu:ContextMenu = new ContextMenu();
```

Figure 4.57 A new ContextMenu object named myZoomMenu has been created.

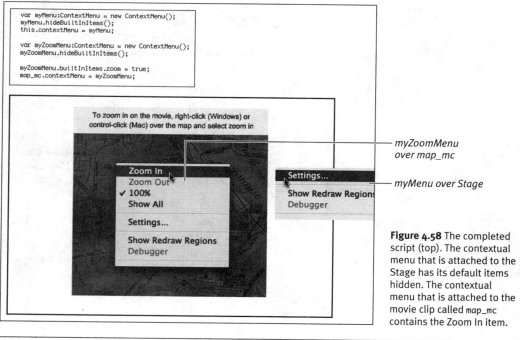

```
var myMenu:ContextMenu = new ContextMenu();
myMenu.hideBuiltInItems();
this.contextMenu = myMenu;

var myZoomMenu:ContextMenu = new ContextMenu();
myZoomMenu.hideBuiltInItems();

myZoomMenu.builtInItems.zoom = true;
map_mc.contextMenu = myZoomMenu;
```

To zoom in on the movie, right-click (Windows) or control-click (Mac) over the map and select zoom in

myZoomMenu over map_mc

myMenu over Stage

Figure 4.58 The completed script (top). The contextual menu that is attached to the Stage has its default items hidden. The contextual menu that is attached to the movie clip called map_mc contains the Zoom In item.

Creating new contextual menu items

You can add your own items in the contextual menu by creating new objects from the `ContextMenuItem` class. Each new item requires that you instantiate a separate `ContextMenuItem` object with a string parameter, as in the following code:

```
var myFirstItem:ContextMenuItem = new
→ ContextMenuItem("First Item");
```

The parameter represents the text that will be displayed for the item in the contextual menu. Because it's a string, use quotation marks around the enclosed text. There are certain size and content restrictions on new menu items—see the sidebar "Custom Item Restrictions" for details.

Next, you must add your new `ContextMenuItem` object to the `customItems` property of your `ContextMenu` object. However, the `customItems` property is different from the `builtInItems` property you learned about in the preceding section. The `customItems` property is an array, which is an ordered list of values or objects. (You can learn more about arrays in Chapter 11, "Manipulating Information.") To add your new `ContextMenuItem` object to the `customItems` array, use the array method `push()`, as in the following code:

```
mymenu.customItems.push(myFirstItem);
```

Finally, you have to create an event handler to respond when the user selects your new contextual item. The `Event` object that is dispatched when an item on the contextual menu is selected is a `ContextMenuEvent` object. You can use `ContextMenuEvent.MENU_ITEM_SELECT` as the specific event type.

To create a new item for the contextual menu:

1. Select the first frame of the main Timeline, and open the Actions panel.

2. In the Script pane, create a new `ContextMenu` object as in previous tasks. The completed code looks like this:

   ```
   var mymenu:ContextMenu = new
   → ContextMenu();
   ```

3. Starting on the next line, hide the default items in the contextual menu:

   ```
   mymenu.hideBuiltInItems();
   ```

4. Next, instantiate a new `ContextMenuItem` object for your first item:

   ```
   var myFirstItem:ContextMenuItem=new
   → ContextMenuItem("Flip");
   ```

   A new `ContextMenuItem` is instantiated. Be sure to enclose the parameter, which represents the title of your item, in quotation marks.

5. On the next line, add a call to the `Array` class's `push()` method with the name of your `ContextMenuItem` as its parameter:

   ```
   mymenu.customItems.push(myFirstItem);
   ```

   The completed statement adds your `ContextMenuItem` object to the `customItems` array of your `ContextMenu` object.

Continues on next page

THE CONTEXTUAL MENU

6. On the following line, assign the ContextMenu object to the `contextMenu` property of an object on the Stage.

`picture_mc.contextMenu = mymenu;`

In this example, your contextual menu now becomes associated with the movie clip called `picture_mc` (**Figure 4.59**).

7. You're not done yet! Finally you must create the event handler. Add the listener:

```
myFirstItem.addEventListener
→ (ContextMenuEvent.MENU_ITEM_SELECT,
→ selectFlip);
```

Note that the listener goes on the `ContextMenuItem` object, not on the object on the Stage or on the `ContextMenu` object.

8. Next, create a function with the `ContextMenuEvent` object as its parameter, like so:

```
function selectFlip
→ (myevent:ContextMenuEvent):void {
    picture_mc.rotation+=180;
}
```

The actions that should happen when the user selects your custom item in the contextual menu go in between the function's curly braces.

The completed code (**Figure 4.60**) attaches a custom item to the contextual menu. When the user right-clicks on the object called `picture_mc` and selects Flip, the object rotates 180 degrees.

```
var mymenu:ContextMenu= new ContextMenu();
mymenu.hideBuiltInItems();
var myFirstItem:ContextMenuItem= new ContextMenuItem("Flip");
mymenu.customItems.push(myFirstItem);
picture_mc.contextMenu = mymenu;
```

Figure 4.59 A new `ContextMenuItem` object called `myFirstItem` is created with one parameter: the name of the item (`"Flip"`). The `ContextMenuItem` called `myFirstItem` is put into the `customItems` array.

```
var mymenu:ContextMenu= new ContextMenu();
mymenu.hideBuiltInItems();
var myFirstItem:ContextMenuItem= new ContextMenuItem("Flip");
mymenu.customItems.push(myFirstItem);
picture_mc.contextMenu = mymenu;
myFirstItem.addEventListener(ContextMenuEvent.MENU_ITEM_SELECT, selectFirstItem);
function selectFirstItem(myevent:ContextMenuEvent):void {
    picture_mc.rotation+=180;
}
```

Figure 4.60 The final code (top) makes the custom item show up at the top of the contextual menu when right-clicked over `picture_mc` (middle). When the custom item is selected, the `MENU_ITEM_SELECT` event occurs and Flash responds by rotating the picture 180 degrees (bottom).

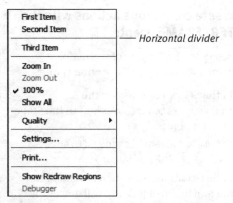

Horizontal divider

Figure 4.61 The custom item called Third Item has been defined with a horizontal divider above it.

✔ Tips

- Custom items always appear above the built-in items and are separated from the built-in items by a horizontal bar.

- If you have many custom items, you can group them by adding another horizontal bar (**Figure 4.61**). Use the property `separatorBefore` and set it to `true` for any `ContextMenuItem` to add a horizontal bar before the item in the list, like so:

  `myFirstItem.separatorBefore=true;`

- You can also use the property `caption` to define the title of a new item. For a new `ContextMenuItem` called `myFirstItem`, you can use the statement `myFirstItem.caption="Flop"`.

Custom Item Restrictions

The contextual menu has a maximum of 15 custom items, and each item can't be more than 100 characters long and must fit on a single line.

Items that are identical to any built-in menu item or another custom item will be ignored.

The following words can't be used in custom items at all: Adobe, Macromedia, Flash Player, Settings.

The following words can't be used alone but can be used in conjunction with other words: Save, Zoom In, Zoom Out, 100%, Show All, Quality, Play, Loop, Rewind, Forward, Back, Movie Not Loaded, About, Print, Show Redraw Regions, Debugger, Undo, Cut, Copy, Paste, Delete, Select All, Open, Open in New Window, Copy Link.

Creating Continuous Actions

So far, you've learned ways to execute an action in response to events that happen when the user does something—whether a mouse click or a keyboard press. But on many occasions, you'll want to perform an action continuously. An if statement, for example, often needs to be performed continuously to check whether conditions in the movie have changed. Another example is if you want to animate an object moving across the Stage purely with ActionScript. In that case, you'll want to perform a command that changes its position continuously.

The Event.ENTER_FRAME event happens continuously. The event is triggered at the frame rate of the movie, so if the frame rate is set to 12 frames per second, the ENTER_FRAME event is triggered 12 times per second (**Figure 4.62**). Even when the Timeline is stopped, the event continues to happen. This setup is an ideal way to make actions run on automatic pilot; they will run as soon as the event handler is established and stop only when the event handler is removed or the object on which it is defined is removed.

To create continuous actions with the ENTER_FRAME event:

1. Select the first frame of the main Timeline, and open the Actions panel.

2. In the Script pane, assign the addEventListener() method to the Stage or to an object:

   ```
   car_mc.addEventListener (Event.
    → ENTER_FRAME, movecar);
   ```

   In this example, the listener is added to the movie clip object and will detect the ENTER_FRAME event, which happens continuously at the frame rate of the Flash movie.

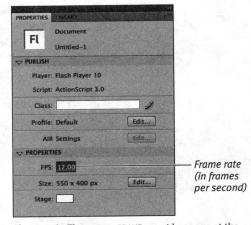

Frame rate (in frames per second)

Figure 4.62 The ENTER_FRAME event happens at the frame rate of the movie, which you can change in the Property inspector. Typical frame rates for online playback are between 12 and 24 frames per second.

```
car_mc.addEventListener(Event.ENTER_FRAME, movecar);
function movecar(myevent:Event):void {
    car_mc.y-=5;
    if (car_mc.y<100) {
        car_mc.removeEventListener(Event.ENTER_FRAME, movecar);
    }
}
```

Figure 4.63 Flash continuously moves the movie clip called car_mc 5 pixels up the Stage. An if statement has been added to check if the movie clip has moved beyond a certain point and if so, removes the event listener.

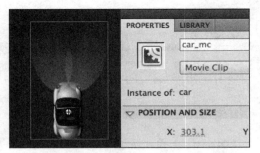

Figure 4.64 The movie clip named car_mc is put on the Stage.

3. On the next line, create a function with the Event object as its parameter:

```
function movecar(myevent:Event):void {
    car_mc.y-=5;
};
```

In this example, when the function is called, the movie clip called car_mc will move 5 pixels upward (**Figure 4.63**).

4. Create a movie clip symbol and place an instance of it on the Stage. In the Property inspector, name it car_mc to match the ActionScript code.

5. Choose Control > Test Movie.

At the frame rate of the Flash movie (12 times a second if the frame rate is 12 fps), the ENTER_FRAME event occurs and your function is called, moving the movie clip on the Stage upward continuously (**Figure 4.64**).

✔ Tip

■ Be careful of overusing the ENTER_FRAME event handler, because it can be processor intensive. After you no longer need the event handler, it's good practice to use removeEventListener() to remove the listener.

Using timers

The ENTER_FRAME event, although easy to use and effective for creating most continuous actions, is restricted to the frame rate of your Flash movie. If you want to perform an action on a continuous basis and do so at an interval that you specify, you should use the Timer class instead.

When you create an object from the Timer class, the new object dispatches a TimerEvent event at regular intervals. You specify how long those intervals are (in milliseconds) and how many intervals there will be. You can then add an event handler to listen and respond to each event.

The TimerEvent has two specific events: a TimerEvent.TIMER event that happens at each interval and a TimerEvent.TIMER_COMPLETE, which happens at the end of the timer.

To create continuous actions with a timer:

1. Select the first frame of the main Timeline, and open the Actions panel.

2. Instantiate a new Timer object. The constructor takes two parameters—the first is a number (in milliseconds) for the timer interval, and the second is the number of intervals. The second parameter is optional, and if left out, your timer will run forever until stopped.

   ```
   var myTimer:Timer=new Timer(10,1000);
   ```

   The function will be called every 10 milliseconds (1/100th of second). There will be 1,000 intervals, so this timer lasts 10 seconds.

3. On the next line, call the start() method to begin the timer:

   ```
   myTimer.start();
   ```

   The two lines of code so far create a Timer object and start it (**Figure 4.65**).

```
var myTimer:Timer=new Timer(10,1000);
myTimer.start();
```

Figure 4.65 A new Timer object called myTimer is created and started.

4. Next, add an event handler to detect the
TimerEvent.TIMER events that are being
dispatched every 10 milliseconds:

```
myTimer.addEventListener
→ (TimerEvent.TIMER, movecar);
function movecar
→ (myevent:TimerEvent):void{
   car_mc.y-=5;
};
```

This listener detects the TimerEvent.TIMER
event and calls the function called movecar,
moving the movie clip upward continuously
until the timer stops.

5. On the Stage, add a movie clip instance
called car_mc. Test your movie by choosing Control > Test Movie (**Figure 4.66**).

✔ Tip

■ Add the command updateAfterEvent to
your function if you're modifying graphics
at a smaller interval than your movie
frame rate. This method forces Flash to
refresh the display, providing smoother

results. The updateAfterEvent command
is called on the Event object, so in this
task, the code for the function would be

```
function movecar
→ (myevent:TimerEvent):void{
   car_mc.y-=5;
   myevent.updateAfterEvent();
};
```

To detect the end of a timer:

◆ Add an event handler to detect the
TimerEvent.TIMER_COMPLETE event. The
following code is an example:

```
myTimer.addEventListener
→ (TimerEvent.TIMER_COMPLETE,
→ stoptimer);
function stoptimer
→ (myevent:TimerEvent):void{
   // do something
};
```

The function called stoptimer is called
only after the timer called myTimer has
completed all of its intervals.

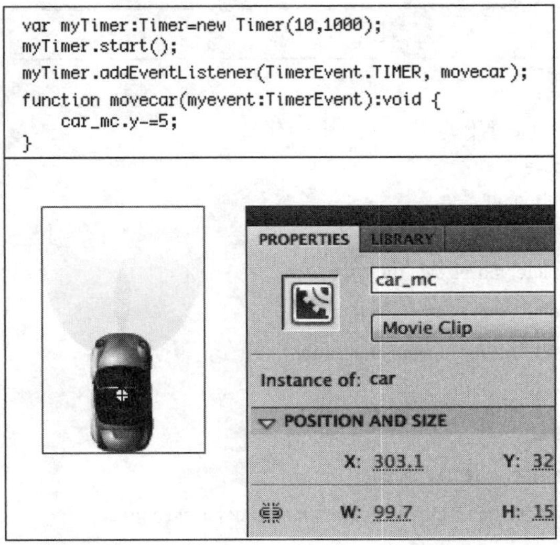

```
var myTimer:Timer=new Timer(10,1000);
myTimer.start();
myTimer.addEventListener(TimerEvent.TIMER, movecar);
function movecar(myevent:TimerEvent):void {
    car_mc.y-=5;
}
```

Figure 4.66 At each 10-millisecond interval for
1,000 intervals, a TIMER event happens. Each time
it happens, the movie clip called car_mc moves
5 pixels up the Stage, animating the graphic.

A Summary of Events

Table 4.4 lists the many basic events discussed in this chapter. You'll learn about many more events in the chapters that follow. For more on the Event class, see Flash Help > ActionScript 3.0 Language and Component Reference > All Classes > Event Class.

Table 4.4

Events	
EVENT	DESCRIPTION
MouseEvent.CLICK	Mouse click
MouseEvent.DOUBLE_CLICK	Mouse double-click
MouseEvent.MOUSE_MOVE	Mouse move
MouseEvent.MOUSE_DOWN	Mouse button pressed
MouseEvent.MOUSE_UP	Mouse button released
MouseEvent.MOUSE_OVER	Mouse pointer moves over the target
MouseEvent.MOUSE_OUT	Mouse pointer moves off of the target
MouseEvent.MOUSE_WHEEL	Mouse wheel moves forward or backward
KeyboardEvent.KEY_DOWN	Key pressed
KeyboardEvent.KEY_UP	Key released
ContextMenuEvent.MENU_ITEM_SELECT	Contextual menu item selected
Event.ENTER_FRAME	Happens at the frame rate of the Flash movie (not user controlled)
TimerEvent.TIMER	Happens at every interval defined by the Timer object
TimerEvent.TIMER_COMPLETE	Happens when the Timer object finishes all of its intervals

CONTROLLING MULTIPLE TIMELINES

To create interactivity and direct your users to see, hear, and experience exactly what you want, you have to know how to control the Flash playhead on different timelines. The playhead displays what is on the Stage at any moment and triggers any actions attached to that keyframe. Jumping from frame to frame on the main movie Timeline is simple enough; you use basic actions you should be familiar with, such as `gotoAndPlay()`, `gotoAndStop()`, `play()`, and `stop()`. But when you include movie clip symbols in your movie, you introduce other independent timelines that can be controlled individually. Your main Timeline can control a movie clip's timeline; a movie clip's timeline can, in turn, control the main Timeline. You can even have the timeline of one movie clip control the timeline of another. Handling this complex interaction and navigation between timelines is the subject of this chapter.

Navigating Timelines with Movie Clips

The independent timelines of movie clip symbols make complicated navigation schemes possible. While the main Timeline is playing, other timelines of movie clips can be playing as well, interacting with one another and specifying which frames to play or when to stop. In fact, it's quite common to have multiple movie clips on the Stage, all talking to one another while the main movie Timeline remains only a single frame. Driving all this navigation between timelines is, of course, ActionScript. The basic actions used to navigate within the main Timeline (gotoAndStop(), gotoAndPlay(), stop(), play(), nextFrame(), and prevFrame()) can also be used to navigate the timeline of any movie clip. This navigation is possible because you can give a name to every movie clip instance on the Stage. As you've seen in previous chapters, you name a movie clip instance in the Property inspector. When an instance is named, you can identify its particular timeline and give instructions on where you want to move its playhead.

Insert Target Path button in Actions panel

Insert Target Path dialog box

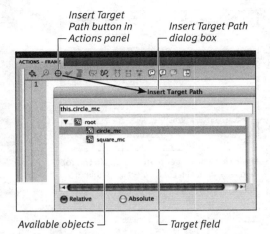

Available objects

Target field

Figure 5.1 The Insert Target Path dialog box allows you to choose a target path by clicking a movie clip, button, or text field within the hierarchy.

Figure 5.2 This movie clip instance on the Stage is named square_mc in the Property inspector.

Target Paths

A *target path* is essentially an object name, or a series of object names separated by dots, that tells Flash where to find a particular object. To control movie clip timelines, you specify the target path for a particular movie clip followed by a dot and then the method you want to call. The target path tells Flash which movie clip instance to look at, and the method tells Flash what to do with that movie clip instance. The methods of the `MovieClip` class that control the playhead are `gotoAndStop()`, `gotoAndPlay()`, `play()`, `stop()`, `nextFrame()`, and `prevFrame()`. If you name a movie clip instance `myClock_mc`, for example, and you write the ActionScript statement `myClock_mc.gotoAndStop(10)`, the playhead within the movie clip instance called `myClock_mc` will move to frame 10 and stop there. `myClock_mc` is the target path, and `gotoAndStop()` is the method.

The Insert Target Path button at the top of the Script pane of the Actions panel opens the Insert Target Path dialog box, which provides a visual way to insert a target path (**Figure 5.1**). All named movie clip instances, button instances, and text fields are shown in a hierarchical fashion in the display window. You can select individual objects, and the correct target paths appear in the Target field.

To target a movie clip instance from the main Timeline:

1. Create a movie clip symbol and place an instance of it on the Stage.

2. In the Property inspector, give the instance a name (**Figure 5.2**).

Continues on next page

3. Select the first keyframe of the main Timeline, and open the Actions panel.

You'll assign an action on the main Timeline that will control the movie clip instance.

4. Click the Insert Target Path above the Script pane.

The Insert Target Path dialog box opens.

5. Choose Relative from the radio buttons at the bottom of the Insert Target Path dialog box.

6. In the display window, select the movie clip as the target path. The target path appears in the top field. Click OK (**Figure 5.3**).

The target path appears in the Script pane, beginning with this, a dot, and then your object name. The word this means *myself* and gives Flash a starting point for the target path, and is optional in this context.

or

Enter the name of your movie clip in the Script pane directly (this is your target path).

7. After the target path, enter a period and then an action for the movie clip, like assigning a new value to one of its properties:

this.square_mc.rotation=45;

This statement changes the angle of the movie clip (called square_mc).

8. Test your movie (Control > Test Movie).

The action you assign on the main Timeline targets your movie clip and tells it to rotate 45 degrees (**Figure 5.4**).

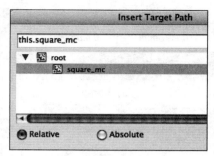

Figure 5.3 The target path appears in the top field when you select an object in the hierarchy within the display window.

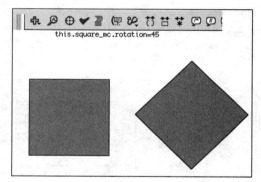

Figure 5.4 The target path is this.square_mc, and the command is to assign the value 45 to the rotation property. The original movie clip instance (left) is rotated 45 degrees (right).

TARGET PATHS

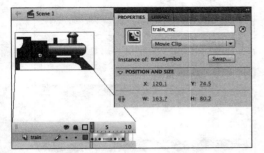

Figure 5.5 The movie clip instance called `train_mc` is on the main Timeline. The movie clip contains an animation (below) of the train shaking back and forth.

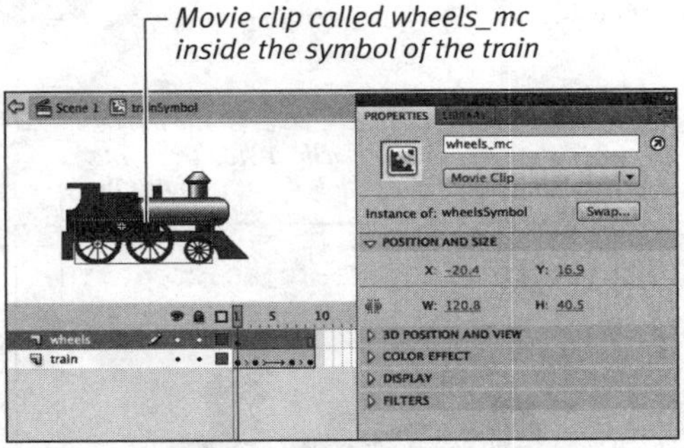

— Movie clip called *wheels_mc* inside the symbol of the train

Figure 5.6 Place an instance of another movie clip inside the train movie clip. Name the child movie clip instance `wheels_mc`.

Target paths for nested movie clips

You can have a movie clip within another movie clip, or as you saw in the previous chapter with pull-down menus, you can have buttons within a movie clip. The outer movie clip is the parent, and the object that's nested inside it is the child. Because the child is part of the parent, any graphical transformations you do to the parent also affect the child. To control the timeline or properties of a child object from the main Timeline, use the parent name followed by the child name separated by a period to form a hierarchical target path. In the following task, the parent movie clip is a train (`train_mc`), and the child movie clip is its wheels (`wheels_mc`).

To target a movie clip within a movie clip:

1. Create a movie clip symbol that contains an animation on its timeline, place an instance on the Stage, and name it in the Property inspector (**Figure 5.5**).

2. Create another movie clip symbol that contains an animation on its timeline.

3. Go to symbol editing mode for the first movie clip, and drag an instance of your second movie clip to the Stage.

4. In the Property inspector, give the second movie clip instance a name (**Figure 5.6**).

   You now have a parent movie clip on the main Stage. The parent movie clip contains a child movie clip.

5. Exit symbol editing mode, and return to the main Stage.

6. Select a keyframe in the main Timeline, and open the Actions panel.

Continues on next page

TARGET PATHS

7. Click the Insert Target Path button.

   The Insert Target Path dialog box opens.

8. Choose Relative from the radio buttons at the bottom of the Insert Target Path dialog box.

9. In the display window, click the plus sign (Windows) or the triangle (Mac) in front of the parent movie clip.

   The hierarchy expands, showing the child movie clip within the parent (**Figure 5.7**).

10. Select the child movie clip as the target path, and click OK.

    or

    Simply enter the target path directly in the Script pane without using the Insert Target Path dialog box.

    The target path, in the form `this.Parent.Child`, appears in the Script pane.

11. Enter a period after the target path and then an action. This example uses

    `this.train_mc.wheels_mc.stop();`

12. Test your movie (Control > Test Movie).

    The animation of the wheels turning plays within the movie clip of the train, which is bobbing up and down. The action you assign on the main Timeline, however, targets the movie clip of the wheels that is inside the movie clip of the train and tells its playhead to stop. The animation of the train continues (**Figure 5.8**). Despite the parent-child relationship, the timelines remain independent. (You could target the parent and tell it to stop, but the child would continue to play.)

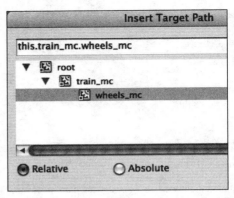

Figure 5.7 The display window of the Insert Target Path dialog box. The hierarchy shows parent-child relationships.

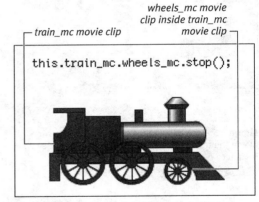

Figure 5.8 The ActionScript statement on the main Timeline tells the `wheels_mc` movie clip inside the `train_mc` movie clip to stop.

TARGET PATHS

Absolute and Relative Paths

Flash gives you two path type options in the Insert Target Path dialog box: Relative and Absolute. In the preceding example, the method `this.train_mc.wheels_mc.stop()` originated from the main Timeline. When Flash executes that method, it looks within its own timeline for the object called `train_mc` that contains another object called `wheels_mc`. This is an example of a relative path. Everything is relative to where the ActionScript statement resides—in this case, the main Timeline. An alternative way of inserting a target path is to use an absolute path, which has no particular frame of reference. You can think of relative target paths as being directions given from your present location, as in "Go two blocks straight; then turn left." Absolute target paths, on the other hand, are directions that work no matter where you are, as in "Go to 555 University Avenue."

Why Relative Paths?

Why use relative paths at all? Absolute paths seem to be a safer construction because they identify an object explicitly no matter where you are.

Relative paths, however, are useful in at least two cases:

◆ If you create a movie clip that contains actions that affect other movie clips relative to itself, you can move the entire ensemble and still have the target paths work by using relative terms. This method makes it easier to work with complex navigation schemes because you can copy, paste, and move the pieces without having to rewrite the target paths. A direct parallel is managing a Web site and maintaining its links. If you were to create absolute paths to links to your résumé and then move your home page to a different server, you'd have to rewrite your links. The more practical method would be to establish relative links within your home page.

◆ Relative paths are also useful when you create movie clips and other objects dynamically. You'll learn how to create movie clip objects and name them on the fly with ActionScript. In these cases, movie clips aren't static, and relative target paths are required to follow them around.

Using this, root, and parent

In relative mode, the current timeline is called this. The keyword this means *myself.* All other timelines are relative to the this timeline.

In absolute mode, the path starts with the main movie Timeline and you drill down to the timeline you want to target. To target the main movie Timeline, you can use the keyword root, but you must explicitly tell Flash that you are using root to reference a timeline. Timelines are a feature of the MovieClip class, so you can reference the main movie Timeline by using the statement MovieClip(root). This is where the Insert Target Path dialog box is no longer relevant. You should only use the Insert Target Path dialog box for targeting visual objects on the Stage in relative mode.

You may find that you want to target a movie clip that is above the current timeline. In that case, you can use the relative term parent. However, just as in the case of root, you must tell Flash that you want to refer to a timeline, so use the full statement MovieClip(parent).

Table 5.1 and **Figure 5.9** summarize the ways you can use absolute and relative paths with the keywords this, MovieClip(root), and MovieClip(parent) to target different movie clips.

✔ Tip

- Using this or an absolute path to target a movie clip's own timeline is unnecessary, just as it's unnecessary to use this or MovieClip(root) when navigating within the main Timeline. It's understood that actions residing in one timeline pertain, or are scoped, to that particular timeline.

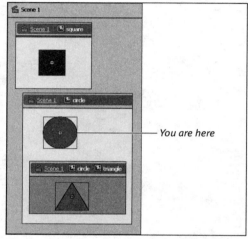

Figure 5.9 A representation of a movie with multiple movie clips. The main Timeline (scene 1) contains the square movie clip and the circle movie clip. The circle movie clip contains the triangle movie clip. These names represent instances. Table 5.1 summarizes the absolute and relative target paths for calls made from the circle movie clip (you are here).

Table 5.1

Absolute vs. Relative Target Paths

To Target... (From Circle)	Absolute Path	Relative Path
Scene 1	MovieClip(root)	MovieClip(parent)
square	MovieClip(root).square	MovieClip(parent).square
circle	MovieClip(root).circle	this
triangle	MovieClip(root).circle.triangle	triangle

Using the with Action to Target Objects

An alternative way to target movie clips and other objects is to use the action with. Instead of creating multiple target paths to the same movie clip, you can use the with action to target the movie clip only once. Imagine creating these statements to make the wheels_mc movie clip inside a train movie clip stop and shrink 50 percent:

```
train_mc.wheels_mc.stop();

train_mc.wheels_mc.scaleX = .5;

train_mc.wheels_mc.scaleY = .5;
```

You can rewrite those statements using the with statement like this:

```
with (train_mc.wheels_mc) {
    stop();
    scaleX = .5;
    scaleY = .5;
}
```

This with action temporarily sets the scope to train_mc.wheels_mc so that the method and properties between the curly braces affect that particular target path. When the with action ends, any subsequent statements refer to the current timeline.

Scope

You've learned that to direct an ActionScript statement to affect a different timeline, you need a target path that defines the *scope*. Without a target path, the ActionScript would affect its own timeline. An ActionScript statement belongs, or is *scoped*, to a particular timeline or a particular object where it resides. Everything you do in ActionScript has a scope, so you must be aware of it. You could be giving the correct ActionScript instructions, but if they aren't scoped correctly, nothing—or, worse, unexpected things—could happen.

When you assign ActionScript to a frame on the main Timeline, the statement is scoped to that timeline. When you assign ActionScript to a frame of a movie clip timeline, the statement is scoped to that movie clip timeline. When you create an ActionScript object by using the constructor function new, that object is scoped to the timeline where it was created. If you create a Date object (as you did in Chapter 3) on the main Timeline with the statement

```
var myDate:Date = new Date();
```

the object myDate is scoped to the main Timeline.

To target objects using the with action:

1. In a keyframe or within an event handler, open the Actions panel.

2. Enter the code as follows with the target path within the parentheses of the with action:

   ```
   with (train_mc.wheels_mc){
   }
   ```

   In this example, the target path is train_mc.wheels_mc.

3. Between the curly braces of the with action, create your statements for the targeted object.

   Note that you don't need to specify a target path or put a dot before the method or property name (**Figure 5.10**).

The scaleY property stretches out the vertical dimension and affects train_mc.wheels_mc.

```
with (train_mc.wheels_mc) {
    scaleY=2;
}
```

Figure 5.10 A with statement is an alternative to writing out a target path in front of objects.

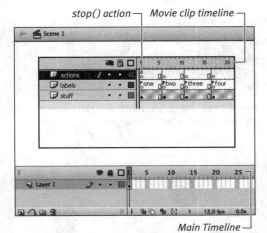

stop() action ⌐   Movie clip timeline ⌐

Main Timeline ⌐

Figure 5.11 The movie clip as a container. This figure represents a main Timeline (scene 1) with a movie clip on its Stage. The movie clip has a stop() action in its first keyframe. The other labeled keyframes can contain buttons, graphics, animations, or any other kind of Flash information, which you can access by targeting the movie clip and moving its playhead to the appropriate keyframe.

stop() action ⌐

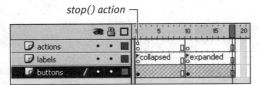

Figure 5.12 The pull-down-menu movie clip contains both collapsed and expanded states.

Movie Clips as Containers

So far in this chapter, you've learned how to name your movie clip objects, target each one, and navigate within their timelines from any other timeline in your movie. But how does the ability to control movie clip timelines translate into meaningful interactivity for your Flash project? The key is to think of movie clips as containers that hold stuff: animation, graphics, sound, and text. By moving the playhead back and forth or playing certain parts of a particular movie clip timeline, you can access those items whenever you want, independently of what else is going on (**Figure 5.11**).

For example, movie clips are commonly used to show objects with different states that toggle from one to the other; the different states are contained in the movie clip's timeline. When you built pull-down menus in Chapter 4, "Advanced Buttons and Event Handling," you used movie clips to serve that purpose. The pull-down menu is essentially a movie clip object that toggles between a collapsed state and an expanded state. The buttons inside the movie clip control which of those two states you see (**Figure 5.12**).

Another example is using different keyframes of a movie clip to hold different states of a main character in a game. Depending on the circumstances, you can tell the playhead to go to a certain frame of the movie clip to display the character in a sad, happy, or sleepy state. The examples are numerous, as are the benefits of organizing your content in this way. By keeping the changing content in a single object, you can better edit and manipulate all the content at once.

The following task demonstrates how to create a toggle button with a movie clip. Building a toggle button is a matter of defining two different keyframes that toggle between an on state and an off state.

To create a toggle button:

1. Create a movie clip symbol.

2. Go to symbol editing mode for the movie clip.

3. In the first keyframe, add a stop() action.

4. Insert another keyframe, and in this second keyframe, add another stop() action.

   The stop() action in both keyframes will prevent this movie clip from playing automatically and will stop the playhead on each keyframe (**Figure 5.13**).

5. Insert a new layer.

6. Create graphics that correspond to the off state in the first keyframe and graphics that correspond to the on state in the second keyframe (**Figure 5.14**).

7. Exit symbol editing mode, and return to the main Stage.

8. Place an instance of your movie clip on the Stage, and give it an instance name in the Property inspector.

9. Create a new layer, select the keyframe on frame 1 of this layer, and open the Actions panel. Make sure you are on the main Timeline.

10. Create an event handler for your movie clip instance as described in Chapter 4 to detect a mouse click. Inside the curly braces of the event handler function, write the target path for your movie clip, then a period, and then the method play() (**Figure 5.15**).

11. Test your movie (Test > Control Movie). When you click the movie clip, Flash targets the movie clip and moves the playhead to the next keyframe and stops. Each click toggles between two different states, just like a toggle button (**Figure 5.16**).

stop() actions

Figure 5.13 The toggle-button movie clip contains a stop() action in both keyframes.

Figure 5.14 The first keyframe contains graphics representing the button's off state, and the second keyframe contains graphics representing the button's on, or depressed, state.

```
toggleButton_mc.addEventListener(MouseEvent.CLICK, doToggle);
function doToggle(myevent:MouseEvent):void {
    toggleButton_mc.play();
}
```

Figure 5.15 The full script on the main Timeline listens for a mouse click and responds by playing the timeline of the movie clip.

Figure 5.16 When the movie clip plays, the playhead moves from the first keyframe (left) to the second keyframe (right). From the second keyframe, the playhead loops back to the first keyframe (the default movie clip behavior when it reaches the end of its timeline).

MOVIE CLIPS AS CONTAINERS

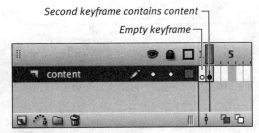

Second keyframe contains content

Empty keyframe

Figure 5.17 A movie clip with an empty first keyframe is invisible on the Stage. The second keyframe contains hidden content.

Creating a movie clip with hidden content

You can do the same thing to a movie clip that you do to a button to make it invisible—that is, leave the first keyframe blank so that the instance is invisible on the Stage initially. If the first keyframe of a movie clip is blank and contains a `stop()` action to keep it there, you can control when to expose the other frames inside that movie clip timeline. You could create a movie clip with an embedded video but keep the first keyframe blank. Then you could place this movie clip on the Stage and, at the appropriate time, advance to the next frame to reveal the video to the user.

Note that you have other ways of using ActionScript to hide or reveal the contents of a movie clip or to place content on the Stage dynamically; you'll learn about these possibilities in upcoming chapters. But being aware of both the simple (frame-based, as described here) and sophisticated (purely ActionScript-based) approaches will help you tackle a broader range of animation and interactivity challenges.

To create an "invisible" movie clip:

1. Create a movie clip symbol.

2. Go to symbol editing mode for the movie clip, and insert a new keyframe on frame 2 of its timeline.

3. Leave the first keyframe of this layer empty, and begin placing graphics and animations in the second keyframe (**Figure 5.17**).

Continues on next page

4. Add a new layer to hold ActionScript. Select the keyframe on frame 1 of this layer, and open the Actions panel.

5. Add a stop() action (**Figure 5.18**).

6. Exit symbol editing mode, and return to the main Timeline.

7. Drag an instance of the movie clip from the Library to the Stage.

   The instance appears on the Stage as an empty circle (**Figure 5.19**). The empty circle represents the registration point of the instance, allowing you to place the instance exactly where you want it.

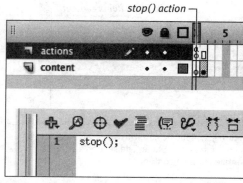

Figure 5.18 This movie clip has a stop() action in its first frame.

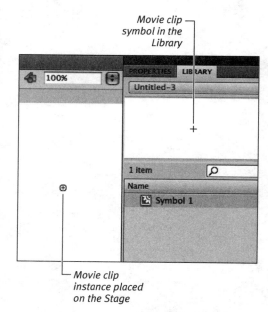

Figure 5.19 An instance of a movie clip with an empty first frame appears as an empty circle.

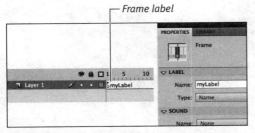

Frame label

Figure 5.20 This timeline (left) has a frame label on its first keyframe. Frame labels are added in the Property inspector (right).

Using Frame Labels

When you navigate different timelines, it's useful to use frame labels, which are names that you give specific keyframes on a timeline. Frame labels are created in the Property inspector in the Frame Label field and appear as tiny flags on the timeline (**Figure 5.20**). By using frame labels, you mark important spots in your animation without worrying about the exact frame numbers.

In ActionScript, you can retrieve the name of any frame label with currentLabel, a property of the MovieClip class. The currentLabel property holds the most recently encountered frame label name (a string). For example, you can construct a conditional statement to check on the location of the playhead, like so:

```
if (this.currentLabel=="SomeLabel"){

    // do something

}
```

Note that the frame label is in quotation marks because it is a string value. If the playhead isn't on a frame with a frame label, the property currentLabel returns the last frame label encountered. The useful counterpart to currentLabel is the property currentFrame, which is the frame number of the playhead.

Continues on next page

USING FRAME LABELS

You can also use ActionScript to retrieve all the frame labels in a timeline and their associated frame numbers. Each frame label that you create on a timeline is automatically represented in ActionScript as an object of the FrameLabel class. These objects have two properties: a name property, which is the name of the frame label, and a frame property, which is the number of the frame. You can access the properties of each FrameLabel object by using the currentLabels property of the MovieClip class. The currentLabels property returns an Array of all the FrameLabel objects in the timeline. (An Array is another type of object that holds data in an orderly manner, which you'll learn more about in Chapter 11, "Manipulating Information.") You access the data in an Array with the square brackets. So, you can find out the name of the first frame label in a timeline with the following statement:

```
this.currentLabels[0].name;
```

And you can find out the frame number of the first frame label with this statement:

```
this.currentLabels[0].frame;
```

The square brackets access the different FrameLabel objects, beginning with the number 0 (**Figure 5.21**).

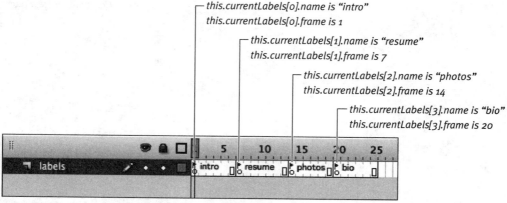

this.currentLabels[0].name is "intro"
this.currentLabels[0].frame is 1

this.currentLabels[1].name is "resume"
this.currentLabels[1].frame is 7

this.currentLabels[2].name is "photos"
this.currentLabels[2].frame is 14

this.currentLabels[3].name is "bio"
this.currentLabels[3].frame is 20

Figure 5.21 Each frame label is an instance of the FrameLabel class. Each instance has a name property and a frame property. Access each instance from the currentLabels array.

To retrieve the current frame label on a timeline:

1. On the timeline, select a keyframe and in the Property inspector, give it a frame label (**Figure 5.22**).

2. Open the Actions panel and in the Script pane, enter

   `trace (this.currentLabel);`

   The `trace` command lets you display expressions in the Output window in Flash authoring mode for testing purposes. This statement displays the name of the current frame label (**Figure 5.23**).

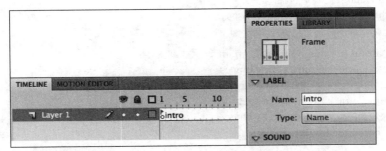

Figure 5.22 The first keyframe of this timeline has the frame label called `intro`.

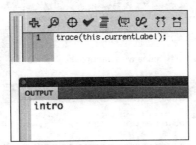

Figure 5.23 The `trace` action in the Actions panel (above) shows up in the Output panel (below).

To retrieve any of the frame labels and numbers on a timeline:

1. On the timeline, create multiple key-frames, each with its own frame label (**Figure 5.24**).

2. Select the first keyframe and open the Actions panel. In the Script pane, first enter a stop() command:

   ```
   stop();
   ```

   The stop() command will prevent the playhead from moving.

3. On the next line, enter the following code:

   ```
   for (var i:uint = 0; i<    this.
   → currentLabels.length; i++) {
     trace("frame " + this.
     → currentLabels[i].frame + ":
     → "+ this.currentLabels[i].name);
   }
   ```

   The for statement is a looping statement that repeats actions within its curly braces. This statement displays the frame label number and frame label name of each FrameLabel object, represented by this. currentLabels[i] (**Figure 5.25**).

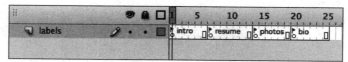

Figure 5.24 Create a timeline with multiple keyframes.

```
stop();
for (var i:uint = 0; i < this.currentLabels.length; i++) {
    trace("frame " + this.currentLabels[i].frame + ": " + this.currentLabels[i].name);
}
```

```
OUTPUT
frame 1: intro
frame 7: resume
frame 13: photos
frame 19: bio
```

Figure 5.25 The code in the Actions panel (above) contains a looping statement that displays all the frame label names and numbers in the Output panel (below).

MANAGING EXTERNAL COMMUNICATION

Flash provides powerful tools to communicate with other applications such as Web browsers and with other files (including images, videos, and other Flash movies). By using Flash to link to the Web, you can send e-mail, communicate with JavaScript, or relay information to and from servers for data-driven applications. While many of these functions that connect to databases are beyond the scope of this book, this chapter introduces you to some of the most popular ways Flash can communicate with HTML and JavaScript through the Web browser.

You'll learn to work with external images, video, and Flash movies. You can use one main Flash movie to load in several external Flash movies to create modular projects that are easier to edit and have smaller file sizes. Your main Flash movie might serve simply as an interface that loads your portfolio of Flash animations when the viewer selects them. You can manage the communication from the main Flash movie to its loaded movie to control its appearance and playback.

Finally, you'll learn to communicate with your movie's playback environment. You'll learn how to detect the amount of data that has downloaded to users' computers so you can tell them how much longer they have to wait before your movie begins. Keeping track of these external factors will help you provide a friendly and customized user experience.

Communicating Through the Web Browser

Flash links to the Web browser through the method navigateToURL(). This method takes one parameter, which is a URLRequest object that contains all the information needed to make the connection, such as the address to the Web site. The *URL* is the address that points to a specific file on the Internet. Use an *absolute URL* (a complete address to a specific file) to link to any Web site, or use a *relative URL* (a path to a file that's described in relation to the current directory) to link to pages in the same Web site or local files contained on your hard drive or a CD or DVD. The navigateToURL() method also provides ways to target different frames you create within the browser window or in new browser windows. You can create Flash movies that navigate between these frames and windows and control what loads in each one.

Linking to the Web

Linking to the Web requires several steps. You must first instantiate the URLRequest object and define the URL as a property of the object, like so:

```
var myURL:URLRequest = new URLRequest();
myURL.url="http://www.adobe.com";
```

Or, you can combine the two statements and define the url property at the same time you instantiate the object, like so:

```
var myURL:URLRequest = new URLRequest
("http://www.adobe.com");
```

Note that the url property is a string, so it must be enclosed within quotation marks. Next, use navigateToURL() with the URLRequest object as its parameter as in the following:

```
navigateToURL(myURL);
```

If you test your Flash movie by choosing Control > Test Movie or play it in Flash Player, the method navigateToURL() automatically launches the default browser and loads the specified Web address in a new window.

To link to a Web site:

1. Create a button symbol, drag an instance from the Library to the Stage, and give it a name in the Property inspector.

   You'll assign the navigateToURL() method to a mouse click on this button.

2. Select the first frame of the main Timeline, and open the Actions panel.

3. Instantiate a new object from the URLRequest class with the Web address as its parameter:

   ```
   var myURL:URLRequest = new URLRequest
   → ("http://www.adobe.com");
   ```

   In this example, the new object called myURL is created and the Adobe Web site is assigned to its url property.

```
var myURL:URLRequest = new URLRequest ("http://www.adobe.com");
mybutton_btn.addEventListener(MouseEvent.CLICK, clickButton);
function clickButton(myevent:MouseEvent):void {
    navigateToURL(myURL);
}
```

Figure 6.1 The `navigateToURL()` method requires a URLRequest object as a parameter. The URLRequest object (called myURL here) contains the Web site address (http://www.adobe.com).

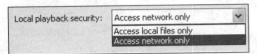

Figure 6.2 In the Publish Settings dialog box, set your SWF file to allow remote (network only) access.

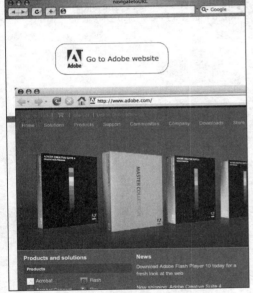

Figure 6.3 The Flash movie (top) links to the Adobe site in a new browser window (bottom).

4. Create an event handler that detects a mouse click on your button (see Chapter 4, "Advanced Buttons and Event Handling," to learn more about event handling), and in the function of your event handler, add the `navigateToURL()` method, as in the following statements:

```
mybutton_btn.addEventListener
→ (MouseEvent.CLICK, clickButton);
function clickButton(myevent:
→ MouseEvent):void {
    navigateToURL(myURL);
}
```

In this example, when the mouse is clicked on `mybutton_btn`, Flash uses the `myURL` object to link to the Web (**Figure 6.1**).

5. Choose File > Publish Settings.
The Publish Settings dialog box opens.

6. On the Flash tab, under the "Local playback security" option, choose "Access network only" (**Figure 6.2**). Click OK.

This will prevent you from getting a security error message when you test your SWF file and the file, which will play locally from your hard drive, tries to access a Web site on the Internet.

7. Publish your Flash movie, and play it in either the Flash Player or a browser.

When you click the button you created, the Web site loads in a new window (**Figure 6.3**). Click the Close button in your browser to close the window and return to your Flash movie.

Continues on next page

COMMUNICATING THROUGH THE WEB BROWSER

✔ Tips

- If you skip steps 5–6 (changing the Publish Settings) and then test the movie in a browser from your hard drive, you may see a security warning when you click the button that calls the navigateToURL() method. For more about working around this issue, see the sidebar "Flash Player Security: Mixing Local and Remote Content," later in this chapter. However, testing the movie within Flash or over the Internet in a Web browser won't cause the security warning to appear.

- You can also link to the Web from a static horizontal text field. Create static text with the Text tool, and in the Property inspector, enter the address of the Web site in the Link field and choose where you want the Web site to load in the Target field (**Figure 6.4**). Your static text will display with an underline to show that it's linked to a URL. When your viewers click the text, the Web site will load in the browser window indicated by the Target field. You can also link to a dynamic text field, but the entire field becomes clickable.

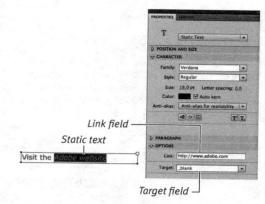

Link field

Static text

Target field

Figure 6.4 A Web address in the Link field of the Property inspector makes the selected text in a static text field link to the site. The Target field in the Property inspector determines where the link will open. In this figure, _blank is selected, so the link will open in a new browser window.

To preaddress an e-mail:

1. Instantiate a new object from the URLRequest class with "mailto:" followed by the e-mail address of the person who should receive the e-mail enclosed in quotation marks as its parameter:

   ```
   var myURL:URLRequest = new
   → URLRequest ("mailto:
   → yourname@domain.com");
   ```

   In this example, the new object is called myURL and its url property is a different scheme for sending e-mail.

2. Make a call to the navigateToURL() method, like so:

   ```
   navigateToURL(myURL, "_self");
   ```

   The second parameter, _self, enclosed in quotation marks, is to prevent a new window from opening (**Figure 6.5**).

When the code executes, the user's default e-mail application opens with a new pre-addressed e-mail message (**Figure 6.6**). The viewer then types a message and clicks Send. Use this method to preaddress e-mail that viewers can use to contact you about your Web site or to request more information.

✔ Tip

- It's a good idea to spell out the e-mail address of the mailto: recipient in your Flash movie (**Figure 6.7**). If a person's browser isn't configured to send e-mail, an error message appears instead of an e-mail form. By spelling out the address, you allow users to enter it in their e-mail applications.

```
var myURL:URLRequest = new URLRequest ("mailto: yourname@domain.com");
mybutton_btn.addEventListener(MouseEvent.CLICK, clickButton);
function clickButton(myevent:MouseEvent):void {
    navigateToURL(myURL, "_self");
}
```

Figure 6.5 Enter e-mail recipients after mailto: for the URLRequest object. When the URLRequest object is passed to the navigateToURL() method, the browser will open the default mail application and preaddress an e-mail message.

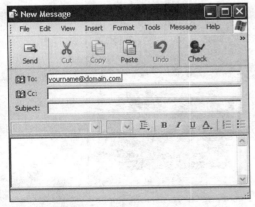

Figure 6.6 A new e-mail message appears in your default mail program.

Contact: yourname@yourdomain.com

Figure 6.7 This e-mail address is also a button that links to the browser via mailto:.

Linking using a relative path

Just as you can with images or hyperlinks in a Web page, you can use relative paths rather than absolute URLs to link to other content. In addition, you can use relative paths rather than complete URLs to specify local files instead of files on the Web. This method lets you distribute your Flash movie on a CD or DVD without requiring an Internet connection. Instead of using the complete URL http://www.myServer.com/ images/photo.jpg, for example, you can specify just images/photo.jpg, and Flash will look inside the folder called images to find the file called photo.jpg.

To link to a file using a relative path:

◆ When specifying the URL in the URLRequest object, use a slash (/) to separate directories and two periods (..) to move up one directory (**Figure 6.8**).

Be sure to place your published SWF and your linked file in the correct level in the folder hierarchy (**Figure 6.9**).

Flash looks for the file using the relative path and loads it into a new browser window (**Figure 6.10**).

✔ Tip

■ When working with relative URLs, the BASE tag in the HTML file that holds your Flash movie can be helpful. The BASE tag defines the base directory or URL used as the starting point for all relative path statements in the Flash movie. This tag is particularly helpful when your Flash movies are in different directories from your other files. For example, in the head of the HTML file, add the following code to have relative paths resolve from the directory www.domain.com/stuff:

```
<HEAD>
<BASE
→ href="http://www.domain.com/stuff/"/>
</HEAD>
```

```
var myURL:URLRequest = new URLRequest ("../images/photo.jpg");
mybutton_btn.addEventListener(MouseEvent.CLICK, clickButton);
function clickButton(myevent:MouseEvent):void {
    navigateToURL(myURL);
}
```

Figure 6.8 This relative URL defined in the URLRequest object goes up one directory level and looks for a folder called images, which contains a file called photo.jpg.

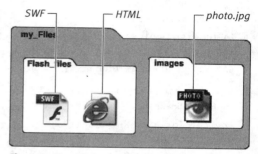

Figure 6.9 Your Flash movie (SWF) and its accompanying HTML file are in a directory that's at the same level as the directory that contains the file photo.jpg.

Figure 6.10 The Flash movie (top) links to the local file in a new browser window (bottom).

Table 6.1

Window Name	Explanation
_self	Current frame of the current browser window
_blank	New browser window; default behavior when parameter is not specified
_parent	Frameset that contains the current frame
_top	Top-level frameset in the current browser window

Window Parameters for navigateToURL

Working with browser framesets and windows

When you play your Flash movie in a browser window, the navigateToURL() method loads the new Web address in a new window if you provide the URLRequest object as its only parameter. To make the Web address load into the same window, a named window, or a different frame of your window, enter a second parameter in the navigateToURL() method for the window, as defined in **Table 6.1**.

What's the difference between a window and a frame? Browser windows can be divided into separate areas, or *frames*, that contain individual Web pages. The collection of frames is called a *frameset*, and the frameset HTML file defines the frame proportions and the name of each frame (**Figure 6.11**).

Continues on next page

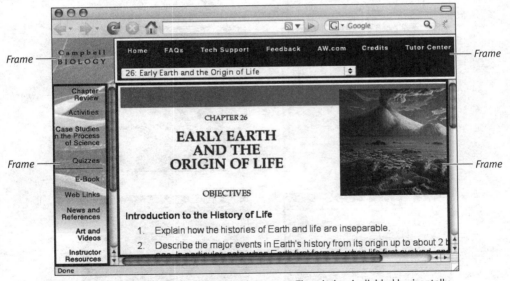

Frame — Frame — Frame — Frame

Figure 6.11 A Web site using frames to divide content. The window is divided horizontally into two frames. The bottom and top frames are divided vertically into two more frames. Ad banners, navigation bars, and content usually are separated in this way.

The navigateToURL() method's second parameter can use the name that the frameset HTML file assigns to a frame to load a URL directly into that specific frame. This method is similar to using the HTML <a href> tag attribute target. If you divide a Web page into two frames, for example, you can call the left frame *navigator* and the right frame *contents*. Place a Flash movie in the navigator frame with the navigateToURL() method targeting the content frame. **Figure 6.12** depicts how each page loads into a frameset.

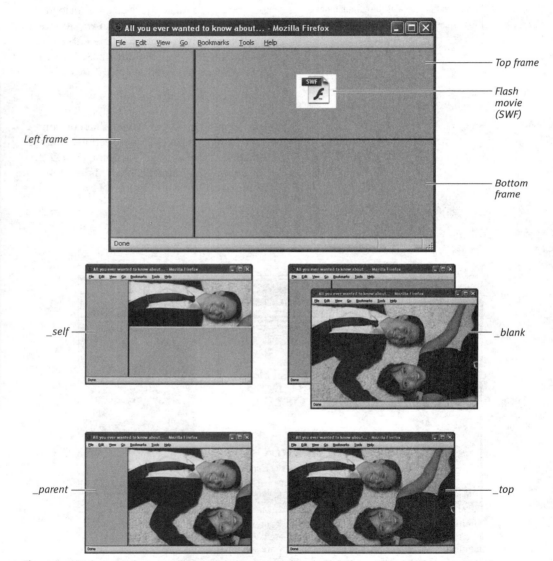

Figure 6.12 At the top, a frameset divides a window into a left and a right frame. The right frame contains another frameset that divides itself into top and bottom frames. The Flash movie (SWF) plays in the top frame of the second frameset. The window names specify where the URL loads.

To open a Web site in a named frame:

1. In an HTML editor such as Adobe Dreamweaver, create an HTML frameset with two frames and unique names for both.

   Your Flash movie will play in one frame, and the Web site links will be loaded into the other frame (**Figure 6.13**).

2. In Flash, create a button symbol, drag an instance from the Library to the Stage, and give it a name in the Property inspector.

3. Select the first frame of the main Timeline, and open the Actions panel.

4. As you have done in previous tasks, instantiate a URLRequest object with a URL as its parameter.

5. Create an event handler for a mouse click on the button.

6. In the body of the function, call the navigateToURL() method. For the first parameter, enter the URLRequest object. For the second parameter, enter the name of the frame established in the HTML frameset (**Figure 6.14**).

   The second parameter, which tells Flash where to load the Web address, must be surrounded by quotation marks.

Continues on next page

```
<!DOCTYPE HTML PUBLIC "-//W3C//DTD HTML 4.01 Frameset//EN" "http://www.w3.org/TR/html4/frameset.dtd">
<html>
<head>
<title>Untitled Document</title>
<meta http-equiv="Content-Type" content="text/html; charset=UTF-8">
</head>
<frameset rows="8" cols="130,*" framespacing="8" frameborder="yes" border="8" bordercolor="#999999">
<frame src="navigator.html" name="navigator" scrolling="NO" noresize>
<frame src="contents.html" name="contents" scrolling="NO">
</frameset>
</html>
```

Figure 6.13 The frameset HTML file (top) divides this window into a left column named navigator, which is 20 percent of the browser width, and a right column named contents, which is 80 percent of the browser width (bottom).

```
var googleURL:URLRequest=new URLRequest("http://www.google.com");
googleButton_btn.addEventListener(MouseEvent.CLICK, googleclick);

function googleclick (myevent:MouseEvent):void {
    navigateToURL(googleURL, "contents");
}
```

Figure 6.14 The second parameter of the navigateToURL() method specifies that the Web site defined in googleURL will load in the contents frame.

COMMUNICATING THROUGH THE WEB BROWSER

7. To prevent a security warning when testing your movie, choose File > Publish Settings; on the Flash tab, set the "Local playback security" field to "Access network only."

   or

   Be sure to test your project from a trusted location on your computer (as described in the sidebar "Flash Player Security: Mixing Local and Remote Content").

8. Publish your Flash movie with its accompanying HTML file.

9. Create another HTML file for the other frame in the frameset.

10. Name both HTML files according to the `<frame src>` tags in the frameset document, and place all files in the same folder (**Figure 6.15**).

11. Open the frameset document in a browser.

    Your Flash movie plays in one frame. The button loads a Web site in the other frame (**Figure 6.16**).

To open a Web site in the same window:

◆ Specify _self, enclosed in quotation marks, as the second parameter in the `navigateToURL()` method, like so:

`navigateToURL(myURL, "_self");`

When you test your movie in a browser, the new Web address loads in the same window as the Flash movie, replacing it. Use the back button to return to your Flash movie.

✔ Tip

■ Security restrictions prevent a Flash movie from linking to a Web site with a window name of _self, _parent, or _top if the SWF is located in a different domain (different Web site address) than its HTML page. This issue is discussed in the sidebar "Flash Player Security: Loading Across Domains," later in this chapter.

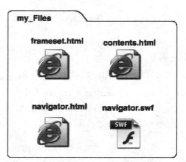

Figure 6.15 The frameset.html file puts the contents.html file in the contents frame and the navigator. html file in the navigator frame. The navigator.html file embeds the Flash movie (navigator.swf).

```
var googleURL:URLRequest=new URLRequest("http://www.google.com");
googleButton_btn.addEventListener(MouseEvent.CLICK, googleclick);
function googleclick (myevent:MouseEvent):void {
    navigateToURL(googleURL, "contents");
}

var yahooURL:URLRequest=new URLRequest("http://www.yahoo.com");
yahooButton_btn.addEventListener(MouseEvent.CLICK, yahooclick);
function yahooclick (myevent:MouseEvent):void {
    navigateToURL(yahooURL, "contents");
}
```

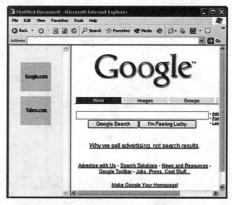

Figure 6.16 The ActionScript for the SWF in the navigator frame is shown (top). The Google and Yahoo! Web sites load in the other frame, keeping the left frame intact.

Flash Player Security: Mixing Local and Remote Content

This chapter is all about how a Flash movie communicates with its external environment to access other scripts, files, and data. However, there are security features that restrict Flash movies from communicating with and loading other files and data from locations other than its own. This protects users from the possibility of a Flash movie secretly loading a file from the user's hard drive and sending it over the Internet, for example.

You'll come across this security issue when you mix local content (when you test Flash files on your computer) with remote content (when you link to a Web site). You will see a security warning message when the locally running SWF file tries to access any network resource (**Figure 6.17**). This includes the navigateToURL() method and many of the other actions I'll discuss in this chapter.

One way to prevent the warning is to change the "Local playback security" setting in the Publish Settings dialog from "Access local files only" to "Access network only," as explained in the task "To link to a Web site." However, you'll have to remember to change this setting for each Flash document you test locally that accesses a remote resource.

You can make a single change to resolve this issue for all your Flash documents. The simplest way is to specify a *trusted* location on your computer—a folder within which any Flash movies are trusted by the Flash Player and don't cause this security warning.

To designate a trusted location on your computer:

1. Create a Flash document containing ActionScript that will cause the security warning. For example, add a navigateToURL() method with a URLRequest that links to a Web site.

2. Test the file in a browser by choosing File > Publish Preview > HTML. Do whatever is necessary to trigger the navigateToURL() method.

3. In the error dialog box that appears, click the Settings button.

   A new browser window opens to the Flash Player Settings Manager page on the Adobe Web site.

4. In the Settings Manager, click the Edit locations menu and choose Add location (**Figure 6.18**).

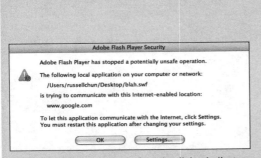

Figure 6.17 The Flash Player Security dialog indicates that a SWF has tried to access the network and isn't allowed to. Click the Settings button to create a trusted location on your computer, which prevents this warning.

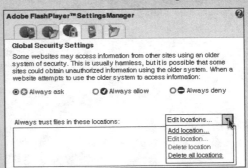

Figure 6.18 You can specify a location on your computer whose contents are trusted by the Flash Player.

Continues on next page

COMMUNICATING THROUGH THE WEB BROWSER

Flash Player Security: Mixing Local and Remote Content *(continued)*

5. In the dialog box that appears, click the "Browse for folder" button (**Figure 6.19**); another dialog box will allow you to choose a folder whose contents will always be trusted by the Flash Player.

In general, you should choose a folder that contains your Flash projects (subfolders of this folder are trusted as well). You also need to be careful to never place in that folder any SWF files that you don't completely trust.

6. Click the Confirm button. The dialog box closes, and you return to the Settings Manager.

Your newly added location appears in the bottom field (**Figure 6.20**). With this setting, the Flash Player will no longer trigger the error message when you test local SWF files that are in the trusted location.

7. Quit the browser that triggered the error message, and then reopen it to test your project.

For more information about this error and some alternative ways of working around it, see the Flash Help section, Programming ActionScript 3.0 > Flash Player Security.

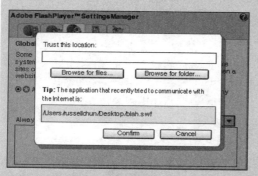

Figure 6.19 Choose a single SWF file or a folder to designate as trusted.

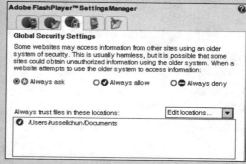

Figure 6.20 The newly designated folder appears in the bottom field and is set to be a trusted location.

COMMUNICATING THROUGH THE WEB BROWSER

Using JavaScript to control new window parameters

When Flash opens new browser windows to load a URL, the appearance and location of these new windows are set by the browser's preferences. If you play a Flash movie in a browser that shows the location bar and the toolbar, for example, and you open a new window, the new window also has a location bar and a toolbar. You can't control these window parameters directly with Flash, but you can control them indirectly with JavaScript.

JavaScript is the scripting language for your Web browser. Most of the time, your Flash movie will play in an HTML file in a Web browser. You can use the ActionScript class `ExternalInterface` to communicate with the JavaScript that is written in the HTML file. Use the `call()` method from the Flash movie, like so:

```
ExternalInterface.call("somefunction");
```

This statement triggers the JavaScript function called `somefunction` in the HTML page that plays your Flash movie. JavaScript is in the head of an HTML file and would look something like this:

```
<script language="javascript">

function somefunction (){

        alert ("hello");

        }

</script>
```

The `call()` method can also pass parameters (`Boolean`, `Number`, or `String` data types) to the JavaScript function. Simply add additional parameters to the `call()` method, like so:

```
ExternalInterface.call("somefunction",
→ param1, param2);
```

Continues on next page

The parameters called param1 and param2 will now be passed to the JavaScript function.

You can use the JavaScript function window. open() to open a new window and control several window properties. The JavaScript function takes three parameters: the URL, the new window name, and the window properties. These properties specify the way the window looks, how it works, and where it's located on the screen (**Figure 6.21**). When you define these window properties, use yes (1), no (0), or a number specifying pixel dimensions or coordinates. **Table 6.2** lists the most common window properties that are compatible with all major Web browsers.

Table 6.2

JavaScript Window Properties

PROPERTY	DESCRIPTION
height	Vertical dimension, in pixels
width	Horizontal dimension, in pixels
left	X-coordinate of left edge
top	Y-coordinate of top edge
resizable	Resizable area in the bottom-right corner that allows the window to change dimensions (yes/no or 1/0)
scrollbars	Vertical and horizontal scroll bars (yes/no or 1/0)
directories	Also called links, where certain bookmarks are accessible (yes/no or 1/0)
location	Location bar, containing URL area (yes/no or 1/0)
menubar	Menu bar, containing drop-down menus such as File and Edit; works only in the Windows operating system (yes/no or 1/0)
status	Status bar in the bottom-left corner, containing browser status and security (yes/no or 1/0)
toolbar	Toolbar, containing the back and forward buttons and other navigation aides (yes/no or 1/0)

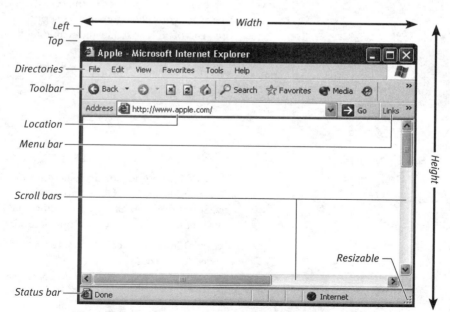

Figure 6.21 You can set the properties of a browser window with JavaScript.

To open a custom window with JavaScript:

1. Create a button symbol and place an instance of it on the Stage. In the Property inspector, give it a name.

   You will assign an event handler for a button click on this button that opens a new custom browser window using JavaScript.

2. Select the first frame of the timeline and open the Actions panel.

3. Add an event listener to detect a mouse click over your button.

4. Create the event handler function. In between the curly braces of the function, declare and initialize three variables for your URL, your new window name, and your window properties, like so:

   ```
   var myurl:String=
   → "http://www.adobe.com";
   var mywindow:String="newwindow";
   var myfeatures:String="width=400,
   → height=400, left=0, right=0,
   → toolbar=0, location=0";
   ```

   These variables will be used as parameters for your JavaScript function.

5. On the next line, still within the event handler function, write the `call()` method of the `ExternalInterface` class

with the name of the JavaScript function and then the three variables as parameters separated by commas, as in the following (**Figure 6.22**):

```
ExternalInterface.call("openwindow",
→ myurl, mywindow, myfeatures)
```

Flash makes the browser execute the JavaScript function called `openwindow` and passes three parameters.

6. Publish your Flash movie. Open the HTML file that gets created in the publishing process in an HTML editing application like Dreamweaver. In the head of the HTML file, add the following JavaScript code (**Figure 6.23**):

```
<script language="javascript">
function openwindow (URL,
→ windowname, windowfeatures){
window.open(URL, windowname,
→ windowfeatures);
}
</script>
```

The `openwindow` function has three parameters: `URL`, `windowname`, and `windowfeatures`. When this function is called, three parameters are passed from Flash and used in this function.

Continues on next page

```
mybutton_btn.addEventListener(MouseEvent.CLICK, clickButton);
function clickButton(myevent:MouseEvent):void {
    var myurl:String="http://www.peachpit.com";
    var mywindow:String="newwindow";
    var myfeatures:String="width=200, height=250, left=80, top=180, toolbar=0, location=0, directories=0";
    ExternalInterface.call("openwindow", myurl, mywindow, myfeatures);
}
```

Figure 6.22 The three variables `myurl`, `mywindow`, and `myfeatures` are strings that provide information to pass to the JavaScript function in the HTML page. The `call()` method triggers the function called openwindow and passes the three parameters to it.

```
<head>
<meta http-equiv="Content-Type" content="text/html; charset=iso-8859-1" />
<title>OpenNewWindow</title>
<body bgcolor="#ffffff">

<script language="javascript">
    function openwindow (URL, windowname, windowfeatures){
        window.open(URL, windowname, windowfeatures);
    }
</script>

</head>
```

Figure 6.23 You must add the JavaScript function (highlighted in gray) in the head of the HTML page that plays your Flash movie.

7. Save the modified HTML page and upload the HTML file and the SWF file to your server to test it on the Web.

When you click the button that you created, Flash passes the three parameters containing the Web address, the window name, and the window features to the JavaScript function in the HTML page called openwindow. Then a new window with those features opens (**Figure 6.24**).

✔ Tips

■ It's important that you test the ExternalInterface.call() method over the Internet, not locally on your hard drive. Security restrictions won't allow you to open a new window to a Web site from your local hard drive.

■ The ExternalInterface class is supported in these environments: Internet Explorer 5.0 and later for Windows, Firefox 1.0 and later, Mozilla 1.7.5 and later, Netscape 8.0 and later, or Safari 1.3 and later for the Mac. The ExternalInterface class is not supported in a stand-alone player.

■ You can use the ExternalInterface. call() method to call other JavaScript functions defined in your HTML page, not just to open custom browser windows.

■ Make sure you don't overwrite your HTML file that contains the added JavaScript function when you republish your Flash movie. If you make changes to your Flash movie, change the Publish Settings so you just publish a SWF file.

■ More JavaScript window properties are available, but many of them work in only one or some of the most popular browsers. The properties innerHeight and innerWidth, for example, define the dimensions of the actual window content area, but these properties are unique to Mozilla-based browsers such as Netscape Navigator and Firefox. You're safe if you stick to the properties listed in Table 6.2.

■ Security restrictions only allow a Flash movie to communicate with JavaScript on an HTML page that is in the same sandbox (see the Flash Player Security sidebars "Mixing Local and Remote Content" and "Loading Across Domains"). You can allow access by changing the AllowScriptAccess parameter to always (for both the embed and object tags) in the HTML page and adding the following statement in Flash: flash.system. Security.allowDomain("domainName").

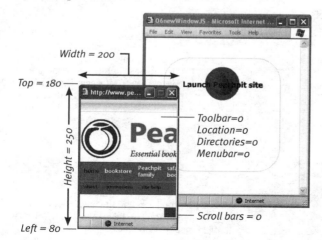

Width = 200
Top = 180
Height = 250
Left = 80

Launch Peachpit site

Toolbar=0
Location=0
Directories=0
Menubar=0

Scroll bars = 0

Figure 6.24 The new window created by the JavaScript function is a customized window without most features. The status bar and resize control are still visible.

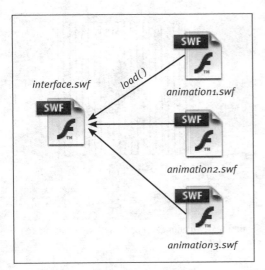

interface.swf   load()

animation1.swf

animation2.swf

animation3.swf

Figure 6.25 You can keep data-heavy content separate by maintaining external SWF files. Here, the interface. swf movie loads the animation files one by one as they're requested.

Loading External Flash Movies

Another way to communicate with external content is to combine other Flash movies into your first Flash movie. You use the Loader class to do this. The Loader class provides the load() method to load many kinds of external content into a Flash movie and integrate it with the current content. The original, container Flash movie establishes the frame rate, the Stage size, and the background color, but you can layer multiple external SWF files and even navigate within their Timelines. In Chapter 5, "Controlling Multiple Timelines," you learned to navigate the Timelines of movie clips in a single Flash movie. Now imagine the complexity of navigating multiple Timelines of multiple Flash movies!

Loading external Flash movies has many benefits. It keeps your Flash project small and lets you maintain quick download times. It also lets you edit the external Flash movies separately for a more modular way of working. For example, if you build a Web site to showcase your Flash animation work, you can keep all your individual animations as separate SWF files. Build the main interface so that your potential clients can load each animation as they request it. That way, your viewers download only the content that's needed, as it's needed. The main interface doesn't become bloated with the inclusion of every one of your Flash animations (**Figure 6.25**).

After you've loaded an external SWF file into Flash with the Loader class, you must add it to the display list, which makes it visible to the viewer. You'll learn more about the display list in the next chapter, "Controlling and Displaying Graphics." You add objects to the display list with the method addChild().

To load an external Flash movie:

1. Create the external Flash movie you want to load.

   For this example, keep the animation at a relatively small Stage size (**Figure 6.26**).

2. Publish your external movie as a SWF file.

3. Open a new Flash document to create the main, container movie that will load your external Flash movie.

4. Select the first frame of the main Timeline, and select the Actions panel.

5. Create a new URLRequest object with the name of the external SWF file as the url property, as in the following:

   ```
   var myrequest:URLRequest=new
   → URLRequest("letterA.swf");
   ```

   In this example, the external SWF that you want to load is called letterA.swf, and it lies in the same folder as the main Flash movie. If your external movie will be in a different directory, you can specify the path by using the slash (/) to drill down a directory or double periods (..) to move up a directory. If your SWF file resides on a Web site, you can enter an absolute path to the file.

6. On the next line, create a new Loader object with the following code:

   ```
   var myloader:Loader=new Loader();
   ```

7. On the next line, call the load() method for your new Loader object and use the URLRequest object as the parameter:

   ```
   myloader.load(myrequest);
   ```

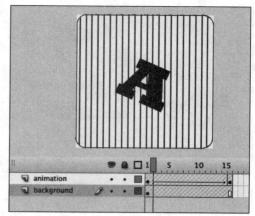

Figure 6.26 An animation of the letter A spins on a vertical grid.

```
var myrequest:URLRequest=new URLRequest("letterA.swf");
var myloader:Loader=new Loader();
myloader.load(myrequest);
stage.addChild(myloader);
```

Figure 6.27 The full code to load an external SWF file called letterA.swf into your Flash movie. The URLRequest object holds the information on what file to get and where to get it, and the load() method loads it into the Loader object. The Loader object finally is displayed on the Stage with the addChild() method.

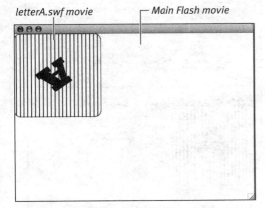

letterA.swf movie   *Main Flash movie*

Figure 6.28 The external movie of the spinning letter loads into the bigger main Flash movie.

8. On the last line, call the addChild() method to add the Loader object to the Stage to display it (**Figure 6.27**).

stage.addChild(myloader);

The Stage is the top-level display object. You can also add the Loader object to other DisplayObjectContainer objects on the Stage, if you desire.

9. Publish your movie.

10. Place the SWF file, its HTML file, and the external SWF file in the same directory.

11. Play the main movie in Flash Player or a browser.

Flash loads the external movie, which sits on top of your original movie and begins playing (**Figure 6.28**).

Flash Player Security: Loading Across Domains

Loading external SWFs and other content and data introduces data security issues and some restrictions you should be aware of. Because SWFs published on the Internet can be loaded into any Flash movie, the potential exists for private information and sensitive data held in variables in the SWF to be accessed. To prevent this abuse, Flash movies operate in their own secure space, called a *sandbox*. Only movies playing in the same sandbox can access and/or control each other's variables and other Flash elements. The sandbox is defined by the domain in which the Flash movie resides. So, a movie on www.adobe.com can access other movies on www.adobe.com without restriction, because they're in the same domain.

If you need to load content or data that reside in different domains, you can call the ActionScript method Security.allowDomain("domainName") within those SWFs, and movies from the specified domain can access their variables. For more specific information and details about domain-based authentication and granting access, see the Flash Help topic Programming ActionScript 3.0 > Flash Player Security. Current information is also available as a white paper on the Adobe Web site.

✔ Tip

■ Be careful when mixing Flash movies authored in ActionScript 3.0 and others authored in previous versions, especially when loading movies. ActionScript 2.0 movies can't load ActionScript 3.0 movies. ActionScript 3.0 movies can load ActionScript 2.0 movies and earlier, but there are limitations, such as not being able to access the loaded movie's variables or functions. In general, it's best to migrate all movies written in ActionScript 2.0 or earlier to ActionScript 3.0 to keep all externally loaded Flash content consistent.

To unload a movie:

◆ Use the unload() method on the Loader object, like so:

```
myloader.unload();
```

This statement unloads the Flash movie that was loaded into myloader from the previous task.

To replace a loaded movie:

◆ Use the load() method with a different URLRequest object. If you instantiate a second URLRequest object with a second SWF as its url property, you can load it into the original Loader object. Continuing with the previous task, add the following code when you want to replace the loaded movie:

```
var myrequest2:URLRequest=new
→ URLRequest("letterB.swf");
```

```
myloader.load(myrequest2);
```

This statement creates a new URLRequest object and loads the second external movie in the same loader, replacing the first movie (**Figure 6.29**).

or

◆ Use the unloadAndStop() method, like so:

```
myloader.unloadAndStop();
```

This statement unloads the Flash movie that was loaded into myloader and shuts down any video or sounds that may continue to play.

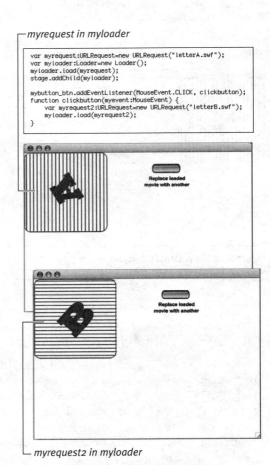

myrequest in myloader

```
var myrequest:URLRequest=new URLRequest("letterA.swf");
var myloader:Loader=new Loader();
myloader.load(myrequest);
stage.addChild(myloader);

mybutton_btn.addEventListener(MouseEvent.CLICK, clickbutton);
function clickbutton(myevent:MouseEvent) {
    var myrequest2:URLRequest=new URLRequest("letterB.swf");
    myloader.load(myrequest2);
}
```

myrequest2 in myloader

Figure 6.29 In the ActionScript code (top), the first external SWF movie (letterA.swf) loads in automatically. Then, when the user clicks the button on the Stage, a second URLRequest object is created for another external SWF movie (letterB.swf). When it is loaded into the same Loader object, the first movie is replaced.

Characteristics of Loaded Flash Movies

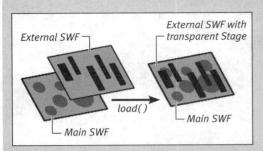

Figure 6.30 The Stage of an external SWF is transparent when the SWF is loaded into the main Flash movie.

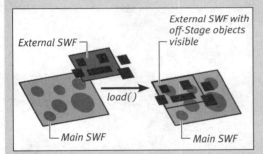

Figure 6.31 Smaller external SWFs are aligned at the top-left corner and display the work area off their Stages. Consider using masks or external SWFs with the same Stage dimensions.

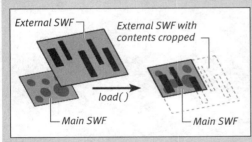

Figure 6.32 Larger external SWFs get cropped when they're loaded in a smaller main Flash movie.

The following is a list of things to keep in mind when you're loading external Flash movies:

◆ Loaded movies have transparent Stages. To have an opaque Stage, create a filled rectangle in the bottom layer of your loaded movie (**Figure 6.30**).

◆ Loaded movies are aligned with the registration point of the object that they are loaded into. That means the loaded movies are aligned to the top-left corner of the Stage (x = 0 and y = 0 for both the loaded movie and the Stage). So, loaded movies with smaller Stage sizes still show objects that are off their Stage (**Figure 6.31**). Create a mask to block objects that may go beyond the Stage and that you don't want your audience to see. Likewise, loaded movies with larger Stage sizes are cropped at the bottom and right boundaries (**Figure 6.32**).

◆ Loader objects can have only one loaded movie, so new calls to load() will bump out the existing loaded movie and replace it with the new loaded movie.

◆ You can have multiple loaded Flash movies as long as you have a unique Loader object for each loaded movie. Each time you use the addChild() method to display the loaded movie, it will be placed on top of the previously loaded movies. See the next section and Chapter 7, "Controlling and Displaying Graphics," for more information about managing depth levels of objects on the display list.

LOADING EXTERNAL FLASH MOVIES

Controlling Loaded Flash Movies

When you load an external Flash movie, you'll likely want to control it or change some of its properties. For example, to better fit your design, you can move the loaded movie to a different location on the Stage. Or, you can stop or play the loaded movie, or navigate to different spots on its Timeline.

Before you can control the loaded Flash movie, however, you have to wait until the entire external SWF has loaded. You can detect when the loading process is complete by accessing the LoaderInfo object of your loaded object. The LoaderInfo object provides events such as Event.COMPLETE or Event.OPEN that tells you the status of the load progress. The LoaderInfo object also provides information such as the amount of data that has loaded, the total amount of data of the loaded object, the loaded movie's SWF version, its frame rate, the URL from where it is being loaded, and other useful properties.

LoaderInfo and contentLoaderInfo

To access the LoaderInfo object, you use the contentLoaderInfo property of your Loader object. For example, consider the following statements that create a URLRequest and a Loader, and then load an external SWF file:

```
var myrequest:URLRequest=new
→ URLRequest("letterA.swf");

var myloader:Loader=new Loader();

myloader.load(myrequest);
```

After the load() call is made, you can access the LoaderInfo and its properties with the contentLoaderInfo property, like so:

```
myloader.contentLoaderInfo.bytesLoaded
```

This statement returns the amount of data that has loaded into the myloader object. The next statement,

```
myloader.contentLoaderInfo.content
```

returns the object (in this case, the external SWF) that is loaded into myloader. **Table 6.3** lists a few of the useful properties and events of the LoaderInfo object.

Table 6.3

LoaderInfo Properties and Events	
PROPERTY	DESCRIPTION
actionScriptVersion	ActionScript version of the loaded SWF
bytesLoaded	Amount of data that is loaded
bytesTotal	Total amount of data in the file
content	The loaded object associated with the LoaderInfo object
loader	The Loader object associated with the LoaderInfo object
frameRate	Frame rate of the loaded file
height	Vertical dimension, in pixels
width	Horizontal dimension, in pixels
loaderURL	URL of the Flash movie that initiated the load
url	URL of the file being loaded
swfVersion	Player version of the loaded SWF
Event.COMPLETE	Dispatches when the file is completely downloaded
Event.OPEN	Dispatches when the file begins to load
ProgressEvent.PROGRESS	Dispatches when the file is loading
Event.UNLOAD	Dispatches when the loaded file is removed or replaced
IOErrorEvent.IO_ERROR	Dispatches when an error in the loading happens

CONTROLLING LOADED FLASH MOVIES

Detecting a successful load

Only after a load is successful is it safe to control the loaded movie. Create an event handler that detects the `Event.COMPLETE` event of the `LoaderInfo` class as follows:

```
myloader.contentLoaderInfo.
addEventListener(Event.COMPLETE,
swfLoaded);

function swfLoaded(myevent:Event):void {
        var mycontent:MovieClip=
    → myevent.target.content;

        // do something with mycontent

}
```

In this example, when Flash detects the completion of a load process into the `myloader` object, it calls the `swfLoaded` function. The content of the event target (the loaded SWF) is assigned to a movie clip variable called `mycontent` for ease of manipulation and control.

To target and control a loaded Flash movie:

1. As in the preceding tasks, create an animation to serve as an external Flash movie, and export it as a SWF file.

2. Open a new Flash document, select the first frame of the timeline, and open the Actions panel.

3. Instantiate a `URLRequest` object and a `Loader` object and make a call to the `load()` method to start loading the external SWF, as in the following code (**Figure 6.33**):

```
var myrequest:URLRequest=new
→ URLRequest("letterA.swf");

var myloader:Loader=new Loader();

myloader.load(myrequest);
```

```
var myrequest:URLRequest=new URLRequest("letterA.swf");
var myloader:Loader=new Loader();
myloader.load(myrequest);
```

Figure 6.33 The external SWF called letterA.swf loads into the Loader object called myloader.

4. On the next available line, create a function with an `Event` type as the parameter. In the body of the function, assign the `target.content` property of the event object to a new movie clip, like so:

```
function
→ swfLoaded(myevent:Event):void {
stage.addChild(myloader);
var mycontent:MovieClip=
→ myevent.target.content;
}
```

This event handler, when executed, puts the external SWF on display on the Stage. Then it puts the content of the event target in a variable typed to a movie clip. The content of the event target is the loaded object, or the external SWF, which you know belongs to the `MovieClip` class. This helps you reference the external SWF, change its properties, and navigate its timeline.

5. Add an event listener to the `myloader.contentLoaderInfo` object (which references the `LoaderInfo` object) and listen for the `Event.COMPLETE` event, as in the following (**Figure 6.34**):

```
myloader.contentLoaderInfo.
→ addEventListener(Event.COMPLETE,
→ swfLoaded);
```

6. Within the body of the event handler function, add additional statements that change the properties or navigate the timeline of the external SWF. For example, consider the following statements:

```
mycontent.x=100;
mycontent.y=100;
mycontent.gotoAndStop(5);
```

The first and second statements change the position of the loaded SWF, and the third statement moves the playhead of the loaded SWF to frame 5 and stops there (**Figure 6.35**).

Continues on next page

```
var myrequest:URLRequest=new URLRequest("letterA.swf");
var myloader:Loader=new Loader();
myloader.load(myrequest);

function swfLoaded(myevent:Event):void {
    stage.addChild(myloader);
    var mycontent:MovieClip=myevent.target.content;
}
myloader.contentLoaderInfo.addEventListener(Event.COMPLETE, swfLoaded);
```

Figure 6.34 When the listener detects the completion of the loading, it triggers the function called swfLoaded. When that function is triggered, the external SWF is displayed on the Stage and is assigned to the variable mycontent.

```
var myrequest:URLRequest=new URLRequest("letterA.swf");
var myloader:Loader=new Loader();
myloader.load(myrequest);

myloader.contentLoaderInfo.addEventListener(Event.COMPLETE, swfLoaded);
function swfLoaded(myevent:Event):void {
    stage.addChild(myloader);
    var mycontent:MovieClip=myevent.target.content;
    mycontent.x=100;
    mycontent.y=100;
    mycontent.gotoAndStop(5);
}
```

Figure 6.35 The highlighted portions of the code change the position and control the playhead of the loaded external SWF.

CONTROLLING LOADED FLASH MOVIES

205

7. Publish your movie, and place the SWF and its HTML in the same directory as the external SWF file.

8. Play the movie in Flash Player or a browser.

Flash loads the external SWF. When it detects the completion of the load, it adds it to the Stage, moves its position, and goes to a different spot on its timeline (**Figure 6.36**).

Managing multiple Flash movies

When you load an external Flash movie and use addChild() to display it on the Stage, Flash adds the object to a display list, which is a list that Flash uses to keep track of the stacking order of objects. You'll learn much more about the display list in Chapter 7, because it is used to display all sorts of objects on the Stage—movie clips, bitmaps, graphics, as well as loaded movies.

Think of the display list as a stack of items, and each time you add an object to the Stage with addChild(), you add to the top of the stack. So the most recent addChild() statement will be the topmost object that overlaps all the other objects. If you want to bring an object that's lower in the stack to the top, simply call addChild() for that object, and Flash will pull it out of the list and put it on the top. If you want to remove an object from the stack entirely, use removeChild() (**Figure 6.37**).

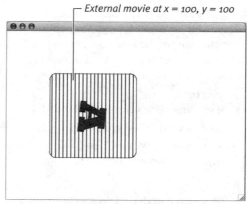

External movie at x = 100, y = 100

Figure 6.36 The loaded external SWF moves to x = 100, y = 100, and the playhead stops at frame 5.

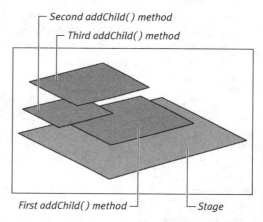

Second addChild( ) method
Third addChild( ) method
First addChild( ) method
Stage

Figure 6.37 The addChild( ) method puts the Loader object on display on the Stage. The most recent addChild( ) method will be on top.

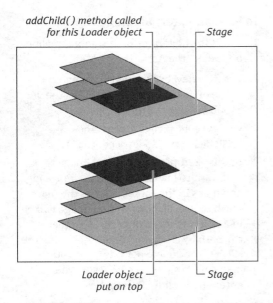

addChild( ) method called
for this Loader object —   — Stage

Loader object —   — Stage
put on top

Figure 6.38 When you call an addChild() method for a Loader object already displayed, it pulls it from the display list and puts it on the top.

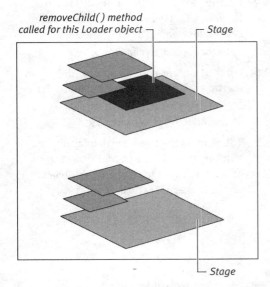

removeChild( ) method
called for this Loader object —   — Stage

—   — Stage

Figure 6.39 When you call a removeChild() method for a Loader object already displayed, it pulls it from the display list so it is no longer visible.

To put a loaded movie on top of others:

◆ Make a call to the addChild() method for the Loader object, like so:

    stage.addChild(myloader);

This statement adds the Flash movie loaded into myloader to the top of the Stage, overlapping other objects that may already be present on the Stage (**Figure 6.38**).

To remove a loaded movie from the Stage:

◆ Make a call to the removeChild() method for the Loader object, like so:

    stage.removeChild(myloader);

This statement removes the myloader object from the Stage so it is no longer visible. The myloader object, however, still exists. It can be added to the Stage at a later point in time or deleted entirely if it is no longer needed (**Figure 6.39**).

Loaded Movies and root

If you've worked with previous versions of ActionScript, you know that the _root property always referred to the main Timeline, even when an external SWF was loaded into another Flash movie. That made loaded Flash movies a little tricky if ActionScript from their timeline made reference to _root. In ActionScript 3.0, the new root property behaves a little differently. The root property within the loaded SWF represents the instance of the main class of that SWF (the main timeline of that SWF, equivalent to the Loader object's content property). Hence, there can be multiple root instances in a Flash movie if external content is loaded into the player with the Loader class.

Loading External Images

Using the same actions that load external Flash files into your movie dynamically, you can load images dynamically, including JPEG, progressive JPEG, GIF, and PNG images. The process is similar: create a URLRequest object to define the URL or path to your image file, create a Loader object, and then use the load() method to pull images into your Loader object. Finally, display the loaded images by adding the Loader object to the display list with addChild(). As is the case with external SWFs, keeping images separate from your Flash movie reduces the size of your Flash movie, saves download time, and makes revisions quicker and easier because you can edit the images without needing to open the actual Flash file.

Loaded images follow many of the same rules that loaded movies do, and those rules are worth repeating here:

◆ Loaded images are aligned at the registration point of the object that they are loaded into. That means images loaded on the Stage are aligned at their top-left corners (x = 0 and y = 0 for both the loaded movie and the Stage).

◆ Loader objects can have only one loaded image, so new calls to load() will bump out the existing loaded image and replace it with the new loaded image.

◆ You can have multiple loaded images as long as you have a unique Loader object for each loaded image. Each time you use the addChild() method to display the loaded image, it will be placed on top of the previously loaded image.

To load an external image:

1. Select the first frame of the main Timeline, and select the Actions panel.

2. Create a new URLRequest object with the name of the external image file as the url property, as in the following:

   ```
   var myrequest:URLRequest=new
   → URLRequest("someimage.jpg");
   ```

   In this example, the external image that you want to load is called someimage.jpg, and it lies in the same folder as the main Flash movie. If your external image will be in a different directory, you can specify the path by changing directories using the slash (/) or double periods (..). If your image file resides on a Web site, you can enter an absolute path to the file.

3. On the next line, create a new Loader object with the following code:

   ```
   var myloader:Loader=new Loader();
   ```

4. On the next line, call the load() method for your new Loader object, and use the URLRequest object as the parameter:

   ```
   myloader.load(myrequest);
   ```

5. On the last line, call the addChild() method to add the Loader object to the Stage to display it (**Figure 6.40**):

   ```
   stage.addChild(myloader);
   ```

   The Stage is the top-level display object. You can also add the Loader object to other DisplayObjectContainer objects on the Stage, if you desire.

```
var myrequest:URLRequest=new URLRequest ("someimage.jpg");
var myloader:Loader = new Loader();
myloader.load(myrequest);
addChild(myloader);
```

Figure 6.40 This ActionScript code loads an image called someimage.jpg and displays it on the Stage.

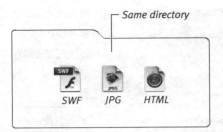

Same directory

SWF   JPG   HTML

External image loaded into SWF

Figure 6.41 The image file, someimage.jpg, is in the same directory as the SWF and HTML (top). When the Flash movie plays, the external image loads (bottom).

6. Publish your movie, and place your image in the correct directory so your Flash movie can find it.

Flash loads the external image, which sits on top of your original movie. The top-left corner of the JPEG aligns with the top-left corner of the Stage (**Figure 6.41**).

To remove or replace a loaded image:

◆ To unload an image, make a call to the unload() method of the Loader object. To remove the image from the display, make a call to the removeChild() method of the Stage.

◆ To replace an image, use the load() method, and load another URLRequest object into the same Loader object. The new image will replace the old one.

To control a loaded image:

◆ Assign new values to the Loader object properties to change the appearance of the loaded image. For example, myloader.x=50 moves the horizontal position of the myloader object and its loaded image. You should assign new properties only after you know the loading is complete with the Event.COMPLETE event (**Figure 6.42**).

To put a loaded image on top of others:

◆ Make a call to the addChild() method for the Loader object, like so:

stage.addChild(myloader);

This statement puts the image loaded into myloader to the top of the Stage, overlapping other objects that may already be present on the Stage.

```
var myrequest:URLRequest=new URLRequest ("someimage.jpg");
var myloader:Loader = new Loader();
myloader.load(myrequest);

myloader.contentLoaderInfo.addEventListener(Event.COMPLETE, imgLoaded);
function imgLoaded(event:Event):void {
    addChild(myloader);
    myloader.x=100;
    myloader.y=100;
    myloader.rotation=45;
}
```

Figure 6.42 When Flash detects the completion of the load, the image someimage.jpg is displayed on the Stage, moves position, and is rotated.

Communicating with External Video

In Chapter 2, "Working with Video," you learned how to embed video in a SWF file and also how to create an external Flash Video (FLV/F4V) file that loads into a player skin in a SWF file. However, you don't have to rely on the preset skins that are provided to you. Using ActionScript, you can control the loading and playback of external video to build your own playback features and use video in a less conventional way.

Once you have an FLV/F4V file, use a NetConnection object and a NetStream object to load the video stream into Flash. The NetConnection object provides the means to play back an FLV file from your local drive or Web address, whereas the NetStream object makes the actual connection and tells Flash to play the video. To receive the streaming video, you must also have a video object on the Stage. You can do this in one of two ways: create a video symbol in your Library and place an instance on the Stage where you want the video to appear, or create a video symbol and attach it to the Stage purely with ActionScript using the Video class.

To dynamically load external video with a video symbol placed on the Stage:

1. Convert your video file to an FLV or F4V file, as described in Chapter 2.

2. Open a new Flash document with its Stage size large enough to accommodate the video file.

3. Open the Library. From the Library panel's Options menu, choose New Video (**Figure 6.43**).

    The Video Properties dialog box appears.

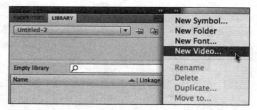

Figure 6.43 Choose New Video from the Library panel's Options menu.

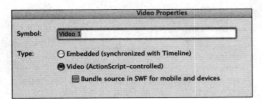

Figure 6.44 The Video Properties of your new video symbol.

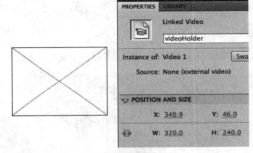

Figure 6.45 A video symbol placeholder named videoHolder is placed on the Stage. The instance looks like a square with an x inside it.

4. Give your symbol a name in the Symbol field; in the Type field, choose Video (ActionScript-controlled) (**Figure 6.44**). A new video symbol appears in the Library.

5. Place an instance of the video symbol on the Stage.

6. Modify its width and height to match the external video file that will be loaded in, and give it an instance name in the Property inspector. In this example, the instance name is videoHolder (**Figure 6.45**). Your external video will play inside this video instance.

7. Select the first frame of the main Timeline, and in the Actions panel, create a new instance from the NetConnection class as follows:

   ```
   var myVideo:NetConnection = new
   → NetConnection();
   ```

   A new NetConnection object is instantiated.

8. On the next line, enter the name of the NetConnection object you just created followed by a period, and then enter the connect() method with null as its parameter:

   ```
   myVideo.connect(null);
   ```

   The null parameter tells Flash that it isn't connecting through the Flash Communication Server but instead to expect a download from the local hard drive or a Web address.

9. On the next line, declare and instantiate a new NetStream object with the NetConnection object as its parameter:

   ```
   var newStream:NetStream = new
   → NetStream(myVideo);
   ```

   A new NetStream object is instantiated.

Continues on next page

COMMUNICATING WITH EXTERNAL VIDEO

10. Enter the instance name of the video symbol instance you placed on the Stage followed by a period. Enter the `attachNetStream()` method with the video source parameter:

```
videoHolder.attachNetStream
⇢ (newStream);
```

In this example, the name of the new `NetStream` object is the video source parameter.

11. On the next line, enter the name of the `NetStream` object followed by a period and then the method, `play()`. As the parameter for the `play()` method, enter the name of the external FLV or F4V file that you want to play on the Stage (**Figure 6.46**).

```
newStream.play("kayak.flv");
```

As in this example, make sure the file-name is enclosed by quotation marks.

12. On the next line, enter the following event listener to detect asynchronous error events and ignore them. See the sidebar "Asynchronous Error Events" for details regarding this error event.

```
newStream.addEventListener
⇢ (AsyncErrorEvent.ASYNC_ERROR,
⇢ asyncErrorHandler);

function asyncErrorHandler
⇢ (myevent:AsyncErrorEvent):void
{
    // ignore error
}
```

13. Publish your movie, and place the SWF file in the same directory as the video file whose name you entered.

Flash attaches your external video file to the instance of the video symbol on the Stage and begins to stream the video (**Figure 6.47**).

```
var myVideo:NetConnection = new NetConnection();
myVideo.connect(null);
var newStream:NetStream = new NetStream(myVideo);
videoHolder.attachNetStream(newStream);
newStream.play("kayak.flv");
```

Figure 6.46 A `NetConnection` object and a `NetStream` object are used to load and play an external FLV.

```
var myVideo:NetConnection = new NetConnection();
myVideo.connect(null);
var newStream:NetStream = new NetStream(myVideo);
videoHolder.attachNetStream(newStream);
newStream.play("kayak.flv");

newStream.addEventListener(AsyncErrorEvent.ASYNC_ERROR, errorhandler);
function errorhandler(myevent:AsyncErrorEvent) {
    //ignore error
}
```

Figure 6.47 The ActionScript code (top) loads the external FLV file named kayak.flv into the `videoHolder` instance on the Stage and plays.

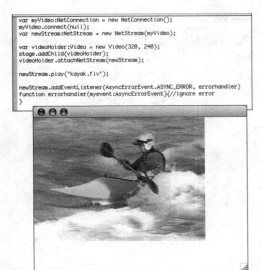

```
var myVideo:NetConnection = new NetConnection();
myVideo.connect(null);
var newStream:NetStream = new NetStream(myVideo);

var videoHolder:Video = new Video(320, 240);
stage.addChild(videoHolder);
videoHolder.attachNetStream(newStream);

newStream.play("kayak.flv");

newStream.addEventListener(AsyncErrorEvent.ASYNC_ERROR, errorhandler)
function errorhandler(myevent:AsyncErrorEvent){//ignore error
}
```

Figure 6.48 The ActionScript code (top) loads the external FLV file named kayak.flv into the dynamically created Video object and plays. The Video object is aligned at the top-left corner of the Stage, but you can change its x and y properties to move it anywhere you want.

To dynamically load external video with a video object:

1. Modify the file created in the previous task by deleting the video instance on the Stage.

2. Instead of creating a video symbol in the Library beforehand (steps 3–6 of the previous task), create a Video object with ActionScript, like so:

   ```
   var videoHolder:Video = new
   → Video(320, 240);
   ```

   This statement creates a new object called videoHolder from the Video class, which is 320 pixels wide by 240 pixels high.

3. Add the new Video object to the Stage with the addChild() method:

   ```
   stage.addChild(videoHolder);
   ```

4. Publish your movie, and place the SWF file in the same directory as the video file whose name you entered.

   The full ActionScript code (**Figure 6.48**) is similar to the one in the previous task, but Flash creates the Video object dynamically.

✔ Tips

■ Move the Video object, whether dynamically generated or placed on the Stage manually, by assigning new values to its x and y properties. You'll learn more about changing graphics displayed on the Stage in the next chapter.

■ When working with FLV or F4V files for playback, you may need to configure your server to handle the file type (by telling the server its MIME type and file extension). Check with your hosting service to make sure the server can handle FLV and F4V files.

COMMUNICATING WITH EXTERNAL VIDEO

Controlling playback of externally loaded video

There are several methods that you can call to control the playback of the video stream. See **Table 6.4** for a description of the various commands. All of these methods are called from the NetStream object. The following task creates buttons for the four methods to control the playback of the video.

Table 6.4

Playback Methods of the NetStream Object

METHOD	DESCRIPTION
pause()	Pauses the video
resume()	Begins playing at the point where the video is paused
seek()	Seeks to any point in the stream provided by the parameter, in seconds
togglePause()	Alternates between pausing or resuming playback of the video

Asynchronous Error Events

Cue points and metadata are information embedded in FLV and F4V files that you can create when you originally encode your video. They provide a way to trigger ActionScript code with the onCuePoint and onMetaData handlers at specific spots along the video stream. Flash requires that you write event handlers for cue points and metadata; otherwise, errors may be generated. However, if you are not interested in cue points or metadata and simply want to play the video, you must add the following bit of code to tell Flash to ignore any asynchronous errors:

```
newStream.addEventListener(AsyncErrorEvent.ASYNC_ERROR, asyncErrorHandler);

function asyncErrorHandler(myevent:AsyncErrorEvent):void
{
    // ignore error
}
```

The sample code adds a listener on the NetStream object called newStream for the asynchronous error event, which happens when no event handler exists to deal with cue points and metadata from an FLV/F4V.

Figure 6.49 Four button instances placed on the Stage.

```
pause_btn.addEventListener(MouseEvent.CLICK, pausefunction);
function pausefunction (myevent:MouseEvent):void{
    newStream.pause();
}

resume_btn.addEventListener(MouseEvent.CLICK, resumefunction);
function resumefunction (myevent:MouseEvent):void{
    newStream.resume();
}

toggle_btn.addEventListener(MouseEvent.CLICK, togglefunction);
function togglefunction (myevent:MouseEvent):void{
    newStream.togglePause();
}

seek_btn.addEventListener(MouseEvent.CLICK, seekfunction);
function seekfunction (myevent:MouseEvent):void{
    newStream.seek(1);
}
```

Figure 6.50 The mouse click event handlers for the four buttons on the Stage. Each button calls a different method of the NetStream object called newStream.

```
var myVideo:NetConnection = new NetConnection();
myVideo.connect(null);
var newStream:NetStream = new NetStream(myVideo);
var videoHolder:Video = new Video(320, 240);
stage.addChild(videoHolder);
videoHolder.attachNetStream(newStream);

newStream.play("kayak.flv");

pause_btn.addEventListener(MouseEvent.CLICK, pausefunction);
function pausefunction (myevent:MouseEvent):void{
    newStream.pause();
}

resume_btn.addEventListener(MouseEvent.CLICK, resumefunction);
function resumefunction (myevent:MouseEvent):void{
    newStream.resume();
}

toggle_btn.addEventListener(MouseEvent.CLICK, togglefunction);
function togglefunction (myevent:MouseEvent):void{
    newStream.togglePause();
}

seek_btn.addEventListener(MouseEvent.CLICK, seekfunction);
function seekfunction (myevent:MouseEvent):void{
    newStream.seek(1);
}

newStream.addEventListener(AsyncErrorEvent.ASYNC_ERROR, errorhandler)
function errorhandler(myevent:AsyncErrorEvent){//ignore error
}
```

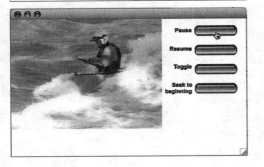

Figure 6.51 The ActionScript code (top) loads the external FLV. The buttons (bottom) control its playback. Create your own playback skin using these methods.

To control playback of externally loaded video:

1. Continue with the file created in the previous task in which you load and play an external video.

2. Create a button symbol, and place four instances of the button symbol on the Stage.

3. In the Property inspector, give unique names to the four instances and add text to describe their function. In this example, name the four instances pause_btn, resume_btn, toggle_btn, and seek_btn (**Figure 6.49**).

4. Select the first frame of the timeline and open the Actions panel.

5. On the next available line in the Script pane, create an event handler for each of the four buttons to detect a mouse click.

6. In the function of each event handler, make a call to a method of the NetStream object (**Figure 6.50**).

7. Publish your movie, and place the SWF file in the same directory as the video file that you want to load.

   The full ActionScript code (**Figure 6.51**) creates the necessary objects to load the video file and provides event handlers to control its playback.

Detecting the status of the video stream

The NetStream object dispatches events (NetStatusEvent) at various points during the data stream. The different NetStatusEvent conditions are captured in its property info. code as a string. For example, if the play() method can't find the correct video file, the info.code property returns a value of "NetStream.Play.StreamNotFound."

Two important string values, "NetStream. Play.Start" and "NetStream.Play.Stop", can help you detect the start and end of a loaded video to better manage the video streams. For example, you could create an event handler to listen for the end of a loaded video. When the video finishes playing, you automatically load the next video in the queue.

To detect the end of externally loaded video:

1. Continue with the file created in the previous task in which you loaded and played an external video.

2. Select the first frame on the timeline and open the Actions panel.

3. On the next available line, add an event listener on your NetStream object to detect the NetStatusEvent.NET_STATUS event as follows:

```
newStream.addEventListener
→ (NetStatusEvent.NET_STATUS,
→ statusHandler);
```

4. On the next line, create the function with the NetStatusEvent as a parameter, like so:

```
function statusHandler
→ (myevent:NetStatusEvent):void {
// do something
}
```

When there is a change in the condition of the video stream, the function called statusHandler will be triggered.

5. In between the curly braces of the function, add a conditional statement that checks whether the info.code property of the event matches a string that indicates the video has finished:

```
if (myevent.info.code ==
→ "NetStream.Play.Stop") {
    // video has stopped
}
```

6. Add additional statements to be carried out when the video finishes (**Figure 6.52**). Publish your movie, and place the SWF file in the same directory as the video file that you want to load.

When Flash detects the end of the video, myevent.info.code matches the string "NetStream.Play.Stop" and additional instructions can be given.

```
newStream.addEventListener(NetStatusEvent.NET_STATUS, statusHandler);
function statusHandler(myevent:NetStatusEvent):void {
    if (myevent.info.code =="NetStream.Play.Stop") {
        newStream.play("video2.flv");
    }
}
```

Figure 6.52 When Flash detects the end of the first video stream, it plays another video, called video2.flv.

Detecting Download Progress: Preloaders

All the hard work you put into creating complex interactivity in your movie will be wasted if your viewers have to wait too long to download the movie over the Web and leave. You can avoid losing viewers by creating short animations that entertain them while the rest of your movie downloads. These diversions, or *preloaders*, tell your viewers how much of the movie has downloaded and how much longer they have to wait. When enough data has been delivered over the Web to the viewers' computers, you can trigger your movie to start. In effect, you hold back the playhead until you know that all the frames are available to play. Only then do you send the playhead to the starting frame of your movie.

Preloaders must be small because you want them to load almost immediately, and they should be informative, letting your viewers know what they're waiting for.

Flash provides many ways to monitor the state of the download progress. You can test for the number of frames that have downloaded with the `MovieClip` class properties `framesLoaded` and `totalFrames`. But the frames of your movie most likely contain data that aren't evenly spread, so testing the amount of data (measured in bytes) is a more accurate gauge of download progress.

As you learned earlier in the section "Controlling Loaded Flash Movies," you can access information about the status of any load with the `LoaderInfo` object. Earlier you used it to determine when an external SWF had completely loaded. But you can also use it to determine when the main SWF (or any loading file) has completely loaded, or check on its download progress. Use the `ProgressEvent` event with the properties `bytesLoaded` and `bytesTotal` to help you monitor the download progress.

The concept of a preloader is simple. You tell Flash to compare the amount of data loaded with the total data in the movie. As this ratio changes, you can display the percentage numerically with a dynamic text field or represent the changing ratio graphically, such as with a growing, horizontal progress bar. Because they often show the progress of the download, these preloaders are sometimes known as *progressive preloaders*.

To create a preloader that graphically shows download progress:

1. Create a long rectangular movie clip symbol.

   Make sure its registration point is at its far-left edge (**Figure 6.53**).

2. Place an instance of the symbol on the Stage, and give it an instance name (this example uses `bar_mc`).

   Your preloader is a rectangle that grows longer according to the percentage of downloaded frames. Flash will dynamically change the properties of the rectangular movie clip to stretch it out. Because the bar should grow from left to right, the registration point is placed on the left edge.

3. Select the first frame of the main Timeline, and open the Actions panel.

4. Enter `stop()`.

   The `stop()` method prevents your movie from playing until it has downloaded completely (**Figure 6.54**).

5. On the next line, add an event listener on the main Timeline's `loaderInfo` property. Listen for the `ProgressEvent.PROGRESS` event, like so:

   ```
   root.loaderInfo.addEventListener
   → (ProgressEvent.PROGRESS,
   → progressHandler);
   ```

The loading of your main Flash movie is happening on the root Timeline, so you can use `loaderInfo` to access its load properties. Whenever download progress is detected, the function called `progressHandler` is called.

6. On the next line, create the function called `progressHandler` with a `ProgressEvent` event as its parameter:

   ```
   function progressHandler
   → (myevent:ProgressEvent):void {
       // show progress
   }
   ```

7. In between the curly braces of the function, declare a variable and assign the ratio of bytes downloaded to total bytes with the following:

   ```
   var myprogress:Number=
   → myevent.bytesLoaded/
   → myevent.bytesTotal;
   ```

   The amount of data loaded is defined in the `ProgressEvent`'s `bytesLoaded` property. The total data is defined in the `ProgressEvent`'s `bytesTotal` property. Dividing the first over the second provides a ratio of the overall progress.

Registration point

Figure 6.53 A rectangular movie clip with its registration point on the far-left edge can be used as a graphical representation of download progress.

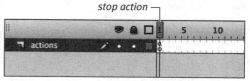
stop action

Figure 6.54 The stop() method is put on the very first frame on the Timeline to pause your movie until all the data has downloaded.

```
stop();
root.loaderInfo.addEventListener(ProgressEvent.PROGRESS, progressHandler);
function progressHandler(myevent:ProgressEvent):void {
    var myprogress:Number=myevent.bytesLoaded/myevent.bytesTotal;
    bar_mc.scaleX=myprogress
}
```

Figure 6.55 As the movie downloads, its progress is captured in the variable `myprogress`, which measures the ratio of `bytesLoaded` to `bytesTotal` of the loading movie. This ratio is used to scale the rectangle on the Stage.

```
stop();
root.loaderInfo.addEventListener(ProgressEvent.PROGRESS, progressHandler);
function progressHandler(myevent:ProgressEvent):void {
    var myprogress:Number=myevent.bytesLoaded/myevent.bytesTotal;
    bar_mc.scaleX=myprogress;
}

root.loaderInfo.addEventListener(Event.COMPLETE, finished);
function finished(myevent:Event):void {
    play();
}
```

Figure 6.56 When the loading process is complete, the function called `finished` is triggered. Flash begins playing the main Timeline.

Rectangular movie clip removed at keyframe 2

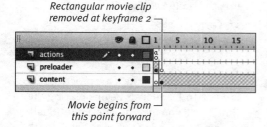

Movie begins from this point forward

Figure 6.57 The real movie begins at keyframe 2 after the rectangular movie clip is removed.

8. On the next line (but still within the function), add the following:

`bar_mc.scaleX=myprogress;`

The bar on the Stage is scaled horizontally according to the download ratio (**Figure 6.55**).

9. On a new line outside the event handler, create a new listener on the root Timeline's `loaderInfo` property to detect the `Event.COMPLETE` event:

`root.loaderInfo.addEventListener`
`→ (Event.COMPLETE, finished);`

This second listener listens for the completion of the download and will call the function called `finished`.

10. On the next line, create the function called `finished` with an `Event` event as its parameter:

`function`
`→ finished(myevent:Event):void {`
`    play();`
`}`

In this example, when the function is called, the Flash movie begins playing (**Figure 6.56**).

11. Begin the actual content of your Flash document from the second keyframe (**Figure 6.57**).

12. Test your movie (Control > Test Movie).

Continues on next page

13. Choose View > Bandwidth Profiler (Ctrl-B for Windows, Cmd-B for Mac) and choose View > Simulate Download.

The Bandwidth Profiler is an information window above your movie in Test Movie mode; it displays the number of frames and the amount of data in each frame as vertical bars. If the vertical bars extend over the bottom of the red horizontal line, there is too much data to be downloaded at the bandwidth setting without causing a stutter during playback. The Simulate Download option simulates actual download performance (**Figure 6.58**). The green bar at the top shows the download progress. The triangle marks the current location of the playhead. The playhead remains in frame 1 until the green progress bar reaches the end of the timeline. Only then does the playhead begin moving.

✔ Tips

- You won't see your preloader working unless you build an animation with many frames containing fairly large graphics that require lengthy download times. If your animation is small, you'll see your preloader whiz by because all the data will download quickly and begin playing almost immediately.

- Explore other graphical treatments of the download progress. Stretching the length of a movie clip is just one way to animate the download process. With subtle changes to your ActionScript, you can apply a variety of animated effects to your preloader.

- Another way of detecting the completion of the load is to insert a conditional statement within the event handler that monitors the progress, like so:

```
if (myprogress==1){
play();
}
```

This statement checks if the progress ratio is equal to 1, and if so, begins playing the timeline. If you include this conditional statement, you don't need to listen for the Event.COMPLETE event.

Data transfer rate   *Current location of playhead*

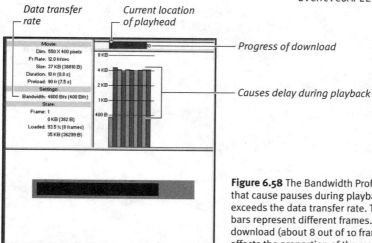

Progress of download

Causes delay during playback

Figure 6.58 The Bandwidth Profiler shows the individual frames that cause pauses during playback because the amount of data exceeds the data transfer rate. The alternating light and dark bars represent different frames. Notice how the progress of the download (about 8 out of 10 frames have loaded completely) affects the proportion of the movie clip (about 80 percent).

Showing numeric download progress

Often, a preloader has an accompanying display of the percentage of download progress. This display is accomplished with a dynamic text field placed on the Stage. You'll learn more about dynamic text in Chapter 10, "Controlling Text," but you can use the steps in the following task now to add a simple numeric display.

The Bandwidth Profiler

The Bandwidth Profiler is a handy option to see how data is distributed throughout your Flash movie and how quickly (or slowly) it will download over the Web. In Test Movie mode (after choosing Control > Test Movie), choose View > Bandwidth Profiler (Ctrl-B for Windows, Cmd-B for Mac) to see this information.

The left side of the Bandwidth Profiler shows movie information, such as Stage dimensions, frame rate, file size, total duration, and preload time in frames and seconds. It also shows the Bandwidth setting, which simulates actual download performance at a specified rate. You can change that rate in the View > Download Settings menu and choose the Internet connection speed that your viewers are likely to have. Flash gives you options for 28.8 and 56K modems, for example.

The bar graph on the right side of the Bandwidth Profiler shows the amount of data in each frame of your movie. You can view the graph as a streaming graph (choose View > Streaming Graph) or as a frame-by-frame graph (choose View > Frame by Frame Graph). The streaming graph indicates how the movie downloads over the Web by showing you how data streams from each frame, whereas the frame-by-frame graph indicates the amount of data in each frame. In Streaming Graph mode, you can tell which frames will cause hang-ups during playback by noting which bar exceeds the given Bandwidth setting.

To watch the actual download performance of your movie, choose View > Simulate Download. Flash simulates playback over the Web at the given Bandwidth setting. A green horizontal bar at the top of the window indicates which frames have been downloaded, and the triangular playhead marks the current frame.

To add a numeric display to the preloader:

1. Continuing with the file from the preceding task, select the Text tool and drag out a text field on the Stage.

2. In the Property inspector, choose Dynamic Text, and give the text field an instance name (**Figure 6.59**).

   As with buttons and movie clip symbols, the instance name of the text field lets you target the text field and control it using ActionScript.

3. Select the first frame of the main Timeline, and open the Actions panel.

4. Within the curly braces of the function called progressHandler, enter the following:

   myTextField_txt.text = Math.
   → round(myprogress*100)+"%";

   The percentage of download progress is rounded to a whole number by the Math. round() method. The percent (%) character is appended to the end, and the result is assigned to the text property of your text field, displaying it on the Stage (**Figure 6.60**).

Detecting download progress of external images and movies

Monitoring the download progress of external images and movies is very similar to monitoring the download progress of the main Flash movie. You can use the identical code, but instead of adding your listener to root.loaderInfo, you'll add your listener to myloader.contentLoaderInfo (provided that your Loader object is named myloader). Recall that your Loader's contentLoaderInfo refers to the LoaderInfo object of the loaded content. You can visualize the relationship in **Figure 6.61**.

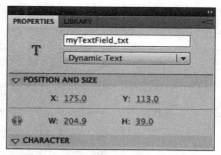

Figure 6.59 This dynamic text field is called myTextField_txt.

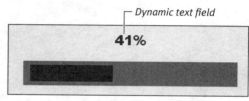

Figure 6.60 The dynamic text field displays the percentage of the download progress along with the graphical representation.

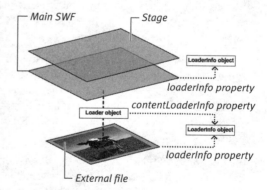

Figure 6.61 In this figure, you can see the relationship between the Loader object, the external file that it loads, and the associated LoaderInfo object that provides information about the content and the loading process (see Table 6.3). The contentLoaderInfo property of the Loader object references the LoaderInfo object. The loaderInfo property of the content also references the LoaderInfo object. So for loading external content, use the contentLoaderInfo property of the Loader object. For the main SWF, use the loaderInfo property of root.

To create a preloader for external images or movies:

1. Create a small rectangular movie clip symbol.

   Make sure its registration point is at the far-left edge.

2. Place an instance of the symbol on the Stage, and give it a name in the Property inspector (**Figure 6.62**).

   The properties of the rectangle will change in proportion to the number of bytes that are downloaded. This will act as a visual indicator to the audience that the movie is loading.

Figure 6.62 A new rectangular movie clip is given an instance name of bar_mc.

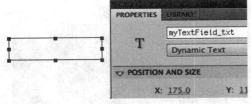

Figure 6.63 A dynamic text field is given an instance name of myTextField_txt.

3. Select the Text tool and drag out a text field on the Stage. In the Property inspector, select Dynamic Text from the drop-down list and give the field an instance name (**Figure 6.63**).

   The dynamic text field will display the percentage of download progress.

4. Select the first frame of the main Timeline, and open the Actions panel.

5. Create a new URLRequest object with the name of the external file as the url property as in the following:

   ```
   var myrequest:URLRequest=new
   → URLRequest("someimage.jpg");
   ```

   In this example, the external file is a JPG that you want to load, and it lies in the same folder as the main Flash movie. You can use an absolute URL to an image or SWF on the Internet as well.

6. On the next line, create a new Loader object with the following code:

   ```
   var myloader:Loader=new Loader();
   ```

7. On the next line, call the load() method for your new Loader object and use the URLRequest object as the parameter (**Figure 6.64**):

   ```
   myloader.load(myrequest);
   ```

8. On the next line, add an event listener to the Loader object's contentLoaderInfo property and listen for the ProgressEvent. PROGRESS event as in the following code:

   ```
   myloader.contentLoaderInfo.
   → addEventListener(ProgressEvent.
   → PROGRESS, progresshandler);
   ```

Continues on next page

```
var myrequest:URLRequest=new URLRequest ("someimage.jpg");
var myloader:Loader = new Loader();
myloader.load(myrequest);
```

Figure 6.64 An external file called someimage.jpg loads into the Loader object called myloader.

DETECTING DOWNLOAD PROGRESS: PRELOADERS

9. On the next line, enter the event handler function as you did for the previous task. The full code so far is shown in **Figure 6.65**.

10. Next, add a second event listener to the Loader object's contentLoaderInfo property and listen for the Event. COMPLETE event as in the following code:

```
myloader.contentLoaderInfo.
→ addEventListener(Event.COMPLETE,
→ alldone);
```

As soon as the Event.COMPLETE event has dispatched from the loading process, the function called alldone will be called.

11. On a new line, enter the function called alldone as follows:

```
function
→ alldone(myevent:Event):void {
    addChild(myloader);
    removeChild(myTextField_txt);
    removeChild(bar_mc);
}
```

When the load is complete, the external file (whether a JPEG or SWF) is added to the Stage to be displayed and the text field and movie clip are removed (**Figure 6.66**).

12. Test your movie.

As your external movie or image loads into your Loader object, the text field displays the percentage of total bytes downloaded, and the rectangular movie clip grows longer. When the entire movie or image has loaded, it appears on the Stage and the text field and elongated rectangular movie clip disappear (**Figure 6.67**).

```
var myrequest:URLRequest=new URLRequest ("someimage.jpg");
var myloader:Loader = new Loader();
myloader.load(myrequest);

myloader.contentLoaderInfo.addEventListener(ProgressEvent.PROGRESS, progresshandler);
function progresshandler(myevent:ProgressEvent):void {
    var myprogress:Number=myevent.bytesLoaded/myevent.bytesTotal;
    bar_mc.scaleX=myprogress;
    myTextField_txt.text = Math.round(myprogress*100)+"%";
}
```

Figure 6.65 When the external file begins to load, the Loader object's contentLoaderInfo property can be used to access the LoaderInfo object. The ProgressEvent.PROGRESS event is dispatched as the load happens, and the ratio of downloaded data to total data is displayed graphically with the movie clip and in a dynamic text field.

```
var myrequest:URLRequest=new URLRequest ("someimage.jpg");
var myloader:Loader = new Loader();
myloader.load(myrequest);

myloader.contentLoaderInfo.addEventListener(ProgressEvent.PROGRESS, progresshandler);
function progresshandler(myevent:ProgressEvent):void {
    var myprogress:Number=myevent.bytesLoaded/myevent.bytesTotal;
    bar_mc.scaleX=myprogress;
    myTextField_txt.text = Math.round(myprogress*100)+"%";
}
myloader.contentLoaderInfo.addEventListener(Event.COMPLETE, alldone);
function alldone(myevent:Event):void {
    addChild(myloader);
    removeChild(myTextField_txt);
    removeChild(bar_mc);
}
```

Figure 6.66 The complete code for a preloader for external content. The last event handler detects when the load is complete. When the load is complete, the external file is displayed on the Stage and the preloader (movie clip and dynamic text field) are removed from the Stage.

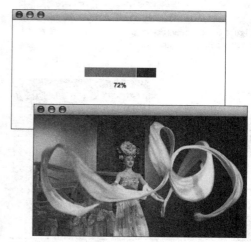

Figure 6.67 During the loading progress, Flash updates the contents of the text field called myTextField_txt and stretches the rectangular movie clip called bar_mc in proportion to the percentage of downloaded bytes (top). When loading is finished, the image called someimage.jpg appears (bottom).

Part III: Transforming Graphics and Sound

CONTROLLING AND DISPLAYING GRAPHICS

ActionScript's fine-tuned ability to create, control, and display graphical elements on the fly and in response to events is what makes Flash truly powerful. You can create and manipulate many objects such as movie clips, buttons, images, and even shapes and masks. Properties that control how these objects appear, such as position, scale, rotation, transparency, color, and blending effects, can all be changed with ActionScript. You can even have control over individual pixels in bitmap images. As a result of these abilities, you can create arcade-style interactivity with characters changing in response to viewer input or conditions, like a game of Tetris where the objects move according to keyboard input. This kind of animation isn't based on tweens you create while authoring the Flash movie. Rather, this is dynamic animation that is essentially created during playback.

Flash also gives you many methods to control an object's behavior. You can make objects draggable so that viewers can pick up puzzle pieces and put them in their correct places, or you can develop a more immersive online shopping experience in which viewers can grab merchandise and drop it into their shopping carts. In this chapter, you'll learn how to control collisions and overlaps with other objects, and you'll learn how to generate different objects dynamically so that new instances appear on the Stage during playback.

In previous versions of ActionScript, much of the dynamic graphics depended on the movie clip object to act as a jack-of-all-trades. However, in ActionScript 3.0, Flash provides more individualized objects, so different objects perform more specific functions. You'll use certain objects to draw shapes, other objects for drag-and-drop interactivity, and others for handling bitmaps. This reduces the overall overhead by avoiding the powerful, yet bulky, object like the movie clip for many tasks that don't require all its capabilities.

Understanding the Display List

The key to successfully manipulating graphics on the Stage is to understand what is known as the *display list*. The display list is the hierarchy of visible objects on the Stage. The display list lets Flash (and you) keep track of what the user sees, the visual relationships between objects, and the stacking order (or overlapping) of the objects.

Conceptually, it's much like the folder structure on your computer desktop and can be represented as a tree structure (**Figure 7.1**). The top-level element is the Stage. Each time you play a Flash movie in a Web browser, the Flash Player opens your SWF and places it on the Stage. So the Stage is the container that holds your main SWF. Inside your main SWF you can place other elements, such as buttons, text, video, bitmaps, and other objects—all of which are instances of a big class known as DisplayObject. You'll be using many of the properties of the DisplayObject class to control the objects' appearances. You can also have elements on your main SWF that contain DisplayObject objects. These are known as DisplayObjectContainer objects and include objects like a Sprite object, a Loader object, a MovieClip object, and the Stage itself. So you can think of the main SWF on the Stage as your desktop, the DisplayObjects as individual files, and the DisplayObjectContainers as folders that can contain additional folders or files.

One of the most important methods of the DisplayObjectContainer class is one that you've already used in previous chapters—addChild(). This method adds an element (either another DisplayObjectContainer or a DisplayObject) to the display list and makes it visible. As you add more DisplayObjects and DisplayObjectContainers to your display list, you need to keep track of how they overlap. Flash keeps track of each object with a number, known as an index, that begins at 0 and increases in whole numbers. Objects with higher display list index numbers overlap those with lower numbers.

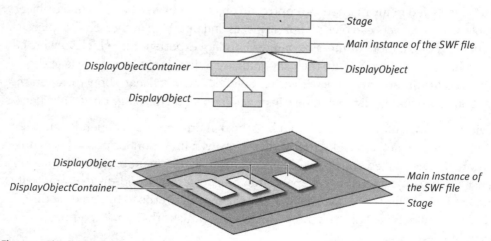

Figure 7.1 The display list can be represented hierarchically like a tree (top) where the Stage is the top-level DisplayObjectContainer. You can also think of the display list like your computer desktop, where the Stage is at the bottom and the objects you add to it are folders (DisplayObjectContainers) or files (DisplayObjects). The folders can contain other folders or files.

Changing Visual Properties

Many `DisplayObject` properties—`alpha`, `rotation`, `scaleX`, `scaleY`—define how the object looks. By using dot syntax, you can target any object of the class and change any of those characteristics during playback. **Table 7.1** summarizes many properties that are available to all the objects in the `DisplayObject` class, which include movie clips, static text, text fields, videos, bitmaps, buttons, dynamically drawn shapes, loaders, sprites, and the Stage. You've already learned about some of these objects in previous chapters, and you'll learn about the others in this chapter and upcoming ones. Note the properties new

in Flash CS4 that control the position of an object in 3D space: `rotationX`, `rotationY`, `rotationZ`, `scaleZ`, and `z`.

The following tasks demonstrate how to change a few of the common properties of an object.

✔ Tip

■ Make note of how the property names and values are different in ActionScript 3.0 from ActionScript 2.0. Properties no longer have an underscore (_) before their names, and some of the values they take are different. For example, the transparency values (`alpha`) in ActionScript 3.0 range from 0 to 1 instead of 0 to 100.

Table 7.1

DisplayObject Properties

PROPERTY	VALUE	DESCRIPTION
alpha	Number (0 to 1)	Transparency, where 0 is totally transparent and 1 is opaque.
visible	true or false	Whether an object can be seen.
name	String	Instance name of the object.
rotation	Number	Degree of rotation in a clockwise direction from the registration point.
rotationX	Number	Degree of rotation around the x-axis from its original orientation.
rotationY	Number	Degree of rotation around the y-axis from its original orientation.
rotationZ	Number	Degree of rotation around the z-axis from its original orientation.
width	Number in pixels	Horizontal dimension.
height	Number in pixels	Vertical dimension.
x	Number in pixels	Horizontal position of the object's registration point.
y	Number in pixels	Vertical position of the object's registration point.
z	Number in pixels	Depth position of the object's registration point.
scaleX	Number (0 to 1)	Percentage of the original object's horizontal dimension.
scaleY	Number (0 to 1)	Percentage of the original object's vertical dimension.
scaleZ	Number (0 to 1)	Percentage of the original object's depth dimension.
blendMode	String	Which blend mode to use to visually combine colors.
cacheAsBitmap	true or false	Whether to redraw the contents of the object every frame (false) or use a static bitmap of the object's contents (true).
opaqueBackground	Numeric color value	Nontransparent background color for the instance.
scrollRect	Rectangle object	Window of visible content of the object, which can be changed to efficiently simulate scrolling.
loaderInfo	LoaderInfo object	Returns a LoaderInfo object containing information about the loading process.
mask	DisplayObject	Sets the mask area (visible area) of the object.
filters	Array of filter objects	Set of graphical filters to apply to this object.
scale9Grid	Rectangle object	Nine regions that control how the movie clip distorts when scaling.
transform	Transform object	Values representing color, size, and position changes applied to the instance.

To change the position of an object:

1. For this example, create a movie clip and place an instance of it on the Stage. In the Property inspector, give it a name (**Figure 7.2**).

2. Select the first frame of the timeline and open the Actions panel.

3. Enter the instance name, then a dot, followed by the property x. Enter an equals sign followed by a number in pixels, like so:

   `myMovieClip_mc.x=100;`

   This statement positions the movie clip called `myMovieClip_mc` 100 pixels from the left edge of the Stage.

4. On a new line, enter the instance name, then a dot, followed by the property y. Enter an equals sign followed by a number in pixels, like so:

   `myMovieClip_mc.y=50;`

   This statement positions the movie clip called `myMovieClip_mc` 50 pixels from the top edge of the Stage.

5. Test your movie (Control > Test Movie).

   Both statements change the original horizontal and vertical position of the movie clip called `myMovieClip_mc` on the Stage (**Figure 7.3**).

Figure 7.2 This movie clip instance on the Stage is called `myMovieClip_mc`.

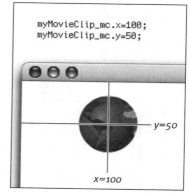

Figure 7.3 The instance moves position.

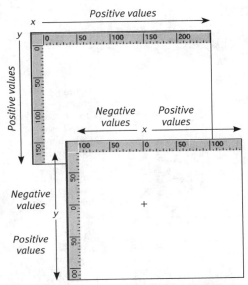

Figure 7.4 The coordinate space for the Stage (top). The x position increases from the left and the y position increases from the top. The coordinate space for a movie clip (bottom) can go into negative values.

```
myMovieClip_mc.rotation=45;
```

Figure 7.5 The original instance (top) rotates clockwise as a result of the new value assigned to the rotation property.

■ The x- and y-coordinate space for the main Timeline is different from movie clip timelines. In the main Timeline, the x-axis begins at the left edge and increases to the right; the y-axis begins at the top edge and increases to the bottom. Thus, x = 0, y = 0 corresponds to the top-left corner of the Stage. For movie clips, the coordinates x = 0, y = 0 correspond to the registration point (the crosshair). The value of x increases to the right of the registration point and decreases into negative values to the left of the registration point. The value of y increases to the bottom and decreases into negative values to the top (**Figure 7.4**).

To change the rotation of an object:

◆ In the Actions panel, assign a number to the property rotation of an instance, like so:

```
myMovieClip_mc.rotation=45;
```

This statement rotates the movie clip called myMovieClip_mc 45 degrees clockwise from its registration point (**Figure 7.5**).

CHANGING VISUAL PROPERTIES

231

To change the 3D rotation of an object:

◆ In the Actions panel, assign a number to the property rotationX, rotationY, or rotationZ of an instance, like so:

`myMovieClip_mc.rotationY=45;`

This statement rotates the movie clip called `myMovieClip_mc` in 3D space around the y-axis (**Figure 7.6**).

To change the size of an object:

◆ In the Actions panel, assign a decimal to the property scaleX or scaleY of an instance, like so:

`myMovieClip_mc.scaleX=.5;`

This statement makes the movie clip called `myMovieClip_mc` scale down in the horizontal direction 50 percent of its original size (**Figure 7.7**).

or

In the Actions panel, assign a number to the property width and height of an instance, like so:

`myMovieClip_mc.width=250;`

This statement makes the movie clip called `myMovieClip_mc` change its horizontal dimension to 250 pixels (**Figure 7.8**).

✔ Tip

■ The scaleX and scaleY properties control the percentage of the original object, which is different from what may be on the Stage. For example, if you place an instance of a movie clip on the Stage and manually shrink it 50 percent with the Free Transform tool, and then you assign 1 to scaleX and assign 1 to scaleY during playback, your movie clip will double in appearance.

`myMovieClip_mc.rotationY=45;`

Figure 7.6 The original instance (top) rotates along the y-axis in 3D (like a door swinging along its vertical hinge) as a result of the new value assigned to the rotationY property.

`myMovieClip_mc.scaleX=.5;`

Figure 7.7 The original instance (top) squishes horizontally as a result of the new value assigned to the scaleX property.

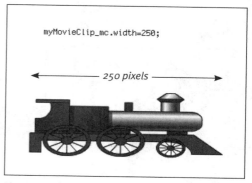
`myMovieClip_mc.width=250;`

← 250 pixels →

Figure 7.8 The instance can squish or stretch to the specified pixel dimension as a result of the new value assigned to the width property.

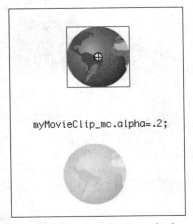

myMovieClip_mc.alpha=.2;

Figure 7.9 The original instance (top) becomes more transparent as a result of the new value assigned to the alpha property.

To change the transparency of an object:

◆ In the Actions panel, assign a decimal to the property `alpha` of an instance, like so:

`myMovieClip_mc.alpha=.2;`

This statement changes the transparency of the movie clip called `myMovieClip_mc` so it is 20 percent opaque (**Figure 7.9**).

✔ Tip

■ There is a difference between an `alpha` of 0 and a `visible` of `false`, although the result may look the same. When the `visible` property is `false`, the object literally can't be seen. Buttons and other interactive objects don't respond. When `alpha` is 0, on the other hand, buttons and other interactive objects are transparent, but can still respond.

CHANGING VISUAL PROPERTIES

Assigning values that are relative

In the previous examples, you assigned a fixed value to change various properties of objects. However, often you'll want to change an object's property relative to its current value or relative to another object's property. You may want to rotate a cannon 10 degrees each time your viewer clicks a button, for example. Or you may want to move an image to align its left edge with another image. To change the property of one object based on another object, simply reference the second object on the right side of the equals sign, like so:

```
myimage.x=myimage2.x + myimage2.width;
```

In this example, the object called myimage moves so that its left edge is aligned with the right edge of myimage2 (**Figure 7.10**).

To change an object's property based on its own current value, you can write the expression

```
myimage.rotation=myimage.rotation+10;
```

This expression adds 10 degrees to the current angle of the object named myimage. A shortcut way of writing this statement is as follows:

```
myimage.rotation+=10;
```

To assign a property that is relative to its current value:

1. Create a movie clip, place an instance on the Stage, and give it an instance name in the Property inspector.

   In this task, you'll assign a new value to the rotation property based on the object's current value of rotation. Each time you click the object, it will add 30 degrees.

2. Select the first frame of the main Timeline, and open the Actions panel.

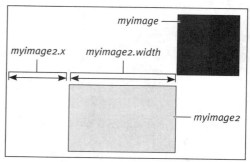

Figure 7.10 The top square (myimage) moves relative to where the bottom square (myimage2) is located.

```
clockhand_mc.addEventListener(MouseEvent.CLICK, rotate);
function rotate(myevent:MouseEvent):void {
    clockhand_mc.rotation+=30;
}
```

Figure 7.11 At each mouse click, 30 degrees is added to the current value of rotation.

Figure 7.12 The instance called clockhand_mc rotates 30 degrees at each mouse click.

3. Create an event handler by adding a listener to the movie clip to detect a mouse click, like so:

clockhand_mc.addEventListener
→ (MouseEvent.CLICK, rotate);

In this example, Flash listens for a mouse click over the movie clip called clockhand_mc and triggers a function called rotate in response.

4. On the next available line, add the event handler function as follows:

function
→ rotate(myevent:MouseEvent):void {
    clockhand_mc.rotation+=30;
}

The addition assignment operator is the plus and equals signs together. It will read the value of the rotation property, add to it the amount written to the right of the operator, and store the result back in the property's value (**Figure 7.11**).

5. Test your movie (Control > Test Movie). Each time the movie clip is clicked, Flash will get the current value of clockhand_mc and rotate it 30 degrees clockwise (**Figure 7.12**).

✔ **Tip**

■ You can use shortcuts like the addition assignment operator in this task to add and subtract values by using combinations of the arithmetic operators. You'll learn about these combinations in Chapter 9, "Controlling Information Flow."

Modifying the Color

To modify the color of a `DisplayObject` object, you can use the `ColorTransform` class, which provides properties to which you assign new colors or new values for the red, blue, green, and alpha channels.

Every `DisplayObject` has a `transform` property, which is an instance of the `Transform` class. The `Transform` object contains a snapshot of all the transformations that have been applied to the object, including color changes, scaling, rotation, and more. The color changes are specifically defined in another property called `colorTransform`, which is an instance of the `ColorTransform` class. So you can retrieve or assign color transformations by referencing the target path `myimage.transform.colorTransform`, where `myimage` would be the name of the object you want to modify.

The first step in modifying an object's color is instantiating a new `ColorTransform` object. Then you define color changes as a new value of the `color` property of your new `ColorTransform` object. Your code would look similar to this:

```
var mynewcolor:ColorTransform = new
ColorTransform();

mynewcolor.color=0x0D69F2;
```

In this example, `mynewcolor` is the name of your new `ColorTransform` object. The new value of the `color` property is in the form 0xRRGGBB (hexadecimal equivalents for the red, green, and blue components of a color). You can find the code for any color in the Color Mixer panel. Choose a color in the color spectrum, and the hexadecimal value for that color appears in the display underneath (**Figure 7.13**).

Finally, once you've defined a new color in the `color` property of your `ColorTransform` instance, you assign it to your object like this:

```
myimage.transform.colorTransform=
→ mynewcolor;
```

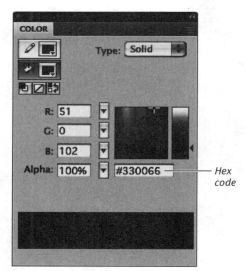

Hex code

Figure 7.13 The Color Mixer panel has a display window to show the selected RGB code in hexadecimal code.

```
var mycolorchange:ColorTransform = new ColorTransform();
```

Figure 7.14 The new `ColorTransform` object is called `mycolorchange`.

```
var mycolorchange:ColorTransform = new ColorTransform();
mycolorchange.color=0x0D69F2;
```

Figure 7.15 A new color is assigned to the `color` property of your `ColorTransform` object.

```
var mycolorchange:ColorTransform = new ColorTransform();
mycolorchange.color=0x0D69F2;
stage.addEventListener(MouseEvent.CLICK, changecolor);
function changecolor(myevent:MouseEvent):void {
    image_mc.transform.colorTransform = mycolorchange;
}
```

Figure 7.16 A mouse click will assign the new color to the `transform.colorTransform` property of the instance called `image_mc`, changing its color.

Figure 7.17 The original instance (top) changes color (bottom) when it is clicked. Notice that the entire object changes color.

To set the color of an object:

1. Create a movie clip symbol whose color you want to modify, place an instance of it on the Stage, and name it in the Property inspector. This example uses a movie clip, but you can change the color of any `DisplayObject` or `DisplayObjectContainer`.

2. Select the first frame of the main Timeline, and open the Actions panel.

3. Create a new instance from the `ColorTransform` class (**Figure 7.14**).

4. On the next line, enter the instance name of your new `ColorTransform` object, then a dot, the `color` property, and equals sign, and then the six-digit hexadecimal code for your new color (**Figure 7.15**).

5. Assign an event handler to detect a mouse click. When you click on the Stage, you will change the color of your movie clip.

6. Within the body of the event handler function, enter a statement that assigns your new `ColorTransform` object to the movie clip's `transform.colorTransform` property. The full code including the event handler is shown in **Figure 7.16**.

7. Test your movie (Control > Test Movie). In the first frame, a `ColorTransform` object is instantiated and a new value is assigned to its `color` property. When you click the Stage, your `ColorTransform` object is assigned to your movie clip, changing its color (**Figure 7.17**).

MODIFYING THE COLOR

237

Making advanced color transformations

The property color lets you change only an object's color. To change its brightness or its transparency, or change each red, green, or blue component separately, you must specify multiplier and offset properties. There is one property to define a multiplier and one to specify an offset value for each of the RGB components as well as the alpha (transparency). These properties are the same as those in the Advanced Effect dialog box that appears when you apply an advanced color effect to an instance (**Figure 7.18**). The only difference is that in the dialog box you specify the multiplier as a percentage (0–100); but in ActionScript, the multiplier properties are set as decimal numbers. A multiplier is usually in the range 0–1, which corresponds to 0–100% (for example, 25% is specified as .25). However, the multiplier can be any decimal number (such as 2 to double the value, for instance).

You can specify multiplier and offset properties in two ways. The ColorTransform class has individual multiplier and offset properties for each color channel, described in **Table 7.2**. To change just one of these properties, assign a new value to the appropriate property.

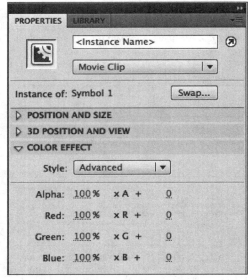

Figure 7.18 The options for advanced effects in the Property inspector control the RGB and alpha percentages and offset values for any instance.

Table 7.2

ColorTransform Properties

PROPERTY	VALUE
redMultiplier	Decimal number to multiply by the red component.
redOffset	Offset (–255 to 255) of the red component.
greenMultipler	Decimal number to multiply by the green component.
greenOffset	Offset (–255 to 255) of the green component.
blueMultiplier	Decimal number to multiply by the blue component.
blueOffset	Offset (–255 to 255) of the blue component.
alphaModifier	Decimal number to multiply by the alpha (transparency).
alphaOffset	Offset (–255 to 255) of the alpha (transparency).
color	Hex color (0xRRGGBB). Setting this property sets the offset and multiplier properties accordingly.

You may want to set several of the multiplier or offset properties for a `ColorTransform` instance, which is cumbersome to do one property at a time. As an alternative, you can specify the multiplier and offset values as parameters when you call the constructor function to create your `ColorTransform` instance. To set the properties as parameters in the constructor function, you must specify all eight in the following order: red multiplier, green multiplier, blue multiplier, alpha multiplier, red offset, green offset, blue offset, alpha offset. Here's an example:

```
var mynewcolor:ColorTransform = new
→ ColorTransform (1,.3, .2, 1, 0, 0,
→ 0, 0);
```

When you call the `ColorTransform` constructor without parameters as you did previously, the `ColorTransform` object is created with the default parameters that maintain the movie clip's color—1 for each multiplier and 0 for each offset.

To transform the color and alpha of an object:

1. Create a movie clip symbol whose color you want to modify, place an instance of it on the Stage, and name it in the Property inspector. This example uses a movie clip, but you can change the color of any `DisplayObject` or `DisplayObjectContainer`.

2. Select the first frame of the main Timeline, and open the Actions panel.

3. Create a new instance from the `ColorTransform` class. Provide eight parameters in the constructor function for the RGB and alpha multipliers and the RGB and alpha offset values (**Figure 7.19**).

   The properties for the color transformation are defined in the parameters of your `ColorTransform` constructor call.

4. Assign an event handler to detect a mouse click. When you click on the Stage, you will change the color of your movie clip.

5. Within the body of the event handler function, enter a statement that assigns your new `ColorTransform` object to the movie clip's `transform.colorTransform` property. The full code, including the event handler, is shown in **Figure 7.20**.

Continues on next page

```
var mycolorchange:ColorTransform = new ColorTransform(1, .3, .2, 1, 0, 0, 0, 0);
```

Figure 7.19 A new `ColorTransform` object is created with red, green, blue, and alpha multiplier and offset values assigned as properties at the same time.

```
var mycolorchange:ColorTransform = new ColorTransform(1, .3, .2, 1, 0, 0, 0, 0);
stage.addEventListener(MouseEvent.CLICK, changecolor);
function changecolor(myevent:MouseEvent):void {
    image_mc.transform.colorTransform = mycolorchange;
}
```

Figure 7.20 A mouse click will assign the color changes to the `transform.colorTransform` property of the instance called `image_mc`, changing its color and/or alpha.

MODIFYING THE COLOR

6. Test your movie (Control > Test Movie).

In the first frame, a `ColorTransform` object is instantiated and the new color properties are defined. When you click your movie clip, your `ColorTransform` object is assigned to your movie clip, changing its color and transparency (**Figure 7.21**).

✔ Tip

■ If you don't want to define the color transformation values when you instantiate your new `ColorTransform` instance, you can do so by specifying a value for each property, like so:

```
var mynewcolor:ColorTransform=new
 → ColorTransform();
mynewcolor.redMultiplier=.3;
mynewcolor.greenMultiplier=.2;
mynewcolor.blueMultiplier=1;
mynewcolor.alphaMultiplier=1;
mynewcolor.redOffset=0;
mynewcolor.greenOffset=0;
mynewcolor.blueOffset=0;
mynewcolor.alphaOffset=0;
image_mc.transform.colorTransform =
 → mynewcolor;
```

In this example, the transparency doesn't change, but the colors shift to a bluer hue.

Figure 7.21 The original image (top) is assigned new color values for its RGB and alpha channels, and as a result, shifts colors (bottom).

To change the brightness of a movie clip:

◆ Increase the offset parameters for the red, green, and blue components equally, but leave the other parameters unchanged.

If your `ColorTransform` object is called mynewcolor, for example, set its properties individually as follows to increase the brightness about 50 percent:

```
mynewcolor.redMultiplier = 1;
mynewcolor.greenMultiplier = 1;
mynewcolor.blueMultiplier = 1;
mynewcolor.alphaMultiplier = 1;
mynewcolor.redOffset = 125;
mynewcolor.greenOffset = 125;
mynewcolor.blueOffset = 125;
mynewcolor.alphaOffset = 0;
```

Or, instantiate your `ColorTransform` object with these parameters:

```
var mynewcolor:ColorTransform= new
→ ColorTransform(1, 1, 1, 1, 125,
→ 125, 125, 0);
```

If you want to increase the brightness completely so your object turns white, you can set the offset parameters of red, green, and blue to their maximum (255), as follows:

```
mynewcolor.redMultiplier = 1;
mynewcolor.greenMultiplier = 1;
mynewcolor.blueMultiplier = 1;
mynewcolor.alphaMultiplier = 1;
mynewcolor.redOffset = 255;
mynewcolor.greenOffset = 255;
mynewcolor.blueOffset = 255;
mynewcolor.alphaOffset = 0;
```

To change the transparency of a movie clip:

◆ Decrease either the offset or the percentage parameter for the alpha component and leave the other parameters unchanged.

Decrease alphaMultiplier to 0 or decrease alphaOffset to −255 for total transparency.

Blending Colors

If you've used a graphics manipulation program such as Photoshop or Fireworks, you've likely seen a *blend mode* option, which is a way to control how the colors of overlapping objects interact. Normally, when one object overlaps another, the object is opaque and completely blocks the object below from view. By applying a blend mode to the top object, you can change this behavior and show a mix of the colors of the two objects rather than just the color of the top object.

You can manually apply a blend mode to a movie clip or a button from within the authoring tool by selecting an instance on the Stage and choosing the desired mode from the Blending menu in the Display section of the Property inspector (**Figure 7.22**). You can also apply a blend mode using ActionScript by setting a value for a DisplayObject's blendMode property.

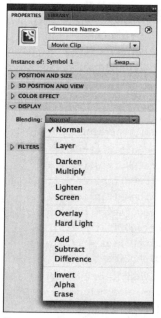

Figure 7.22 The Blending mode menu in the Property inspector.

Each of the blend modes works by examining the overlapping portions of graphical objects. The color value of each pixel from the top (or *blend*) object is taken together with the color of the pixel directly below it in the bottom (or *base*) object. The two color values are then plugged into a mathematical formula to determine the resulting color displayed in that pixel location on the screen. The blend mode you choose determines the mathematical formula that's used (and hence the output color). **Table 7.3** describes the blend modes available in Flash.

To designate a blend mode for an instance, set the blendMode property to the appropriate string, or alternatively, use the properties from the BlendMode class. The following two statements are identical:

```
myMovieClip.blendMode = "darken";
```

```
myMovieClip.blendMode =
→ BlendMode.DARKEN;
```

Figure 7.23 The top image is a movie clip called cow_mc.

Note that the `blendMode` property of the `DisplayObject` starts with a lowercase letter, but the `BlendMode` class that you reference to assign different blend modes starts with an uppercase letter.

To change color blending between two objects:

1. Create two movie clip symbols whose colors will be blended.

2. Put one instance of each symbol on the Stage, overlapping as desired. Give the top (blend) movie clip an instance name in the Property inspector (**Figure 7.23**).

3. Select the first keyframe, and open the Actions panel.

4. Enter the target path of your blend movie clip, a dot, the property `blendMode`, and then an equals sign.

Continues on next page

Table 7.3

Blend Mode Properties		
BLEND MODE	**ACTIONSCRIPT VALUE**	**DESCRIPTION**
Darken	`BlendMode.DARKEN` or `"darken"`	Color values are compared and the darker of the two is displayed, resulting in a darker image overall. Often used to create a background for (light) text.
Lighten	`BlendMode.LIGHTEN` or `"lighten"`	Lighter of the two color values is displayed, leading to a lighter image overall. Often used to create a background for (dark) text.
Multiply	`BlendMode.MULTIPLY` or `"multiply"`	Color values are multiplied to get the result, which is usually darker than either value.
Screen	`BlendMode.SCREEN` or `"screen"`	Opposite of Multiply; the result is lighter than either original color. Typically used for highlighting or flare effects.
Overlay	`BlendMode.OVERLAY` or `"overlay"`	Uses Multiply if the base color is darker than middle gray or Screen if it's lighter.
Hard Light	`BlendMode.HARDLIGHT` or `"hardlight"`	Opposite of overlay; uses Screen if the base color is darker than middle gray or Multiply if it's lighter.
Add	`BlendMode.ADD` or `"add"`	Adds the two colors together, making a lighter result. Often used for a transition between images.
Subtract	`BlendMode.SUBTRACT` or `"subtract"`	Subtracts the blend color from the base color, making the resulting color darker. Often used as a transition effect.
Difference	`BlendMode.DIFFERENCE` or `"difference"`	Darker color is subtracted from the lighter one, resulting in a brighter image, often with unnatural results.
Invert	`BlendMode.INVERT` or `"invert"`	Displays the inverse of the base color anywhere the blend clip overlaps.
Alpha	`BlendMode.ALPHA` or `"alpha"`	Creates an alpha mask. The blend clip doesn't show, but any alpha values of the blend clip are applied to the base clip, making those areas transparent. The clips must be inside another clip with Layer mode applied.
Erase	`BlendMode.ERASE` or `"erase"`	Inverse of Alpha mode. The blend clip doesn't show. Under opaque areas on the blend clip, the base clip becomes transparent; beneath transparent areas on the blend image, the base clip is visible, creating a stencil or cookie-cutter effect. The clips must be inside a Layer mode clip.
Layer	`BlendMode.LAYER` or `"layer"`	Special container blend mode in Flash. Any blends inside a display object set to Layer don't affect images outside the layer clip.
Normal	`BlendMode.NORMAL` or `"normal"`	Blend image is opaque (no blending takes place).
Shader	`BlendMode.SHADER` or `"shader"`	Used to specify a custom blending effect created with Pixel Bender (see the sidebar "What Is Pixel Bender?").

BLENDING COLORS

5. Continuing on the same line, enter a string value for the desired blend mode, or use the equivalent property from the `BlendMode` class (**Figure 7.24**).

The blend mode is applied to the blend movie clip, altering the color interaction between the two movie clips.

6. Test your movie.

The colors of the movie clips on the Stage blend together according to the blend mode selected (**Figure 7.25**).

✔ Tips

■ Blend modes can only be applied to movie clips and button instances in the authoring environment of Flash, but can be applied to all objects of the `DisplayObject` or `DisplayObjectContainer` class with ActionScript.

■ It's helpful to use the Flash authoring environment to experiment with different blend modes using the images you want to combine, even if you ultimately plan to apply the effect using ActionScript.

■ The `blendMode` properties `"erase"` and `"alpha"` (`BlendMode.ERASE` and `BlendMode.ALPHA`) work a little differently in that you need to assign `BlendMode.LAYER` or the value `"layer"` to the `blendMode` property of the parent. If you have your two movie clips on the main Stage, you can set `MovieClip(root).blendMode=BlendMode.LAYER`.

```
cow_mc.blendMode=BlendMode.MULTIPLY
```

Figure 7.24 Assign the value `BlendMode.MULTIPLY` to the `blendMode` property of your instance. `BlendMode.MULTIPLY` is a constant of the `BlendMode` class that makes it easier for you to assign values.

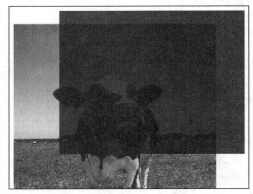

Figure 7.25 The top image interacts with the bottom image in more complex ways with color blending.

Applying Special Effects with Filters

Flash graphics can look nice, but it's the little finishing touches that make a good graphic into a great one. These finishing touches are usually subtle—the soft glow of light emanating from a mysterious orb or the drop shadow behind an object that creates a sense of depth. As mentioned in Chapter 1, "Building Complexity," Flash includes a number of filter effects that can be used to create these finishing touches as well as complex graphic manipulation. These filter effects are built into the Flash Player, so using them adds nothing to the download size of your SWF file. Because this is Flash, you can add these effects not only within the authoring environment but also dynamically using ActionScript. In fact, in addition to the filters available with the drawing tools, four filters—the Convolution filter, the Color Matrix filter, the Displacement Map filter, and the Shader filter—can only be applied using ActionScript.

Each filter is represented as a class in ActionScript (**Table 7.4**). To apply a filter effect to an object, you first create an instance of the filter you want. Each filter can be customized with several values, which are usually set as parameters of the constructor function that is called to create the filter object, like this:

```
var myBlur:BlurFilter = new BlurFilter
→ (3, 0, 1);
```

Once you have defined one or more filter objects, you apply them to a `DisplayObject` instance to take effect. Objects of the `DisplayObject` class have a `filters` property that takes an `Array` (an object that is a set of objects or values) containing one or more filter objects. (You'll learn more about the `Array` class in Chapter 11, "Manipulating Information.") This allows a single `DisplayObject` to be affected by multiple filters—for example, an object can have a beveled edge and also cast a drop shadow. Most often, you can create the `Array` instance and assign it to the `filters` property in a single statement. Pass your filter object or objects as parameters of the new `Array` constructor function, like this:

```
myimage_mc.filters = new Array(myBlur);
```

When you pass objects as parameters to the `Array` constructor, those objects are automatically added into the `Array` object; in this example, the `new Array()` constructor function creates a new `Array` object, and the object passed as a parameter (the filter object) is added into the array. The `Array` instance is then

Continues on next page

Table 7.4

Filter Classes

FILTER CLASS NAME	DESCRIPTION
BevelFilter	Adds a beveled edge to an object, making it look three dimensional
BlurFilter	Makes an object looked blurred
ColorMatrixFilter	Performs complex color transformations on an object
ConvolutionFilter	A highly customizable filter that can be used to create unique filter effects beyond those included with Flash by combining pixels with neighboring pixels in various ways
DisplacementMapFilter	Shifts pixel values according to values in a map image to create a textured or distorted effect
DropShadowFilter	Adds a drop shadow to an object
GlowFilter	Adds a colored halo around an object
GradientBevelFilter	Like the Bevel filter, with the additional ability to specify a gradient color for the bevel
GradientGlowFilter	Like the Glow filter, with the additional ability to specify a gradient color for the glow
ShaderFilter	Applies a custom filter made with Pixel Bender (see the sidebar "What Is Pixel Bender?")

stored in the object's `filters` property, causing any filter objects it contains (just one, in this case) to be applied to the target object.

In the next task, you'll see how to apply a drop-shadow filter to a movie clip. The procedure for applying any other filter to a `DisplayObject` is the same; the only difference is that with each one, you use the specific parameters for that filter when calling the constructor function to create the filter object.

To dynamically add a drop-shadow filter effect:

1. For this example, create a movie clip symbol; place an instance on the Stage, and give it an instance name in the Property inspector.

2. Select the first keyframe, and open the Actions panel.

3. Instantiate a `DropShadowFilter`, like so:

   ```
   var dropshadow:DropShadowFilter=new
   → DropShadowFilter();
   ```

   The filter's constructor function is added without parameters. (You'll add them next.)

4. Between the parentheses, enter values separated by commas as parameters for the constructor function (**Figure 7.26**).

   The `DropShadowFilter` constructor takes up to 11 parameters, which match different options. However, they're all optional, and you can specify just some of them if you wish. To get you started, the first six are the offset distance (a number of pixels), the shadow angle (a number of degrees), the shadow color (a hexadecimal numeric color value), alpha (a number from 0 to 1), and `blurX` and `blurY` (both numbers).

5. On the next line, enter your target object's name, a dot, and then the property `filters`.

6. On the same line, enter an equals sign and the constructor `new Array()`.

   This creates a new `Array` object.

7. Between the parentheses of the `Array` constructor, enter the name of your filter object (**Figure 7.27**).

   Your filter object is added into the new `Array` as it's created. The `Array` is assigned to the `filters` property of your movie clip and the filter takes effect.

```
var dropshadow:DropShadowFilter=new DropShadowFilter(25, 45, 0x000000, .7,20, 20);
```

Figure 7.26 Create a new filter. Each filter has its own set of properties that you define when you create a new instance. This `DropShadowFilter` object makes a shadow at 25 pixels distance, 45 degrees, with a black color, at 70% alpha, and with a horizontal and vertical blur of 20.

```
var dropshadow:DropShadowFilter=new DropShadowFilter(25, 45, 0x000000, .7,20, 20);
myimage_mc.filters=new Array(dropshadow);
```

Figure 7.27 The new filter object is put in the `filters` array of your movie clip.

Figure 7.28 This image of a ball has a drop shadow automatically generated from the `DropShadowFilter`.

8. Test your movie.

Your movie clip instance on the Stage has a drop shadow applied with the properties you specified (**Figure 7.28**).

To dynamically remove a filter effect:

1. Enter the target path for your object, a dot, and then the property `filters`.

2. On the same line, enter an equals sign and the constructor `new Array()`.

You assign a new array with no filters, effectively removing any existing filters on your object.

✔ Tips

- Because the `filters` property accepts an `Array`, you can apply multiple filters to an object. To add multiple filters to an object, instantiate all the filter objects first, and then add them all as parameters to the `new Array()` constructor that is assigned to the `filters` property (step 7). For instance, if you create two filter objects named `filter1` and `filter2`, this line of code applies both filters to a movie clip named `myimage_mc`:

  ```
  myimage_mc.filters = new
  → Array(filter1, filter2);
  ```

- When applying filters to a `BitmapData` object, you must use the method `applyFilter()` instead of the `filters` property.

Creating Drag-and-Drop Interactivity

Drag-and-drop behavior gives the viewer one of the most direct interactions with the Flash movie. Nothing is more satisfying than grabbing a graphic on the screen, moving it around, and dropping it somewhere else. It's a natural way of interacting with objects, and you can easily give your viewers this experience. Creating drag-and-drop behavior in Flash involves two basic steps: creating the graphic and then assigning an event handler that triggers the drag action on the graphic.

Usually, during drag-and-drop interactivity, the dragging begins when the viewer presses the mouse button with the pointer over the graphic. When the mouse button is released, the dragging stops. Hence, the action to start dragging is tied to a `MouseEvent.MOUSE_DOWN` event, and the action to stop dragging is tied to a `MouseEvent.MOUSE_UP` event.

In many cases, you may want the draggable graphic to snap to the center of the user's pointer as it's being dragged rather than wherever the user happens to click, described in the task "To center the draggable object," or you may want to limit the area where viewers can drag graphics, as described in the task "To constrain the draggable object."

The methods `startDrag()` and `stopDrag()` are methods of the `Sprite` class, which is a general `DisplayObjectContainer` class for handling graphics. It is similar to the `MovieClip` class, but it does not contain a Timeline. Movie clip objects are a subclass of the `Sprite` class. In these examples, you'll use movie clips as the draggable graphics.

To start dragging an object:

1. Create a movie clip symbol, place an instance of it on the Stage, and name it in the Property inspector (**Figure 7.29**).

2. Select the first frame of the main Timeline, and open the Actions panel.

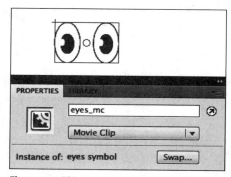

Figure 7.29 This movie clip instance on the Stage is called eyes_mc.

```
eyes_mc.addEventListener(MouseEvent.MOUSE_DOWN, startDragging);
function startDragging(myevent:MouseEvent):void {
    eyes_mc.startDrag();
}
```

Figure 7.30 The `MouseEvent.MOUSE_DOWN` event handler to make the movie clip instance start dragging.

```
eyes_mc.addEventListener(MouseEvent.MOUSE_UP, stopDragging);
function stopDragging(myevent:MouseEvent):void {
    eyes_mc.stopDrag();
}
```

Figure 7.31 The `MouseEvent.MOUSE_UP` event handler to make the movie clip instance stop dragging.

3. Enter the name of your movie clip, a dot, and then the method `addEventListener()`. In between the parentheses of the method, enter `MouseEvent.MOUSE_DOWN` and a name for a function, as follows:

```
eyes_mc.addEventListener
→ (MouseEvent.MOUSE_DOWN,
→ startDragging);
```

The completed statement listens for a `MOUSE_DOWN` event and triggers the function called `startDragging` if it detects that event.

4. On the next line, create the function called `startDragging` with a `MouseEvent` parameter. In between the curly braces of the function, enter the name of your movie clip followed by the method `startDrag()`, like so:

```
function
→ startDragging(myevent:MouseEvent):
→ void{
    eyes_mc.startDrag();
}
```

The movie clip called `eyes_mc` will be dragged when this function is called (**Figure 7.30**).

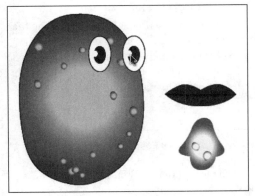

Figure 7.32 The movie clip instances of the eyes, lips, and nose can be dragged and dropped around the Stage to build a simple interaction.

5. Test your movie.

When your pointer is over the movie clip and you press your mouse button, you can drag the clip around.

To stop dragging an object:

1. Using the file you created in the preceding task, select the first frame of the timeline and open the Actions panel.

2. On a new line, enter the name of your movie clip, a dot, and then the method `addEventListener()`. In between the parentheses of the method, enter `MouseEvent.MOUSE_UP` and a name for a function, as follows:

```
eyes_mc.addEventListener
→ (MouseEvent.MOUSE_UP, stopDragging);
```

The completed statement listens for a `MOUSE_UP` event and triggers the function called `stopDragging` if it detects that event.

3. On the next line, create the function called `stopDragging` with a `MouseEvent` parameter. In between the curly braces of the function, enter the name of your movie clip followed by the method `stopDrag()`, like so:

```
function
→ stopDragging(myevent:MouseEvent):
→ void{
    eyes_mc.stopDrag();
}
```

The movie clip called `eyes_mc` will stop being dragged when this function is called (**Figure 7.31**).

4. Test your movie.

When your pointer is over the movie clip and you press your mouse button, you can drag it. When you release your mouse button, the dragging stops (**Figure 7.32**).

Continues on next page

✔ Tips

- Only one movie clip or sprite can be dragged at a time using this method.

- If you have multiple objects that you want the user to drag and drop, you can make your function more generic and refer to the target of the mouse click. Use the target property of the MouseEvent object to call the startDrag() and stopDrag() methods, like so:

```
function
→ startDragging(myevent:MouseEvent):
→ void{
    myevent.target.startDrag();
}
function stopDragging(myevent:
→ MouseEvent):void{
    myevent.target.stopDrag();
}
```

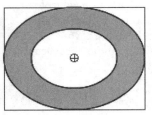

Figure 7.33 If this movie clip (which has an empty space in the middle) were to be dragged and the lockCenter parameter set to true, the mouse pointer would hover over the middle and not be able to stop the dragging motion.

To center the draggable object:

◆ Place your pointer inside the parentheses for the startDrag() method, and enter the Boolean value true, as in startDrag(true).

The startDrag() method's first parameter, lockCenter, is set to true. After you press the mouse button when your pointer is over the movie clip to begin dragging, the registration point of your movie clip snaps to the mouse pointer.

✔ Tip

- If you set the lockCenter parameter to true, make sure the area of your object covers its registration point. If it doesn't, then after the object snaps to your mouse pointer, your pointer will no longer be over any graphic area and Flash won't be able to detect when to stop the drag action (**Figure 7.33**).

To constrain the draggable object:

1. Insert a new line in the Actions panel and create a new object of the Rectangle class with four parameters—x-position, y-position, width, and height—like so (**Figure 7.34**):

```
var myBoundaries:Rectangle=new
→ Rectangle(20,30,100,50);
```

The Rectangle object is used to define the boundaries of the draggable motion. The Rectangle object isn't an actual visible graphic, but just an abstract object to help do geometric manipulations.

```
var myBoundaries:Rectangle=new Rectangle(20,30,100,50);
```

Figure 7.34 The boundaries of a dragging motion can be restricted by first creating a Rectangle object to act as the boundaries.

2. Place your pointer inside the parentheses for the startDrag() method, and enter true or false for its first parameter (the lockCenter parameter), then a comma, and then the name of your Rectangle object (**Figure 7.35**).

The pixel coordinates of your Rectangle object are relative to the container object in which the movie clip resides. If the draggable movie clip sits on the Stage, the pixel coordinates correspond to the Stage. If the draggable movie clip is within another object, the coordinates refer to the registration point of the parent (**Figure 7.36**).

✔ Tips

■ You can use the dimensions of the Rectangle object to force a dragging motion along a horizontal or a vertical track, as in a scroll bar. Set the width of your Rectangle object to 1 pixel to restrict the motion to up and down, or set the height of your Rectangle object to 1 pixel to restrict the motion to left and right.

■ To define the Rectangle object as the second parameter to constrain the draggable motion, you must also set the startDrag() method's first parameter (lockCenter) to true or false.

■ A shortcut to coding the Rectangle boundary is to create the new Rectangle object within the startDrag() method. The following statement is also valid:

```
eyes_mc.startDrag (false, new
→ Rectangle(0,0,100,20));
```

```
var myBoundaries:Rectangle=new Rectangle(20,30,100,50);
eyes_mc.startDrag(true, myBoundaries);
```

Figure 7.35 Use the Rectangle object as the second parameter in the startDrag() method to constrain the drag motion.

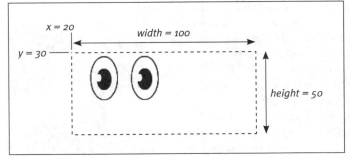

Figure 7.36 The x- and y-coordinates of the eyes_mc object are constrained by the bounds of the Rectangle object.

CREATING DRAG-AND-DROP INTERACTIVITY

Detecting Collisions

Now that you can make an object that can be dragged around the Stage, you'll want to know where the user drops it. If the objects are puzzle pieces, for example, you need to know whether those pieces are dragged and dropped on the correct spots.

It's also valuable to check whether an object intersects another object. The game of Pong, for example, detects collisions between the ball, the paddles, and the wall.

To detect dropped objects or colliding objects, use one of two methods of the DisplayObject class: hitTestObject() or hitTestPoint(). The first method lets you check whether the bounding boxes of any objects intersect. The *bounding box* of an object is the minimum rectangular area that contains the graphics. This method is ideal for graphics colliding with other graphics, such as a ball with a paddle, a ship with an asteroid, or a puzzle piece with its correct resting spot. In the following example, if the object ball intersects with the object called paddle, the method returns a value of true:

```
ball.hitTestObject(paddle);
```

The second method checks whether a certain x-y coordinate intersects with an object. This method is point specific, which makes it ideal for checking whether only the registration point of a graphic or the mouse pointer intersects with an object. In this case, the hitTestPoint() method is used, and you provide an x value, a y value, and the shapeflag parameter (which is true or false). The shapeflag parameter indicates whether Flash should use the bounding box of an object (false) or the shape of the graphics it contains (true) in deciding if the point is in contact with the object (**Figure 7.37**).

The hitTestObject() and hitTestPoint() methods work for all objects in the DisplayObject class, but in the following examples, you'll just use movie clip objects.

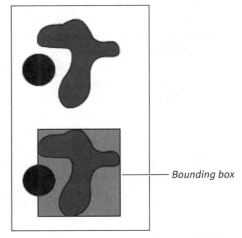

Figure 7.37 When the shapeFlag is true (top), then according to Flash, the two objects aren't intersecting; only the shapes are considered. When the shapeFlag parameter is false (bottom), the two objects are intersecting because the bounding box is considered.

To detect an intersection between two objects:

1. Create a movie clip, place an instance of it on the Stage, and name it in the Property inspector.

2. Create another movie clip, place an instance of it on the Stage, and name it in the Property inspector.

3. Select the first frame of the main Timeline and open the Actions panel; assign actions to make the second movie clip instance draggable.

4. Create a new line in the Script pane at the end of the current script, and add an event listener to detect the `Event.ENTER_FRAME` event (**Figure 7.38**).

   The `Event.ENTER_FRAME` event occurs at the frame rate of the movie, which makes it ideal for checking the `hitTestObject()` method continuously.

5. On the next line, create the function that gets triggered for the `ENTER_FRAME` event. In between the curly braces of the function, enter the word `if`, then a set of parentheses.

6. For the condition (between the parentheses), enter the name of the draggable movie clip followed by a period, and then enter `hitTestObject()`.

7. Within the parentheses of the `hitTestObject()` method, enter the name of the stationary movie clip.

8. Immediately after the `hitTestObject()` method, enter two equals signs followed by the Boolean value `true`.

9. Enter a set of curly braces to complete the `if` statement. In between those curly braces, choose an action to be performed when this condition is met.

   The final script should look like **Figure 7.39**.

10. Test your movie (**Figure 7.40**).

Continues on next page

```
spaceship_mc.startDrag(true);
stage.addEventListener(Event.ENTER_FRAME, detectCollision);
```

Figure 7.38 The `Event.ENTER_FRAME` event happens continuously at the frame rate of your Flash movie.

```
spaceship_mc.startDrag(true);
stage.addEventListener(Event.ENTER_FRAME, detectCollision);

function detectCollision(myevent:Event):void {
    if (spaceship_mc.hitTestObject(asteroid_mc)==true) {
        spaceship_mc.nextFrame();
    }
}
```

Figure 7.39 Flash monitors the intersection between the two objects `spaceship_mc` and `asteroid_mc`. If there is a collision, the `spaceship_mc` movie clip advances to the next frame.

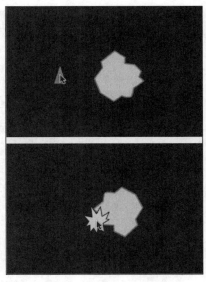

Figure 7.40 Dragging the `spaceship_mc` movie clip into the bounding box of the `asteroid_mc` movie clip advances the spaceship movie clip to the next frame, which displays an explosion.

DETECTING COLLISIONS

✔ Tips

■ When you're checking `true`/`false` values (known as *Boolean values*) in an `if` statement as you do in this task, you can test the value and leave out the last part, `== true`. Flash returns `true` or a `false` when you call the `hitTestObject()` method, and the `if` statement tests `true` and `false` values. You'll learn more about conditional statements in Part IV, "Working with Information."

■ It doesn't matter whether you test the moving movie clip to the target or the target to the moving movie clip. The following two statements detect the same collision:

```
spaceship.hitTestObject(asteroid);
asteroid.hitTestObject(spaceship);
```

To detect an intersection between a point and an object:

1. Continuing with the same file you created in the preceding task, select the first frame of the main Timeline and open the Actions panel.

2. Place your pointer within the parentheses of the `if` statement.

3. Change the condition so it reads as follows:

   `asteroid_mc.hitTestPoint`
   → `(spaceship_mc.x, spaceship_mc.y,`
   → `true)`

   The `hitTestPoint()` method now checks whether the x and y positions of the draggable movie clip `spaceship_mc` intersect with the shape of the movie clip `asteroid_mc` (**Figure 7.41**).

4. Test your movie.

✔ Tip

■ The properties `mouseX` and `mouseY` are values of the current x and y positions of the pointer on the screen. You can use these properties in the parameters of the `hitTestPoint()` method to check whether the pointer intersects a movie clip. This expression returns `true` if the pointer intersects the movie clip `asteroid_mc`:

   `asteroid_mc.hitTestPoint(mouseX,`
   → `mouseY, true)`

```
spaceship_mc.startDrag(true);
stage.addEventListener(Event.ENTER_FRAME, detectCollision);

function detectCollision(myevent:Event):void {
    if (asteroid_mc.hitTestPoint(spaceship_mc.x, spaceship_mc.y, true)==true) {
        spaceship_mc.nextFrame();
    }
}
```

Figure 7.41 The ActionScript (above) tests whether the registration point of the `spaceship_mc` movie clip intersects with any shape in the `asteroid_mc` movie clip. Notice that the spaceship is safe from collision because its registration point is within the crevice and clear of the asteroid.

Generating Graphics Dynamically

Creating graphics on the fly—that is, during playback—opens a new world of exciting interactive possibilities. Imagine a game of Asteroids in which enemy spaceships appear as the game progresses. You can store those enemy spaceships as movie clip symbols in your Library and create instances on the Stage with ActionScript as you need them. Or, if you want an infinite supply of a certain draggable item (such as merchandise) to be pulled off the shelf of an online store, you can make a duplicate of the object each time the viewer drags it away from its original spot. Or you can create entirely new graphics by drawing lines, shapes, and curves with solid color or gradients. All the while, you maintain the power to modify properties and control color, blending, and filters for those objects.

Flash provides many different ways to dynamically generate graphics, and in the previous chapter, you learned about some of them (by loading external images). All the processes begin with creating a new `DisplayObject` or `DisplayObjectContainer` with the constructor function, `new`. To create a new `Sprite` object, for example, you can use `var myNewSprite:Sprite=new Sprite()`. The next step would be to do something with the new object (which depends on what kind of object you decided to create), and then display the object by putting it on the display list with `addChild()`. The challenge is knowing which object of the `DisplayObject` or `DisplayObjectContainer` class to choose from. Among the considerations:

◆ Create a new `Loader` object to load in an external image or SWF (discussed in the previous chapter).

◆ Create a new `Sprite` object or `MovieClip` object for interactivity like drag-and-drops, for dynamic drawing, and for attaching other `DisplayObject` or `DisplayObjectContainer` objects with `addChild()`. The `MovieClip` object differs from the `Sprite` object in that it has a Timeline.

◆ Create a new `Shape` object if you just want to use ActionScript to draw lines, curves, and shapes.

◆ Create a new `BitMap` object to display bitmap images and manipulate the data at a pixel level.

Creating new movie clips

You can dynamically create new instances of existing movie clip symbols in your Library.

You must first identify the movie clip symbol in your Library so you can reference it in ActionScript and make new instances. You do so by setting the Linkage properties in the Symbol Properties dialog box. In this panel, you indicate the class name for your movie clip and the preexisting class that you want Flash to extend to it. In essence, you are creating your own custom class for your movie clip symbol and extending a preexisting class to share its methods and properties.

To create a movie clip instance from a Library symbol:

1. Create a movie clip symbol.

   The movie clip symbol is stored in your Library.

2. From the Library Options menu, choose Properties (**Figure 7.42**).

   The Symbol Properties dialog box appears.

3. Click the Advanced button to expand the dialog box. In the Linkage section, select the Export for ActionScript check box. Leave "Export in frame 1" selected.

4. In the Class field, enter a name to identify your movie clip. Leave the Base class as flash.display.MovieClip and click OK (**Figure 7.43**).

   A dialog box may appear that warns you that your class could not be found and one will automatically be generated for you (**Figure 7.44**). Click OK. In this example, the class name for your Library symbol is BaldMan. This new class inherits from the MovieClip class, which means it has all the same methods and properties of the MovieClip class. Your class name will be used to create new instances of your movie clip. Make sure that your class name doesn't contain any periods.

5. Select the first frame of the main Timeline, and open the Actions panel.

6. On the first line, create a new instance of your movie clip symbol, referencing its class name (created in step 4), like so:

   `var Larry:BaldMan=new BaldMan();`

   A new instance of a movie clip, specifically the movie clip in your Library, is created.

Figure 7.42 Choose Properties from the Options menu in the Library.

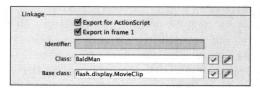

Figure 7.43 The new class name for your Library symbol here is BaldMan, and it has all the same methods and properties of the MovieClip class.

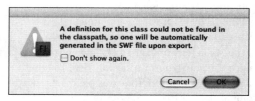

Figure 7.44 The warning dialog box, which you can ignore.

```
var Larry:BaldMan=new BaldMan();
stage.addChild(Larry);
```

Figure 7.45 Create a new instance of your Library symbol and add it to the display list.

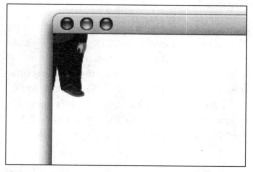

Figure 7.46 When the new instance is put on the display list, its registration point is aligned with the registration point of the `DisplayObjectContainer`. Since this instance was added to the Stage, its center point is at the top-left corner of the Stage.

7. On the next line, enter `stage`, a period, and then the method `addChild()`. Within the parentheses, put your new movie clip instance (**Figure 7.45**).

The `addChild()` method is required to add your new instance to the display list to see it. The new instance called `Larry` is put on the Stage.

8. Test the movie (**Figure 7.46**).

The default position of your new instance is at the registration point of its parent (the `DisplayObjectContainer`). So, in this example, the registration point of the new movie clip instance is at the top-left corner of the Stage. Use the properties x and y to move the new instance to your desired position.

✔ Tips

■ When you add objects to the display list, they are affected by the properties of the `DisplayObjectContainer` that you add them to. For example, suppose you create a new `Sprite` object, add it to the Stage, and change its transparency to 50 percent, like so:

```
var mySprite:Sprite=new Sprite();
stage.addChild(mySprite)
mySprite.alpha=.5
```

Now, if you created your new `BaldMan` instance and attached it to the `Sprite` object, the `BaldMan` instance would be 50 percent transparent:

```
var Larry:BaldMan=new BaldMan();
mySprite.addChild(Larry);
```

■ Objects are also affected by ActionScript that may be assigned to the `DisplayObjectContainer`. If the `DisplayObjectContainer` is draggable, for example, the added object is also draggable.

Controlling Stacking Order

When you are generating multiple DisplayObjects and putting them on the display list, you need a way to control how each one overlaps the other. If you have multiple draggable objects, you'll notice that the objects maintain their depth level even while they're being dragged, which can seem a little odd. In a drag-and-drop interaction, you expect that the item you pick up will come to the top, which requires that you control the stacking order.

Controlling the stacking order is a simple matter of reordering the objects on the display list. Recall that Flash maintains a tree-like hierarchy of the objects on the display list, giving each object an index number that determines which object is overlapping others (**Figure 7.47**).

The methods of the DisplayObjectContainer class provide several ways to access the objects on the Stage and to move them to different levels, add new objects, or remove them completely. These methods work for both dynamically generated objects as well as objects you create on the Stage manually. See **Table 7.5** for a description of the various methods.

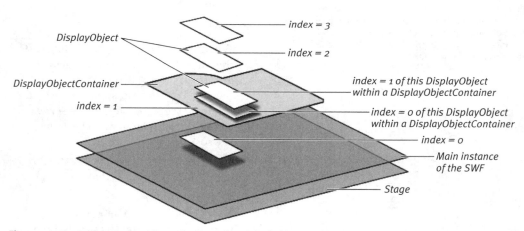

Figure 7.47 Controlling the stacking order or overlapping of objects on the display list depends on each object's index number.

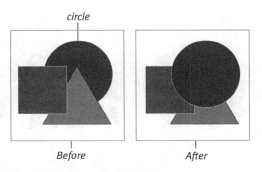

circle

Before   *After*

Figure 7.48 The result of the statement addChild(circle).

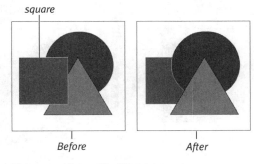

square

Before   *After*

Figure 7.49 The result of the statement setChildindex(square, 0).

To move an object to the front:

◆ Call the addChild() method as in:

addChild(circle)

The circle object is added to the top of the display list. If the object is already present on the display list, it is pulled from its current position and added to the top, and all the objects are shuffled downward and reassigned the appropriate index numbers automatically (**Figure 7.48**).

To move an object to the back:

◆ Call the setChildIndex() method and use the object name and the index number 0 as its parameters, as in:

setChildindex(square, 0)

The square object is placed at the bottom of the display list. The object must already be present on the display list (**Figure 7.49**).

or

Call the addChildAt() method and use the name of the object and the index number 0 as its parameters, as in:

addChildAt(square, 0)

Continues on next page

CONTROLLING STACKING ORDER

Table 7.5

DisplayObjectContainer Methods	
METHOD	**DESCRIPTION**
addChild(child)	Adds a child object
addChildAt(child, index)	Adds a child object at the specified index
getChildAt(index)	Retrieves the child object at the specified index
getChildByName(name)	Retrieves the child object at the specified name (a string)
getChildIndex(child)	Retrieves the index position of the child object
getObjectsUnderPoint(point)	Returns an array of objects that lie under the specified point (a Point object)
removeChild(child)	Removes a child object
removeChildAt(index)	Removes a child object at the specified index level
setChildIndex(child, index)	Changes the position of an existing child to the specified index
swapChildren(child1, child2)	Swaps the stacking order of the two specified child objects
swapChildrenAt(index1, index2)	Swaps the stacking order of two child objects at the specified index numbers

The `square` object is placed at the bottom of the display list. If the object is already present on the display list, it is pulled from its current position and placed at the bottom, and all the objects are shuffled and reassigned the appropriate index numbers automatically.

To swap two objects:

◆ Call the `swapChildren()` method and use the two objects as its parameters, as in:

`swapChildren(circle, square)`

The `circle` and the `square` objects switch places in the stacking order (**Figure 7.50**).

To remove an object:

◆ Call the `removeChild()` method and use the object as its parameter, as in:

`removeChild(triangle)`

The `triangle` object is removed from the display list and disappears from the Stage (**Figure 7.51**).

or

If you don't know the name of the object but know its index (for example, it is at the very bottom with an index of 0), use the `removeChildAt()` method and use the index number 0 as its parameter, as in:

`removeChildAt(0)`

The object at the very bottom of the display list (index 0) is removed and disappears (**Figure 7.52**).

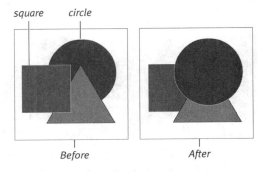

Figure 7.50 The result of the statement `swapChildren(circle, square)`.

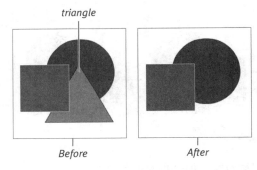

Figure 7.51 The result of the statement `removeChild(triangle)`.

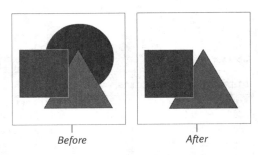

Figure 7.52 The result of the statement `removeChildAt(0)`.

Creating Vector Shapes Dynamically

Drawing vector lines, curves, and shapes, and using colors or gradients to fill those shapes, is a process that you can do with Flash's drawing tools or purely with ActionScript using the `graphics` property of the `Shape`, `Sprite`, or `MovieClip` objects. You can use the drawing methods to create your own simple paint and coloring application, or you can draw bar graphs or pie charts or connect data points to visualize numerical data that your viewer inputs.

To use the drawing methods, you must start with a new object, and the simplest is the `Shape` object. You create a new `Shape` object like any other object, with a statement such as `var myShape:Shape = new Shape()`. You can also use a `Sprite` object or a `MovieClip` object if you plan to have your object contain other objects within it (the `Shape` class is a subclass of the `DisplayObject` class, whereas

the `Sprite` and `MovieClip` classes are subclasses of the `DisplayObjectContainer` class) or if you want additional functionality that the `Shape` class doesn't provide (such as drag-and-drop). Your new object acts as the canvas that holds the drawing you create. It also acts as the point of reference for all your drawing coordinates. If you place your object at the top-left corner of the Stage (at x = 0, y = 0), all the drawing coordinates are relative to that registration point.

The `Shape`, `Sprite`, and `MovieClip` classes have a property called `graphics`. This property is an instance of the `Graphics` class, which provides many methods that enable you to create vector graphics. The process is straightforward: You define the styles of your graphics (colors, line weights, etc.), then you give Flash coordinates as to where to begin the drawing, and then you draw your lines, curves, or shapes. See **Table 7.6** for a description of the `Graphics` class drawing methods.

Table 7.6

Graphics Methods	
METHOD	**DESCRIPTION**
`beginBitmapFill(bitmap, matrix, repeat, smooth)`	Fills a drawing area with a bitmap image
`beginFill(color, alpha)`	Specifies the fill color as a hex code and transparency
`beginGradientFill(type, colors, alphas, ratios, matrix, spread, interpolation, focalpoint)`	Specifies the gradient fill
`clear()`	Clears the drawing and resets the fill and line style settings
`curveTo(controlx, controly, x, y)`	Draws a curve to the x, y point with the control points `controlx` and `controly` that determine curvature
`drawCircle(x, y, radius)`	Draws a circle at location x, y with a specified radius
`drawEllipse(x, y, width, height)`	Draws an ellipse at location x, y with a specified width and height
`drawRect(x, y, width, height)`	Draws a rectangle at location x, y with a specified width and height
`drawRoundRect(x, y, width, height, ellipsewidth, ellipseheight)`	Draws a rectangle at location x, y with a specified width and height and rounded corners
`endFill()`	Applies a fill
`lineGradientStyle(type, colors, alphas, ratios, matrix, spread, interpolation, focalpoint)`	Specifies a gradient for the line style
`lineStyle(thickness, color, alpha, pixelhinting, scalemode, caps, joints, miter)`	Specifies a line style
`lineTo(x, y)`	Draws a line to the specified x, y location
`moveTo(x, y)`	Moves the drawing position to the specified x, y location

Creating lines and curves

The lineStyle() method sets the characteristics of your stroke, such as its point size, color, and transparency. The moveTo() method sets the beginning point of your line or curve, like placing a pen on paper. The lineTo() and curveTo() methods draw lines and curves by setting the end points and, in the case of curves, determine its curvature. The clear() method erases all the drawing on an object.

Color, line width, and transparency are just the beginning of the ways you can style lines you draw in ActionScript. Flash provides additional line-style properties to control how lines scale and the style of the corners (*joints*) and ends (*caps*) of the lines you draw. You can also create lines that use a gradient rather than a solid color. All these techniques are demonstrated in the next several tasks.

To create lines:

1. Select the first frame of the main Timeline, and open the Actions panel.

2. Declare a variable with the data type Shape, enter an equals sign, and then enter new Shape() to create a new Shape instance.

   An empty Shape object is created.

3. On the next line, enter the name of your Shape object, followed by a period, followed by the property graphics; then call the lineStyle() method.

4. For the parameters of the lineStyle() method, enter a number for thickness, a hex number for the color (in the form 0xRRGGBB), and a number for the transparency (**Figure 7.53**).

   The thickness is a number from 0 to 255; 0 is hairline thickness, and 255 is the maximum point thickness.

   The RGB parameter is the hex code referring to the color of the line. You can find the hex code for any color in the Color Mixer panel below the color picker. Red, for example, is 0xFF0000.

   The transparency is a number from 0 to 1 for the line's alpha value; 0 is completely transparent, and 1 is completely opaque.

   The lineStyle() method can take up to 8 parameters, but only the first (thickness) is required.

5. On the next line, enter your Shape object's name followed by a period and the property graphics, and then call the moveTo() method.

6. With your pointer between the parentheses, enter the x- and y-coordinates where you want your line to start, separating the parameters with a comma (**Figure 7.54**).

7. On the next line, enter your Shape object's name followed by a period and the property graphics, and then call the lineTo() method.

```
var myShape:Shape = new Shape();
myShape.graphics.lineStyle(4, 0x000000, 1);
```

Figure 7.53 Define the line style (stroke thickness, color, and transparency) before you begin drawing.

```
var myShape:Shape = new Shape();
myShape.graphics.lineStyle(4, 0x000000, 1);
myShape.graphics.moveTo(0, 100);
```

Figure 7.54 The beginning of this line is at x = 0, y = 100.

8. With your pointer between the parentheses, enter the x- and y-coordinates of the end point of your line, separating the parameters with a comma (**Figure 7.55**).

The end point of your line segment automatically becomes the beginning point for the next, so you don't need to use the moveTo() method to move the coordinates.

9. If you wish, continue adding more lineTo() methods to draw more line segments.

10. On the last line, enter stage, a period, and the method addChild() with the name of your Shape object within the parentheses (**Figure 7.56**).

The lines that you drew won't be visible unless you add them to the display list.

11. Test your movie (Control > Test Movie).

```
var myShape:Shape = new Shape();
myShape.graphics.lineStyle(4, 0x000000, 1);
myShape.graphics.moveTo(0, 100);
myShape.graphics.lineTo(400, 100);
```

Figure 7.55 This straight line is drawn with a 4-point black stroke. The virtual pen tip is now positioned at x = 400, y = 100 and ready for a new lineTo() method.

```
var myShape:Shape = new Shape();
myShape.graphics.lineStyle(4, 0x000000, 1);
myShape.graphics.moveTo(0, 100);
myShape.graphics.lineTo(400, 100);
stage.addChild(myShape);
```

Figure 7.56 The code (top) draws and displays the Shape object on the Stage when you choose Control > Test Movie (below).

✔ Tips

■ You can change the line style at any time, so multiple line segments can have different thicknesses, colors, transparencies, and so forth. Add a lineStyle() method before the lineTo() method whose line you want to modify.

■ After you finish your drawing, you can modify its properties by modifying the properties of the Shape object. Or, you can affect the behavior of your drawing by calling a method. For example, if you used a Sprite or MovieClip object instead of a Shape, you could make your drawing draggable by calling its startDrag() method!

To create paths with square corners and ends:

◆ Add additional parameters to the lineStyle() call for pixel hinting, scale mode, cap style, joint style, and miter limit:

Pixel hinting takes a true/false value. With pixel hinting on, Flash draws anchor and curve points on exact pixels rather than fractions of pixels, leading to smoother curves.

Scale mode determines what happens to the line when the object's size is scaled up or down. It can be one of four values: LineScaleMode.NORMAL means lines scale normally; LineScaleMode.NONE means line thickness doesn't scale; LineScaleMode.VERTICAL means line thickness doesn't scale in the vertical direction; and LineScaleMode.HORIZONTAL means line thickness doesn't scale horizontally.

The remaining three parameters, cap style, joint style, and miter limit, are described in the sidebar "Cap and Joint Styles" on the next page.

Cap and Joint Styles

When line thickness becomes large, the corners and ends are rounded off unless you control the cap and joint styles. Three parameters of the `lineStyle()` method allow greater control over this aspect of line styling.

Figure 7.57 The three cap styles are (left to right) no caps, round, and square, drawn here with a thick line. The overlaid thin line shows the actual end point.

The **cap style** parameter controls what the start and end of the lines will look like. The three options are (**Figure 7.57**) as follows:

◆ **No cap (CapStyle.NONE):** The end falls exactly at the end coordinate, resulting in a squared-off end.

◆ **Round (CapStyle.ROUND):** The end is rounded and extends slightly beyond the end x, y coordinate to add thickness to the end.

◆ **Square (CapStyle.SQUARE):** The end is squared off and extends slightly beyond the end x, y coordinate to add thickness to the end.

Figure 7.58 The three joint styles, bevel (left), round (middle), and miter (right).

The **joint style** parameter determines the appearance of corners where two line segments are joined. These are the three options (**Figure 7.58**):

◆ **Bevel (JointStyle.BEVEL):** The corner is flattened off perpendicular to the center of the angle and extends only slightly beyond the corner x, y coordinate.

◆ **Round (JointStyle.ROUND):** The corner is rounded off and extends beyond the corner x, y coordinate.

◆ **Miter (JointStyle.MITER):** The lines continue to a point beyond the corner coordinate. The point may be chopped short depending on the miter limit setting.

The **miter limit**, which is used only when the joint style is set to `JointStyle.MITER`, determines how far an angle extends beyond the true corner point before it's chopped short. For small angles without some sort of limit, the miter joint could extend across the width of the Stage or farther; the miter limit sets constraints on the joint.

The value you set is a number between 1 and 255. How this value translates into the actual distance that the angle extends before being cut short depends on the angle of the corner and the line thickness. In general, with small angles (smaller than 45 degrees), the default limit of 3 causes some trimming. It's a good idea to experiment with the specific line thickness and angle before using miter limits in a Flash movie. **Figure 7.59** shows some examples of different miter limits.

Figure 7.59 This small angle is chopped off with miter limits of 1, 2, and 3 but extends fully with a limit of 4 or greater.

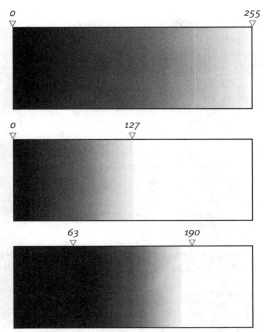

Figure 7.60 Ratios determine the mixing of colors for your gradient. The entire width of your gradient (or radius, for a radial gradient) is represented on a range from 0 through 255. Ratio values of (0,255) represent the typical gradient where each color is at one of the far sides (top). Ratio values of (0,127) create a tighter mixing in the first half of the gradient (middle). Ratio values of (63,190) create a tighter mixing in the middle of the gradient (bottom).

Creating gradient lines

Creating a solid-colored line is simple: specify the color and alpha parameters in the `lineStyle()` method. To create a line that is drawn with a *gradient* color (a color that smoothly blends between two or more colors) is more involved. To create a gradient, after calling `lineStyle()` to indicate the line thickness, you then call the `lineGradientStyle()` method, which takes various parameters that control the gradient's appearance:

Gradient type is either the value `GradientType.RADIAL` or `GradientType.LINEAR`. A radial gradient's colors are defined in rings from the inside to the outside. With a linear gradient, the colors are defined from left to right.

Colors takes an `Array` object of numeric color values. You must create an `Array` object and put the hex codes for the gradient colors into the array in the order in which you want them to appear. If you want blue on the left side of a linear gradient and red on the right side, for example, your array is created like this:

```
var colors:Array=new
 → Array(0x0000FF,0xFF0000);
```

Alphas is also an `Array` object and contains the alpha values (0 through 1) corresponding to the colors in the order in which you want them to appear. If you want your blue on one side to be 50 percent transparent, you create an array like this:

```
var alphas:Array= new Array (.5,1);
```

Ratios is an `Array` object containing values (0 through 255) that correspond to the colors, determining how they mix. The ratio value defines the point along the gradient where the color is at 100 percent. An array like `ratios = new Array(0, 127)` means that the blue is 100 percent at the left side and the red is 100 percent starting at the middle (**Figure 7.60**).

Continues on next page

CREATING VECTOR SHAPES DYNAMICALLY

Matrix type is an object that represents size, position, scale, and rotation information. You can define properties that determine the size, position, and orientation of your gradient. You create a matrix and specify width and height properties (in pixels), an angle property (in radians), and x and y offset (position) coordinates (**Figure 7.61**).

Spread method determines how the gradient behaves when the shape is larger than the gradient matrix. The parameter takes a string with one of three values: SpreadMethod.PAD fills out the shape with solid color, using the end color of the gradient; SpreadMethod.REPEAT causes the gradient pattern to repeat; and SpreadMethod.REFLECT causes the pattern to repeat in a mirror image of itself (**Figure 7.62**).

Interpolation method instructs Flash how to calculate the blend between colors. The two values are InterpolationMethod.RGB, which blends colors more directly, resulting in a less spread-out appearance, and InterpolationMethod.LINEAR_RGB, which includes intermediate colors as part of blending colors, resulting in a more spread-out gradient.

Focal point ratio controls the *focal point* (center point) of a radial gradient and takes a number between -1 and 1. Normally, the focal point is the center of the gradient (0); a value between 0 and 1 (or -1) shifts the center toward one or the other edge by that percentage. For instance, a value of -.05 shifts the focal point 50 percent between the center and the outer edge (**Figure 7.63**).

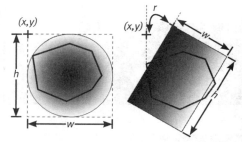

Figure 7.61 Parameters for the matrix type. A radial gradient (left) and a linear gradient (right) are shown superimposed on a shape they would fill. Its width and height are indicated by w and h; r is the clockwise angle that it makes from the vertical; x and y are the position offset coordinates for the top-left corner of the gradient.

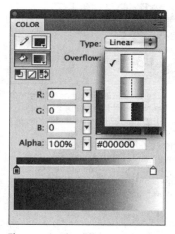

Figure 7.62 The different spread methods are the same options in the Color panel gradient Overflow options. The top option is PAD, the second is REFLECT, and the third is REPEAT.

Figure 7.63 The focal point of the gradient on the left is 0. The focal point of the gradient on the right is -0.5.

To create gradient lines:

1. As you did in the previous task, create a new `Shape` object to serve as the drawing space.

2. On the next line, call the `lineStyle()` method of the `graphics` property of your `Shape` object, and enter the line thickness parameter between the parentheses.

   The other parameters are optional and don't apply when creating gradient lines.

3. On the next line, declare and instantiate a new `Array` object to hold your gradient's colors. In the parentheses of the constructor function, enter the numeric color values (**Figure 7.64**).

4. Create another `Array` object, adding the alpha value corresponding to each color as a parameter.

   The constructor function call for this `Array` object should have the same number of parameters as the colors `Array` (**Figure 7.65**).

5. Create a third `Array` object, entering ratio values defining the distribution of the colors in the gradient.

6. Declare and instantiate a new `Matrix` object. Don't enter any parameters in the constructor function call.

7. On the next line, enter the name of your267`Matrix` object and call the `createGradientBox()` method.

   The `Matrix` class's `createGradientBox()` method is specially designed for creating `Matrix` objects to use when drawing gradients. The parameters you enter in this method call determine the size and position of the gradient.

   Continues on next page

```
var myShape:Shape = new Shape();
myShape.graphics.lineStyle(8);
var colors:Array = new Array(0x009900, 0xCC0066, 0x999999);
```

Figure 7.64 The `Array` holds the set of color values that will make up the gradient.

```
var myShape:Shape = new Shape();
myShape.graphics.lineStyle(8);
var colors:Array = new Array(0x009900, 0xCC0066, 0x999999);
var alphas:Array = new Array(1, 1, 1);
```

Figure 7.65 For each value in the colors `Array`, there is a corresponding value in the alphas `Array`.

8. Inside the parentheses of the
createGradientBox() method call, enter
parameters for width, height, rotation,
x offset position, and y offset position
(**Figure 7.66**):

Width and **height** (numbers in pixels)
determine the size of the gradient. Outside
those dimensions, the colors will end or
repeat according to the spread method
you choose.

Rotation (number in radians) indicates
how much to rotate the gradient—by
default, linear gradients go from left to
right, so if you want the gradient to go
from top to bottom or at an angle, you
must specify a rotation parameter.
Otherwise, use 0.

X and y offset (numbers in pixels) indicate at what coordinate (relative to the
Shape object's registration point) to begin
the gradient.

9. On the following line, enter your Shape
object's name, then the property graphics,
and call the lineGradientStyle() method.

The gradient properties you've specified
will be added as parameters to this
method.

10. In the parentheses, add the following
parameters: the gradient type
(GradientType.LINEAR or
GradientType.RADIAL), your colors
Array, your alphas Array, your ratios
Array, and your Matrix object. Be
sure to separate the parameters with
commas.

11. Still in the parentheses, if you wish to
do so, enter a gradient spread method,
interpolation method, and focal point
ratio (**Figure 7.67**).

```
var myShape:Shape = new Shape();
myShape.graphics.lineStyle(8);
var colors:Array = new Array(0x009900, 0xCC0066, 0x999999);
var alphas:Array = new Array(1, 1, 1)
var ratios:Array = new Array(0, 127, 255);
var matrix:Matrix = new Matrix();
matrix.createGradientBox(150, 150, 0, 10, 10);
```

Figure 7.66 The Matrix class's createGradientBox() method takes
parameters that control the gradient's position and rotation properties.

```
var myShape:Shape = new Shape();
myShape.graphics.lineStyle(8);
var colors:Array = new Array(0x009900, 0xCC0066, 0x999999);
var alphas:Array = new Array(1, 1, 1)
var ratios:Array = new Array(0, 127, 255);
var matrix:Matrix = new Matrix();
matrix.createGradientBox(150, 150, 0, 10, 10);
myShape.graphics.lineGradientStyle(GradientType.LINEAR, colors,
    alphas, ratios, matrix, SpreadMethod.REFLECT, InterpolationMethod.RGB, 0);
```

Figure 7.67 The lineGradientStyle() method takes several parameters to indicate how the
gradient will be drawn.

12. Add `moveTo()` and `lineTo()` method calls to draw lines on your Shape object's `graphics` property.

13. On the last line, enter the `addChild()` method to add the Shape object to the display list.

14. Test your movie (**Figure 7.68**).

✔ Tip

■ You must call the `lineStyle()` method before the `lineGradientStyle()` to define the stroke.

To create curved lines:

1. As you did in the previous task, create a new Shape object to serve as the drawing space.

2. On the next line, call the `lineStyle()` method of the `graphics` property of your Shape object, and enter the line thickness parameter and other optional parameters between the parentheses.

3. On the next line, enter your Shape object's name followed by a period and the property `graphics`, and then call the `moveTo()` method.

4. With your pointer between the parentheses, enter the x- and y-coordinates where you want your line to start, separating the parameters with a comma.

5. On the next line, enter your Shape object's name followed by a period and the property `graphics`, and then call the `curveTo()` method.

Continues on next page

```
var myShape:Shape = new Shape();
myShape.graphics.lineStyle(8);
var colors:Array = new Array(0x009900, 0xCC0066, 0x999999);
var alphas:Array = new Array(1, 1, 1);
var ratios:Array = new Array(0, 127, 255);
var matrix:Matrix = new Matrix();
matrix.createGradientBox(150, 150, 0, 10, 10);
myShape.graphics.lineGradientStyle(GradientType.LINEAR, colors,
    alphas, ratios, matrix, SpreadMethod.REFLECT, InterpolationMethod.RGB, 0);
myShape.graphics.moveTo(0, 200);
myShape.graphics.lineTo(300, 300);
myShape.graphics.lineTo(0, 400);
addChild(myShape)
```

Figure 7.68 The complete script (top) creates a gradient line style and uses it to color the lines that are drawn (bottom).

6. With your pointer between the parentheses, enter x- and y-coordinates for the control point and x- and y-coordinates for the end of the curve (**Figure 7.69**).

The *control point* is a point that determines the amount of curvature. If you were to extend a straight line from the control point to the end point of the curve, you would see that it functions much like the handle of a curve (**Figure 7.70**).

7. On the last line, enter the addChild() method to add the Shape object to the display list.

8. Test your movie (**Figure 7.71**).

✔ Tip

- To reduce the repetition of writing the graphics property of the Shape object, use a with statement to change the scope temporarily. For example, note the savings in having not to repeat the target path:

```
with (myShape.graphics) {
lineStyle(5, 0xff0000, 100);
moveTo(200, 100);
curveTo(300, 100, 300, 200);
curveTo(300, 300, 200, 300);
curveTo(100, 300, 100, 200);
curveTo(100, 100, 200, 100);
}
```

```
var myShape:Shape = new Shape()
myShape.graphics.lineStyle(2, 0xFF0000, 1);
myShape.graphics.moveTo(200, 200);
myShape.graphics.curveTo(300, 100, 400, 200);
```

Figure 7.69 The curveTo() method requires x- and y-coordinates for its control point and for its end point. This curve starts at (200,200) and ends at (400,200), with the control point at (300,100) (see Figure 7.70).

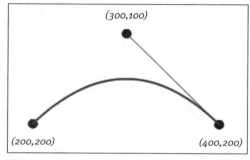

Figure 7.70 By drawing a straight line from the control point to the end point, you can visualize the curve's Bézier handle. The dots have been added to show the two anchor points and the control point.

```
var myShape:Shape = new Shape()
myShape.graphics.lineStyle(2, 0xFF0000, 1);
myShape.graphics.moveTo(200, 200);
myShape.graphics.curveTo(300, 100, 400, 200);
addChild(myShape)
```

Figure 7.71 The complete script draws and displays the curved line on the Stage.

Updating a drawing

The clear() method erases the drawings made with the Graphics drawing methods. In conjunction with an Event.ENTER_FRAME event or a Timer object, you can make Flash continually erase a drawing and redraw itself. This is how you can create curves and lines that aren't static but change.

The following task shows the dynamic updates you can make in a drawing by continuously redrawing lines.

To update a drawing dynamically:

1. As you did in the previous task, create a new Shape object to serve as the drawing space.

2. On the next line, declare a variable called counter to hold an integer data type, and assign the number 0 to it.

3. On the next line, add an event listener to detect the Event.ENTER_FRAME event (**Figure 7.72**).

4. On the next line, create the event handler function. In between the curly braces of the function, add the following statements (**Figure 7.73**):

```
myShape.graphics.clear();
myShape.graphics.lineStyle(4);
myShape.graphics.moveTo(100,100);
myShape.graphics.curveTo (150, 100+counter, 200, 100);
stage.addChild(myShape);
counter++;
```

Each time the ENTER_FRAME event happens, Flash clears the current drawing in the myShape object and creates a new curve. The curves are always a little different than the one before it, because the variable called counter adds a small amount to the curvature.

5. Test your movie (**Figure 7.74**).

The line bends dynamically, creating a smile!

```
var myShape:Shape = new Shape();
var counter:int=0;
stage.addEventListener(Event.ENTER_FRAME, updateDrawing);
```

Figure 7.72 The Event.ENTER_FRAME event will provide a way to continuously update a drawing.

```
var myShape:Shape = new Shape();
var counter:int=0;
stage.addEventListener(Event.ENTER_FRAME, updateDrawing);
function updateDrawing(myevent:Event):void {
    myShape.graphics.clear();
    myShape.graphics.lineStyle(4);
    myShape.graphics.moveTo(100,100);
    myShape.graphics.curveTo(150, 100+counter, 200, 100);
    stage.addChild(myShape);
    counter++;
}
```

Figure 7.73 Within the function, the drawing is cleared and a new curve is drawn with an increasing control point, which increases the curvature.

Figure 7.74 The curve (top) is dynamically erased and redrawn to create an animation as it bends (bottom).

Creating fills and gradients

You can fill shapes with solid colors, transparent colors, or radial or linear gradients by using the methods beginFill(), beginGradientFill(), and endFill(). Begin the shape to be filled by calling either the beginFill() or the beginGradientFill() method, and mark the end of the shape with endFill(). If your path isn't closed (the end points don't match the beginning points), Flash automatically closes it when the endFill() method is applied.

Applying solid or transparent fills with beginFill() is fairly straightforward; specify a hex code for the color and a value from 0 to 1 for the transparency. Gradients are more complex. You control the gradient by adding up to eight parameters to the beginGradientFill() method call. These parameters are the same ones used for creating gradient lines, as described earlier in this chapter.

To fill a shape with a solid color:

1. As you did in the previous task, create a new Shape object.

2. On the next line, call the lineStyle() method of the graphics property of your Shape object, and enter the line thickness parameter and other optional parameters between the parentheses.

3. On the next line, enter your Shape object's name followed by a period and the property graphics, and then call the beginFill() method.

4. With your pointer between the parentheses, enter the hex code for a color and a value for the alpha, separating your parameters with a comma (**Figure 7.75**).

5. On a new line, enter your Shape object's name followed by a period and the property graphics, and then call the moveTo() method to identify the beginning of your drawing.

```
var myShape:Shape = new Shape()
myShape.graphics.lineStyle(1, 0xFF0000, 1);
myShape.graphics.beginFill(0x7E6AE3, 1);
```

Figure 7.75 This fill is light blue at 100 percent opacity.

```
var myShape:Shape = new Shape()
myShape.graphics.lineStyle(1, 0xFF0000, 1);
myShape.graphics.beginFill(0x7E6AE3, 1);
myShape.graphics.moveTo(100, 100);
myShape.graphics.lineTo(100, 200);
myShape.graphics.lineTo(200, 200);
myShape.graphics.lineTo(200, 100);
myShape.graphics.lineTo(100, 100);
myShape.graphics.endFill();
addChild(myShape)
```

(100,100)   (200,100)

(100,200)   (200,200)

Figure 7.76 The end point of the last lineTo() method (100,100) matches the beginning point (100,100), creating a closed shape that can be filled. A blue box appears as a result of this code. The box was drawn counterclockwise from its top-left corner, but the order of line segments is irrelevant.

```
var myShape:Shape = new Shape()
var colors:Array = new Array(0xFF0000, 0x0000FF);
```

Figure 7.77 The colors array is created with blue on one side and red on the other. If this gradient will be a linear gradient, blue (0x0000FF) will be on the left. If it will be a radial gradient, blue will be in the center.

```
var myShape:Shape = new Shape()
var colors:Array = new Array(0xFF0000, 0x0000FF);
var alphas:Array = new Array(1, 1);
```

Figure 7.78 The alphas array is created with 100 percent opacity for both the blue and the red. The ratios array is created with blue on the far left side (or the center, in the case of a radial gradient) and with red on the far right side (or the edge of a radial gradient).

6. Use the lineTo() or curveTo() method to draw a closed shape.

7. When the end point matches the beginning point of your shape, enter your Shape object's name followed by a period and the property graphics, and call the method endFill().

No parameters are required for the endFill() method. Flash fills the closed shape with the specified color.

8. On the last line, enter the addChild() method to add the Shape object to the display list.

9. Test your movie (**Figure 7.76**).

To fill a shape with a gradient:

1. As you did in the previous task, create a new Shape object.

2. On the next line, declare and instantiate a new Array object to hold your gradient's colors. In the parentheses of the constructor function, enter the numeric color values (**Figure 7.77**).

By adding parameters to the new Array() statement, you instantiate a new Array object and populate the array at the same time. The first color refers to the left side of a linear gradient or the center of a radial gradient.

3. Create another Array object, adding the alpha value corresponding to each color as a parameter.

The constructor function call for this Array objects should have the same number of parameters as the colors Array (**Figure 7.78**).

4. Create a third Array object, entering ratio values defining the distribution of the colors in the gradient.

Continues on next page

5. Declare and instantiate a new `Matrix` object. Don't enter any parameters in the constructor function call.

6. On the next line, enter the name of your `Matrix` object and call the `createGradientBox()` method.

The `Matrix` class's `createGradientBox()` method is specially designed for creating `Matrix` objects to use when drawing gradients. The parameters you enter in this method call determine the size and position of the gradient.

7. Inside the parentheses of the `createGradientBox()` method call, enter parameters for width, height, rotation, x offset position, and y offset position (**Figure 7.79**):

Width and **height** (numbers in pixels) determine the size of the gradient. Outside those dimensions, the colors will end or repeat according to the spread method you choose.

Rotation (number in radians) indicates how much to rotate the gradient—by default, linear gradients go from left to right, so if you want the gradient to go from top to bottom or at an angle, you must specify a rotation parameter. Otherwise, use 0.

X and y offset (numbers in pixels) indicate at what coordinate (relative to the movie clip's registration point) to begin the gradient.

8. On the next line, call the `lineStyle()` method of the `graphics` property of your `Shape` object, and enter the line thickness parameter between the parentheses.

```
var myShape:Shape = new Shape()
var colors:Array = new Array(0xFF0000, 0x0000FF);
var alphas:Array = new Array(1, 1)
var ratios:Array = new Array(0, 255);
var matrix:Matrix = new Matrix();
matrix.createGradientBox(100, 100, 0, 100, 100);
```

Figure 7.79 The width, height, rotation, and x, y coordinates of the gradient are defined as parameters of the `createGradientBox` method call.

```
var myShape:Shape = new Shape()
var colors:Array = new Array(0xFF0000, 0x0000FF);
var alphas:Array = new Array(1, 1);
var ratios:Array = new Array(0, 255);
var matrix:Matrix = new Matrix();
matrix.createGradientBox(100, 100, 0, 100, 100);
myShape.graphics.lineStyle(5, 0xFF0000, 1);
myShape.graphics.beginGradientFill(GradientType.LINEAR,
                       colors, alphas, ratios, matrix);
```

Figure 7.80 The `beginGradientFill()` method takes several parameters that define how the gradient will be applied to the fill.

9. On the following line, enter your Shape object's name and the property graphics, and call the beginGradientFill() method. In the parentheses, add the following parameters: the gradient type (GradientType.LINEAR or GradientType.RADIAL), your colors Array, your alphas Array, your ratios Array, and your Matrix object. Be sure to separate the parameters with commas.

All the information about your gradient that you defined in your arrays and Matrix object is fed into the parameters of the beginGradientFill() method (**Figure 7.80**).

10. Still in the parentheses, if you wish to do so, enter a gradient spread method, interpolation method, and focal point ratio.

11. Add moveTo() and lineTo() method calls to draw a series of lines to create a closed shape.

12. On a new line, enter the name of your Shape object, a period, and the graphics property, and then call the endFill() method.

13. On the last line, enter the addChild() method to add the Shape object to the display list.

14. Test your movie.

Flash fills your shape with the gradient (**Figure 7.81**).

✔ Tip

■ The rotation parameter of the createGradientBox() method takes radians, not degrees. Using radians is a way to measure angles using the mathematical constant pi. To convert degrees to radians, multiply by the number pi and then divide by 180. Using the Math class for pi (Math.PI), you can use the formula:

radians = degrees * (Math.PI / 180)

```
var myShape:Shape = new Shape()
var colors:Array = new Array(0xFF0000, 0x0000FF);
var alphas:Array = new Array(1, 1)
var ratios:Array = new Array(0, 255);
var matrix:Matrix = new Matrix();
matrix.createGradientBox(100, 100, 0, 100, 100);
myShape.graphics.lineStyle(5, 0xFF0000, 1);
myShape.graphics.beginGradientFill(GradientType.LINEAR,
                    colors, alphas, ratios, matrix);
myShape.graphics.moveTo(100, 100);
myShape.graphics.lineTo(100, 200);
myShape.graphics.lineTo(200, 200);
myShape.graphics.lineTo(200, 100);
myShape.graphics.lineTo(100, 100);
myShape.graphics.endFill();
addChild(myShape)
```

Figure 7.81 The complete ActionScript code (top) creates a box with a linear gradient from blue to red (bottom).

Creating rectangles and circles

The Graphics class provides some methods to create common types of shapes—circles, rectangles, ellipses, and rectangles with rounded corners—saving you much time and effort. The following tasks lead you through creating a circle and rectangle, but the same process applies to ellipses and rounded rectangles with only different methods to consider. Refer to Table 7.6 earlier in this chapter for a description of all these methods.

When you use these methods, you still need to define the line style and the fill colors.

To create a circle:

1. Select the first frame of the main Timeline, and open the Actions panel.

2. As you did in the previous task, create a new Shape object.

3. On the next line, enter the name of your Shape object, a period, and the property graphics; then call the lineStyle() method. Enter parameters in between the parentheses to define the thickness, color, and/or transparency.

4. On the next line, enter your Shape object's name followed by a period and the property graphics, and then call the beginFill() method.

5. With your pointer between the parentheses, enter the hex code for a color and a value for the alpha, separating your parameters with a comma (**Figure 7.82**).

6. On a new line, enter your Shape object's name followed by a period and the property graphics, and then call the drawCircle() method.

7. With your pointer between the parentheses, enter a number for the x location, a number for the y location, and a number for the radius of the circle (**Figure 7.83**).

```
var myShape:Shape = new Shape();
myShape.graphics.lineStyle(1, 0xFF0000, 1);
myShape.graphics.beginFill(0x7E6AE3, 1);
```

Figure 7.82 Create a new Shape and define the line style and fill color.

```
var myShape:Shape = new Shape();
myShape.graphics.lineStyle(1, 0xFF0000, 1);
myShape.graphics.beginFill(0x7E6AE3, 1);
myShape.graphics.drawCircle(50,60,30);
```

Figure 7.83 The drawCircle() method is an easy way to create circles at any x and y position with a certain radius. This one is at x = 50, y = 60 with a 30-pixel radius.

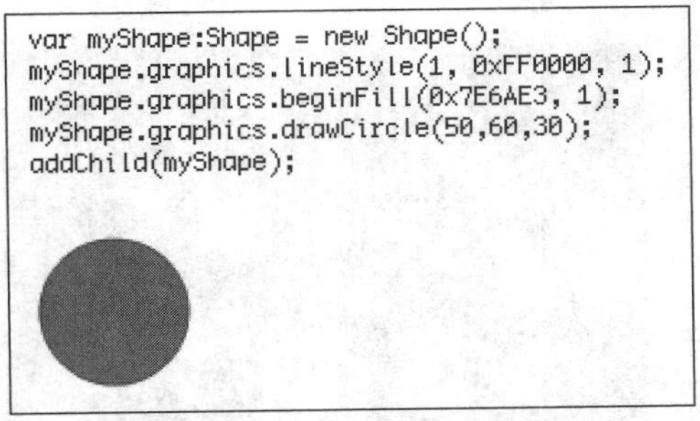

```
var myShape:Shape = new Shape();
myShape.graphics.lineStyle(1, 0xFF0000, 1);
myShape.graphics.beginFill(0x7E6AE3, 1);
myShape.graphics.drawCircle(50,60,30);
addChild(myShape);
```

Figure 7.84 The full code (top) includes the addChild() method to display the shape.

8. On the last line, enter the addChild() method to add the Shape object to the display list.

9. Test your movie.

Flash draws a circle positioned at the x and y location with the specified radius (**Figure 7.84**).

To create a rectangle:

◆ Replace steps 6–7 in the previous task with the method drawRect().

The four parameters of this method are the x and y positions of the top-left corner, and the width and height in pixels. The following statement creates a rectangle 200 pixels wide, 50 pixels tall, and snuggled in the top-left corner.

```
myShape.graphics.
drawRect(0,0,200,50)
```

✔ Tip

■ The endFill() method is unnecessary when you use the methods that automatically draw circles and squares.

Advanced Drawing Methods

In addition to the drawing methods that you've learned here, Flash Player 10 supports some new advanced drawing methods that greatly expand the dynamic drawing capabilities.

In particular, drawPath() is a new method that consolidates the moveTo(), lineTo(), and curveTo() methods in a single call to make defining shapes less code heavy. The drawPath() method relies on a special kind of an array called a *vector* and represents the drawing methods as numeric identifiers. The method also keeps track of the direction of how a shape is drawn, which is called *winding*. You can draw a shape in either a clockwise direction or a counterclockwise direction, which has implications for intersecting shapes.

Another new method, drawTriangles(), can render triangles and map images to those triangles with the purpose of distorting images for 3D rendering.

These are two of several new important additions to the ActionScript drawing tools. Although they are substantially more complicated than the methods covered here, they can be very powerful and greatly enhance what can be dynamically rendered. See the Adobe Help site for more information on the advanced methods of the Graphics class.

Using Dynamic Masks

You can turn any `DisplayObject` into a mask and specify another `DisplayObject` to be masked with `mask`, a property of the `DisplayObject` class. To do so, you simply assign one object as the `mask` property of the other. For example, in the statement `mypicture.mask=mywindow`, the object `mywindow` acts as a mask over the object `mypicture`. Recall that a mask is an area that defines the "hole" through which you can see content.

Because you can control all the properties of `DisplayObjects`, you can make your mask move or grow and shrink in response to viewer interaction. You can even combine a dynamic mask with the drawing methods you learned earlier in the chapter to create masks that change shape.

An effective combination assigns `startDrag()` and `stopDrag()` methods to a mask and creates a draggable mask. When you add `startDrag()` to a `MouseEvent.MOUSE_DOWN` handler and `stopDrag()` to a `MouseEvent.MOUSE_UP` handler, your viewer can control the position of the mask.

To set an object as a mask:

1. Create a `DisplayObject` for the object that will be masked. For this example, import a bitmap to the Stage and convert it to a movie clip symbol. In the Property inspector, give it a name (**Figure 7.85**). This movie clip will be masked.

2. Create another `DisplayObject` for the object that will act as the mask. For this example, you will create a `Shape` object and dynamically draw a shape with the `Graphics` class methods.
   This `Shape` object will act as a mask.

3. Select the first frame of the main Timeline, and open the Actions panel.

Figure 7.85 A movie clip containing a cityscape image will be the masked movie clip.

Traditional Masks

It seems counterintuitive that a mask is the area in which the masked object is visible. But if you think of a mask in terms of how a photographer or a painter uses one, it makes more sense. In traditional darkroom photography or in painting, a mask is something that protects the image and keeps it visible. A photographer would shield areas of light-sensitive paper from exposure to the light, and a painter would shield certain areas of the canvas from paint.

```
var myShape:Shape = new Shape();
myShape.graphics.beginFill(0x7E00E3, 1);
myShape.graphics.drawCircle(200,200,120);
```

Figure 7.86 A dynamic circle is drawn with the Sprite object.

```
var myShape:Shape = new Shape();
myShape.graphics.beginFill(0x7E00E3, 1);
myShape.graphics.drawCircle(200,200,120);
addChild(myShape);
cityscape_mc.mask=myShape;
```

Figure 7.87 The mask property makes the circle act as a mask over the cityscape_mc object.

✔ Tips

■ You can specify the main Timeline as the object to be masked, and all the graphics on the main Timeline will be masked. To do so, enter MovieClip(root) as the target path for the mask property.

■ The stacking order of the mask object and the masked object doesn't matter when you use ActionScript to create a mask. Either of them can be in front or in back of the other, although it is more intuitive to always keep the mask in front of the masked object.

■ If the mask object is dynamically created, it doesn't necessarily have to be added to the display list. However, if you want to change the Stage (and the objects contained in it) or if you want the user to interact with the mask, you must put it on the display list before assigning the mask property.

4. Create a new Shape object.

5. On the next line, call the beginFill() method of the Shape object's graphics property to define the color of the fill.

The actual color of the fill won't matter for the mask object, since it simply defines the area of the masked object that is visible. However, you still need to define a color.

6. On a new line, enter your Shape object's name followed by a period and the property graphics, and then call the drawCircle() method.

7. With your pointer between the parentheses, enter a number for the x location, a number for the y location, and a number for the radius of the circle (**Figure 7.86**).

8. On the next line, enter the addChild() method to add the Shape object to the display list.

Flash draws a circle positioned at the x and y locations at the specified radius.

9. On the next line, enter the name of the object that will be masked (your movie clip on the Stage), a dot, the property mask, an equals sign, and then the object that will be the mask (the Shape object).

Flash assigns the Shape object as the mask of the movie clip on the Stage.

10. Test your movie.

The circle of the Shape reveals portions of the masked movie clip (**Figure 7.87**).

To remove a mask:

◆ To remove a mask, assign the null keyword to the masked object's mask property, as follows:

```
myImage.mask=null;
```

The object called myImage will no longer be masked.

USING DYNAMIC MASKS

Transparent masks

Holes and areas with alpha transparency in the mask aren't recognized and don't normally affect the mask (**Figure 7.88**). To make the mask function with holes and/or alpha, you must set both masked and mask DisplayObjects to use runtime bitmap caching, either by selecting the "Use runtime bitmap caching" check box in the Property inspector (for objects on the Stage) or by setting the cacheAsBitmap property to true in ActionScript. Bitmap caching is a mode in which Flash treats the images as bitmaps, storing them in memory so it does not have to continuously redraw them.

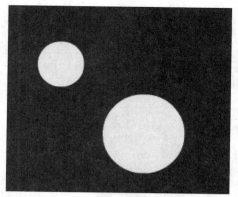

Figure 7.88 If this shape were to be assigned as the mask property, Flash would recognize only a square for the mask unless runtime bitmap caching was enabled for the objects.

Transparent masks will reveal the masked object in gradations, depending on the alpha value of the mask. This allows you to create masks with soft, feathered edges and vignette images.

To make a transparent mask:

◆ Set the cacheAsBitmap property of the mask and the masked object to true before you assign the mask property, like so:

myImage.cacheAsBitmap = true;

myShape.cacheAsBitmap = true;

myImage.mask=myShape;

The object called myShape will reveal portions of the object called myImage, according to its transparent gradient (**Figure 7.89**).

✔ Tip

■ Transparent masks only work in ActionScript. Masks created on the timeline by defining the Layer properties (described in Chapter 1) don't support alpha transparencies even when "Use runtime bitmap caching" is turned on in the Property inspector.

Figure 7.89 An object with alpha transparency (above) can create a softer, more graduated mask (below) if cacheAsBitmap is set to true.

Figure 7.90 You'll create a draggable mask to uncover this movie clip of New York City called map_mc.

```
var mySprite:Sprite = new Sprite();
mySprite.graphics.beginFill(0x7E00E3, 1);
mySprite.graphics.drawCircle(200,200,100);
addChild(mySprite);
```

Figure 7.91 A simple circle created dynamically will act as the mask. Use the Sprite object to create the circle because the Sprite class includes the startDrag() and stopDrag() methods, and the Shape object does not.

To create a draggable mask:

1. Create a DisplayObject for the object that will be masked. For this example, import a bitmap to the Stage and convert it to a movie clip symbol. In the Property inspector, give it a name (**Figure 7.90**). This movie clip will be masked.

2. Create another DisplayObject for the object that will act as the mask. For this example, you will create a Sprite object and dynamically draw a shape with the Graphics class methods.

   This Sprite object will act as a draggable mask. (You can't use a Shape object in this example because it is too simple of an object, and it doesn't support drag-and-drop methods).

3. Select the first frame of the main Timeline, and open the Actions panel.

4. Create a new Sprite object.

5. On the next line, call the beginFill() method of the Sprite object's graphics property to define the color of the fill.

6. On a new line, enter your Sprite object's name followed by a period and the property graphics, and then call the drawCircle() method.

7. With your pointer between the parentheses, enter a number for the x location, a number for the y location, and a number for the radius of the circle.

8. On the next line, enter the addChild() method to add the Sprite object to the display list.

   Flash draws a circle positioned at the x and y locations at the specified radius (**Figure 7.91**).

Continues on next page

9. On the next line, set the `buttonMode` property of the `Sprite` object to `true`.

   This allows the `Sprite` object to receive `MouseEvent` events, like the `MOUSE_DOWN` event that will be needed for a drag action.

10. On the next line, enter the name of the object that will be masked (your movie clip on the Stage), a dot, the property `mask`, an equals sign, and then the object that will be the mask (the `Sprite` object) (**Figure 7.92**).

    Flash assigns the `Sprite` object as the mask of the movie clip on the Stage.

```
var mySprite:Sprite = new Sprite();
mySprite.graphics.beginFill(0x7E00E3, 1);
mySprite.graphics.drawCircle(200,200,100);
addChild(mySprite);

mySprite.buttonMode=true;
map_mc.mask=mySprite;
```

Figure 7.92 Make sure that the `buttonMode` property for your Sprite object is set to true.

```
var mySprite:Sprite = new Sprite();
mySprite.graphics.beginFill(0x7E00E3, 1);
mySprite.graphics.drawCircle(200,200,100);
addChild(mySprite);

mySprite.buttonMode=true;
map_mc.mask=mySprite;

mySprite.addEventListener(MouseEvent.MOUSE_DOWN, startdragging);
function startdragging(myevent:MouseEvent):void {
    mySprite.startDrag();
}
mySprite.addEventListener(MouseEvent.MOUSE_UP, stopdragging);
function stopdragging(myevent:MouseEvent):void {
    mySprite.stopDrag();
}
```

Figure 7.93 The event handlers for the `MouseEvent.MOUSE_DOWN` and `MouseEvent.MOUSE_UP` events trigger the dragging and dropping actions on the `Sprite` object.

Figure 7.94 The circle becomes a draggable mask.

11. On the next lines, create the event handler to detect the MouseEvent.MOUSE_DOWN event that triggers a startDrag() method on the Sprite object as follows:

```
mySprite.addEventListener
→ (MouseEvent.MOUSE_DOWN,
→ startdragging);
function startdragging
→ (myevent:MouseEvent):void{
    mySprite.startDrag();
}
```

When the mouse button is pressed on the mask, it becomes draggable.

12. On the next lines, create the event handler to detect the MouseEvent.MOUSE_UP event that triggers a stopDrag() method on the Sprite object as follows:

```
mySprite.addEventListener
→ (MouseEvent.MOUSE_UP,
→ stopdragging);
function stopdragging
→ (myevent:MouseEvent):void{
    mySprite.stopDrag();
}
```

When the mouse is released on the mask, it stops being dragged (**Figure 7.93**).

13. Test your movie.

The Sprite acts as a mask, and the MOUSE_DOWN and MOUSE_UP handlers provide the drag-and-drop interactivity (**Figure 7.94**).

USING DYNAMIC MASKS

Customizing Your Pointer

When you understand how to control graphics on the display list, you can build your own custom mouse pointer. Think about all the different pointers you use in Flash. As you choose different tools in the Tools panel—the Paint Bucket, the Eyedropper, the Pencil—your pointer changes to help you understand and apply them. Similarly, you can tailor the pointer's form to match its function in your Flash projects.

Customizing the pointer involves first hiding the default mouse pointer. Then you must match the location of your new graphic to the location of the hidden (but still functional) pointer. To do this, continuously assign the `mouseX` and `mouseY` properties to the x and y properties of a `DisplayObject`.

To hide the mouse pointer:

1. Select the first frame and open the Actions panel.

2. Enter `Mouse.hide()`.

   When you test your movie, the mouse pointer becomes invisible.

To show the mouse pointer:

◆ Use the statement, `Mouse.show()`.

To create your own mouse pointer:

1. Create any `DisplayObject` for your pointer. For this example, create a movie clip, place an instance of it on the Stage, and name it in the Property inspector.

   This movie clip will become your pointer.

2. Select the first frame of the root Timeline, and open the Actions panel.

3. Enter `Mouse.hide()`.

   When this movie begins, the mouse pointer disappears.

4. On the next line, add an event listener to the Stage to detect the `MouseEvent.MOUSE_MOVE` event like the following:

   ```
   stage.addEventListener
   ⇢ (MouseEvent.MOUSE_MOVE,
   ⇢ moveCursor);
   ```

   When the mouse pointer moves on the Stage, the function called `moveCursor` is triggered.

5. On the next line, create the function called `moveCursor`, like so:

   ```
   function
   ⇢ moveCursor(myevent:MouseEvent):
   ⇢ void {
      cursor_mc.x=mouseX;
      cursor_mc.y=mouseY;
      myevent.updateAfterEvent();
   }
   ```

   The first two lines of the function assign the location of the mouse pointer to the position of the movie clip called `cursor_mc`. The third line adds the `updateAfterEvent()` method of the event object, which forces Flash to redraw the screen whenever the event happens, independently of the frame rate. This will create a smoother motion of your mouse pointer because your user may be moving the pointer faster than the screen refresh rate.

```
Mouse.hide();

stage.addEventListener(MouseEvent.MOUSE_MOVE, moveCursor);
function moveCursor(myevent:MouseEvent):void {
    cursor_mc.x=mouseX;
    cursor_mc.y=mouseY;
    myevent.updateAfterEvent();
}
```

Figure 7.95 The x and y properties for the movie clip cursor_mc follow the mouse pointer's position. Add the updateAfterEvent() method to the event object to force Flash to refresh the display and create smoother motion.

6. Test your movie.

When the mouse pointer moves on the Stage, the movie clip follows to act as the custom pointer (**Figure 7.95**).

✔ Tip

■ To reactivate the hand cursor when rolling over buttons or other interactive objects, you must create new event handlers that set the visibility of your custom cursor to false for each button. The statement Mouse.show() can then reactivate the hand cursor. Use a MouseEvent.MOUSE_OUT event handler to restore your original settings. For example, if you have a custom cursor cursor_mc but still want the hand cursor to appear over a button button1_btn, use the code shown in **Figure 7.96**.

```
Mouse.hide();

stage.addEventListener(MouseEvent.MOUSE_MOVE, moveCursor);
function moveCursor(myevent:MouseEvent):void {
    cursor_mc.x=mouseX;
    cursor_mc.y=mouseY;
    myevent.updateAfterEvent();
}

button1_btn.addEventListener(MouseEvent.MOUSE_OVER, showHandCursor);
function showHandCursor(myevent:MouseEvent):void {
    cursor_mc.visible=false;
    Mouse.show();
    myevent.updateAfterEvent();
}

button1_btn.addEventListener(MouseEvent.MOUSE_OUT, hideHandCursor);
function hideHandCursor(myevent:MouseEvent):void {
    cursor_mc.visible=true;
    Mouse.hide();
    myevent.updateAfterEvent();
}
```

Figure 7.96 This code restores the hand cursor when your custom cursor moves over a button, and then returns the custom cursor when moving off the button.

CUSTOMIZING YOUR POINTER

Putting It Together: Animating Graphics with ActionScript

The methods and properties discussed so far in this chapter—scripts that let you control and test virtually all aspects of objects on display on the Stage (appearance, position, draggability, collisions, depth level, creation, drawing capability, and masking capability)—are the basic tools for animating entirely with ActionScript. Whereas motion tweens and shape tweens are created before playback, ActionScript animation is generated during playback, so it can respond to and change according to your viewer's actions. You can use the mouse properties mouseX and mouseY as parameters in methods or to control properties so that the location of your viewer's pointer determines the behavior and appearance of graphics onscreen.

The following tasks show how to use the mouse properties mouseX and mouseY to create responsive animations. The first task combines mouseX and mouseY with the drawing methods of a Shape object so you can draw with the pointer. The second task creates a scrolling menu that moves according to the pointer's location.

To draw with the pointer:

1. Select the first frame of the main Timeline, and open the Actions panel.

2. Create a new Shape object.

3. Call the moveTo() method of the graphics property of your Shape object. For the parameters, use mouseX and mouseY (**Figure 7.97**).

   Flash moves the starting position of your drawing to the current position of your mouse pointer.

4. On the next line, enter the name of the Shape object followed by a period and the property graphics. Then enter the lineStyle() method.

5. With your pointer between the parentheses, enter a thickness, a hex-code value, and an alpha value.

6. On the next line, add an event listener to the Stage to detect the MouseEvent.MOUSE_MOVE event like the following:

   ```
   stage.addEventListener
   → (MouseEvent.MOUSE_MOVE,
   → startdraw);
   ```

   The function called startdraw is triggered when the mouse pointer moves over the Stage.

```
var myShape:Shape=new Shape();
myShape.graphics.moveTo(mouseX, mouseY);
```

Figure 7.97 The start of the drawing begins at the position of the mouse cursor.

7. On the next line, create the function called startdraw.

8. Within the function, enter the Shape object followed by a period and the property graphics. Then enter the lineTo() method.

9. With your pointer between the parentheses, enter mouseX, a comma, and mouseY.

Whenever the pointer moves, Flash draws a line segment from the previous position to the current position of the pointer.

10. On a new line but still within the MOUSE_MOVE event handler function, call the updateAfterEvent() method of your event (**Figure 7.98**).

This method forces Flash to redraw the screen every time the event happens (every time the mouse pointer moves).

11. On a new line outside the function, enter the addChild() method to add the Shape object to the display list.

12. Test your movie (**Figure 7.99**).

```
var myShape:Shape=new Shape();
myShape.graphics.moveTo(mouseX, mouseY);
myShape.graphics.lineStyle(1, 0xFF0000);

stage.addEventListener(MouseEvent.MOUSE_MOVE, startdraw);
function startdraw(myevent:MouseEvent):void {
    myShape.graphics.lineTo(mouseX, mouseY);
    myevent.updateAfterEvent();
}
addChild(myShape);
```

Figure 7.98 The lineTo() method draws a segment to the x, y position of the mouse pointer whenever the mouse pointer moves.

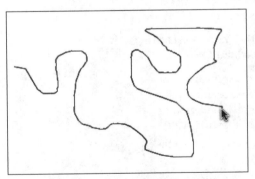

Figure 7.99 Whenever your mouse pointer moves, a new line segment is drawn, creating a simple drawing program.

To create a scrolling menu that responds to the mouse pointer:

1. Create a movie clip that contains a long row of buttons or graphics (**Figure 7.100**), put it on the Stage, and name it in the Property inspector.

2. Select the first frame of the main Timeline, and open the Actions panel.

3. Create a Shape object.

   You will use the drawing methods to create a square that will mask the scrolling menu.

4. On the next line, enter the name of the Shape object, a period, and the graphics property, and then call the beginFill() method. Enter a hex number as the parameter for the method.

5. On the next line, enter the name of the Shape object, a period, and the graphics property, and then call the drawRect() method. Enter the x and y positions of the upper-left corner and the width and height of the rectangle (**Figure 7.101**).

   A rectangular shape is drawn.

6. On the next line, add the Shape object to the display list with addChild().

7. On the following line, enter the name of your movie clip on the Stage, add a period and then the property mask, and then assign the Shape object (**Figure 7.102**).

   The rectangular shape becomes the mask for your movie clip.

8. On the next line, add an event listener to the Stage to detect the Event.ENTER_FRAME event like the following:

   ```
   stage.addEventListener (Event.ENTER_FRAME, movemenu);
   ```

   The function called movemenu is triggered continuously at the frame rate of the movie.

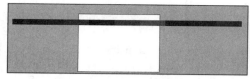

Figure 7.100 A movie clip with a long row of buttons extends off the Stage. To provide access to the buttons, the movie clip will scroll to the right or to the left, depending on where the mouse pointer is located.

```
var myShape:Shape = new Shape();
myShape.graphics.beginFill(0x7E00E3);
myShape.graphics.drawRect(50,10,450, 100);
```

Figure 7.101 A Shape object is created and a rectangle drawn.

```
var myShape:Shape = new Shape();
myShape.graphics.beginFill(0x7E00E3);
myShape.graphics.drawRect(50,10,450, 100);

addChild(myShape);
menu_mc.mask=myShape;
```

Figure 7.102 A Shape object masks the movie clip.

9. On the next line, create the function called movemenu.

10. Between the curly braces of the function, enter the following expression:

menu_mc.x = menu_mc.x + (0.5 *
→ myShape.width - mouseX) / 20;

When you subtract the horizontal position of the mouse pointer from half of the mask width, you get a number that is positive if the pointer is on the left or negative if the pointer is on the right. Use this value to move the x position of your movie clip. The division by 20 makes the increments smaller and, hence, the movement of the movie clip slower (**Figure 7.103**).

11. Test your movie (**Figure 7.104**).

✔ Tip

- The next step for this scrolling menu would be to script boundaries so the movie clip can't scroll off the screen. You'll learn about creating if statements in Chapter 9, "Controlling Information Flow."

```
var myShape:Shape = new Shape()
myShape.graphics.beginFill(0x7E00E3);
myShape.graphics.drawRect(50,10,450, 100)

addChild(myShape)
menu_mc.mask=myShape

stage.addEventListener(Event.ENTER_FRAME, movemenu);
function movemenu(myevent:Event):void {
    menu_mc.x = menu_mc.x + (0.5 * myShape.width - mouseX) / 20;
}
```

Figure 7.103 The horizontal position of the mouse pointer is used to calculate the new position of the movie clip menu_mc.

Figure 7.104 As the mouse pointer moves left or right from the center line, the movie clip scrolls behind a rectangular mask.

Generating Motion Tweens Dynamically

In addition to dynamically assigning new values to individual properties to create animations, you can use the classes AnimatorFactory, Motion, and MotionBase to generate motion tweens. For complex motions, you can create the tween on the Timeline first, and then simply copy the ActionScript for the motion. To do so, right-click (Windows) or Ctrl-click (Mac) on the tween span or the object of the tween and choose Copy Motion as ActionScript 3.0 (**Figure 7.105**).

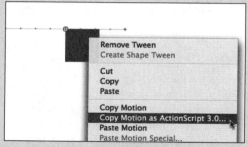

Figure 7.105 Choose Copy Motion as ActionScript 3.0 to copy the code for any motion tween that you create.

```
import fl.motion.AnimatorFactory;
import fl.motion.MotionBase;
import flash.filters.*;
import flash.geom.Point;
var __motion_box_mc:MotionBase;
if(__motion_box_mc == null) {
    import fl.motion.Motion;
    __motion_box_mc = new Motion();
    __motion_box_mc.duration = 12;

    // Call overrideTargetTransform to prevent the scale, skew,
    // or rotation values from being made relative to the target
    // object's original transform.
    // __motion_box_mc.overrideTargetTransform();

    // The following calls to addPropertyArray assign data values
    // for each tweened property. There is one value in the Array
    // for every frame in the tween, or fewer if the last value
    // remains the same for the rest of the frames.
    __motion_box_mc.addPropertyArray("x", [0,27.2727,54.5454,81.8181,109.091,136.364,
163.636,190.909,218.182,245.455,272.727,300]);
    __motion_box_mc.addPropertyArray("y", [0,0,0,0,0,0,0,0,0,0,0,0]);
    __motion_box_mc.addPropertyArray("scaleX", [1.00]);
    __motion_box_mc.addPropertyArray("scaleY", [1.00]);
    __motion_box_mc.addPropertyArray("skewX", [0]);
    __motion_box_mc.addPropertyArray("skewY", [0]);
    __motion_box_mc.addPropertyArray("rotationConcat", [0]);
    __motion_box_mc.addPropertyArray("blendMode", ["normal"]);

    // Create an AnimatorFactory instance, which will manage
    // targets for its corresponding Motion.
    var __animFactory_box_mc:AnimatorFactory = new AnimatorFactory(__motion_box_mc);

    // Call the addTarget function on the AnimatorFactory
    // instance to target a DisplayObject with this Motion.
    // The second parameter is the number of times the animation
    // will play - the default value of 0 means it will loop.
    // __animFactory_box_mc.addTarget(<instance name goes here>, 0);
}
```

Figure 7.106 Flash provides all the necessary code with thorough comments.

Continues on next page

Generating Motion Tweens Dynamically *(continued)*

In a new Flash file, paste the copied ActionScript code into the first keyframe (**Figure 7.106**). Flash provides all the code to dynamically generate the motion tween for a different object. Use the `addTarget()` method to specify what object on the Stage you want to apply the motion tween to (**Figure 7.107**).

You can alter the parameters of the `addPropertyArray()` methods to affect the motion tween. The first parameter of the `addPropertyArray()` method is the name of the property (in quotes), and the second parameter is an array of values for each frame of the tween (**Figure 7.108**).

```
__animFactory_box_mc.addTarget(mytrain_mc, 0);
```

Figure 7.107 The `addTarget()` method targets a different object for the motion tween. Here, a movie clip called `mytrain_mc` will go through the same motion as shown in Figure 7.105.

```
__motion_box_mc.addPropertyArray("x", [0,27.2727,54.5454,81.8181,109.091,136.364,
163.636,190.909,218.182,245.455,272.727,300]);
__motion_box_mc.addPropertyArray("y", [0,0,0,0,0,0,0,0,0,0,0,0]);
```

Figure 7.108 Change the `addPropertyArray()` method to modify the motion tween. The values within the square brackets refer to the values of properties at each frame.

About Bitmap Images

One of the hallmark characteristics of Flash is that the images you create are vector images, whether you use the drawing tools in the authoring environment or the drawing methods of the Graphics class. For computer-based drawing, vectors are convenient because they allow you to deal with lines, shapes, text, and other objects as a single unit rather than as a collection of pixels that must be controlled individually. However, as part of the process of displaying the Flash movie on a computer screen, the Flash Player has always converted those vectors to bitmap images behind the scenes.

ActionScript allows you to directly manipulate bitmap images. You've already seen some of the power of bitmap manipulation when you learned to apply filters. Filters are a bitmap manipulation technique, and inside the Flash Player a vector-based object is converted to a bitmap before any filter effect is applied to it. Controlling bitmap images requires that you use the BitmapData class. Using the properties and methods of the BitmapData class, you can create your own filters and graphical effects to enhance your Flash projects. You can add subtle touches, like converting an image to grayscale or fading two images together. Add textures and static to give it a worn look. Or go wild, invert images, chop them into pieces like a puzzle, and envelop them in a cloud of flame!

Creating and Accessing Bitmap Data

A bitmap image consists of a series of rows and columns of colored dots known as *pixels*. Each pixel is assigned a single color value containing a mix of red, green, blue, and possibly alpha (transparency) values. Although the image's pixels often form shapes that humans recognize, such as a rectangle, a sweeping landscape, or a person's smiling face, the computer is only aware of the individual pixel values and knows nothing about what the content of the bitmap represents. When you use the BitmapData class to manipulate image information, all the changes are made to the individual pixel's color values.

The first step to manipulating a bitmap image is to create an instance of the BitmapData class. Sometimes you'll want to start with a new, blank image, and many times you'll want to manipulate an existing image such as a digital photo.

As with most objects in ActionScript, to create a new BitmapData object you use the constructor function as in var myBitmapData: BitmapData = new BitmapData(100, 200). This statement creates an object with a width of 100 pixels and a height of 200 pixels. The BitmapData constructor takes up to four parameters. You must use the first two parameters: a width and height for the image. You can optionally add two more parameters to specify whether the image will use transparency (alpha channel) information and what color to fill the image with initially.

Previously, you used hexadecimal numbers to specify color values in the form 0x*RRGGBB*, where *RR* is a two-digit value for the amount of red in the image, *GG* for the amount of green, and *BB* for the amount of blue. Several of the BitmapData methods require you to provide a numeric color parameter. For a BitmapData object with no alpha channel, the six-digit hexadecimal format is still used. If the BitmapData object has an alpha channel, however, use eight digits instead of six, like this: 0x*AARRGGBB*. In this case, you add two extra digits that represent the alpha value after the 0x prefix but before the two red digits. These two digits indicate the amount of transparency the color will have. As with the other color values, the possible alpha values range from 0 (00) to 255 (FF). Note that this is different from the alpha property of a DisplayObject, which uses a decimal from 0 to 1.

After you create a BitmapData object, you can use methods from the BitmapData class to manipulate its pixels and colors. The next step is to assign the BitmapData object as the bitmapData property of a Bitmap object. The Bitmap object is the DisplayObject that you must add to the display list to make your image visible.

To create new bitmap data:

1. Select the first frame of the Timeline and open the Actions panel.

2. Create a new instance of the `BitmapData` class, as in:

   ```
   var myBitmapData:BitmapData=new
   → BitmapData(200, 100, false,
   → 0x33ee44)
   ```

   The four parameters are width, height, alpha transparency, and color. Only the first two are required. This instance, called `myBitmapData`, is a 200-by-100-pixel rectangle filled with a certain solid color.

   If you set the alpha transparency parameter to false, you should use a six-digit number; otherwise, use an eight-digit number to include the transparency information.

   At this point, no image is visible. The `BitmapData` object is simply information about a collection of pixels that you can manipulate and then, at a later point, put into a `Bitmap` object to display on the Stage (explained later).

✔ Tip

■ If you leave off the fourth parameter for color in the `BitmapData` constructor function, the `BitmapData` object is filled with solid white pixels by default.

Accessing images dynamically

In addition to creating an image filled with a single color, as in the previous task, you can create a `BitmapData` object with more interesting image information. You can create a new `BitmapData` object from a bitmap symbol in your Library. Or, you can use the `load()` method of the `Loader` class to retrieve an image from an external image file, and then copy a snapshot of the `Loader` object into a `BitmapData` object. This transfer of image information from the `Loader` object to the `BitmapData` object requires the method `draw()`.

To create bitmap data from a Library symbol:

1. In your Flash document, add an image to the Library by choosing File > Import > Import to Library, browsing to your image file in the dialog box, and clicking OK.

   Your image appears in the Library and is identified as a bitmap item.

2. Select the bitmap in the Library panel. In the Library panel's Options menu, choose Properties.

   The Symbol Properties dialog box appears.

3. Click the Advanced button to reveal the Linkage section.

4. In the Linkage section, select the Export for ActionScript check box. Leave "Export in frame 1" selected.

5. In the Class field, enter a name to identify your bitmap. Leave the Base class as flash display.BitmapData and click OK (**Figure 7.109**).

   A dialog box may appear, warning you that your class could not be found so one will automatically be generated. Click OK. In this example, the class name for your Library symbol is `Jumper`. This new class inherits from the `BitmapData` class, which means it has all the same methods and properties of the `BitmapData` class. Your class name will be used to create new instances of your `BitmapData`. Make sure that your class name doesn't contain any periods.

6. Select the first frame of the main Timeline, and open the Actions panel.

7. On the first line, create a new instance of your `BitmapData` object, referencing its class name (created in step 5), like so:

```
var myBitmapData:Jumper=new
→ Jumper(384, 256);
```

Include two parameters for its width and height. These parameters are required as they are for all `BitmapData` objects. A new instance of your `Jumper` class, which has all the characteristics of the `BitmapData` class, is created. The name of your new instance is `myBitmapData` (**Figure 7.110**).

The bitmap image from the Library is now stored in a `BitmapData` object.

To create bitmap data from an externally loaded image:

1. As in the previous tasks covered in Chapter 6, create a `URLRequest` object; then create a `Loader` object and call the `load()` method to load an external image (**Figure 7.111**).

2. Create the event handler to detect the completion of the loading process (**Figure 7.112**).

Continues on next page

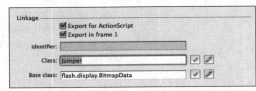

Figure 7.109 The Linkage section of the Symbol Properties dialog box. This Library symbol can be referenced with the class name `Jumper`. It will have all the same properties and methods of the `BitmapData` class.

```
var myBitmapData:Jumper=new Jumper(384,256);
```

Figure 7.110 Create a new `BitmapData` object with the class name that you defined in the Linkage section of the Symbol Properties dialog box. The first two parameters of the constructor specify the width and height of the bitmap, and are required.

```
var myrequest:URLRequest=new URLRequest ("gymnast.jpg");
var myloader:Loader = new Loader();
myloader.load(myrequest);
```

Figure 7.111 Create a new `Loader` object and load an external file as described in the `URLRequest` object.

```
var myrequest:URLRequest=new URLRequest ("gymnast.jpg");
var myloader:Loader = new Loader();
myloader.load(myrequest);

myloader.contentLoaderInfo.addEventListener(Event.COMPLETE, imgLoaded);
function imgLoaded(event:Event):void {

}
```

Figure 7.112 Create an event handler to detect when the loading is complete.

CREATING AND ACCESSING BITMAP DATA

3. In between the curly braces of the event handler function, create a new `BitmapData` object and reference your `Loader` object's width and height properties to specify its exact dimensions, like so:

```
var myBitmapData:BitmapData = new
→ BitmapData(myloader.width,
→ myloader.height);
```

4. On the next line, still within the curly braces of the function, enter the name of your `BitmapData` object, and then call the `draw()` method. Provide the `Loader` object as its parameter as in the following:

```
myBitmapData.draw(myloader)
```

This `draw()` method copies the image from the `Loader` object into the `BitmapData` object.

Your `BitmapData` object now contains the image information from the externally loaded file (**Figure 7.113**).

✔ Tips

■ You can use the `draw()` method to copy image data from any `DisplayObject` source into your `BitmapData` object, not just a `Loader` object. For example, you can copy an image from a text field and put it into your `BitmapData` object and manipulate text at the pixel level.

■ The `draw()` method has additional optional parameters so you can alter the image before putting it into your `BitmapData` object. The full parameters for the `draw()` method are as follows:

source: The `BitmapData` object from which to copy pixel information. This is the first, required parameter.

matrix: The `Matrix` object designating the transformations to the image.

colorTransform: The `ColorTransform` object designating the color changes to the image.

blendMode: The way in which the resulting bitmap will interact with colors below it. Use constants from the `BlendMode` class such as `BlendMode.MULTIPLY`.

clipRect: The `Rectangle` object designating the portion of the source bitmap to copy.

smoothing: A true or false value indicating whether the image will be smoothed when scaled or rotated.

You can pass `null` values for the parameters if you want to pass values for some but not all the parameters.

```
var myrequest:URLRequest=new URLRequest ("gymnast.jpg");
var myloader:Loader = new Loader();
myloader.load(myrequest);

myloader.contentLoaderInfo.addEventListener(Event.COMPLETE, imgLoaded);
function imgLoaded(event:Event):void {
    var myBitmapData:BitmapData = new BitmapData(myloader.width, myloader.height);
    myBitmapData.draw(myloader);

}
```

Figure 7.113 When the loading is complete, create a `BitmapData` object with dimensions that match the `Loader` object. Then copy the image data from the `Loader` into the `BitmapData` object.

To remove bitmap data from a BitmapData object:

◆ In the Script pane, enter the name of your BitmapData object and a period; then call the method dispose().

This frees up Flash's memory by setting the width and height of the BitmapData object to 0.

✔ Tip

■ Be careful not to try to manipulate or access a BitmapData object once you have called its dispose method; at that point, its width and height are set to 0, and its methods and properties won't work.

Displaying the bitmap data

So far, you've only learned to create bitmap data or load in bitmap data from another source, either from a Library symbol or an external file. To display your bitmap data, you must assign the data to the bitmapData property of a new object, the Bitmap object. The Bitmap object is a subclass of the DisplayObject class, which are the objects that you add to the display list.

To display bitmap data:

1. Create an instance of the Bitmap class, like so:

   var myBitmap:Bitmap=new Bitmap();

   In this example, your new Bitmap object is called myBitmap.

2. Assign your BitmapData object to the Bitmap object's bitmapData property, like so:

   myBitmap.bitmapData=myBitmapData;

3. Call the addChild() method to add the Bitmap object to the display list:

   addChild(myBitmap);

   The bitmap data is now visible on the Stage (**Figure 7.114**).

   Continues on next page

```
var myrequest:URLRequest=new URLRequest ("gymnast.jpg");
var myloader:Loader = new Loader();
myloader.load(myrequest);

myloader.contentLoaderInfo.addEventListener(Event.COMPLETE, imgLoaded);
function imgLoaded(event:Event):void {
    var myBitmapData:BitmapData = new BitmapData(myloader.width, myloader.height);
    myBitmapData.draw(myloader);
    var myBitmap:Bitmap=new Bitmap;
    myBitmap.bitmapData=myBitmapData;
    addChild(myBitmap);
}
```

Figure 7.114 The highlighted code creates a new Bitmap object, puts the BitmapData object into it, and displays the image on the Stage (below). Although the image appears the same as if you added the Loader object to the Stage, the image is bitmap data and you can manipulate all the color and transparency information for each pixel.

✔ Tips

■ As a shortcut, you can pass the `BitmapData` object as a parameter when you create your `Bitmap` object, and it will be assigned as the `bitmapData` property, like so:

```
var myBitmap:Bitmap=new
→ Bitmap(myBitmapData);
```

■ You can set the `smoothing` property of a `Bitmap` object to `true` to smooth out the image when it is scaled (**Figure 7.115**).

```
myBitmap.smoothing=true;
```

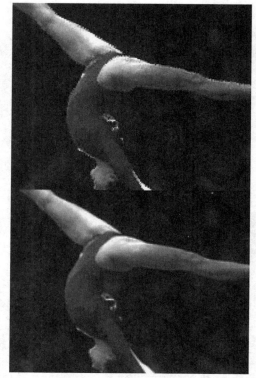

Figure 7.115 The `smoothing` property of the `Bitmap` object helps smooth out rough edges due to scaling and rotations. The top image has no smoothing, and the image appears pixilated. The bottom image has smoothing set to true.

Manipulating Bitmap Images

There is little use in creating a `BitmapData` object just to hold an image and display it through a `Bitmap` object. The real fun is in manipulating the image's pixels. The most basic way to do this is to draw color onto the bitmap.

You can change the color of a single pixel at a time using the `setPixel()` and `setPixel32()` methods. To cover a larger area, use the `fillRect()` method to set all the pixels in a rectangular portion of a `BitmapData` object to the same color; the `floodFill()` method lets you fill in a region of color with a different color, similar to the Paint Bucket tool in many graphics programs. Finally, using the `getPixel()` and `getPixel32()` methods, you can identify the color of a pixel in a `BitmapData` object, much like the Eyedropper tool that is common in image-editing programs.

To draw single pixels:

1. Select the first keyframe on the Timeline, and open the Actions panel.

2. As you have done in the previous tasks, declare and instantiate a new `BitmapData` object with `width` and `height` parameters like the following:

   `var myBitmapData:BitmapData = new`
   `→ BitmapData(300, 300);`

   This new `BitmapData` object is called `myBitmapData` and is 300 pixels by 300 pixels.

3. On a new line, enter the name of your `BitmapData` object and a period; then call the `setPixel()` method. For its parameters, specify an x-coordinate, a y-coordinate, and a color in hex code, like so:

   `myBitmapData.setPixel(100, 100,`
   `→ 0x993300);`

   This method creates a single pixel at x = 100, y = 100 at a certain color specified by the hex code (**Figure 7.116**).

4. On the next line, create a new `Bitmap` object.

5. On the next line, assign the `BitmapData` object to the `bitmapData` property of your `Bitmap` object.

6. On the last line, add a call to the `addChild()` method to display the `Bitmap` object on the Stage (**Figure 7.117**).

   You may have to squint to find the lone pixel, but you'll see a single dot rendered on your `Bitmap` object on the Stage.

Continues on next page

```
var myBitmapData:BitmapData = new BitmapData(300, 300);
myBitmapData.setPixel(100, 100, 0x993300);
```

Figure 7.116 A new `BitmapData` object called `myBitmapData` is created, which is 300 pixels square. The `setPixel()` method is called. The three parameters of the `setPixel()` method are the x- and y-coordinates and the color.

```
var myBitmapData:BitmapData = new BitmapData(300, 300);
myBitmapData.setPixel(100, 100, 0x993300);
var myBitmap:Bitmap=new Bitmap();
myBitmap.bitmapData=myBitmapData;
addChild(myBitmap);
```

Figure 7.117 The final code draws a red pixel at x = 100, y = 100. The bitmap information is put in a `Bitmap` object and displayed.

✔ Tip

■ The setPixel() method only accepts color values without an alpha channel; that is, color values specified as six-digit hexadecimal values. To change a pixel's color to a color that is partially transparent, use the setPixel32() method instead and specify an eight-digit hexadecimal code.

To fill a rectangle with a color:

1. Select the first keyframe on the Timeline, and open the Actions panel.

2. As you have done in the previous tasks, declare and instantiate a new BitmapData object with width and height parameters, and parameters for alpha and the color.

3. On the next line, create a Rectangle object with parameters for the x and y location, and the width and height (**Figure 7.118**).

4. On a new line, enter the name of your BitmapData object and a period; then call the fillRect() method with two parameters, like so:

   ```
   myBitmapData.fillRect(myRectangle,
   → 0x993300);
   ```

   For the first parameter, enter the name of your Rectangle object, indicating the section of the BitmapData object that should be colored.

   For the second parameter, enter a numeric color value indicating what color to set the pixels in the rectangle.

   The fillRect() method fills a rectangular region with a solid color.

5. On the next line, create a new Bitmap object.

6. On the next line, assign the BitmapData object to the bitmapData property of your Bitmap object.

7. On the last line, add a call to the addChild() method to display the Bitmap object on the Stage (**Figure 7.119**).

```
var myBitmapData:BitmapData = new BitmapData(500, 500, false, 0x33ee44);
var myRectangle:Rectangle = new Rectangle(0, 0, 100, 200);
```

Figure 7.118 A new Rectangle object called myRectangle is created. This object represents a rectangular region at the coordinate (o, o) that is 100 pixels wide and 200 pixels high.

```
var myBitmapData:BitmapData = new BitmapData(500, 500, false, 0x33ee44);
var myRectangle:Rectangle = new Rectangle(0, 0, 100, 200);

myBitmapData.fillRect(myRectangle, 0xAA3300);
var myBitmap:Bitmap=new Bitmap();
myBitmap.bitmapData=myBitmapData;
addChild(myBitmap);
```

Figure 7.119 The fillRect() method fills the region defined by a Rectangle object with the color 0xAA3300.

Figure 7.120 A rectangular portion of the BitmapData object is filled with a color.

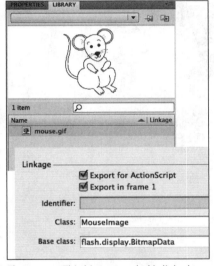

Figure 7.121 This bitmap symbol is linked to the class called MouseImage, which inherits the methods and properties of the BitmapData class.

```
var myBitmapData:MouseImage=new MouseImage(422, 492);
```

Figure 7.122 A new BitmapData object is created from your custom class (from the Library).

```
var myBitmapData:MouseImage=new MouseImage(422, 492);
myBitmapData.floodFill(10, 30, 0x55cc33);
```

Figure 7.123 The BitmapData class's floodFill() method takes three parameters: the x and y location of the starting point of the fill and the fill color.

8. Test your movie.

The Bitmap object is drawn on the Stage, and the rectangular region is filled in with the color you chose (**Figure 7.120**).

To fill a region with a color:

1. As in the previous tasks, create a BitmapData object. For this particular example, import an image that has one or more regions of solid color into the Library. In the Linkage section of the Symbol Properties dialog box, identify the Library symbol with its own class name that extends the BitmapData class (**Figure 7.121**).

2. In the Actions panel, create a new instance of your Library symbol, giving parameters for its width and height (**Figure 7.122**). The new instance is a BitmapData object.

3. On a new line, enter the name of your BitmapData object and a period; then call the floodFill() method with three parameters (**Figure 7.123**).

x: The x-coordinate of the pixel to use as the starting point for the fill operation

y: The y-coordinate of the starting pixel

color: The numeric color to set as the color for the affected pixels

When the floodFill() call is made, regions of similar color connected to the x- and y-coordinates are filled with the new color specified.

4. On the next line, create a new Bitmap object.

5. On the following line, assign your BitmapData object (the one from the Library) to the bitmapData property of your Bitmap object.

Continues on next page

6. On the last line, add a call to the addChild() method to display the Bitmap object on the Stage (**Figure 7.124**).

7. Test your movie.

Flash first creates an instance of your Library symbol, which is a BitmapData object. Then, at the specified coordinate, the region of similar color is filled with a new color. Finally, the BitmapData is assigned to a Bitmap object and displayed on the Stage (**Figure 7.125**).

✔ Tip

■ Unlike many image-editing programs, which allow you to specify a tolerance level for filling a region, the floodFill() method only fills pixels whose color is exactly the same as the starting pixel.

To get a color from an image:

◆ Call the getPixel() method as in:

myBitmapData.getPixel(100,200)

The color information for the particular pixel at x = 100, y = 100 for the BitmapData object called myBitmapData is returned. The returned value, however, is not in the familiar hexadecimal code. To convert the returned value, use the method toString(16).

✔ Tip

■ The color value provided by the getPixel() method only includes the red, green, and blue color information for the chosen pixel. If you want to know the alpha channel value as well, you must use the getPixel32() method instead.

```
var myBitmapData:MouseImage=new MouseImage(422, 492);
myBitmapData.floodFill(10, 30, 0x55cc33);

var myBitmap:Bitmap=new Bitmap(myBitmapData);
addChild(myBitmap);
```

Figure 7.124 The final code, which displays the manipulated bitmap data in a Bitmap object.

Figure 7.125 In this example, the BitmapData object is filled with continuous regions of color starting at x = 10, y = 30.

Copying, layering, and blending images

In addition to setting colors directly on an image, a common image-manipulation task is to incorporate part or all of one image into another image. Perhaps you want to duplicate an image in multiple places on the screen, or you want to copy several images onto one for a collage effect. Or maybe you want to copy a BitmapData object so that you can make changes to it without modifying the original. The BitmapData class offers several ways to accomplish the task of copying image data.

Figure 7.126 This bitmap symbol is linked to the class called Daisies, which inherits the methods and properties of the BitmapData class.

You have already used the draw() method to copy a source image to a BitmapData object; that same method can be used to copy all or part of a BitmapData object onto another using the optional parameters of the draw() method to manipulate the image.

In addition, you can make an exact copy of a BitmapData object with the clone() method, copy all the colors with the copyPixels() method (or just a single color channel using copyChannel()), and even combine the colors of two BitmapData objects with the merge() method. The following tasks demonstrate the use of these methods.

To make an exact copy of a bitmap:

◆ Call the clone() method and assign the returned value to another BitmapData object, like so:

```
var myCopy:BitmapData =
→ myBitmapData.clone()
```

This statement creates an exact duplicate of the myBitmapData object and assigns it to the object called myCopy, another BitmapData object.

To copy part of an image onto another image:

1. As in the previous tasks, create a BitmapData object. For this particular example, import a bitmap image into the Library. In the Linkage section of the Symbol Properties dialog box, identify the Library symbol with its own class name that extends the BitmapData class (**Figure 7.126**).

2. In the Actions panel, create a new instance of your Library symbol, giving parameters for its width and height.

   The new instance is a BitmapData object. Don't forget the width and height parameters, because they are required to create a new BitmapData object.

Continues on next page

3. On a new line, create another `BitmapData` object, specifying parameters for its width, height, alpha, and color. This `BitmapData` object will be the one that first image will be copied onto. This `BitmapData` object can contain an image, a solid color, or any other bitmap information.

In this example, the second `BitmapData` object will simply have a solid background color (**Figure 7.127**).

4. On the next line, create a `Rectangle` object with four parameters: the x, y, width, and height values corresponding to the rectangular portion of the source `BitmapData` object that you want to copy.

5. On the next line, create a `Point` object with two parameters, which are the x- and y-coordinates of the pixel in the destination `BitmapData` object where you want the top-left corner of the copied pixels to be placed (**Figure 7.128**).

6. On a new line, enter the name of the second `BitmapData` object (the colored rectangle) and then a period. Then call the `copyPixels()` method with three parameters (**Figure 7.129**).

sourceBitmap: The `BitmapData` object from which to copy pixel information (in this example, the new instance of the Library symbol)

sourceRect: The `Rectangle` object designating the portion of the source bitmap to copy

destPoint: The `Point` object designating the x- and y-coordinates on the destination image where the top-left corner of the copied rectangle should be positioned

7. On the next line, create a new `Bitmap` object.

Continues on next page

```
var srcBitmapData:Daisies = new Daisies (320,212);
var destBitmapData:BitmapData = new BitmapData(290, 212, false, 0xff0000);
```

Figure 7.127 The `BitmapData` object from the Library (the daisies picture) will be the source bitmap, and another `BitmapData` object that is 290 wide by 212 high filled with a red color will be the destination bitmap.

```
var srcBitmapData:Daisies = new Daisies (320,212);
var destBitmapData:BitmapData = new BitmapData(290, 212, false, 0xff0000);

var cropping:Rectangle = new Rectangle(75, 35, 103, 126);
var destBitmapDataPoint:Point = new Point(43, 43);
```

Figure 7.128 The source cropping `Rectangle` and destination `Point` objects are created, with values entered in their constructor functions.

```
var srcBitmapData:Daisies = new Daisies (320,212);
var destBitmapData:BitmapData = new BitmapData(290, 212, false, 0xff0000);

var cropping:Rectangle = new Rectangle(75, 35, 103, 126);
var destBitmapDataPoint:Point = new Point(43, 43);

destBitmapData.copyPixels(srcBitmapData, cropping, destBitmapDataPoint);
```

Figure 7.129 Using the source bitmap, cropping rectangle, and destination point parameters for the `copyPixels()` method gives you fine-tuned control over the copying and pasting of image data.

MANIPULATING BITMAP IMAGES

8. On the following line, assign your
`BitmapData` object (the one that contains
the copied pixels) to the `bitmapData`
property of your `Bitmap` object.

9. On the last line, add a call to the
`addChild()` to display the `Bitmap`
object on the Stage.

10. Test your movie.

Flash copies the pixels from the first
`BitmapData` object onto the second
according to the boundaries indicated
by the `Rectangle` object and placed at
the point indicated by the `Point` object.
The `BitmapData` with the copied pixels is
assigned to a `Bitmap` object and displayed on the Stage (**Figure 7.130**).

✔ Tips

- If you want to copy the entire source
image, the easiest way to indicate this is
to use the source `BitmapData` object's `rect`
property as the second parameter, like
this: `sourceImage.rect`. Any `BitmapData`
object's `rect` property contains a `Rectangle`
object whose size and boundaries match
those of the `BitmapData` object.

- To place the copied pixels at the top-left
corner of the destination image, use the
`topLeft` property of the destination
`BitmapData` object's `rect` property for the
third parameter, like this: `destImage.rect.topLeft`.

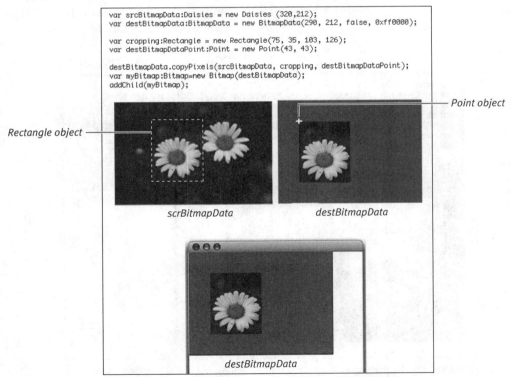

```
var srcBitmapData:Daisies = new Daisies (320,212);
var destBitmapData:BitmapData = new BitmapData(290, 212, false, 0xff0000);

var cropping:Rectangle = new Rectangle(75, 35, 103, 126);
var destBitmapDataPoint:Point = new Point(43, 43);

destBitmapData.copyPixels(srcBitmapData, cropping, destBitmapDataPoint);
var myBitmap:Bitmap=new Bitmap(destBitmapData);
addChild(myBitmap);
```

Rectangle object

Point object

scrBitmapData

destBitmapData

destBitmapData

Figure 7.130 The final code (top) copies a cropped portion of the original
image and places it at a point 43 pixels over and 43 pixels down from the
top-left corner of the destination image.

To copy one color channel of an image onto another image:

1. Continue working with the same document from the previous task.

2. In the line with the `copyPixels()` method call, change the method `copyPixels()` to `copyChannel()`.

   The `copyChannel()` method works like the `copyPixels()` method except that it copies only one of the source image's color channels (red, green, blue, or alpha) onto a single channel of the destination image.

   This is similar to the command in some image-manipulation programs that allows you to separate an image into its component channels.

3. Inside the parentheses of the `copyChannel()` method call, add two additional parameters after the three parameters that are currently there (**Figure 7.131**). These two parameters are as follows:

   sourceChannel: A Number indicating which color channel should be copied from the source image. The value must be 1 (red), 2 (green), 4 (blue), or 8 (alpha).

   destChannel: A Number indicating the color channel in the destination image into which the copied pixels should be placed. The possible values are the same as for the `sourceChannel` parameter (1, 2, 4, or 8).

4. Test your movie.

   This time, instead of copying the entire image, only one of the color channels is copied onto the destination image.

```
var srcBitmapData:Daisies = new Daisies (320,212);
var destBitmapData:BitmapData = new BitmapData(290, 212, false, 0xff0000);
var cropping:Rectangle = new Rectangle(75, 35, 103, 126);
var destBitmapDataPoint:Point = new Point(43, 43);
destBitmapData.copyChannel(srcBitmapData, cropping, destBitmapDataPoint, 4, 2);
var myBitmap:Bitmap=new Bitmap(destBitmapData);
addChild(myBitmap);
```

Figure 7.131 The `copyChannel()` method works like the `copyPixels()` method, but it copies only a single color channel from the source image onto a single channel of the destination image. Here the blue channel (4) of the source image has been copied into the green channel (2) of the destination image.

✔ Tips

■ The copied color channel is still only one of four channels in the destination image. Any color that was already present in the other channels of the destination image will be used together with the copied channel to determine the actual color displayed. If you want the destination image to show only the copied channel, create the destination image as solid black, which has a value of 0 in all color channels.

■ For an interesting effect, try using the same image as the source and destination, and copy one channel (for example, red) into a different channel (such as green). Depending on the selected color channels and the brightness of the colors in the original image, this can create a muted effect or a wildly vivid one.

■ To create a grayscale representation of a single color channel from the source BitmapData object, call the copyChannel() method three times. Use the same source channel for all three method calls, and use a different destination channel (1, 2, and 4) in each. For example, to create a grayscale image of the red channel, copy channel 1 to destination channel 1, copy channel 1 to destination channel 2, and finally, copy channel 1 to destination channel 4.

To blend an image onto another image:

1. As in previous tasks, create two BitmapData objects that will be blended together into a single image.

   The source image will be combined onto the destination image. The dimensions of the destination image will be used for the final image.

2. Declare and instantiate a Rectangle object with parameters indicating the portion of the source image to copy onto the destination image.

   If you want the entire source image to be used, remember that you can use the rect property for the Rectangle object.

3. Declare and instantiate a Point object with parameters indicating the x- and y-coordinates where the source image should be placed in the destination image.

   If you want to position the image at the top-left corner of the destination object, remember that you can use the rect.topLeft property for the Point parameter.

4. On a new line, enter the name of the destination BitmapData object followed by a period; then enter the method merge().

5. Inside the parentheses of the merge() method, enter seven parameters to control how the BitmapData objects will be blended together (**Figure 7.132**).

   Continues on next page

```
var srcBitmapData:Surfer1 = new Surfer1 (500,800);
var destBitmapData:Surfer2 = new Surfer2(500,800);
destBitmapData.merge(srcBitmapData,srcBitmapData.rect,
                destBitmapData.rect.topLeft,128,128,128,128);
```

Figure 7.132 To use the merge() method, you must create two BitmapData objects and define the source rectangle and destination points. In this example, the source rectangle is the entire dimension of the source image (using the rect property), and the destination point is the top-left corner (using the rect.topLeft property). Entering 128 for the merge() method's final four (multiplier) parameters creates an even blend between the two BitmapData objects.

The first three parameters, `sourceBitmap`, `sourceRect`, and `destPoint`, are equivalent to those parameters in the `copyPixels()` and `copyChannel()` methods, as explained in the previous tasks.

The last four parameters are multiplier numbers between 0 and 255, which control the balance of the colors between the two images. Each parameter represents the color balance of a single channel (in the order red, green, blue, and alpha). The larger the value, the more the balance favors the source image. For instance, entering 255 for all the values shows only the source image. For an even blend between the two images, enter 128 for each parameter.

6. Enter the remaining script to create a `Bitmap` object, and assign the destination `BitmapData` object to its `bitmapData` property.

7. To see the resulting image, call `addChild()` to put the `Bitmap` object on the display list.

When you test your movie, you see a new image composed of the two original images blended together (**Figure 7.133**).

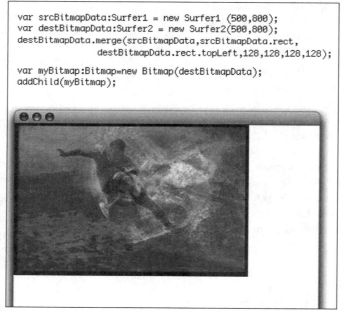

```
var srcBitmapData:Surfer1 = new Surfer1 (500,800);
var destBitmapData:Surfer2 = new Surfer2(500,800);
destBitmapData.merge(srcBitmapData,srcBitmapData.rect,
            destBitmapData.rect.topLeft,128,128,128,128);

var myBitmap:Bitmap=new Bitmap(destBitmapData);
addChild(myBitmap);
```

Figure 7.133 Using the `merge()` method, the two surfer images are blended together. The destination image determines the size constraints.

Using Filters on Bitmap Images

Previously, you learned how filters can be applied to movie clips to add visual interest. The same filters can be applied to bitmap graphics as well, using the BitmapData class's applyFilter() method. There are a few important differences between applying filters to a BitmapData object versus DisplayObjects like movie clips.

First, with DisplayObjects, you use the filters property, which you can use to layer multiple filters at a time. Second, the filters are just an enhancement; they can be added or removed at any time without altering the underlying object. However, when a filter is applied to a BitmapData object, the object (that is, the information it contains about pixels and color values) is directly modified; there is no way to undo the change or remove a filter from a BitmapData object.

However, you have a greater degree of control over the end result when you apply a filter to a BitmapData object. Because the filter modifies the pixels of the BitmapData object directly, any rotation, scaling, or other transformations applied to the BitmapData object are reflected in the filtered result.

The applyFilter() method takes four parameters. The first three parameters are the source bitmap, the source rectangle, and the destination point; these are the same three parameters you used in the copyPixels() method and the related methods you learned about in the previous tasks. The fourth parameter is the filter object that is to be applied to the BitmapData object.

To apply a filter to a bitmap image:

1. Using any of the techniques described previously, create your source `BitmapData` object (the one that contains the bitmap to which the filter will be applied).

2. On the next line, declare and instantiate a destination `BitmapData` object, into which the output of the filter operation will be placed (**Figure 7.134**).

   If you don't need to preserve the original image, you can use the source `BitmapData` object as the destination object as well.

   Whether you're using the source `BitmapData` object or a new `BitmapData` object as the destination object, there are a few important details to keep in mind—see the Tips following this task.

3. As you did in previous tasks, create a `Rectangle` object to define the region of the source bitmap to which the filter will be applied and a `Point` object defining the point where the result will be placed within the destination `BitmapData` object.

   If you want the entire image to be filtered and positioned to fill the entire source `BitmapData` object, remember that you can use the `rect` property for the `Rectangle` object and the `rect.topLeft` property for the `Point` property.

4. On the following line, declare and instantiate the filter object that will be used to alter the bitmap. Enter parameters in the constructor function to set the filter's properties, or set the properties directly (**Figure 7.135**).

5. On a new line, enter the name of your destination `BitmapData` object followed by a period, and then enter `applyFilter()`.

6. Enter as parameters for the `applyFilter()` method the name of your source `BitmapData` object, the name of your source `Rectangle` object, the name of your destination `Point` object, and the name of your filter object (**Figure 7.136**).

```
var srcBitmapData:Daisies = new Daisies (320,212);
var destBitmapData:BitmapData = new BitmapData (320,212);
```

Figure 7.134 A source bitmap (which will be filtered) and a destination bitmap (where the filter's result will be placed) are created.

```
var srcBitmapData:Daisies = new Daisies (320,212);
var destBitmapData:BitmapData = new BitmapData (320,212);

var myBlur:BlurFilter=new BlurFilter(15,15);
```

Figure 7.135 A new `BlurFilter` object is created.

```
var srcBitmapData:Daisies = new Daisies (320,212);
var destBitmapData:BitmapData = new BitmapData (320,212);

var myBlur:BlurFilter=new BlurFilter(15,15);
destBitmapData.applyFilter(srcBitmapData, srcBitmapData.rect,
                            destBitmapData.rect.topLeft, myBlur);
```

Figure 7.136 In this example the filter will be applied to the entire source bitmap, and it will be placed in the top-left corner of the destination bitmap.

USING FILTERS ON BITMAP IMAGES

7. Enter the remaining script to create a `Bitmap` object, and assign the destination `BitmapData` object to its `bitmapData` property.

8. To see the resulting image, call `addChild()` to put the `Bitmap` object on the display list.

The destination `BitmapData` object, which contains a copy of the source `BitmapData` object with the filter applied to it, appears on the Stage (**Figure 7.137**).

✔ Tips

■ Several of the filters (bevel, gradient bevel, glow, gradient glow, blur, and drop shadow) use alpha channel values; consequently, the destination `BitmapData` object must be able to store alpha channel values (its `transparent` property must be `true`). If your source `BitmapData` object doesn't have alpha channel information (its `transparent` is `false`), you must create a new `BitmapData` object rather than using the source object as the destination object.

■ Often, the output of a filter such as an outer glow or drop shadow is larger than the size of the `BitmapData` object (or the designated `Rectangle`). If the destination `BitmapData` object isn't large enough (for example, if its dimensions are identical to the source bitmap's dimensions), the filter will be cropped and may not be displayed.

To know the output size of the filter beforehand, use the `generateFilterRect()` method on the source bitmap. It takes two parameters—the cropping rectangle and the filter object that will be used—and returns a `Rectangle` object whose dimensions match the size of the output from the filter. Use those dimensions to define the size of your destination `BitmapData` object and the destination point to prevent the filter's result from being cropped.

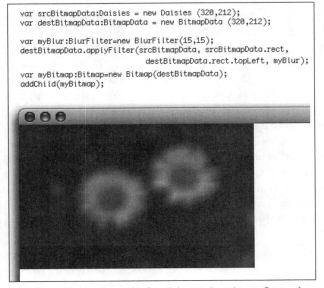

```
var srcBitmapData:Daisies = new Daisies (320,212);
var destBitmapData:BitmapData = new BitmapData (320,212);

var myBlur:BlurFilter=new BlurFilter(15,15);
destBitmapData.applyFilter(srcBitmapData, srcBitmapData.rect,
                           destBitmapData.rect.topLeft, myBlur);

var myBitmap:Bitmap=new Bitmap(destBitmapData);
addChild(myBitmap);
```

Figure 7.137 The final code (top) and the resultant image (bottom).

Putting It Together: Animating Bitmap Images

Throughout the latter part of this chapter, you've seen ways that bitmap images can be created, drawn onto, copied, combined, and changed. These techniques allow for interesting and exciting effects. But this is Flash—it's an animated, interactive medium, and bitmap images can animate and be part of interactivity just like any Flash elements.

As you explore the bitmap-manipulation capabilities of Flash, chances are you'll continue to be impressed by their power and by how quickly they perform. Not only can you blend images and apply a filter effect to them, but you can also do it in real time, over and over again.

To help give your creativity a head start, the following task demonstrates how to combine the various bitmap manipulation capabilities of Flash to create an animated flame that follows the mouse pointer.

Creating animated flame

This task integrates several of the techniques you have learned about `BitmapData` objects. First, the `draw()` method copies a movie clip, the source of the fire color and shape, into a `BitmapData` object. By default, the `draw()` method copies the pixels into the top-left corner of a destination `BitmapData` object. In this case, the copied pixels will be placed at the mouse pointer, so an additional parameter is used with the `draw()` method to control the positioning. Unlike many methods that accept a `Point` object to indicate the destination point, the `draw()` method requires a `Matrix` object for that purpose.

Once the initial fire colors are drawn into the bitmap, the `copyPixels()` method animates the flame moving upward. To do this, the image is copied onto itself, but the destination point is set to (0, -3), which copies the image three pixels above its current location and creates the illusion of upward movement.

Finally, a blur filter is applied to the entire image. As the image is blurred, the orange of the flame blends with the black background, making the flame gradually blend into the black and disappear.

These three tasks—drawing the flame color, shifting the pixels upward, and blurring the image—are placed in an `Event.ENTER_FRAME` event handler function that is called repeatedly, creating the animation.

To create an animated flame:

1. Choose Insert > New Symbol to create a new movie clip symbol that will provide the initial color and shape for the fire.

2. In symbol editing mode, select the Oval tool and draw a small oval shape. Give the shape a radial gradient fill.

In this example, the three gradient colors are `FFCC00` (75 percent alpha) on the left, `FF6600` (90 percent alpha) in the middle, and `FFFFFF` (0 percent alpha) on the right. These values create a radial gradient that is yellow in the center and then dark orange fading to transparent (**Figure 7.138**).

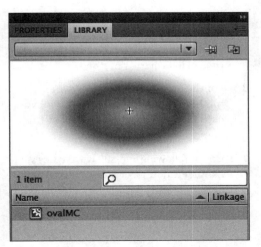

Figure 7.138 A radial gradient with shades of yellow and orange is used to create a movie clip oval to serve as the basis of the flame.

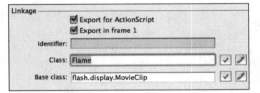

Figure 7.139 In the Linkage section of the Symbol Properties dialog box for the movie clip symbol, give it a class name and extend the `MovieClip` class.

3. Using the Align panel, center the oval over the registration point.

4. Exit symbol editing mode.

5. Select your new movie clip symbol in the Library, and select Properties from the Options menu. In the Linkage section (you may have to expand the dialog box by clicking the Advanced button), identify the Library symbol with its own class name that extends the `MovieClip` class (**Figure 7.139**).

6. Select the first keyframe, and open the Actions panel.

7. Create a new instance of your movie clip symbol in the Library.

8. On the next line, create a new instance of a `BitmapData` object with parameters for width, height, alpha, and color.

   Use the dimensions of the Stage for the width and height, false for alpha, and `0x000000` for the color, making it black (**Figure 7.140**).

9. Next, add a listener and function to handle the `Event.ENTER_FRAME` event.

10. Inside the curly braces of the event handler function, create a new `Matrix` object.

    A `Matrix` object contains information about transformations (position and size changes) that have been or will be applied to an object. In this case, it will define the destination position where the fire movie clip is copied into the `BitmapData` object.

Continues on next page

```
var myFlame:Flame=new Flame();
var myBitmapData:BitmapData = new BitmapData(400, 500, false, 0x000000);
```

Figure 7.140 An instance of the gradient oval movie clip is created, and a new `BitmapData` object is created that is 400 pixels by 500 pixels and filled with black.

11. On the following line, still within the function, enter the name of the `Matrix` object and a period; then call its `translate()` method.

12. Inside the parentheses of the `translate()` method, enter two parameters separated by commas: `mouseX` and `mouseY + 3` (**Figure 7.141**).

The `translate()` method adds a position change to the transformations in the `Matrix` object.

The `Matrix` object is assigned the instruction to change position to the x- and y-coordinates of the mouse pointer. Whatever object the `Matrix` object is applied to will have that position change applied to it.

The extra three pixels on the y-axis compensate for the three-pixel upward motion that will be applied later to keep the flame centered on the mouse pointer.

13. On the next line, still within the event handler function, enter the name of your `BitmapData` object and a period, and then call its `draw()` method.

14. For the parameters of the `draw()` method, enter the name of your movie clip (the color source) followed by the name of your `Matrix` object.

15. On the following line, still within the event handler function, create a `BlurFilter` object with the parameters 2, 10, and 2 as in:

```
var myBlur:BlurFilter=new
→ BlurFilter(2,10,2);
```

This constructor creates a new `BlurFilter` object that blurs two pixels horizontally and ten pixels vertically, and has a quality setting of 2.

16. Enter the name of your `BitmapData` object and then a period, and then call the `applyFilter()` method.

```
var myFlame:Flame=new Flame();
var myBitmapData:BitmapData = new BitmapData(400, 500, false, 0x000000);

stage.addEventListener(Event.ENTER_FRAME, drawFlame);
function drawFlame(myevent:Event):void {
    var myMatrix:Matrix = new Matrix();
    myMatrix.translate(mouseX, mouseY + 3);
}
```

Figure 7.141 A new `Matrix` object is created, and its `translate()` method is called. The chosen parameters cause a copy of the oval movie clip to be placed at the mouse pointer's coordinates.

17. Inside the parentheses of the `applyFilter()` method, enter these four parameters (**Figure 7.142**):

▲ The `BitmapData` object

▲ The `BitmapData` object's `rect` property

▲ The `BitmapData` object's `rect.topLeft` property

▲ The `BlurFilter` object

18. On the next line, create a `Point` object with parameters 0 and -3, as in `var myPoint:Point=new Point(0,-3)`.

This point will be used by the `copyPixels()` method to copy the image over itself three pixels higher than before.

19. On the following line, enter the name of the `BitmapData` object, a period, and then call the `copyPixels()` method.

20. Enter the following parameters for the `copyPixels()` method (**Figure 7.143**):

▲ The `BitmapData` object

▲ The `BitmapData` object's `rect` property

▲ The `Point` object

21. On a new line outside the event handler function, create a new `Bitmap` object and assign the `BitmapData` object to the Bitmap object's `bitmapData` property.

22. On the next line, call the `addChild()` method to add the `Bitmap` object to the display list.

Continues on next page

```
var myFlame:Flame=new Flame();
var myBitmapData:BitmapData = new BitmapData(400, 500, false, 0x000000);

stage.addEventListener(Event.ENTER_FRAME, drawFlame);
function drawFlame(myevent:Event):void {
    var myMatrix:Matrix = new Matrix();
    myMatrix.translate(mouseX, mouseY + 3);
    myBitmapData.draw(myFlame, myMatrix);
    var myBlur:BlurFilter = new BlurFilter(2, 10, 2);
    myBitmapData.applyFilter(myBitmapData, myBitmapData.rect, myBitmapData.rect.topLeft, myBlur);
}
```

Figure 7.142 The `draw()` method is used to copy the gradient oval into the `BitmapData` object. The transformations in the `Matrix` object (a position change in this example) determine the placement of the copied pixels. A blur filter is created and applied to the `BitmapData` object. This causes the color to fade away as it moves upward.

```
var myFlame:Flame=new Flame();
var myBitmapData:BitmapData = new BitmapData(400, 500, false, 0x000000);

stage.addEventListener(Event.ENTER_FRAME, drawFlame);
function drawFlame(myevent:Event):void {
    var myMatrix:Matrix = new Matrix();
    myMatrix.translate(mouseX, mouseY + 3);
    myBitmapData.draw(myFlame, myMatrix);
    var myBlur:BlurFilter = new BlurFilter(2, 10, 2);
    myBitmapData.applyFilter(myBitmapData, myBitmapData.rect, myBitmapData.rect.topLeft, myBlur);
    var myPoint:Point = new Point(0, -3);
    myBitmapData.copyPixels(myBitmapData, myBitmapData.rect, myPoint);
}
```

Figure 7.143 The `copyPixels()` method, using a destination `Point` object of (o, -3), copies the image onto itself, shifted three pixels upward.

23. Test your movie.

With each passing frame, the movie clip is copied onto the bitmap at the point beneath the mouse cursor, blurred, and shifted upward three pixels, creating an interactive flame effect (**Figure 7.144**).

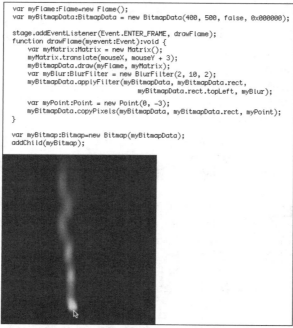

```
var myFlame:Flame=new Flame();
var myBitmapData:BitmapData = new BitmapData(400, 500, false, 0x000000);

stage.addEventListener(Event.ENTER_FRAME, drawFlame);
function drawFlame(myevent:Event):void {
    var myMatrix:Matrix = new Matrix();
    myMatrix.translate(mouseX, mouseY + 3);
    myBitmapData.draw(myFlame, myMatrix);
    var myBlur:BlurFilter = new BlurFilter(2, 10, 2);
    myBitmapData.applyFilter(myBitmapData, myBitmapData.rect,
                             myBitmapData.rect.topLeft, myBlur);

    var myPoint:Point = new Point(0, -3);
    myBitmapData.copyPixels(myBitmapData, myBitmapData.rect, myPoint);
}

var myBitmap:Bitmap=new Bitmap(myBitmapData);
addChild(myBitmap);
```

Figure 7.144 The final code (above) and the result (below) is a flame that trails from the mouse pointer.

What Is Pixel Bender?

You've seen how you can create special visual effects (such as blurs and drop shadows) with the various filter classes and apply them to various images. If you want to create your own filters, you can use a new technology from Adobe called Pixel Bender. Pixel Bender is actually a separate development platform and a separate language that is more specialized than ActionScript.

Essentially, with Pixel Bender you can write code for your own custom filter and save it as a .pbj file. In Flash, you load the .pbj filter and use two new classes, the Shader class and the ShaderFilter class, to apply the new filter to an image.

Pixel Bender is an exciting tool that is sure to open new visual possibilities and unleash the creativity of the Flash community.

Controlling Sound

Incorporating sound into your Flash movie can enhance the animation and interactivity, and add excitement to even the simplest project by engaging more of the user's senses. You can play background music to establish the mood of your movie, use narration to accompany a story, or give audible feedback to interactions such as button clicks and drag-and-drop actions. Flash supports several audio formats for import, including WAV, AIF, and MP3, which enables you to work with a broad spectrum of sounds. Flash also gives you the option of dynamically loading external MP3 files, providing an easy way to manage data-heavy sound files.

This chapter explores sound and its associated classes—`Sound`, `SoundChannel`, `SoundMixer`, `SoundTransform`, and `SoundEvent`. You'll learn how to play sounds from the Library dynamically without having to assign them to keyframes. You'll learn how to load sounds that reside outside your movie, enabling efficient management of your Flash and sound content. Using ActionScript, you can start, stop, and adjust the sound volume or its stereo effect, giving you control based on user interactions or movie conditions. You'll learn to access your sound's properties and events to time your sounds with animations or with other sounds.

All these features give you the flexibility and power to integrate sounds into your movies creatively. You can create a slider bar that lets your viewers change the volume, for example, or add sounds to an arcade game that are customized to the game play. Develop dynamic slide shows synchronized to music or narration, or even make your own jukebox to play MP3 tunes.

Using Sounds

There are several ways you can use sounds in your Flash movie. The simplest approach is to import a sound file into Flash and manually put it on a keyframe of your Timeline when you want it to play. The sound waveform shows up on your Timeline to give you an idea of when and how long your sound plays (**Figure 8.1**). Another way is to import a sound file into Flash and dynamically play it when your Flash movie plays. Your sound file remains in your Library until you use ActionScript to play it (**Figure 8.2**). A third way to use sound is to dynamically load and play an external sound (**Figure 8.3**). This chapter explores the second and third ways to use sounds. They allow you to control when a sound plays, change its volume and playback through the left and right speakers dynamically, or retrieve information about the loading progress or sound playback progress with ActionScript.

Each sound that you play requires an instance of the Sound class. After you have a sound instance, you can use the play() method to play the sound. When you play an individual sound, an instance of the SoundChannel class is created, which provides you with properties to control the sound. One of the properties of the SoundChannel object is a SoundTransform object, which provides additional controls for volume and balance between the left and right speakers.

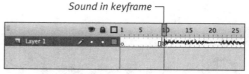

Figure 8.1 A sound placed in a keyframe on the Timeline is the simplest way to play sound and requires no ActionScript.

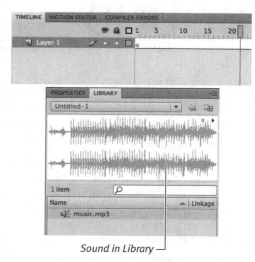

Figure 8.2 Imported sounds in the Library that are not placed on the Timeline can still be played at runtime with ActionScript.

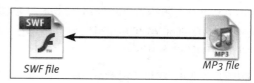

Figure 8.3 A separate MP3 sound file can load into a Flash (SWF) file and play using ActionScript.

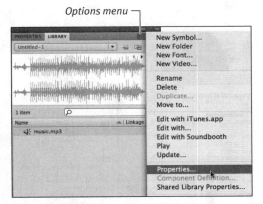

Options menu

Figure 8.4 Choose Properties from the Library options menu for each sound you want to control with ActionScript.

Playing Sounds from the Library

You can import your sound files into your Library during authortime, and use ActionScript to play them when you want at runtime. This requires that you make your sound symbols in the Library available to be called upon in ActionScript. You do this just as you did in Chapter 7, "Controlling and Displaying Graphics," when you dynamically made an instance of a movie clip or a bitmap symbol from the Library. You extend the functionality of a preexisting class to your Library symbol, so you can dynamically create new instances of it with the constructor function. In the case of a sound symbol, the Sound class is extended. Set the class name for your sound symbol from the Linkage section of the Symbol Properties dialog box, which is accessed from your Library.

To prepare a sound symbol for playback with ActionScript:

1. Import a sound file by choosing File > Import > Import to Library and selecting an audio file.

   Your selected audio file appears in the Library. You can import these sound formats: AIF (Mac), WAV (Windows), and MP3 (Mac and Windows). More formats may be available if QuickTime is installed on your system.

2. Select the sound symbol in your Library.

3. From the Options menu, choose Properties (**Figure 8.4**).

   The Symbol Properties dialog box appears.

4. Click the Advanced button. In the Linkage section of the expanded dialog box, select the Export for ActionScript check box. Leave "Export in frame 1" selected.

Continues on next page

5. In the Class field, enter a name to identify your sound class. Leave the Base class as `flash.media.Sound` and click OK (**Figure 8.5**).

A dialog box might appear that warns you that your class could not be found and will automatically be generated (**Figure 8.6**). Click OK. In this example, the class name for your Library symbol is `GuitarsLoop`. This new class inherits from the Sound class, which means it has all the same methods and properties of the Sound class. Your class name will be used to create new instances of your sound. Make sure that your class name doesn't contain any periods.

To play a sound from the Library:

1. Continue with the previous task, and select the first frame of the main Timeline. Then open the Actions panel.

2. On the first line, create a new instance of your sound symbol, referencing its class name, like so:

`var mySound:GuitarsLoop=new`
`→ GuitarsLoop()`

A new instance of a Sound object, specifically the sound in your Library, is created.

3. Enter the name of your new sound instance followed by a period and then the method `play()` (**Figure 8.7**).

Your sound instance begins to play. The sound will play through once and then stop.

✔ Tip

■ The `play()` method plays the sound instance whenever it's called, even when the sound is already playing. This situation can produce multiple, overlapping sounds. To prevent overlaps of this type, use the `stopAll()` method of the SoundMixer class before playing the sound again. This technique ensures that a sound always stops before it plays again.

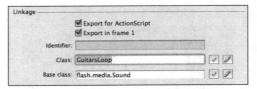

Figure 8.5 The new class `GuitarsLoop` will be created for this SWF file. It inherits the properties and methods of the Sound class.

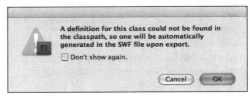

Figure 8.6 Click OK to dismiss the warning box. It tells you that your custom class will be created for you.

```
var mySound:GuitarsLoop = new GuitarsLoop();
mySound.play();
```

Figure 8.7 A new instance of the `GuitarsLoop` class is created and given the name `mySound`. This is an instance of the sound in your Library. Then the `play()` method plays the sound.

Loading and Playing External Sounds

Each time you import a sound into your Library, that sound is added to your SWF file, increasing its size. Sounds take up an enormous amount of space, even with MP3 compression, so you have to be judicious with your inclusion of sounds. One way to manage sounds so that your file stays small is to keep sounds as separate files outside your Flash movie. Use the method load() to bring MP3 audio files into Flash and play them only when you need them. (MP3 is the only allowable format.)

The method load() requires one parameter, which is a URLRequest object that provides the path to the MP3 file.

```
var myRequest:URLRequest=new URLRequest ("music.mp3");
```

Figure 8.8 A URLRequest object defines the path to the file that you want to load. In this example, the file is called music.mp3, and it resides in the same folder as the Flash movie.

```
var myRequest:URLRequest=new URLRequest ("music.mp3");
var mySound:Sound = new Sound();
```

Figure 8.9 The second line of code creates an object called mySound, an instance of the Sound class.

```
var myRequest:URLRequest=new URLRequest ("music.mp3");
var mySound:Sound = new Sound();
mySound.load(myRequest);
mySound.play();
```

Figure 8.10 The load() method loads the sound file from the location provided in the URLRequest object, and the play() method plays the sound.

To load and play an external sound:

1. Declare and instantiate a URLRequest object with the constructor function new URLRequest(). Provide the path to the MP3 file as the parameter (**Figure 8.8**).

   The path is a string, so enclose it in quotation marks. You can load an MP3 file locally or from the Internet with an absolute URL. If the file resides in the same directory as your Flash movie, you can enter just the name of the file.

2. Declare and instantiate a Sound object with the constructor function new Sound() (**Figure 8.9**).

3. On the next line, enter the name of your Sound object followed by a period. Enter the method load() and provide the URLRequest object as the parameter.

4. On the next line, enter the name of your Sound object followed by a period. Enter the method play() and provide optional parameters for the initial offset or looping (**Figure 8.10**).

   As soon as your movie begins, it will load the MP3 file and play.

5. Save your Flash file in the same folder as the MP3 file. Test your movie.

   As soon as your movie begins, Flash uses the URLRequest object to find your external MP3 file, and then uses the Sound object to load and play it.

AAC Sound Files

You can also dynamically load and play AAC sound files by using the NetStream class just as you do with external videos, as described in Chapter 6, "Managing External Communication." The AAC format is the successor to the MP3 format and is the same sound codec used in the H.264 format for F4V video files.

Controlling Sound Playback

The play() method of the Sound object can take three optional parameters. The first parameter is the offset, which is a number that determines how many milliseconds into the sound it should begin playing. You can set the sound to start from the beginning or at some later point. If you have a 20-second sound, for example, calling the method play(10000) makes the sound play from the middle at 10 seconds. It doesn't delay the sound for 10 seconds but begins immediately at the 10-second mark.

The second parameter is a number that determines how many times the sound loops. A setting of 2 plays the entire sound two times with no delay in between. This is useful for sounds that are specifically created where the end matches seamlessly with the beginning, so you can loop it over and over again.

The third parameter for the play() method takes a SoundTransform object, which provides control over the volume and left-right balance. You'll learn more about the SoundTransform object later in this chapter.

If no parameters are defined for the play() method, Flash plays the sound from the beginning and plays one loop.

```
var myRequest:URLRequest=new URLRequest ("music.mp3");
var mySound:Sound = new Sound();
mySound.load(myRequest);
mySound.play(14000);
```

Figure 8.11 In this example, the play() method has a parameter of 14000, which makes the sound play beginning at 14 seconds.

To set the initial starting time for a sound:

◆ Assign the first parameter of the play() method of your Sound object in milliseconds.

Your sound plays from that point (in milliseconds) forward (**Figure 8.11**).

To set the number of loops:

◆ Assign the second parameter of the play() method of your Sound object to the number of times you want the sound to loop.

Your sound loops the specified number of times (**Figure 8.12**).

✔ Tip

■ Unfortunately, you have no way of telling the play() method to loop a sound indefinitely. Instead, set the second parameter to a ridiculously high number, such as 99999.

Stopping sounds

You stop a sound from playing by using a method of the SoundChannel class. When you call the play() method of a Sound object, an instance of the SoundChannel class is generated. There is one SoundChannel instance for each sound that plays.

```
var myRequest:URLRequest=new URLRequest ("music.mp3");
var mySound:Sound = new Sound();
mySound.load(myRequest);
mySound.play(0,3);
```

Figure 8.12 In this example, the play() method has its first parameter set at 0 and its second parameter set at 3, which makes the sound play from the beginning and loop three times.

To assign the SoundChannel instance to a variable that you can later reference, use the following syntax:

myChannel:SoundChannel=mySound.play();

This statement plays the sound associated with the object called mySound. The returned SoundChannel object is put in the variable called myChannel. You can now stop the sound by calling the stop() method of the SoundChannel object, like so:

myChannel.stop();

Stop sound

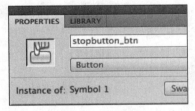

Figure 8.13 This button instance on the Stage is named stopbutton_btn.

```
var myRequest:URLRequest=new URLRequest ("music.mp3");
var mySound:Sound = new Sound();
mySound.load(myRequest);
var myChannel:SoundChannel=mySound.play();
```

Figure 8.14 When the play() method of a Sound object is called, it returns a SoundChannel object. In this example, the SoundChannel object is put in the variable named myChannel.

```
stopbutton_btn.addEventListener(MouseEvent.CLICK, stopsound);
function stopsound(myevent:MouseEvent) {
    myChannel.stop();
}
```

Figure 8.15 The event handler for the stopbutton_btn button on the Stage. The stop() method to stop a sound is called from the SoundChannel object called myChannel.

To stop a sound:

1. Continue with the file you used in the preceding task, "To load and play an external sound."

2. Create a button symbol and place an instance of it on the Stage. In the Property inspector, give it a name (**Figure 8.13**).

   In this example, you'll assign an event handler for a mouse click on the button to stop the sound from playing.

3. Select the first frame of the main Timeline, and open the Actions panel.

4. Replace the statement with the play() method with this one:

   var myChannel:SoundChannel=mySound.
   → play()

   This statement plays the sound and puts the returned SoundChannel object of the play() method in a new variable (of a SoundChannel type) called myChannel (**Figure 8.14**).

5. Create an event handler to detect a mouse click on the button on the Stage.

6. In between the curly braces of the event handler function, enter the name of your SoundChannel object, a period, and then the method stop(), like so (**Figure 8.15**):

   myChannel.stop();

7. Test your movie.

   The external sound begins to play. When you click your button, the sound stops.

✔ Tip

- You can also use the stopAll() method of the SoundMixer class. This stops all sounds in your Flash movie. Use the statement like so: SoundMixer.stopAll().

Resuming sounds

You can keep track of the exact position of your sound playback with a SoundChannel property, position. The position property indicates the current position in milliseconds. This is a useful property if you want to keep track of when a sound was stopped so you can resume playback at that same position.

When a user stops a sound, you can capture the SoundChannel position property at that moment by putting it in a variable. Then, when the user wants to resume the sound, you can call the play() method of the Sound object and provide the number of offset seconds as the first parameter.

To resume playback of a sound:

1. Continuing with the file you used in the preceding task, place another instance of the button symbol on the Stage, and give it an instance name in the Property inspector (**Figure 8.16**).

   In this example, you'll assign an event handler for a mouse click on this second button to resume the sound at the point where it was stopped.

2. Select the first frame of the main Timeline, and open the Actions panel.

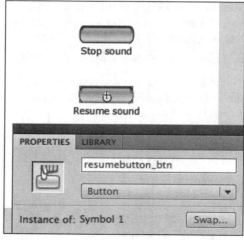

Figure 8.16 A second button instance on the Stage is named resumebutton_btn.

```
var myRequest:URLRequest=new URLRequest ("music.mp3");
var mySound:Sound = new Sound();
mySound.load(myRequest);
var myChannel:SoundChannel=mySound.play();
var pausedposition:int;
```

Figure 8.17 The highlighted statement declares a new variable called pausedposition, which will hold an integer data type.

```
stopbutton_btn.addEventListener(MouseEvent.CLICK, stopsound);
function stopsound(myevent:MouseEvent) {
    pausedposition = myChannel.position;
    myChannel.stop();
}
```

Figure 8.18 Before the sound stops, capture the current position in the sound and assign that value (in milliseconds) to the variable called pausedposition.

```
resumebutton_btn.addEventListener(MouseEvent.CLICK, resumesound);
function resumesound(myevent:MouseEvent) {
    myChannel=mySound.play(pausedposition);
}
```

Figure 8.19 The event handler for the resumebutton_ btn button on the Stage. The play() method uses the variable pausedposition to start playing at the point at which it stopped.

3. Insert a statement at the beginning of your ActionScript code to declare a variable of an integer data type (**Figure 8.17**). This variable will hold the current position of the sound playback.

4. In the event handler for the button that stops the sound, insert a statement before the stop() method, like so (**Figure 8.18**):

   pausedposition=myChannel.position;

   Before the sound is stopped, the current position in the playback of the sound is assigned to your variable.

5. Create another event handler to detect a mouse click on your second button on the Stage.

   This event handler will resume playback of the sound.

6. In between the curly braces of the event handler for the resume function, enter the following statement (**Figure 8.19**):

   myChannel:SoundChannel= mySound. → play(pausedposition);

   The current position of the paused sound is used as the first parameter of the play method, which determines the offset point. The sound plays at the point where it was paused.

7. Test your movie.

   The external sound begins to play. When you click the first button, the sound stops. When you click the second button, the sound resumes.

Tracking Sound Progress

You can also compare the `position` property of a sound with the total `length` of a sound to keep track of its current progress while it's playing.

The `position` is a property of the SoundChannel object, and the `length` is a property of the Sound object. However, keep in mind that the `length` property reflects the total length of the *downloaded* file. If the sound hasn't completely downloaded, the length property will be shorter than the actual length. To track the sound accurately, create an event handler to wait for the sound to completely download.

In the following example, you check whether the sound has been completely downloaded using the `Event.COMPLETE` event. Once the download is complete, you begin playing the sound and display the ratio of SoundChannel `position` to Sound `length` as a proportion of a horizontal bar, much like the progress bar of a preloader.

To track the sound progress:

1. Continue with the file you used in the task, "To load and play an external sound."

2. Delete the last line of code (the `play()` method), and replace it with a statement that declares a SoundChannel object (**Figure 8.20**).

3. Add an event handler to the Sound object that detects the `Event.COMPLETE` event.

4. In the event handler function, respond by playing the sound and adding another listener for the `Event.ENTER_FRAME` event (**Figure 8.21**).

   The ENTER_FRAME event happens at the frame rate of your movie. You can use this event to continuously monitor the progress of your sound.

```
var myRequest :URLRequest=new URLRequest("soulLoop.mp3" );
var mySound:Sound = new Sound();
mySound.load(myRequest);
var myChannel :SoundChannel;
```

Figure 8.20 The file called soulLoop.mp3 is loaded by a Sound object called mySound. On the last line, a new SoundChannel object called myChannel is then declared.

```
var myRequest :URLRequest=new URLRequest("soulLoop.mp3" );
var mySound:Sound = new Sound();
mySound.load(myRequest);
var myChannel :SoundChannel;

mySound.addEventListener (Event.COMPLETE , loaded);
function loaded(myevent:Event):void {
    myChannel =mySound.play();
    stage.addEventListener (Event.ENTER_FRAME , showprogress );
}
```

Figure 8.21 The listener on mySound listens for the completion of the loading of the sound. When that happens, the sound plays and a new listener is added.

5. In the ENTER_FRAME event handler function, divide the SoundChannel position property by the Sound length property and assign the fraction to the horizontal scale of a movie clip, like so (**Figure 8.22**):

   ```
   bar_mc.scaleX= myChannel.position/
   → mySound.length
   ```

   The position measures the current location of the sound in milliseconds, and the length is the total length of the song in milliseconds. The division creates a fraction that changes the width of a movie clip called bar_mc.

6. Create a rectangular movie clip and place it on the Stage. In the Property inspector name it bar_mc.

7. Choose Control > Test Movie (**Figure 8.23**). The bar_mc movie clip slowly grows to its full width as the song progresses.

```
var myRequest:URLRequest=new URLRequest("soulLoop.mp3");
var mySound:Sound = new Sound();
mySound.load(myRequest);
var myChannel:SoundChannel;

mySound.addEventListener(Event.COMPLETE, loaded);
function loaded(myevent:Event):void {
    myChannel=mySound.play();
    stage.addEventListener(Event.ENTER_FRAME, showprogress);
}

function showprogress(myevent:Event) {
    bar_mc.scaleX=myChannel.position/mySound.length;
}
```

Figure 8.22 The function called showprogress scales a movie clip on the Stage in proportion to the progress of the sound.

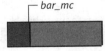
bar_mc

Figure 8.23 The dark bar on the left is a movie clip called bar_mc.

Modifying Volume and Balance

Flash gives you full control of its volume and its output through either the left or right speaker, which is known as *pan control*. With this level of sound control, you can let your users set the volume to their own preferences, and you can create environments that are more realistic. In a car game, for example, you can vary the volume of the sound of cars as they approach or pass you. Playing with the pan controls, you can embellish the classic Pong game by making the sounds of the ball hitting the paddles and the walls play from the appropriate sides.

To modify the volume and balance in a sound, you must provide a third parameter in the `play()` method (recall that the first parameter determines the playback offset, and the second parameter determines the number of loops). The third parameter requires an object of the `SoundTransform` class, like so:

```
var newVolume:SoundTransform=new
→ SoundTransform();
```

Assign a new value for the `volume` property, and then pass the object as the third parameter of the `play()` method, like so:

```
newVolume.volume=.5;
mySound.play(0,0,newVolume);
```

To change the volume or pan of a sound that's already playing, you can assign the `SoundTransform` object to the `soundTransform` property of the `SoundChannel` object. For example:

```
var newVolume:SoundTransform=new
→ SoundTransform();

newVolume.volume=.5;

myChannel.soundTransform=newVolume;
```

The first statement creates a new `SoundTransform` object called `newVolume`. Next, the `volume` property of the new `SoundTransform` object is changed. Finally, the `SoundTransform` object is assigned to the `soundTransform` property of the `SoundChannel` object associated with the sound that's playing.

The `SoundTransform` class has properties such as `volume` for modifying the volume and `pan` for modifying the left-right speaker balance. See **Table 8.1** for a description of these and other properties of the `SoundTransform` class.

Table 8.1

SoundTransform Properties	
PROPERTY	DESCRIPTION
volume	Number (0=silent to 1=full volume)
pan	Number (-1=left to 1=right)
leftToLeft	Number(0 to 1) determining how much of the left input plays in the left speaker
leftToRight	Number(0 to 1) determining how much of the left input plays in the right speaker
rightToLeft	Number(0 to 1) determining how much of the right input plays in the left speaker
rightToRight	Number(0 to 1) determining how much of the right input plays in the right speaker

```
var myRequest:URLRequest=new URLRequest ("music.mp3");
var mySound:Sound = new Sound();
mySound.load(myRequest);

var newSetting:SoundTransform = new SoundTransform();
newSetting.volume=0.5;
```

Figure 8.24 The volume property of this SoundTransform object is set to 50% of the full volume.

```
var myRequest:URLRequest=new URLRequest ("music.mp3");
var mySound:Sound = new Sound();
mySound.load(myRequest);

var newSetting:SoundTransform = new SoundTransform();
newSetting.volume=0.5;

var myChannel:SoundChannel=mySound.play(0,5,newSetting);
```

Figure 8.25 Pass the SoundTransform object called newSetting as the third parameter in the play() method. This sound will play from the beginning, loop five times, and play at 50% of its full volume.

To change the volume or balance before playback:

1. Declare and instantiate a URLRequest object with the constructor function new URLRequest() and provide the path to an MP3 file as the parameter.

2. On the next line, declare and instantiate a Sound object with the constructor function new Sound().

3. On the next line, enter the name of your Sound object followed by a period. Enter the method load() and provide the URLRequest object as the parameter.

   Flash loads the external MP3 file requested in the URLRequest object.

4. On a new line, declare and instantiate a SoundTransform object with the constructor function new SoundTransform().

   The SoundTransform object will provide the properties to change a sound's volume and balance.

5. On the next line, enter the name of your SoundTransform object followed by a period. Enter the property volume (to control volume level) or pan (to control balance) followed by an equals sign and a value (**Figure 8.24**).

6. On a new line, enter the name of your Sound object followed by a period. Enter the method play(). For the parameters, enter 0, 5, and then the name of your SoundTransform object (**Figure 8.25**). Assign the returned value of the play() method to a SoundChannel object.

7. Test your movie.

   The play method plays your sound, and it uses the SoundTransform object to modify the volume or pan.

MODIFYING VOLUME AND BALANCE

To change the volume or balance during playback:

1. Create a button and place an instance on the Stage. In the Property inspector, give the button instance a name (**Figure 8.26**).

   You will assign an event handler to a mouse click over this button that will change the volume of a sound as it plays.

2. On the first frame of the Timeline in the Actions panel, declare and instantiate a URLRequest object with the constructor function new URLRequest() and provide the path to an external MP3 file as the parameter.

3. On the next line, declare and instantiate a Sound object with the constructor function new Sound().

4. On the next line, enter the name of your Sound object followed by a period. Enter the method load() and provide the URLRequest object as the parameter.

   Flash loads the external MP3 file requested in the URLRequest object.

5. On a new line, declare and instantiate a SoundTransform object with the constructor function new SoundTransform().

   The SoundTransform object will provide the properties to change a sound's volume and balance. In this example, the SoundTransform object is called newSetting.

6. On the next line, enter the code:

   ```
   var myChannel:SoundChannel=mySound.
   → play()
   ```

   This statement plays the sound and puts the returned SoundChannel object of the play() method in a new variable (of a SoundChannel type) called myChannel (**Figure 8.27**).

7. On the next line, create an event handler that detects a mouse click on the button on the Stage. In between the curly braces of the function, add the statement:

   ```
   newSetting.volume-=0.1;
   ```

   This statement subtracts 0.1 from the volume property of the SoundTransform object each time the button is clicked.

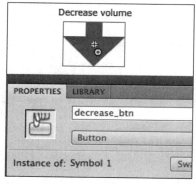

Figure 8.26 This button instance on the Stage is named decrease_btn.

```
var myRequest:URLRequest=new URLRequest ("music.mp3");
var mySound:Sound = new Sound();
mySound.load(myRequest);

var newSetting:SoundTransform = new SoundTransform();
var myChannel:SoundChannel=mySound.play();
```

Figure 8.27 The external MP3 sound called music.mp3 plays.

```
decrease_btn.addEventListener(MouseEvent.CLICK, decreaseVolume);
function decreaseVolume(myevent:MouseEvent):void {
    newSetting.volume-=0.1;
    myChannel.soundTransform=newSetting;
}
```

Figure 8.28 The event handler for the decrease_btn button on the Stage. Each time the button is clicked, the volume property of the SoundTransform object called newSetting decreases by 0.1. The SoundTransform object is assigned to the soundTransform property of the SoundChannel object to take effect.

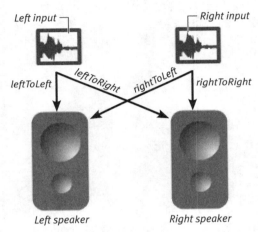

Figure 8.29 The properties of the SoundTransform object that determine the distribution of sounds between the left and right speakers. The values are measured between 0 and 1.

8. On the next line, still within the function of the event handler, add the statement:

myChannel.soundTransform=newSetting;

This statement assigns the soundTransform property of the sound to the settings in your newSetting SoundTransform object to decrease the volume level (**Figure 8.28**).

9. Test your movie.

The external MP3 file loads and plays. Each time the user clicks the button, the volume property of the SoundTransform object called newSetting decreases by 0.1. The new volume is then set while the sound still plays.

To switch the left and right speakers:

◆ Assign the following values for a SoundTransform object:

leftToLeft=0;

leftToRight=1;

rightToRight=0;

rightToLeft=1;

Changing these properties of the SoundTransform object and passing it to the soundTransform property of the SoundChannel object or as the third parameter of the play() method redistributes the sound inputs to switch the speakers (**Figure 8.29**).

✔ Tip

■ As a shortcut, you can also set the properties of a new SoundTransform object at the time you instantiate it. For example, var myNewSettings:SoundTransform=new SoundTransform(.5, 1); is the same as the following code:

var myNewSettings:SoundTransform=new → SoundTransform();

myNewSettings.volume=.5;

myNewSettings.pan=1;

MODIFYING VOLUME AND BALANCE

331

Detecting Sound Events

You can detect when a sound finishes playing by using the Event.SOUND_COMPLETE event of the SoundChannel class. For example, consider the following script:

```
myChannel.addEventListener
  (Event.SOUND_COMPLETE, finished);

function finished(myevent:Event):void {

    // sound finished

}
```

In this script, when the sound associated with the SoundChannel object called myChannel is complete, Flash triggers the function called finished and executes any actions there.

The Event.SOUND_COMPLETE event lets you control and integrate your sounds in several powerful ways. Imagine creating a jukebox that randomly plays selections from a bank of songs. When one song finishes, Flash knows to load a new song. Or you could build a business presentation in which the slides are timed to the end of the narration. In the following task, the completion of the sound triggers the loading and playing of a second sound.

Warning!
Event.SOUND_COMPLETE
on Windows Vista

At the time of this writing, the SOUND_COMPLETE event does not work reliably on Windows Vista. You should keep your eyes (and ears) close to the Adobe Flash forums and developer blogs for any new developments and fixes to this problem.

One workaround would be to use the SoundChannel object's position property and the Sound object's length property to keep track of the progress of the sound (see the task, "To track the sound progress").

```
var myRequest:URLRequest=new URLRequest ("music1.mp3");
var mySound:Sound = new Sound();
mySound.load(myRequest);
var myChannel:SoundChannel=mySound.play();
```

Figure 8.30 The external MP3 sound called music1.mp3 plays.

```
var myRequest:URLRequest=new URLRequest ("music1.mp3");
var mySound:Sound = new Sound();
mySound.load(myRequest);
var myChannel:SoundChannel=mySound.play();

myChannel.addEventListener(Event.SOUND_COMPLETE, finished);
```

Figure 8.31 The event listener detects when the sound is completed and will trigger the function (not yet written here) called `finished`.

```
var myRequest:URLRequest=new URLRequest ("music1.mp3");
var mySound:Sound = new Sound();
mySound.load(myRequest);
var myChannel:SoundChannel=mySound.play();

myChannel.addEventListener(Event.SOUND_COMPLETE, finished);

function finished(myevent:Event) {
    var myRequest2:URLRequest=new URLRequest ("music2.mp3");
    var mySound2:Sound = new Sound();
    mySound2.load(myRequest2);
    myChannel2=mySound2.play();
}
```

Figure 8.32 The function called `finished` begins playing a second sound file.

To detect the completion of a sound:

1. Declare and instantiate a `URLRequest` object with the constructor function `new URLRequest()` and provide the path to an MP3 file as the parameter.

2. On the next line, declare and instantiate a `Sound` object with the constructor function `new Sound()`.

3. On the next line, enter the name of your Sound object followed by a period. Enter the method `load()` and provide the `URLRequest` object as the parameter.

   Flash loads the external MP3 file requested in the `URLRequest` object.

4. On a new line enter the name of your Sound object followed by a period. Enter the method `play()` without any parameters. Assign the returned value to a new `SoundChannel` object (**Figure 8.30**).

   The `play()` method plays your sound.

5. On the next line, add an event listener to the `SoundChannel` object. Listen for the `Event.SOUND_COMPLETE` event (**Figure 8.31**).

6. Add the function that gets triggered at the `Event.SOUND_COMPLETE` event (**Figure 8.32**).

   When the sound finishes, the function is called. In this example, a new Sound object is created and loads and plays a second sound.

✔ Tip

■ If a sound is looping, the `Event.SOUND_COMPLETE` event is triggered when all the loops have finished.

DETECTING SOUND EVENTS

Working with MP3 Song Information

MP3 files are the most popular format for storing and playing digital music. The MP3 compression gives a dramatic decrease in file size, yet the quality is maintained at near-CD levels. Another virtue of MP3 files is that they are capable of carrying simple information about the actual audio file. This *metadata* (descriptive information about data) tag was originally appended to the end of an MP3 file and called ID3 version 1. Information about the music file (such as song title, artist, album, year, comment, and genre) could be stored at the end of the song file in the ID3 tag and then detected and read by decoders.

Over time and slight version upgrades, ID3 is currently at version 2. One of the more notable improvements was moving the data to the beginning of the song file to better support streaming. It now also supports several new fields, such as composer, conductor, media type, copyright message, and recording date.

Flash can read the ID3v2 data of an MP3 file. Each bit of information about the song, or *tag*, corresponds to a property of the id3 object of the Sound object. So, for example, mySound.id3.TALB refers to the album name of the MP3 file. **Table 8.2** covers all the ID3 version 2 Sound properties.

How do you retrieve these ID3 properties? You must first create an event handler that is triggered when available ID3 tags are present after a play() method is called. Using the event Event.ID3 is the only way you can access the ID3 data.

In the following task, you'll load an external MP3 file and display the track information in the Output panel.

Table 8.2

ID3v2 Sound Properties	
PROPERTY	DESCRIPTION
id3.COMM	Comment
id3.TALB	Album/movie/show title
id3.TBPM	Beats per minute
id3.TCOM	Composer
id3.TCOP	Copyright message
id3.TDAT	Date
id3.TDLY	Playlist delay
id3.TENC	Encoded by
id3.TEXT	Lyricist/text writer
id3.TFLT	File type
id3.TIME	Time
id3.TIT1	Content group description
id3.TIT2	Title/song name/description
id3.TIT3	Subtitle/description refinement
id3.TKEY	Initial key
id3.TLAN	Languages
id3.TLEN	Length
id3.TMED	Media type
id3.TOAL	Original album/movie/show title
id3.TOFN	Original filename
id3.TOLY	Original lyricists/text writer
id3.TOPE	Original artists/performers
id3.TORY	Original release year
id3.TOWN	File owner/licensee
id3.TPE1	Lead performers/soloists
id3.TPE2	Band/orchestra/accompaniment
id3.TPE3	Conductor/performer refinement
id3.TPE4	Interpreted, remixed, or otherwise modified by
id3.TPOS	Part of a set
id3.TPUB	Publisher
id3.TRCK	Track number/position in set
id3.TRDA	Recording dates
id3.TRSN	Internet radio station name
id3.TRSO	Internet radio station owner
id3.TSIZ	Size
id3.TSRC	International Standard Recording Code (ISRC)
id3.TSSE	Software/hardware and settings used for encoding
id3.TYER	Year
id3.WXXX	URL link frame

```
var myRequest:URLRequest=new URLRequest ("music.mp3");
var mySound:Sound = new Sound();
mySound.load(myRequest);
mySound.play();
```

Figure 8.33 The external MP3 sound called music.mp3 plays.

```
mySound.addEventListener(Event.ID3, gotmetadata);
function gotmetadata(myevent:Event):void {
    trace( "title="+mySound.id3.TIT2);
}
```

Figure 8.34 The Event.ID3 event happens when metadata from the MP3 file is received. The property id3.TIT2 refers to the artist's name.

To retrieve song information about an MP3 file:

1. Declare and instantiate a URLRequest object with the constructor function new URLRequest() and provide the path to an MP3 file as the parameter.

2. On the next line, declare and instantiate a Sound object with the constructor function new Sound().

3. On the next line, enter the name of your Sound object followed by a period. Enter the method load() and provide the URLRequest object as the parameter.

   Flash loads the external MP3 file requested in the URLRequest object.

4. On the next line, enter the name of your Sound object followed by a period. Enter the method play() without any parameters (**Figure 8.33**).

   The play() method plays your sound.

5. Add an event listener to your Sound object. Listen for the Event.ID3 event as in the following:

   mySound.addEventListener(Event.ID3, → gotmetadata);

   When Flash receives the ID3 metadata from the loading MP3 file, it triggers the function called gotmetadata.

6. Add the function called gotmetadata that gets triggered by the Event.ID3 event. In between the curly braces of the function, add a trace statement that displays the ID3 property, like this (**Figure 8.34**):

   function gotmetadata(myevent:Event): → void{

   trace("title="+mySound.id3.TIT2);

   }

   In this example, the trace action displays the title information of the MP3 song and appends it to the string "title=".

Continues on next page

7. Add more trace statements within the curly braces of the function to retrieve all the ID3 information you want (**Figure 8.35**).

8. Save your FLA file in the location where it can find your MP3 file based on the target path you entered for your URLRequest object.

When you test your movie in the Flash authoring environment, the Output panel displays the ID3 information (**Figure 8.36**).

✔ Tips

- Using dynamic text fields, you can have Flash dynamically populate text fields and display the ID3 information on the Stage (rather than in the Output panel). You'll learn more about dynamic text fields in Chapter 10, "Controlling Text."

- When an MP3 file contains a mix of ID3v2 and ID3v1 tags, the event handler onID3 is triggered twice.

- To view the ID3 files of your MP3 files outside of Flash:

  In Windows XP: Right-click the MP3 file, and select Properties > Summary > Advanced.

  Using Mac OS X: In iTunes, select the song in your playlist, and press Cmd-I.

```
var myRequest:URLRequest=new URLRequest ("music.mp3");
var mySound:Sound = new Sound();
mySound.load(myRequest);
mySound.play();

mySound.addEventListener(Event.ID3, gotmetadata);
function gotmetadata(myevent:Event):void {
    trace( "title="+mySound.id3.TIT2);
    trace( "artist="+mySound.id3.artist);
}
```

Figure 8.35 The two trace statements display the artist's name and song title in the Output panel in test movie mode when the Event.ID3 event occurs.

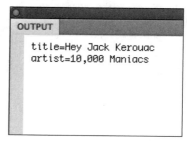

Figure 8.36 The Output panel in Flash test movie mode.

Visualizing Sound Data

You've probably seen sound represented visually as waves or vertical spikes like mountain peaks, or perhaps even vibrating, shimmering lines and colors on a computer screen saver or a laser light show. These graphical effects are tied to different aspects of a sound; as the sound changes, so do the graphics, giving the users a direct visual representation of what they're hearing. This kind of visualization is an effective way of providing feedback that a sound is playing.

You can provide similar graphical representations of your sound in Flash. The SoundChannel class provides two properties, leftPeak and rightPeak, that indicate the volume levels for the left speaker and right speaker at any given moment during the sound. By continuously retrieving both properties with the Event.ENTER_FRAME event, or with a Timer object, you can display their values graphically, perhaps by scaling a vertical bar proportionately, for example.

In the following task, an external MP3 file is loaded and plays dynamically, and two rectangular movie clips change their scaleY properties to reflect the values of leftPeak and rightPeak.

Figure 8.37 Two rectangular movie clips on the Stage, the left named barleft_mc and the right (shown selected) named barright_mc. Their registration points are at the bottom edge.

To visualize left and right volume levels:

1. Create a movie clip symbol of a vertical bar and place two instances on the Stage. In the Property inspector, give each instance a different name. Make sure that the registration point for both movie clips is at the bottom edge (**Figure 8.37**).

   These two bars will change in height to reflect the volume levels of the right and left speakers.

2. Declare and instantiate a Sound object with the constructor function new Sound().

3. Instantiate a URLRequest object with the constructor function new URLRequest() and provide the path to an MP3 file as the parameter.

4. Enter the name of your Sound object followed by a period. Enter the method load() and provide the URLRequest object as the parameter.

   Flash loads the external MP3 file requested in the URLRequest object.

5. Call the play() method for your Sound object and assign the returned value to a new variable typed to a SoundChannel object, as follows:

   ```
   var myChannel:SoundChannel=mySound.
   ↵ play();
   ```

   Flash plays the sound and a new SoundChannel object is created for it (**Figure 8.38**).

   Continues on next page

```
var mySound:Sound = new Sound();
var myRequest:URLRequest = new URLRequest("music.mp3");
mySound.load(myRequest);

var myChannel:SoundChannel= mySound.play();
```

Figure 8.38 The external MP3 sound called music.mp3 plays.

6. Add an event listener to the stage that detects the `Event.ENTER_FRAME` event, like so:

```
stage.addEventListener
→ (Event.ENTER_FRAME, everyframe);
```

Flash triggers the function called `everyframe` at the frame rate of the Flash movie.

7. Add the function to respond to the `Event.ENTER_FRAME` event.

8. In between the curly braces of the function, enter the statements that change the movie clips, like so (**Figure 8.39**):

```
everyframe(event:Event):void{
    barleft_mc.scaleY=
→ (myChannel.leftPeak);
    barright_mc.scaleY=
→ (myChannel.rightPeak);
}
```

The `leftPeak` and `rightPeak` properties of the `SoundChannel` object vary from 0 to 1. They are assigned to the `scaleY` property of the movie clips to vary their heights.

9. Make sure your external MP3 file is in the location where your Flash file can find it based on the information you provided in the `URLRequest` object. Test your movie (Control > Test Movie) (**Figure 8.40**).

✔ Tip

■ Flash provides an even more sophisticated way of looking at raw sound data with the `computeSpectrum()` method of the `SoundMixer` class. This method returns data for the frequency spectrum, which is the measure of the strength of the sound at each tone (where low frequencies are low-pitched tones and high frequencies are high-pitched tones). For more information and examples, look in Flash Help. Choose the category ActionScript 3.0 and Components > Programming ActionScript 3.0 > Working with Sound > Accessing raw sound data.

```
stage.addEventListener(Event.ENTER_FRAME, everyframe);
function everyframe(event:Event):void {
    barleft_mc.scaleY=(myChannel.leftPeak);
    barright_mc.scaleY=(myChannel.rightPeak);
}
```

Figure 8.39 The `Event.ENTER_FRAME` event handler continuously scales both rectangular movie clips according to the sound's `leftPeak` and `rightPeak` properties.

Figure 8.40 The two rectangular movie clips move up and down synchronized to the sound.

Putting It Together: Dynamic Sound Controls

One of the most effective uses of the Sound class and its related classes is to create dynamic controls that allow the user to set the desired volume level or speaker balance. A common strategy is to create a draggable object that acts as a sliding controller. By correlating the position of the draggable object with the volume property of the soundTransform property of the SoundChannel object, you can make the volume change dynamically as the viewer moves the slider bar.

For a slider bar that controls volume, you must create two elements: the handle or slider and the track or groove it runs along (**Figure 8.41**). Create a movie clip called groove_mc. To make things easy, make the

groove_mc movie clip 100 pixels wide with its registration point at the left of the rectangle. Making the groove_mc 100 pixels wide will make it simpler to correlate the position of the slider on the groove_mc with the volume property. To create the draggable slider, create a movie clip called slider_mc and assign the startDrag() method with constraints on the motion relative to the area of the groove_mc movie clip.

To create the volume and balance interface:

1. Create a movie clip of a wide rectangle that is 100 pixels wide and whose registration point lies at the left edge.

2. Place an instance of the clip on the Stage, and name it volumegroove_mc in the Property inspector.

3. Create another movie clip of a slider.

4. Place the slider clip on the volumegroove_mc movie clip, and name it volume_mc in the Property inspector (**Figure 8.42**).

5. Repeat steps 2–4, but name the groove and slider balancegroove_mc and balance_mc, respectively.

   The two sliders will be draggable objects that determine the volume and balance of the sound (**Figure 8.43**).

Continues on next page

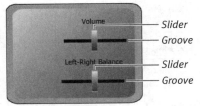

Figure 8.41 The components of both volume and balance controls are a slider and the groove it moves along.

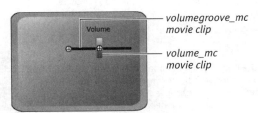

Figure 8.42 The movie clip instance called volume_mc will be a draggable movie clip along another movie clip called volumegroove_mc. Make sure that the registration point of the volumegroove_mc movie clip lies at its left edge.

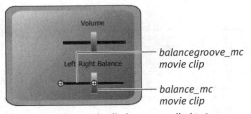

Figure 8.43 The movie clip instance called balance_mc will be a draggable movie clip along another movie clip called balancegroove_mc. Make sure that the registration point of the balancegroove_mc movie clip lies at its left edge.

6. In the Actions panel, create a new Rectangle object whose top-left corner matches the volumegroove_mc, whose width matches volumegroove_mc, and whose height is 1, like so:

```
var myvolumebounds:Rectangle=new
→ Rectangle(volumegroove_mc.x,
→ volumegroove_mc.y,
→ volumegroove_mc.width, 1);
```

The Rectangle object will constrain the draggable sliders in the area of the grooves.

7. On the next line, create a second Rectangle object that matches the location and dimensions of the balancegroove_mc (**Figure 8.44**).

8. On the next line, create an event listener that detects a MouseEvent.MOUSE_DOWN event over the volume_mc slider.

The MOUSE_DOWN event will call on a startDrag action for the slider.

9. On the next line, create an event listener that detects a MouseEvent.MOUSE_UP event over the volume_mc slider.

The MOUSE_UP event will call on a stopDrag action for the slider.

10. Repeat steps 8–9 and create MOUSE_DOWN and MOUSE_UP event listeners for the balance_mc slider. The MOUSE_UP event handler for both the volume_mc and balance_mc can call on the same function (**Figure 8.45**).

11. On the next line, create the event handler functions that begin the dragging and stop the dragging. For the startDrag() methods, use the Rectangle object as constraints on the dragging (**Figure 8.46**).

The dragging and dropping of the sliders are complete. Continue with the next task to play the sound and link the positions of the sliders to volume and balance.

```
var myvolumebounds:Rectangle=new Rectangle(volumegroove_mc.x, volumegroove_mc.y, volumegroove_mc.width, 1);
var mybalancebounds:Rectangle=new Rectangle(balancegroove_mc.x, balancegroove_mc.y, balancegroove_mc.width, 1);
```

Figure 8.44 Two Rectangle objects are created that will be used to limit the dragging action of the sliders. The rectangle is positioned at the left edge of the grooves, is as wide as the grooves, and is only 1 pixel high.

```
volume_mc.addEventListener(MouseEvent.MOUSE_DOWN, startdragvolume);
volume_mc.addEventListener(MouseEvent.MOUSE_UP, stopdrag);
balance_mc.addEventListener(MouseEvent.MOUSE_DOWN, startdragbalance);
balance_mc.addEventListener(MouseEvent.MOUSE_UP, stopdrag);
```

Figure 8.45 The addEventListener() methods for the MOUSE_DOWN and MOUSE_UP events will initiate the drag-and-drop behavior.

```
function startdragvolume(myevent:MouseEvent):void {
    myevent.target.startDrag(false, myvolumebounds);
}
function startdragbalance(myevent:MouseEvent):void {
    myevent.target.startDrag(false, mybalancebounds);
}
function stopdrag(myevent:MouseEvent):void {
    myevent.target.stopDrag();
}
```

Figure 8.46 The event handlers for the drag-and-drop behavior for both the volume slider and the balance slider. Pass the Rectangle objects for the parameter in the startDrag() methods to constrain the slider along a 1-pixel track as wide as each of the grooves.

To correlate slider position with volume and balance:

1. On the next line in the Actions panel, instantiate a URLRequest object, a Sound object, a SoundChannel object, and a SoundTransform object (**Figure 8.47**).

2. Call the load() method of the Sound object and call the play() method of the Sound object, and assign the returned value to the SoundChannel object (**Figure 8.48**).

3. On the next line, add an event listener for the Event.ENTER_FRAME event.

4. On the next line, create the event handler function for the Event.ENTER_FRAME event.

This function will be triggered continuously, so you will put the actions to link slider position to volume and balance within this function.

```
var myRequest:URLRequest=new URLRequest ("music.mp3");
var mySound:Sound = new Sound();
var myChannel:SoundChannel;
var newSetting:SoundTransform = new SoundTransform();
```

Figure 8.47 This block of code creates the objects required for playing and controlling an external MP3 file.

```
mySound.load(myRequest);
myChannel=mySound.play();
```

Figure 8.48 In this block of code, the sound plays.

```
stage.addEventListener(Event.ENTER_FRAME, everyframe);
function everyframe(myevent:Event):void {
    var newvolume:Number = (volume_mc.x-volumegroove_mc.x)/100;
    var newbalance:Number = ((balance_mc.x-balancegroove_mc.x)/50)-1;
    newSetting.volume=newvolume;
    newSetting.pan=newbalance;
    myChannel.soundTransform=newSetting;
}
```

5. In between the curly braces of the function, enter the following statement:

`var newvolume:Number = (volume_mc.` `x-volumegroove_mc.x)/100;`

The position of the volume groove is subtracted from the position of the slider, giving you a range of 0–100. Dividing the result by 100 gives you a number between 0 and 1, which you can use as the value for the volume property. The result is assigned to a new variable called newvolume.

6. On the next line, still within the curly braces of the function, enter the following statement:

`var newbalance:Number =` `((balance_mc.x-balancegroove_` `mc.x)/50)-1;`

The position of the balance groove is subtracted from the position of the balance slider, giving you a range of 0–100. Dividing the result by 50 gives you a number between 0 and 2, and finally subtracting 1 results in a range from -1 to 1. This result is assigned to a new variable called newbalance and can be used for the value of the pan property.

7. Assign new values for the volume and pan properties of the SoundTransform object, and then set the soundTransform property to the new SoundTransform object, like so (**Figure 8.49**):

`newSetting.volume=newvolume;`

`newSetting.pan=newbalance;`

`myChannel.soundTransform=newSetting;`

Continues on next page

Figure 8.49 In this block of code, you connect the position of the slider to the volume or balance levels. Within the Event.ENTER_FRAME event handler, do some calculations to get the range for the volume property between 0 and 1 and the range for the pan property between -1 and 1, and then assign the SoundTransform object to the soundTransform property of the SoundChannel object.

8. Make sure your external MP3 file is in the location where your Flash file can find it based on the information you provided in the URLRequest object. Test your movie (Control > Test Movie).

Flash loads and plays the sound. You can drag either the volume or balance slider across the length of its groove and dynamically control the volume and left-right speaker balance (**Figure 8.50**).

```
//
// define rectangles for dragging constraints
//
var myvolumebounds:Rectangle=new Rectangle(volumegroove_mc.x, volumegroove_mc.y, volumegroove_mc.width, 1);
var mybalancebounds:Rectangle=new Rectangle(balancegroove_mc.x, balancegroove_mc.y, balancegroove_mc.width, 1);
//
//drag volume sliders
//
volume_mc.addEventListener(MouseEvent.MOUSE_DOWN, startdragvolume);
volume_mc.addEventListener(MouseEvent.MOUSE_UP, stopdrag);
balance_mc.addEventListener(MouseEvent.MOUSE_DOWN, startdragbalance);
balance_mc.addEventListener(MouseEvent.MOUSE_UP, stopdrag);
function startdragvolume(myevent:MouseEvent):void {
    myevent.target.startDrag(false, myvolumebounds);
}
function startdragbalance(myevent:MouseEvent):void {
    myevent.target.startDrag(false, mybalancebounds);
}
function stopdrag(myevent:MouseEvent):void {
    myevent.target.stopDrag();
}
//
// create objects
//
var myRequest:URLRequest=new URLRequest ("music.mp3");
var mySound:Sound = new Sound();
var myChannel:SoundChannel;
var newSetting:SoundTransform = new SoundTransform();
//
// load and play sound
//
mySound.load(myRequest);
myChannel=mySound.play();
//
// change volume and balance continuously
//
stage.addEventListener(Event.ENTER_FRAME, everyframe);
function everyframe(myevent:Event):void {
    var newvolume:Number = (volume_mc.x-volumegroove_mc.x)/100;
    var newbalance:Number = ((balance_mc.x-balancegroove_mc.x)/50)-1;
    newSetting.volume=newvolume;
    newSetting.pan=newbalance;
    myChannel.soundTransform=newSetting;
}
```

Figure 8.50 The full code (left) creates the dynamic volume and balance slider controls (right).

Part IV: Working with Information

CONTROLLING INFORMATION FLOW

9

As your Flash movie displays graphics and animation and plays sounds, a lot can be happening behind the scenes that is not apparent to the viewer. Your Flash document may be tracking many bits of information, such as the number of lives a player has left in a game, a user's login name and password, or the items a customer has placed in a shopping cart. Getting and storing this information requires *variables,* which are containers for information. Variables are essential in any Flash movie that involves complex interactivity because they let you create scenarios based on information that changes. You can modify variables and use them in *expressions*—formulas that can combine variables with other variables and values—and then test the information against certain conditions to determine how the Flash movie will unfold. This testing is done in *conditional statements,* which control the flow of information. Conditional statements are the decision makers of your Flash movie; they evaluate information that comes in and then tell Flash what to do based on that information. You can use conditional statements to make a ball bounce back if it collides with a wall, for example, or to increase the speed of the ball if the game time exceeds one minute.

This chapter is about managing information by using variables, expressions, and conditional statements. You've dealt with all three in earlier chapters, but here you'll learn how to work with them in more detail. When you understand how to get, modify, and evaluate information, you can direct your Flash movie and change the graphics, animation, and sound in dynamic fashion.

Using Variables and Expressions

In Chapter 3, "Getting a Handle on ActionScript," you learned the basics of variables—how to declare them, assign values to them, and combine them in expressions. Now that you have more experience with variables in different contexts, this chapter takes another, more refined look at using variables and expressions in ActionScript.

You use variables and expressions as placeholders for parameters within your ActionScript. In virtually every method that requires you to enter a parameter, you can place a variable or an expression instead of a fixed value. For example, you can enter an expression instead of a frame number as the parameter for the basic method gotoAndStop(). This expression may be a variable myCard that holds a number from 1 to 52. Frames 1 through 52 in the Timeline can contain graphics of the 52 playing cards, so changing the variable myCard in the gotoAndStop() method makes Flash display different cards.

You can also use a variable as a simple counter. Rather than taking the place of a parameter, a counter variable keeps track of how many times certain things occur for later retrieval and testing. A player's score can be stored in a variable so that Flash knows when the player reaches enough points to win the game. Or a variable can keep track of a certain state. You can set the variable myShield = true if a character's force field is turned on, for example, and change the variable to myShield = false if the force field is turned off.

The Scope of Variables

When you initialize variables, they belong to the timeline where you create them. This is known as the *scope* of a variable. If you initialize a variable on the main Timeline, the variable is scoped to the main Timeline. If you initialize a variable inside a movie clip's timeline, the variable is scoped to that movie clip.

Think of a variable's scope as being its home. Variables live on certain timelines, and if you want to use the information inside a variable, first you must find it with a target path. This process is analogous to targeting objects. To access either an object or a variable, you identify it with a target path.

```
var frameNumber:Number = 5;
```

Figure 9.1 The variable `frameNumber` is initialized to 5.

```
var frameNumber:Number = 5;

stage.addEventListener(MouseEvent.CLICK, goframe);
function goframe(myevent:MouseEvent):void {
    gotoAndStop(frameNumber);
}
```

Figure 9.2 The variable `frameNumber` is the parameter for the `gotoAndStop()` method. Instead of a predefined fixed number, the `gotoAndStop()` method will use the value of the variable.

ActionScript in frame 1

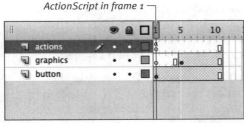

Figure 9.3 When the user clicks the Stage, Flash goes to the value of `frameNumber`, which is 5.

✔ Tip

■ To use a frame label instead of a frame number to identify the frame you want Flash to go to, declare your variable with the `String` data type. Assign the string "Conclusion" to the variable `myFrameLabel`, for example. By using `myFrameLabel` as the parameter in the `gotoAndPlay()` method, you can have Flash go to the frame labeled `Conclusion`.

To create and use a variable:

1. In the first keyframe of the main Timeline, declare a variable as described in Chapter 3, using the `var` statement, entering the name of the variable and a colon, and then specifying a data type. This example uses the data type `Number`. Assign a numerical value to your variable (**Figure 9.1**).

   In this example, you'll use the variable to hold a specific frame number.

2. Now to use the variable, on the next line, assign a `MouseEvent.CLICK` event handler to the Stage.

3. Between the curly braces of the event handler function, enter the method `gotoAndStop()`. For its parameter, enter the name of the variable you initialized in the main Timeline (**Figure 9.2**).

4. On a new line, add a `stop()` method to prevent the playhead from moving until the mouse button is clicked.

5. Provide additional frames so the playhead has somewhere to go.

6. Test your movie (**Figure 9.3**).

   Your variable contains a number. When Flash performs the `gotoAndStop()` method, it uses the information contained in the variable as the frame to go to. If you change the value of the variable, Flash will go to a different frame. This strategy lets you change parameters in code that may be spread throughout your movie by just changing variables initialized on the first keyframe.

USING VARIABLES AND EXPRESSIONS

347

Loading External Variables

You don't have to store the initial value of a variable inside your Flash movie. Flash lets you keep variables outside your Flash movie in a text document that you can load whenever you need the variables. This way, you can change the variables in the text document easily and thereby change the Flash movie without having to edit the movie. You can build a quiz, for example, with variables holding the questions and answers. Keep the variables in a text document, and when you want to change the quiz, edit the text document. You can also set up the variables in the text document to be generated automatically with server-side scripts based on other external data. Then your Flash movie can read the variables in the text document with only the most recent or user-customized values.

There are many ways in which data can be structured in an external document. One common way is to write variables and their values in the Multipurpose Internet Mail Extensions (MIME) URL-encoded format (or simply, URL variable format), which is a standard format that HTML forms and CGI scripts use. In the URL variable format, variables are written in the following form:

```
variable1=value1&variable2=
→ value2&variable3=value3
```

Each variable/value pair is separated from the next by a single ampersand (&) symbol.

```
caption1=Here's the new baby!&caption2=Our
trip to the Great Wall of China.&caption3=A
beautiful shot of the beach at sunset.
```

Figure 9.4 Three variables and their values written in URL variable format. In this example, the variables are saved in a text document called data.txt.

The URLLoader and URLVariables classes

To access the variables in your external text document, use the URLLoader class. It provides properties, methods, and events to handle and manage incoming (and outgoing) data. It is similar to the Loader class that you learned about in Chapter 6, "Managing External Communication," to load in external images and SWF files. You use the method load() to begin loading the data from the external text document. The location of the file is provided in a URLRequest object.

You can test how much of the external data has loaded with the ProgressEvent.PROGRESS event, or define actions to take when external data finishes loading with the Event.COMPLETE event handler.

When the download is complete, the contents of the text file are put in the data property of your URLLoader object, where you can further process the data to get it in the correct form that you want it in with the URLVariables class.

To load external variables:

1. Launch a text editor, and create a new document.

2. Write your variable names and their values in the standard URL variable format (**Figure 9.4**).

3. Save your text document in the same directory where your Flash movie will be saved.

   It doesn't matter what you name your file, but it helps to keep the name simple and to stick to a standard three-letter extension.

4. In Flash, open a new document.

5. Select the first keyframe of the root Timeline, and open the Actions panel.

6. In the Script pane, create a `URLLoader` object. Don't pass any parameters for the constructor.

7. On a new line of the Script pane, create a `URLRequest` object with the path to the text file that contains your variables.

If your SWF file and the text file will reside in the same directory, you can enter just the text file's name, as in this example. Enclose the path or filename in quotation marks (**Figure 9.5**).

8. On the next line, enter the name of your `URLLoader` object, and then call the method `load()`.

9. As a parameter of the `load()` method, enter the `URLRequest` object (**Figure 9.6**).

Flash calls the `load()` method, which loads the variable and value pairs from the external text file into the `URLLoader` object. The data comes into the `URLLoader` object's *data* property.

```
var myURLLoader:URLLoader = new URLLoader();
var myURLRequest:URLRequest = new URLRequest("data.txt");
```

Figure 9.5 The new `URLLoader` object and the `URLRequest` object are created. The `URLRequest` object points to the external file with the variables.

```
var myURLLoader:URLLoader = new URLLoader();
var myURLRequest:URLRequest = new URLRequest("data.txt");
myURLLoader.load(myURLRequest);
```

Figure 9.6 The `load()` method loads the data.txt file into Flash.

```
var myURLLoader:URLLoader = new URLLoader();
var myURLRequest:URLRequest = new URLRequest("data.txt");
myURLLoader.load(myURLRequest);

myURLLoader.addEventListener(Event.COMPLETE, dataOK);
function dataOK(myevent:Event):void {
    // do something with the loaded data
}
```

Figure 9.7 The `Event.COMPLETE` event handler for the `URLLoader` object will be triggered when the loading operation completes. Nothing is written inside the event handler yet.

Receiving the loaded data

After you call the `load()` method for your `URLLoader` object, the data isn't always immediately available to the Flash Player. For instance, the data is often loaded from a Web server, meaning it has to travel across the Internet to reach the Flash Player. You shouldn't try to do anything with the data until you know all of it has downloaded. You can detect when the data is completely loaded using the `Event.COMPLETE` event handler of the `URLLoader` object. Always wait for the `Event.COMPLETE` event handler to be called before attempting to use the loaded data. Typically, this means that you place the actions that use the loaded data within the event handler function.

To detect the completion of loaded data:

1. Continuing with the file you used in the preceding task, select the first frame of the main Timeline, and open the Actions panel.

2. On a new line at the end of the current script, enter the name of your `URLLoader` object followed by a period, and then call the `addEventListener()` method to detect the `Event.COMPLETE` event.

3. On the next line, enter the function for the event handler. In between the curly braces of the function, add actions to be performed using the loaded data (**Figure 9.7**).

The loaded variables are added as the *data* property of the `URLLoader` object. To access a variable and its value pair, you use a `URLVariables` object, as described in the next task.

Decoding the loaded data

If your external text document contains data in the form of variable/value pairs as in the example discussed earlier, you can use the URLVariables object to parse the data so you can use the variables. There are several ways you can go about this. You can create a URLVariables object, and then call the decode() method and pass the URLLoader object's data property as the parameter. This will put the variables in the URLVariables object.

```
var myURLVariables:URLVariables =
→ new URLVariables();
```

```
myURLVariables.decode(myURLLoader.data);
```

You can also pass the URLLoader object's data property directly to the URLVariables object when you create it. The preceding statements can also be written as:

```
var myURLVariables:URLVariables=
→ new URLVariables (myURLLoader.data);
```

Now the loaded variables and values can be used as long as you include your URLVariables object in the target path, such as:

```
myURLVariables.caption1
```

Another way to access the variable/value pairs from your URLLoader object is to define the dataFormat property of the URLLoader object before you load the data from the text document. You can set the property like so:

```
myURLLoader.dataFormat=
→ URLLoaderDataFormat.VARIABLES;
```

Your variables would be available to you through the data property of the URLLoader object, such as:

```
myURLLoader.data.caption1
```

To decode URL-encoded data:

1. Continuing with the file you used in the preceding task, select the first frame of the main Timeline and open the Actions panel.

2. Inside the function of the Event.COMPLETE event handler, create a new URLVariables object and pass the URLLoader.data property to the constructor (**Figure 9.8**).

   A new URLVariables object is created, and the data from the URLLoader object is decoded.

3. Add statements to reference and use the variables in the URLVariables object. In this example, the variables caption1, caption2, and caption3 are used to assign text to three dynamic text fields on the Stage (**Figure 9.9**).

   or

1. Continuing with the file you used in the preceding task, select the first frame of the main Timeline and open the Actions panel.

```
var myURLLoader:URLLoader = new URLLoader();
var myURLRequest:URLRequest = new URLRequest("data.txt");
myURLLoader.load(myURLRequest);

myURLLoader.addEventListener(Event.COMPLETE, dataOK);
function dataOK(myevent:Event):void {
    var myURLVariables:URLVariables= new URLVariables (myURLLoader.data);
}
```

Figure 9.8 The URLLoader.data object is passed to the URLVariables object for handling URL-encoded information.

```
var myURLLoader:URLLoader = new URLLoader();
var myURLRequest:URLRequest = new URLRequest("data.txt");
myURLLoader.load(myURLRequest);

myURLLoader.addEventListener(Event.COMPLETE, dataOK);
function dataOK(myevent:Event):void {
    var myURLVariables:URLVariables= new URLVariables (myURLLoader.data);
    textfield1.text=myURLVariables.caption1;
    textfield2.text=myURLVariables.caption2;
    textfield3.text=myURLVariables.caption3;
}
```

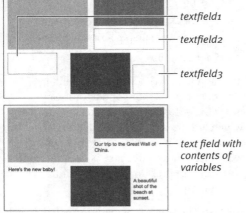

— textfield1

— textfield2

— textfield3

— text field with contents of variables

Figure 9.9 The full code (top) assigns the values of each of the variables in the external text document to three dynamic text fields on the Stage. These text fields are captions to images (shown as generic gray squares). Change the external text document to change the captions without having to open and edit your Flash document.

```
var myURLLoader:URLLoader = new URLLoader();
var myURLRequest:URLRequest = new URLRequest("data.txt");
myURLLoader.dataFormat=URLLoaderDataFormat.VARIABLES;
myURLLoader.load(myURLRequest);
myURLLoader.addEventListener(Event.COMPLETE, dataOK);
function dataOK(myevent:Event):void {
}
```

Figure 9.10 An alternative way of loading URL-encoded data is to set the dataFormat property of your URLLoader object to the string "variables" or the equivalent constant URLLoaderDataFormat. VARIABLES.

```
var myURLLoader:URLLoader = new URLLoader();
var myURLRequest:URLRequest = new URLRequest("data.txt");
myURLLoader.dataFormat=URLLoaderDataFormat.VARIABLES;
myURLLoader.load(myURLRequest);
myURLLoader.addEventListener(Event.COMPLETE, dataOK);
function dataOK(myevent:Event):void {
    textfield1.text=myURLLoader.data.caption1;
    textfield2.text=myURLLoader.data.caption2;
    textfield3.text=myURLLoader.data.caption3;
}
```

2. Insert a new line before the load() method of the URLLoader object. Assign the URLLoaderDataFormat.VARIABLES property to the dataFormat property of the URLLoader object (**Figure 9.10**).

The dataFormat property determines how the data from the external text file will load. Other options include BINARY or TEXT. (TEXT is the default value.)

3. Inside the Event.COMPLETE event handler function, add statements to reference and use the variables in the URLLoader's data object. In this example, the variables caption1, caption2, and caption3 are used to assign text to three dynamic text fields on the Stage (**Figure 9.11**).

✔ Tips

- If you are loading numeric data from external text files, you need to convert the values into numeric values by using methods such as int(), uint(), or Number().

- The default value for the dataFormat property of the URLLoader object is URLLoaderDataFormat.TEXT.

- Write your variable and value pairs in an external text file without any line breaks, spaces, or other punctuation except the ampersand. Although you may have a harder time reading the file, Flash will have an easier time understanding it.

Figure 9.11 If you set the dataFormat of your URLLoader, you can access the variables directly from the data property.

LOADING EXTERNAL VARIABLES

351

Using XML data

The previous examples showed you how to load and decode URL-encoded variables that are in the format of variable/value pairs. However, when you have more complex data, using XML is a better way to structure, read, and use the data.

XML is similar to a traditional markup language such as HTML, which contains information surrounded by tags that are interpreted by a computer. HTML tells the Web browser how to display information—make this text bold, put this image on the left, and so on. XML is more generic than HTML in that it lets you define information according to its content rather than its appearance. For example, you can identify one piece of information as a name and another piece of information as an address. XML also lets you order the data in an outline, or tree-like, structure. For example, the data that was loaded in the previous tasks (the caption text for three pictures on the Stage) were represented in URL-encoded format, like so:

```
caption1=Here's the new baby!&caption2=
→ Our trip to the Great Wall of China.
→ &caption3=A beautiful shot of the
→ beach at sunset.
```

In XML, you could write the same data as:

```
<slidecaptions>

<mycaption>Here's the new
→ baby!</mycaption>

<mycaption>Our trip to the Great Wall
→ of China.</mycaption>

<mycaption>A beautiful shot of
→ the beach at sunset.</mycaption>

</slidecaptions>
```

The data within the XML document is clearer and gives more opportunities to order the data. XML consists of nodes, which are the individual parts that can be arranged in a hierarchy. In the previous example, <slidecaptions> is the root node with <mycaption> and the text values as child nodes.

In Flash, the process of loading XML data is similar to other methods of loading data: You use the URLLoader class and its load() method to start loading an XML document, and you define an Event.COMPLETE event handler so you know when all the data is loaded. Once the data is loaded, you can use the methods of the XML object to *parse*, or decode, the data and retrieve the values. Use the dot operator (.) and the array access operator ([]) to traverse parent and child nodes to access their properties.

Although it's beyond the scope of this book to cover XML in depth, the following example will help you understand how Flash can load simple XML data and extract the information.

```
<slidecaptions>

<mycaption> Here is the new baby!</mycaption>
<mycaption> Our trip to the Great Wall of China.</mycaption>
<mycaption> A beautiful shot of the beach at sunset.</mycaption>

</slidecaptions>
```

Figure 9.12 Data in an XML format. This is a text document that is saved in the same directory as your Flash file.

```
var myURLLoader:URLLoader = new URLLoader();
var myURLRequest:URLRequest = new URLRequest("data.xml");
myURLLoader.load(myURLRequest);
myURLLoader.addEventListener(Event.COMPLETE, dataOK);
function dataOK(myevent:Event):void {
    // do something with data
}
```

Figure 9.13 Loading an XML document is the same as loading one in URL variables format—creating the URLLoader object, creating the URLRequest object, loading the document, and listening for the completion of the load.

```
var myURLLoader:URLLoader = new URLLoader();
var myURLRequest:URLRequest = new URLRequest("data.xml");
myURLLoader.load(myURLRequest);
myURLLoader.addEventListener(Event.COMPLETE, dataOK);
function dataOK(myevent:Event):void {
    var myXML:XML=new XML(myURLLoader.data);
}
```

Figure 9.14 Pass the URLLoader's *data* property to the new XML object.

To decode XML data:

1. Launch a text editor, and create a new document.

2. Write your data in XML format, as shown in **Figure 9.12.**

3. Save your text document in the same directory where your Flash movie will be saved.

4. In Flash, open a new document.

5. Select the first keyframe of the main Timeline, and open the Actions panel.

6. As described in the earlier tasks, create a URLLoader and load the external XML document. Create an event handler to detect the completion of the loading process (**Figure 9.13**).

7. Inside the function of the Event.COMPLETE event handler, create a new XML object and pass the URLLoader.data property to the constructor (**Figure 9.14**).

   Data from the external XML document is put inside the XML object. You can now use dot syntax to access the nodes and information in the XML object (here, it's called myXML).

   Continues on next page

LOADING EXTERNAL VARIABLES

8. On the next line still within the function, access the first piece of information in the `mycaption` object of the `XML` object with square brackets, and assign it to a text field on the Stage, like so:

`textfield1.text=myXML.mycaption[0]`

The square brackets access the first item—which is the text "Here's the new baby!"—and displays it in a text field on the Stage. The square brackets are a way of accessing the contents of an `Array` or of an object that has multiple elements inside it. You'll learn more about the square brackets later in this chapter and about the `Array` object in Chapter 11, "Manipulating Information."

9. Continue accessing the rest of the information and assign the results to the text fields on the Stage (**Figure 9.15**).

10. Create three dynamic text fields on the Stage and give them names in the Property inspector that match the names you used in your ActionScript.

11. Test your movie.

The data from the external XML document is loaded into your `URLLoader` object and then into the `XML` object. Using dots and square brackets, you can access the different information in the XML, and in this example, populate dynamic text fields for picture captions. Simply change the information in the XML document to have the changes be reflected in your Flash movie.

✔ Tip

■ If your XML element has an attribute, as in `<mycaption fontsize="14">`, you can access its value with the `@` symbol. For example, the statement `myXML.mycaption[0].@fontsize` would retrieve the value 14.

```
var myURLLoader:URLLoader = new URLLoader();
var myURLRequest:URLRequest = new URLRequest("data.xml");
myURLLoader.load(myURLRequest);
myURLLoader.addEventListener(Event.COMPLETE, dataOK);
function dataOK(myevent:Event):void {
    var myXML:XML=new XML(myURLLoader.data);
    textfield1.text=myXML.mycaption[0];
    textfield2.text=myXML.mycaption[1];
    textfield3.text=myXML.mycaption[2];
}
```

Figure 9.15 The information in the XML document can be accessed with dot operators and square brackets (array access operators).

Storing and Sharing Information

Although variables enable you to keep track of information, they do so only within a single playing of a Flash movie. When your viewer quits the movie, all the information in variables is lost. When the viewer returns to the movie, the variables are again initialized to their starting values or are loaded from external sources.

You can have Flash remember the current values of your variables even after a viewer quits the movie, however. The solution is to use the SharedObject class. SharedObject instances save information on a viewer's computer, much like browsers save information in cookies. When a viewer returns to a movie that has saved a SharedObject, that object can be loaded back in and the variables from the previous visit can be used.

You can use the SharedObject class in a variety of ways to make your Flash site more convenient for repeat visitors. Store visitors' high scores in a game, or store their login names so they don't have to type them again. If you've created a complex puzzle game, you can store the positions of the pieces for completion at a later date; for a long animated story, you can store the user's current location; or for a site with a collection of articles,

you can store information about which ones your visitor has already read.

To store information in a SharedObject instance, add a new property to the SharedObject's data property object. You then store the information that you want to keep in your new property. The statement mySharedObject.data.highscore = 200 stores the high-score information in the SharedObject instance. The method getLocal() creates or retrieves a SharedObject, and the method flush() causes the data properties to be written to the computer's hard drive.

In the following task, you'll save a login name from a text field (you'll learn more about text fields in the next chapter). When you quit and then return to the movie, your login name is retrieved and displayed.

To store information on a user's computer:

1. Select the Text tool, and drag a text field onto the Stage.

2. In the Property inspector, select Input Text, and give the text field the instance name myLogin_txt (**Figure 9.16**).

   This input text field allows users to enter information via the keyboard.

   Continues on next page

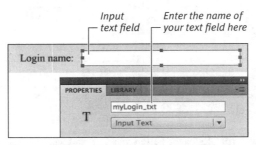

Input text field

Enter the name of your text field here

Figure 9.16 Create an input text field with the Text tool, and give it a name in the Property inspector.

3. Create a button, place an instance of it on the Stage, and give it an instance name in the Property inspector.

You'll assign actions to this button to save the information in your text field in a SharedObject.

4. Select the first frame of the main Timeline, and open the Actions panel.

5. In the Script pane, declare a new SharedObject by entering var mySharedObject:SharedObject followed by an equals sign.

6. On the right side of the equals sign, enter SharedObject.getLocal("myCookie") (**Figure 9.17**).

Flash looks for a SharedObject, and if it does not find one, it creates a SharedObject instance that will be stored on the user's local hard drive.

7. On the next line, create a MouseEvent.CLICK event handler for your button.

8. Between the curly braces of the event handler function, enter the following:

mySharedObject.data.loginData =
→ myLogin_txt.text

The content of your text field on the Stage is saved in a property named loginData on the data property of your SharedObject.

9. On the next line, enter mySharedObject.flush() (**Figure 9.18**).

Calling the flush() method saves all the information in the data property of your SharedObject on the viewer's computer.

✔ Tips

■ If the flush() method isn't called explicitly, the information in the data object of your SharedObject is saved automatically when the viewer quits the movie. The flush() method lets you choose when to save information.

■ Many kinds of information can be stored in the data object of a SharedObject, such as numbers, strings, and even objects such as an array.

Just remember to assign the information to the data object of a SharedObject, as in

mySharedObject.data.name = "Russell"

rather than

mySharedObject.data = "Russell"

```
var mySharedObject:SharedObject = SharedObject.getLocal("myCookie");
```

Figure 9.17 The getLocal() method creates a SharedObject that will be stored on the user's computer.

```
var mySharedObject:SharedObject = SharedObject.getLocal("myCookie");

saveButton_btn.addEventListener(MouseEvent.CLICK, savedata);
function savedata(myevent:MouseEvent):void {
  mySharedObject.data.myLoginData = myLogin_txt.text;
  mySharedObject.flush();
}
```

Figure 9.18 Clicking the button called saveButton_btn puts the contents of the input text field in the myLoginData property of the data property of your SharedObject and saves it on the user's computer.

To retrieve information from a user's computer:

1. Continuing with the file you used in the preceding task, create a second button, place an instance of it on the Stage, and give it a name in the Property inspector.

   You'll assign actions to this second button, which will retrieve `mySharedObject.data` and the most recently saved contents of your text field.

2. Select the main Timeline, and in the Actions panel, assign a `MouseEvent.CLICK` event handler to this second button.

3. Between the curly braces of the event handler function, enter the following statement:

   ```
   myLogin_txt.text =
   → mySharedObject.data.myLoginData;
   ```

   This statement retrieves the information in `myLoginData` that was saved on the viewer's computer in a `SharedObject`. That information is used to change the contents of your text field (**Figure 9.19**).

4. Test your movie.

   Enter your name in the text field on the Stage, and then click the button to save the information into a `SharedObject`. Quit the movie. When you open the movie again and click the second button, your name appears in the text field because Flash retrieved the information from your previous session (**Figure 9.20**).

To clear information on a user's computer:

◆ Call the method `clear()` to clear information saved in a `SharedObject`.

   The statement

   ```
   mySharedObject.clear();
   ```

   removes all the data from the `SharedObject`.

```
var mySharedObject:SharedObject = SharedObject.getLocal("myCookie");

saveButton_btn.addEventListener(MouseEvent.CLICK, savedata);
function savedata(myevent:MouseEvent):void {
  mySharedObject.data.myLoginData = myLogin_txt.text;
  mySharedObject.flush();
}

loadButton_btn.addEventListener(MouseEvent.CLICK, loaddata);
function loaddata(myevent:MouseEvent):void {
    myLogin_txt.text = mySharedObject.data.myLoginData;
}
```

Figure 9.19 Clicking the button called `loadButton_btn` puts the saved data into the input text field for display.

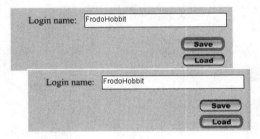

Figure 9.20 Enter your login name in the input text field and click the button to save it (top). Close the Flash movie, and then open it again to return to it. When you click the second button, your login name appears again so you don't have to retype it (bottom).

Sharing information among multiple movies

Flash keeps track of a SharedObject saved on the viewer's computer by remembering the name of the object as well as the location of the movie in which it was created. The location of the movie is known as the SharedObject's *local path*. By default, the local path is the relative path from the domain name to the filename. If your movie is at www.myDomain.com/flash/myMovie.swf, the local path is /flash/myMovie.swf. Flash lets you specify a different local path when you use the getLocal() method so that you can store a SharedObject in a different place. Why would you do this? If you have multiple movies, you can define one SharedObject and a common local path, allowing all the movies to access the same SharedObject and share its information.

Valid local paths for a SharedObject include the directory in which your movie or any of its parent directories sits. Don't include the domain name, and don't specify any other directories in the domain. Remember, you aren't telling Flash to store information on the server; you're telling Flash to store information locally on the viewer's computer (the host), and the local path helps Flash keep track of the SharedObject. Because local paths are relative to a single domain, a SharedObject can be shared only with multiple movies in the same domain.

To store information that multiple movies can share:

1. Continuing with the file that you created in the preceding task, in the Actions panel add a forward slash as the second parameter to the getLocal() method. Make sure the forward slash is between quotation marks (**Figure 9.21**).

   Flash will save the SharedObject mySharedObject_so with the local path "/". This entry represents the top-level directory.

2. In a new Flash document, create an input text field on the Stage, and give it the name myLogin2_txt in the Property inspector.

   This input text field will display information stored in the SharedObject you created in your first movie.

```
var mySharedObject:SharedObject = SharedObject.getLocal("myCookie", "/");
```

Figure 9.21 The second parameter of the getLocal() method determines the local path of the SharedObject and its location on the viewer's computer. The single slash indicates the top-level directory of the domain where the Flash movie resides.

3. Select the first frame of the main Timeline, and open the Actions panel.

4. In the Script pane, enter the following statement:

```
var mySharedObject2:SharedObject =
→ SharedObject.getLocal("myCookie",
→ "/");
```

Flash retrieves the SharedObject with the local path "/" from the viewer's computer. Notice that the parameter "myCookie" must be identical to the one used in the first Flash movie, but the SharedObject variable's name mySharedObject2 can be different.

5. On a new line of the Script pane, assign the property myLoginData in the data property of the SharedObject to the contents of your input text field with the following statement (**Figure 9.22**):

```
myLogin2_txt.text =
→ mySharedObject2.data.myLoginData;
```

This statement retrieves the myLoginData information from the SharedObject and displays it in the text field.

6. Test your movies.

Play the first movie, enter your name in the text field, click the first button to save its position in a SharedObject, and close the movie. Now open your second movie. Flash reads the information in the SharedObject created by the first movie and displays your name (**Figure 9.23**).

```
var mySharedObject2:SharedObject = SharedObject.getLocal("myCookie", "/");
myLogin2_txt.text = mySharedObject2.data.myLoginData;
```

Figure 9.22 In this second Flash movie, the getLocal() method retrieves the same SharedObject that was saved in the first Flash movie, because the same name and local path are given in its parameters for both movies.

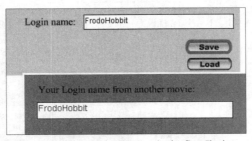

Figure 9.23 When the login name in the first Flash movie is saved (top), you can open the second Flash movie (bottom), and its input text field displays the same login name. Both movies access the same SharedObject on the user's hard drive.

SharedObjects, Permission, and Local Disk Space

The default amount of information that Flash Player allows a single domain to store on a viewer's computer is set at 100 KB, and users can configure the amount of space they allow to be used by SharedObject data. When you call the flush() method, depending on the amount of data you're trying to store and the viewer's settings, different things happen. If the new data doesn't exceed the amount the viewer allows, the SharedObject is saved and flush() returns true. If the new data exceeds the allowable amount and the viewer's Flash Player is set to block requests for more space, the SharedObject isn't saved and flush() returns a value of false. Finally, if the SharedObject data exceeds the amount the user has allowed and the Flash Player isn't set to block requests for more space, a dialog box appears over the Stage asking the viewer for permission to store information (**Figure 9.24**). In that case, the flush() method returns the string "pending" or SharedObjectFlushStatus.PENDING. The viewer can allow the request or deny it.

Viewers can change their local storage settings at any time by right-clicking (Windows) or Ctrl-clicking (Mac) the movie and then choosing Settings from the context menu (**Figure 9.25**). The viewer can choose never to accept information from a particular domain or to accept varying amounts (10 KB, 100 KB, 1 MB, 10 MB, or unlimited). Local storage permission is specific to the domain (which appears in the dialog box), so future movies from the same domain can save SharedObjects according to the same settings.

If you know that the information you save to a viewer's computer will grow, you can request more space ahead of time by defining a minimum disk space for the flush() method. Calling the method mySharedObject.flush(1000000) saves the SharedObject and reserves 1,000,000 bytes (1 MB) for the information. If Flash asks the viewer to allow disk space for the SharedObject, it will ask for 1 MB. After the permission is given, Flash won't ask for more space until the data in all that domain's SharedObject exceeds 1 MB or the viewer changes his local storage settings.

Figure 9.24 Flash asks to store more information than the viewer currently allows. This request comes from local, which is the viewer's computer.

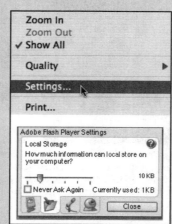

Figure 9.25 From the Flash Player context menu (with your mouse pointer over a Flash movie, right-click for Windows or Ctrl-click for Mac), access the Settings dialog box. You can decide how much information a particular domain can save on your computer. This setting is for local, which is the viewer's computer.

Loading and Saving Files on the Hard Drive

You can get and save information on the user's local hard drive by making Flash open a file browser and having the user choose a particular file. This works well for creating more complex applications that depend on data that the user can save, modify, and retrieve, just like a word processing program or an image-editing program like Adobe Photoshop.

You can directly have your users load and save files with the FileReference class. The method browse() opens a file browser to choose a file, and the method load() loads in the data from a selected file. The method save() opens a file browser to save a file.

```
var myfile:FileReference = new FileReference();
load_btn.addEventListener(MouseEvent.CLICK, loadfile);
function loadfile(myevent:MouseEvent):void {
    myfile.browse();
}
```

Figure 9.26 When you click the button called load_ btn, Flash opens the file browser (below) so the user can choose a file from the hard drive.

Event handlers for the events Event.SELECT and Event.COMPLETE are necessary to detect when a file has been selected and when the loading or saving process has been completed.

✔ Tip

■ The methods of the FileReference class can only be used if the user initiates the process (such as clicking with the mouse or pressing a key on the keyboard). This is a safeguard so that malicious Flash code cannot automatically open files on a user's hard drive or save files to the user's hard drive. Any attempt to call the methods without user interaction will result in an error.

To open the file browser to select a text file:

1. Create a button, place an instance of it on the Stage, and give it an instance name in the Property inspector.

   You'll assign actions to this button to open the file browser to let users choose a file to load from their hard drive.

2. Select the first frame of the main Timeline, and open the Actions panel.

3. In the Script pane, declare a new FileReference object by entering var myfile:FileReference followed by an equals sign and new FileReference().

4. On the next line, create a MouseEvent. CLICK event handler for your button.

5. Between the curly braces of the event handler function, enter the following:

   myfile.browse()

   When the user clicks the button, the file browser will open (**Figure 9.26**).

To load a selected text file:

1. Continue with the previous task, "To open the file browser to select a text file."

   To load a file, you must create an event handler to detect when the user selects a file.

2. On the next line, create an `Event.SELECT` event handler for your `FileReference` object.

3. Between the curly braces of the event handler function, enter the following:

   `myfile.load()`

   When the user selects a file from the file browser, Flash begins loading that file (**Figure 9.27**).

To retrieve the contents of the text file:

1. Continue with the previous task, "To load a selected text file."

   To retrieve the contents of a loaded file, you must create an event handler to detect the completion of the load.

2. On the next line, create an `Event.COMPLETE` event handler for your `FileReference` object.

3. Between the curly braces of the event handler function, enter the following:

   `mytextfield_txt.text=myfile.data.`
   `→ readUTFBytes(myfile.data.length);`

   When the loading process is complete, Flash reads the data in the file and puts it in a textfield called `mytextfield_txt`.

   The data is in the `data` property of the `FileReference` object, but because the `data` property is a `ByteArray` object, you must use the method `readUTFBytes()` to extract the information. The `length` property refers to the total size of the file, so passing `myfile.data.length` as the parameter of `readUTFBytes()` makes Flash load the entire contents of the file (**Figure 9.28**).

4. On the Stage, choose the Text tool and create a text field.

```
var myfile:FileReference = new FileReference();
load_btn.addEventListener(MouseEvent.CLICK, loadfile);
function loadfile(myevent:MouseEvent):void {
    myfile.browse();
}

myfile.addEventListener(Event.SELECT, selectfile);
function selectfile(myevent:Event):void {
    myfile.load();
}
```

Figure 9.27 The second event handler detects when the user selects a file. When that happens, the file is loaded into Flash.

```
var myfile:FileReference = new FileReference();
load_btn.addEventListener(MouseEvent.CLICK, loadfile);
function loadfile(myevent:MouseEvent):void {
    myfile.browse();
}

myfile.addEventListener(Event.SELECT, selectfile);
function selectfile(myevent:Event):void {
    myfile.load();
}

myfile.addEventListener(Event.COMPLETE, completeloading);
function completeloading(myevent:Event):void {
    mytextfield_txt.text=myfile.data.readUTFBytes(myfile.data.length);
}
```

Figure 9.28 The third event handler detects when the file has completely loaded into Flash. When that happens, the entire data in the file is assigned to a text field on the Stage.

Input text field

Figure 9.29 In this example, the text document called "sometext.txt" is selected by the user (top). The contents of the text document is displayed in the text field next to the button.

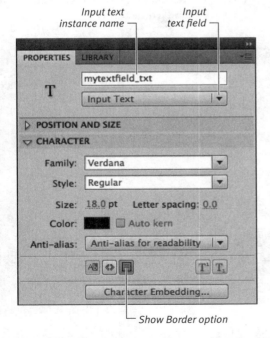

Input text instance name — Input text field —

Show Border option

Figure 9.30 Name the input text field on the Stage mytextfield_txt and select the Show Border option to display a black border around the text.

5. In the Property inspector, choose Dynamic Text and name the text field mytextfield_txt.

6. Choose Control > Test Movie (**Figure 9.29**).

To save a text file:

1. In a new Flash file, create a button, place an instance of it on the Stage, and give it an instance name in the Property inspector.

You'll assign actions to this button to open the file browser to let users save a file on their hard drive.

2. Choose the Text tool and create a text field on the Stage.

3. In the Property inspector, choose Dynamic Text, name the text field mytextfield_txt, and select the Show Border icon (**Figure 9.30**).

You'll allow users to enter text in the text field, and then save the results in a file to their hard drive.

4. Select the first frame of the main Timeline, and open the Actions panel.

5. In the Script pane, declare a new FileReference object by entering var myfile:FileReference followed by an equals sign and new FileReference().

6. On the next line, create a MouseEvent. CLICK event handler for your button.

Continues on next page

7. Between the curly braces of the event handler function, enter the following:

```
myfile.save(mytextfield_txt.text)
```

When the user clicks the button, the file browser will open, allowing the user to save the contents of the text field to a file on the hard drive (**Figure 9.31**).

✔ Tips

- If you want to pre-populate the file browser with a filename, you can provide a second parameter for the save() method. The method save(mytextfield_txt.text, "hello.txt") opens the file browser with the filename hello.txt in the Save As field (**Figure 9.32**).

- The Event.COMPLETE and Event.SELECT events are triggered for both the save() and the load() methods. If the event handlers reference the same FileReference object, you will likely get an error. So, a good idea is to have two separate FileReference objects if you are going to perform both methods.

- You can load and save many other kinds of files—not just text files. See the Flash Help and ActionScript 3.0 reference for ways to handle other file types.

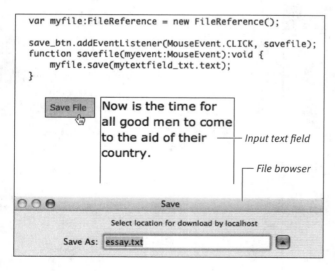

```
var myfile:FileReference = new FileReference();

save_btn.addEventListener(MouseEvent.CLICK, savefile);
function savefile(myevent:MouseEvent):void {
    myfile.save(mytextfield_txt.text);
}
```

Input text field

File browser

Figure 9.31 When the user clicks the save_btn button, the contents of the input text field can be saved to a file on the hard drive. The user can choose the name of the file.

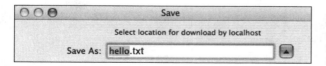

Figure 9.32 By adding a second parameter to the save() method, a suggested filename appears in the file browser.

Table 9.1

Common Operators

Symbol	Description
+	Addition
–	Subtraction
*	Multiplication
/	Division
%	Modulo division; calculates the remainder of the first number divided by the second number. 7 % 2 results in 1.
++	Increases the value by 1. x++ is equivalent to x = x + 1.
––	Decreases the value by 1. x–– is equivalent to x = x – 1.
+=	Adds a value to and assigns the result to the variable. x += 5 is equivalent to x = x + 5.
–=	Subtracts a value from and assigns the result to the variable. x –= 5 is equivalent to x = x – 5.
*=	Multiplies by a value and assigns the result to the variable. x *= 5 is equivalent to x = x * 5.
/=	Divides by a value and assigns it to the variable. x /= 5 is equivalent to x = x / 5.

Modifying Variables

Variables are useful because you can always change their contents with updated information about the status of the movie or your viewer. Sometimes, this change involves assigning a new value to the variable. At other times, the change means adding, subtracting, multiplying, or dividing the variable's numeric values or modifying a string by adding characters. The variable myScore, for example, may be initialized at 0. Then, for every goal a player makes, the myScore variable changes in increments of 1. The job of modifying information contained in variables falls upon *operators*—symbols that operate on data.

Assignment and arithmetic operators

The assignment operator (=) is a single equals sign that assigns a value to a variable. You've already used this operator in initializing variables and creating new objects. **Table 9.1** lists the other common operators.

Operators are the workhorses of Flash interactivity. You'll use them often to perform calculations behind the scenes—adding the value of one variable to another or changing the property of one object by adding or subtracting the value of a variable, for example.

To incrementally increase the value of a variable:

◆ Enter the name of your variable followed by two plus symbols, such as `myVariable++`.

The value of `myVariable` increases by one.

or

Enter the name of your variable followed by a plus symbol and an equals sign followed by the value of the increment, such as `myVariable+=20`.

The value of `myVariable` increases by 20.

To incrementally decrease the value of a variable:

◆ Enter the name of your variable followed by two minus signs, such as `myVariable--`.

The value of `myVariable` decreases by one.

or

Enter the name of your variable followed by a minus symbol and an equals sign followed by the value of the increment, such as `myVariable-=20`.

The value of `myVariable` decreases by 20.

✔ Tips

■ To perform more complicated mathematical calculations (such as square root, sine, and cosine) or string manipulations on your variables and values, you must use the `Math` class or the `String` class. You'll learn about these objects in Chapters 10 and 11.

■ Remember that you can always change the values of variables, but you can't change the type of data that the variables hold. So if you've created a variable to hold a number, you can't assign a string to it.

■ The arithmetic rules of precedence (remember them from math class?) apply when Flash evaluates expressions, which means that certain operators take priority over others. The most important rule is that multiplication and division are performed before addition and subtraction. `3 + 4 * 2`, for example, gives a very different result than `3 * 4 + 2`.

■ Use parentheses to group variables and operators so those portions are calculated before other parts of the expression are evaluated. `(3 + 2) * 4` returns a value of 20, but without the parentheses, `3 + 2 * 4` returns a value of 11.

■ Use the modulo division operator (`%`) to check whether a variable is an even or an odd number. The statement `myNumber % 2` returns 0 if `myNumber` is even and 1 if `myNumber` is odd. You can use this logic to create toggling functionality. You can count the number of times a viewer clicks a light switch, for example. If the count is even, you can turn on the light; if the count is odd, you turn off the light.

Concatenating Variables and Dynamic Referencing

The addition operator (+) adds the values of numeric data types. But it can also put together string values. The expression `"Hello " + "world"`, for example, results in the string "Hello world". This kind of operation is called *concatenation*.

One use of concatenation is to mix strings, numbers, and variables to create expressions that allow you to dynamically create and access objects or variables. For example, you can concatenate a string with a variable to make Flash go to a specified frame, depending on the current value of the variable, as in:

```
gotoAndStop("Chapter"+myChapterNumber);
```

The result of the concatenation is that Flash goes to a frame labeled something like `Chapter1` or `Chapter2`, depending on the value of the variable called `myChapterNumber`. The frame label is assigned dynamically with a concatenation expression.

This kind of concatenation works because the concatenated string is used as a parameter of a method. Flash knows to resolve the expression before using it as the parameter. What happens in other cases? Consider this statement in the Script pane of the Actions panel:

```
var "myVariable" + counter = 5;
```

This statement doesn't make sense to Flash and causes an error. To construct a dynamic variable name and assign a value to that variable, you must instruct Flash to resolve (or "figure out") the left side first and then treat the result as a concatenated variable name before assigning a value to it. The way to do that is to use the array access operator.

Array access operator

To reference a variable or an object dynamically, use the *array access operators*. The array access operator is the square brackets (`[ ]`, located on the same keys as the curly braces). It is called the array access operator because it is typically used to access the contents of an `Array` object, but it can also be used to dynamically access the contents of other objects.

What does this capability mean? Think of the main Timeline as being a `root` object; variables and objects sitting on the main Timeline are its contents. A variable `myVariable` initialized on the main Timeline can be targeted with the array access operator as follows:

```
root["myVariable"]
```

Notice that there is no dot between the object (`root`) and the square brackets. The array access operator automatically resolves concatenated expressions within the square brackets. For example, the following statement puts together a single variable name based on the value of `counter` and then assigns the numeric value of 5 to the variable:

```
root["myVariable" + counter] = 5;
```

If the value of `counter` is 7, Flash accesses the variable named `root.myVariable7` and assigns the value 5 to that variable.

Using the array access operators also enables you to call methods and change the properties of dynamically referenced objects with dot syntax. For example, you can modify an object's transparency this way:

```
root["mushroom_mc" + counter].alpha = .5
```

If the value of `counter` is 3, the movie clip in the root Timeline named `root.mushroom_mc3` becomes 50 percent transparent. To make the movie clip play, call the designated method, like this:

```
root["myClip_mc" + counter].play()
```

To reference a variable dynamically and assign a value:

◆ In the Script pane of the Actions panel, enter the parent of the variable followed by an opening square bracket, an expression, a closing square bracket, an equals sign, and a value.

Flash resolves the expression within the square brackets and assigns the value to the variable with that name (**Figure 9.33**).

To reference an object dynamically and call a method:

1. In the Script pane of the Actions panel, enter the parent of the object followed by an opening square bracket, an expression, and a closing square bracket.

2. On the same line, enter a period, and then enter the method name (**Figure 9.34**).

Flash resolves the expression between the square brackets and calls the method on that object.

To reference an object dynamically and change a property:

◆ In the Script pane of the Actions panel, enter the parent of the object followed by an opening square bracket, an expression, a closing square bracket, a dot, a property, an equals sign, and a value (**Figure 9.35**).

Flash resolves the expression between the square brackets and assigns the value on the right of the equals sign to the object.

```
root["myVariable"+counter]=5;
```

Figure 9.33 Flash resolves the expression in the square brackets first, so if the value of counter is 0, the variable called myVariable0 will be assigned the value of 5.

```
root["myMovieClip" + counter].play();
```

Figure 9.34 Use the array access operators to dynamically reference an object and then call one of its methods. If the value of counter is 0, the movie clip called myMovieClip0 will begin to play.

```
root["myMovieClip" + counter].rotation=45;
```

Figure 9.35 Use the array access operators to dynamically reference an object and then evaluate or modify one of its properties. If the value of counter is 0, the movie clip called myMovieClip0 will rotate 45 degrees clockwise.

✔ Tip

■ A useful method to consider when dynamically accessing objects is the method of the DisplayObject class called getChildByName(). This method returns the DisplayObject that exists with the specified name, which you can construct dynamically with an expression. For example, getChildByName("car"+counter) would return the object whose name is based on the string "car" and the value of the variable counter. Assign the returned object into a DisplayObject to manipulate, as in the following example:

```
var myObject:DisplayObject =
→ getChildByName("car"+counter);
myObject.alpha=.5;
```

Testing Information with Conditional Statements

Variables and expressions go hand in hand with conditional statements. The information you retrieve, store in variables, and modify in expressions is useful only when you can compare it with other pieces of information. Conditional statements let you do this kind of comparison and carry out instructions based on the results. The logic of conditional statements is the same as the logic in the sentence "If abc is true, then do xyz," and in Flash, you define abc (the condition) and xyz (the consequence).

Conditional statements are in the form, if() {}. You put a condition between the parentheses, and the consequences between the curly braces. The *condition*—a statement that can be resolved to a true or false value, usually compares one thing with another. Is the variable myScore greater than the variable alltimeHighScore? Does the bytesLoaded property equal the bytesTotal property? Does the variable myPassword equal "Abracadabra"? These are typical examples of the types of things that are compared in conditions.

How do you compare values? You use comparison operators.

Comparison operators

A *comparison operator* evaluates the expressions on both sides of itself and returns a value of true or false. **Table 9.2** summarizes the comparison operators.

When the statement is evaluated and the condition holds true, Flash performs the consequences within the if statement's curly braces. If the condition turns out to be false, all the actions within the curly braces are ignored (**Figure 9.36**).

In the following task, you'll create a graphic that moves to the right. You want to constrain the position of the graphic so it doesn't run off the Stage, so you'll construct a conditional statement to have Flash test whether the value of its *x* position is greater than 200 pixels. If it is, you'll keep its current position.

To create a conditional statement:

1. For this example, create a Shape object, define a line style and fill style, and call the drawRect() method to draw a square.

2. Call the addChild() method to add the Shape object to the display list.

Continues on next page

```
if (condition) {
    consequence1;
    consequence2;
    consequence3;
}
```

Figure 9.36 If, and only if, the condition within the parentheses is true, consequence1, consequence2, and consequence3 are all performed. If the condition is false, all three consequences are ignored.

Table 9.2

Comparison Operators

SYMBOL	DESCRIPTION
==	Equality
===	Strict equality (value and data type must be equal)
<	Less than
>	Greater than
<=	Less than or equal to
>=	Greater than or equal to
!=	Not equal to
!==	Strict inequality

3. Create an `Event.ENTER_FRAME` event handler and, in the function of the event handler, move the position of the `Shape` to the right (**Figure 9.37**).

The rectangle moves to the right continuously.

```
var myShape:Shape=new Shape();
myShape.graphics.lineStyle(1);
myShape.graphics.beginFill(0xff0000);
myShape.graphics.drawRect(100,100,50,50);
addChild(myShape);

stage.addEventListener(Event.ENTER_FRAME, moveSquare);
function moveSquare(myevent:Event):void {
    myShape.x+=5;
}
```

Figure 9.37 The code draws a square and moves the myShape object continuously to the right across the Stage.

4. Inside the event handler function, after the statement that adds to the position of the rectangle, enter:

```
if (myShape.x >200) {

}
```

Flash tests to see whether the rectangle's *x* position is greater than 200.

5. Between the curly braces of the `if` statement, assign the value 200 to the `Shape`'s `x` property (**Figure 9.38**).

If the `x` property exceeds 200, Flash resets it to 200. This setting prevents the rectangle from moving past the 200-pixel point.

```
var myShape:Shape=new Shape();
myShape.graphics.lineStyle(1);
myShape.graphics.beginFill(0xff0000);
myShape.graphics.drawRect(100,100,50,50);
addChild(myShape);

stage.addEventListener(Event.ENTER_FRAME, moveSquare);
function moveSquare(myevent:Event):void {
    myShape.x+=5;
    if (myShape.x>200) {
        myShape.x=200;
    }
}
```

Figure 9.38 Add a condition that tests the x property of myShape to see if its value exceeds 200. If so, Flash keeps it at 200, preventing the square from moving off the Stage.

6. Test your movie (**Figure 9.39**).

✔ Tip

■ A common mistake is to mix up the assignment operator (=) and the comparison operator for equality (==). The single equals sign assigns whatever is on the right side of it to whatever is on the left side. Use the single equals sign when you're setting and modifying properties and variables. The double equals sign compares the equality of two things; use it in conditional statements.

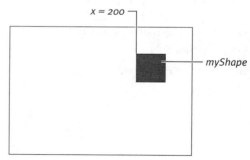

Figure 9.39 The myShape object is limited at x = 200.

Creating a continuous-feedback button

A simple but powerful and widely applicable use of the if statement is to monitor the state of a MouseEvent.MOUSE_DOWN event and provide continuous actions as long as the mouse button is held down. An object or button that provides this kind of functionality is sometimes called a *continuous-feedback button*. When you click and hold down a button, for example, you can increase the sound volume (like a television remote control) until you let go. A simple event handler can't accomplish this functionality.

Creating this functionality requires that you toggle the value of a variable based on the state of the button. When the button is depressed, the toggle variable is set to true. When the button is released or the pointer is moved away from the button, the variable is set to false. Within an Event.ENTER_FRAME handler, you can monitor the status of the variable continuously with an if statement. If the toggle variable is true, the code performs an action. As long as the toggle variable remains true (the button continues to be held down), those actions continue to be executed.

```
var pressing:Boolean = false;
button_btn.addEventListener(MouseEvent.MOUSE_DOWN, pressdown)
function pressdown (myevent:MouseEvent):void{
    pressing = true;
}
```

Figure 9.40 The variable pressing keeps track of whether the button is being pressed or released. When the button is pressed, pressing is set to true.

```
var pressing:Boolean = false;
button_btn.addEventListener(MouseEvent.MOUSE_DOWN, pressdown)
function pressdown (myevent:MouseEvent):void{
    pressing = true;
}
button_btn.addEventListener(MouseEvent.MOUSE_UP, letgo)
function letgo (myevent:MouseEvent):void{
    pressing = false;
}
```

Figure 9.41 When the button is released, pressing is set to false.

To create a continuous-feedback button:

1. Create a button symbol (or any other object that can receive MouseEvents), place an instance of it on the Stage, and give it an instance name in the Property inspector.

2. Select the first frame of the main Timeline, and open the Actions panel.

3. Declare a Boolean variable, and set its initial value to false.

   This will be the toggle variable that tracks whether the button is being held down.

4. Add an event listener to your button to detect the MouseEvent.MOUSE_DOWN event.

5. Add the function that responds to the MouseEvent.MOUSE_DOWN event. In between the curly braces of the function, assign the value true to your toggle variable (**Figure 9.40**).

   The variable is set to true whenever the button is pressed. Note that there are no quotation marks around the word *true*, so true is treated correctly as a Boolean data type, not a string data type.

6. Add another event listener to your button to detect the MouseEvent.MOUSE_UP event.

7. Add the function that responds to the MouseEvent.MOUSE_UP event. In between the curly braces of the function, assign the value false to your toggle variable (**Figure 9.41**).

   The variable is set to false whenever the button is released.

8. Add another event listener to the Stage to detect the Event.ENTER_FRAME event.

   Continues on next page

9. Add the function that responds to the Event.ENTER_FRAME event. In between the curly braces of the function, enter the statement if(){}.

10. For the condition (in between the parentheses of the if statement), enter the toggle variable name followed by two equals signs and then true.

    The condition tests whether the button is being pressed.

11. In between the curly braces of the if statement, choose an action as a consequence that you want to be performed as long as the button is held down (**Figure 9.42**).

✔ Tips

- To refine the continuous-feedback interaction, add a MouseEvent.MOUSE_OUT event to your handler, as follows:

  button_btn.addEventListener
  (MouseEvent.MOUSE_OUT, letgo);

  Now if the pointer wanders off the button, the continuous action will stop.

- You can use a shorthand way of testing whether a variable is true or false by eliminating the comparison operator (==). The if statement automatically tests whether its condition is true, so you can test whether a variable is true by entering the variable name within the parentheses of the if statement, like this:

  if (myVariable) {
  // myVariable is true
  }

  You can test whether a variable is false by preceding the variable name with an exclamation point, which means "not," like so:

  if (!myVariable) {
  // myVariable is not true
  }

```
var pressing:Boolean = false;
button_btn.addEventListener(MouseEvent.MOUSE_DOWN, pressdown)
function pressdown (myevent:MouseEvent):void{
    pressing = true;
};

button_btn.addEventListener(MouseEvent.MOUSE_UP, letgo)
function letgo (myevent:MouseEvent):void{
    pressing = false;
};

stage.addEventListener(Event.ENTER_FRAME, continuousAction)
function continuousAction(myevent:Event):void{
    if (pressing==true){
        // add actions here
    }
}
```

```
stage.addEventListener(Event.ENTER_FRAME, continuousAction)
function continuousAction(myevent:Event):void{
    if (pressing==true){
        root.gotoAndPlay(currentFrame-2)
    }
}
```

```
stage.addEventListener(Event.ENTER_FRAME, continuousAction)
function continuousAction(myevent:Event):void{
    if (pressing==true){
        scrollBar.y+=5;
    }
}
```

Figure 9.42 The status of the pressing variable can be monitored continuously by an if statement inside an Event.ENTER_FRAME handler. This is a useful method that has wide-ranging application. For example, you can create a rewind button to control the timeline (middle image) by subtracting a few frames from the current frame as long as the button is held down (bottom code). Another example shown in the bottom code is moving an object on the Stage as long as the button is held down.

Providing Alternatives to Conditions

In many cases, you need to provide an alternative response to the conditional statement. The `else` statement lets you create consequences when the condition in the `if` statement is false. The `else` statement takes care of any condition that the `if` statement doesn't cover.

The `else` statement must be used in conjunction with the `if` statement and follows the syntax and logic of this hypothetical example:

```
if (daytime) {
        goToWork();
} else {
        goToSleep();
}
```

Use `else` for either-or conditions—something that can be just one of two options. In the preceding example, there are only two possibilities: It's either daytime or nighttime. Situations in which the `else` statement can be useful include collision detection, true/false or right/wrong answer checking, and password verification.

For this task, you'll build an `if-else` statement to detect the keyboard input given to the question "Is the earth round?" The answer can be only right or wrong—there are no other alternatives.

To use else for the false condition:

1. Select the first frame of the main Timeline, and open the Actions panel.

2. Add an event listener to the Stage to detect the `KeyboardEvent.KEY_DOWN` event.

3. On the next line, create the function that gets triggered by the `KeyboardEvent.KEY_DOWN` event.

4. Between the curly braces of the function, create an `if` statement as follows:

```
if (myevent.keyCode==89) {
    answer_txt.text="correct!"
}
```

The function checks to see if the key pressed matches the keycode for the Y key, and if so, a message is displayed in a text field called `answer_txt`.

5. On the same line as the closing curly brace of the `if` statement, enter `else` followed by an opening curly brace.

Continues on next page

6. On the next line, choose another action as a response to the false condition, and then close the `else` statement with a closing curly brace, like so (**Figure 9.43**):

```
if (myevent.keyCode==89) {
    answer_txt.text="correct!"
} else {
    answer_txt.text="wrong!"
}
```

In this example, if the key pressed is Y, the correct-answer message is sent. Otherwise, the incorrect-answer message is sent. The `else` statement covers any key other than Y.

7. On the Stage, create a dynamic text field and give it the name `answer_txt` in the Property inspector.

8. Test your movie (**Figure 9.44**).

✔ Tip

■ By convention, the `else` statement cuddles the closing brace of the `if` statement to show that they belong together. In the Auto Format options, however, you can change the Script pane's formatting to put the `else` statement on its own line.

```
stage.addEventListener(KeyboardEvent.KEY_DOWN, detectText);
function detectText(myevent:KeyboardEvent):void {
    if (myevent.keyCode==89) {
        answer_txt.text="correct!";
    } else {
        answer_txt.text="wrong!";
    }
}
```

Figure 9.43 The `if` statement within the `detectText` event handler checks whether the Y key, which corresponds to the key code value of 89, is pressed. The `else` statement triggers the "wrong!" message if a key other than Y is pressed. Note how the `else` statement is commonly written in a group with the `if` statement, beginning on the same line as the ending curly brace of the `if` statement.

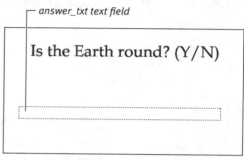

— answer_txt text field

Is the Earth round? (Y/N)

Figure 9.44 The message is displayed in a text field on the Stage.

Branching Conditional Statements

If you have multiple possible conditions and just as many consequences, you need to use more complicated branching conditional statements that provide functionality a single `else` statement can't. If you create an interface to a Web site or a game that requires keyboard input, for example, you need to test which keys are pressed and respond appropriately to each keypress. Flash gives you the `else if` statement, which lets you construct multiple responses, as in the following hypothetical example:

```
if (sunny) {
        bringSunglasses();
} else if (raining) {
        bringUmbrella();
} else if (snowing) {
        bringSkis();
}
```

Each `else if` statement has its own condition that it evaluates and its own set of consequences to perform if that condition returns true. Only one condition in the entire `if-else if` code block can be true. If more than one condition is true, Flash performs the consequences for the first true condition it encounters and ignores the rest. In the preceding example, even if it's both sunny *and* snowing, Flash can perform the consequence only for the sunny condition (`bringSunglasses()`) because it appears before the snowing condition. If you want the

possibility of multiple conditions to be true, you must construct separate `if` statements that are independent, like the following:

```
if (sunny) {
        bringSunglasses();
}
if (raining) {
        bringUmbrella();
}
if (snowing) {
        bringSkis();
}
```

The following example uses `KeyboardEvent.KEY_DOWN` event handlers and branching conditional statements to move and rotate a movie clip according to different keypresses.

To use else if for branching alternatives:

1. Create a movie clip symbol, place an instance of it on the Stage, and give it an instance name in the Property inspector. In this example, the movie clip is named `beetle_mc`.

2. Select the first frame of the main Timeline, and open the Actions panel.

3. Add an event listener to the Stage to detect the `KeyboardEvent.KEY_DOWN` event.

4. On the next line, create the function that gets triggered by the `KeyboardEvent.KEY_DOWN` event.

Continues on next page

5. Between the curly braces of the function, create an if statement as follows:

```
if (myevent.keyCode==Keyboard.UP) {
    beetle_mc.rotation = 0;
    beetle_mc.y -=30;
}
```

As in the previous task, the if statement checks if the key pressed on the keyboard matches a particular key and executes the two statements within the curly braces to rotate and move the object.

The two statements within the if statement rotate the movie clip so that the head faces the top and subtract 30 pixels from its current *y* position, making it move up the Stage. Recall that the operator -= means "subtract this amount and assign the result to myself" (**Figure 9.45**).

6. On the same line as the closing curly brace of the if statement, enter else if and another condition in parentheses and consequences in curly braces as in the following:

```
if (myevent.keyCode==Keyboard.UP){
    beetle_mc.rotation = 0;
    beetle_mc.y -=30;
} else if (myevent.
keyCode==Keyboard.LEFT) {
    beetle_mc.rotation = -90;
    beetle_mc.x -=30;
}
```

7. Add two more else if statements in the manner described earlier to test whether Key.DOWN is being pressed and whether Key.RIGHT is being pressed. Change the rotation and position of the movie clip accordingly.

8. Test your movie.

Your series of if and else if statements tests whether the user presses the arrow keys and moves the movie clip accordingly (**Figure 9.46**). You now have the beginnings of a game!

```
stage.addEventListener(KeyboardEvent.KEY_DOWN, detectText);
function detectText(myevent:KeyboardEvent):void {
    if (myevent.keyCode==Keyboard.UP) {
        beetle_mc.rotation = 0;
        beetle_mc.y -=30;
    }
}
```

Figure 9.45 If the up arrow key is pressed, this movie clip is rotated to 0 degrees and is repositioned 30 pixels up the Stage.

```
stage.addEventListener(KeyboardEvent.KEY_DOWN, detectText);
function detectText(myevent:KeyboardEvent):void {
    if (myevent.keyCode==Keyboard.UP) {
        beetle_mc.rotation = 0;
        beetle_mc.y -=30;
    } else if (myevent.keyCode==Keyboard.LEFT) {
        beetle_mc.rotation = -90;
        beetle_mc.x -=30;
    } else if (myevent.keyCode==Keyboard.RIGHT) {
        beetle_mc.rotation = 90;
        beetle_mc.x += 30;
    } else if (myevent.keyCode==Keyboard.DOWN) {
        beetle_mc.rotation = 180;
        beetle_mc.y += 30;
    }
}
```

Figure 9.46 The else if statement provides alternatives to the first condition. The complete script has four conditions that use if and else if to test whether the up, left, right, or down arrow key is pressed. The rotation and position of the movie clip change depending on which condition holds true.

The switch, case, and default actions

Another way to create alternatives to conditions is to use the `switch`, `case`, and `default` statements instead of the `if` statement. These statements provide a different way to test the equality of an expression. The syntax and logic are shown in this hypothetical example:

```
switch (weather) {
        case sun :
                bringSunglasses();
                break;
        case rain :
                bringUmbrella();
                break;
        case snow :
                bringSkis();
                break;
        default :
                stayHome();
                break;
}
```

Flash compares the expression in the `switch` statement's parentheses to each of the expressions in the `case` statements. If the two expressions are equal, the actions after the colon are performed (for example, if `weather` is equal to `sun`, `bringSunglasses` happens). The `break` action is necessary to break out of the `switch` code block after a `case` has matched. Without it, Flash runs through all the actions. The `default` action, which is optional, provides the actions to be performed if no case matches the `switch` expression.

In the following example, you'll create the same functionality as the previous task (moving a movie clip instance around the Stage with different keypresses), but you'll use the `switch` and `case` statements instead of the `if` and `else if` statements.

To use switch and case for branching alternatives:

1. Create a movie clip symbol, place an instance of it on the Stage, and give it an instance name in the Property inspector. In this example, the movie clip is named `beetle_mc`.

2. Select the first frame of the main Timeline, and open the Actions panel.

3. Add an event listener to the Stage to detect the `KeyboardEvent.KEY_DOWN` event.

4. On the next line, create the function that gets triggered by the `KeyboardEvent. KEY_DOWN` event.

5. Between the curly braces of the function, enter `switch` followed by a pair of parentheses with a condition inside followed by curly braces, like so:

```
switch (myevent.keyCode) {

}
```

Continues on next page

6. In between the curly braces of the `switch` statement, add the following:

```
case Keyboard.UP :
beetle_mc.y -= 30;
beetle_mc.rotation = 0;
break;
```

The `switch` statement will compare the equality of the `myevent.keyCode` to `Keyboard.UP`, and if they are equivalent, the movie clip's position and rotation will be changed. The `break` action discontinues the current code block and makes Flash go on to any ActionScript after the `switch` statement.

7. Repeat step 6, but use different `Keyboard` properties for the case statements and different consequences (**Figure 9.47**).

8. Test your movie.

```
stage.addEventListener(KeyboardEvent.KEY_DOWN, detectText);
function detectText(myevent:KeyboardEvent):void {
    switch (myevent.keyCode) {
        case Keyboard.UP :
            beetle_mc.y -= 30;
            beetle_mc.rotation = 0;
            break;
        case Keyboard.LEFT :
            beetle_mc.x -= 30;
            beetle_mc.rotation = -90;
            break;
        case Keyboard.RIGHT :
            beetle_mc.x += 30;
            beetle_mc.rotation = 90;
            break;
        case Keyboard.DOWN :
            beetle_mc.y += 30;
            beetle_mc.rotation = 180;
    }
}
```

Figure 9.47 The full script to move a beetle movie clip with the arrow keys, using `switch` and `case` instead of the `if` statement.

Combining Conditions with Logical Operators

You can create compound conditions with the logical operators && (AND), | | (OR), and ! (NOT). These operators combine two or more conditions in one if statement to test scenarios involving combinations of conditions. You can test whether somebody has entered the correct login and password, for example. Or you can test whether a draggable movie clip is dropped on one valid target or another. You can use the NOT operator to test whether a variable contains a valid e-mail address whose domain isn't restricted.

```
if (yourAge>=21 && yourGender=="Male") {
}
```

Figure 9.48 The logical && operator joins these two expressions so that both must be true for the whole condition to be true.

```
if (yourAge>=18 || parentalApproval==true) {
}
```

Figure 9.49 The logical | | operator joins these two expressions so that either must be true for the whole condition to be true.

To test if more than one expression is true:

◆ In the Script pane of the Actions panel, enter the if statement, then an open parenthesis, followed by the first expression. Enter two ampersands (&&) followed by your second expression and a closing parenthesis. Enter a pair of curly braces and consequences in between them (**Figure 9.48**).

Flash checks whether both expressions on either side of the && operator are true before the consequences within the curly braces are executed. Think of the && operator as the word *and*.

To test if one of many expressions is true:

◆ In the Script pane of the Actions panel, enter the if statement, then an open parenthesis, followed by the first expression. Enter two vertical bars (| |) followed by your second expression and a closing parenthesis. Enter a pair of curly braces and consequences in between them (**Figure 9.49**).

Flash checks whether one of the expressions on either side of the | | operator is true before the consequences within the curly braces are executed. Think of the | | operator as the word *or*.

To test if an expression is not true:

◆ In the Script pane of the Actions panel, enter the if statement, then an open parenthesis, followed by the exclamation point (!) followed by an expression and a closing parenthesis. Enter a pair of curly braces and consequences in between them (**Figure 9.50**).

Flash checks whether the expression following the ! operator is false before the consequences within the curly braces are executed. Think of the ! operator as the word *not*.

✔ Tip

■ You can nest if statements within other if statements, which is equivalent to using the logical && operator in a single if statement. These two scripts test whether both conditions are true before setting a new variable:

```
if (yourAge >= 12){
  if (yourAge <= 20) {
    status = "teenager";
  }
}
```

or

```
if (yourAge >= 12 && yourAge <= 20) {
  status = "teenager";
}
```

```
if (!parentalApproval) {
}
```

Figure 9.50 The logical ! operator can be used to check if the expression is false. If there is *not* parental approval, then something will happen.

Looping Statements

With looping statements, you can create an action or set of actions that repeats. For example, you may have actions repeat a certain number of times or as long as a certain condition holds true. Repeating actions are often used together with an *array*, which is a special kind of object that holds multiple values in a structured, easily accessible way. Using a looping action lets you add or retrieve the pieces of data in a particular order. You'll learn more about arrays in Chapter 11.

In general, use looping statements to execute actions automatically a specific number of times by using an incrementing counter variable. The counter variable is used in parameters of methods called in the loop or to modify properties of objects that are created. For example, you can generate intricate patterns by duplicating dynamically drawn shapes with looping statements. Use looping statements to change the properties of a whole series of DisplayObjects, modify multiple sound settings, or alter the values of a set of variables.

```
var i:int = 0;
while (i<361) {
}
```

Figure 9.51 Initialize the variable i and create the condition that must be true for the loop to continue. As long as the variable i is less than 361, this loop will run.

```
var i:int = 0;
while (i<361) {
    var myShape:Shape = new Shape();
    myShape.graphics.lineStyle(1);
    myShape.graphics.drawEllipse(0,0,200,90);
    addChild(myShape);
    myShape.x=200;
    myShape.y=200;
    myShape.rotation =i;
}
```

Figure 9.52 The myShape object is created and an ellipse is drawn and rotated based on the counter variable.

There are three kinds of looping statements—the while, do while, and for statements—but they all accomplish the same task. The first two loop types repeat as long as a certain condition holds true. The third statement repeats using a counter variable and a condition that is checked each time the loop repeats. In this example, a new shape is drawn on the Stage and rotated in each loop, creating an overlapping, complex pattern.

To use the while statement to repeat a set of statements:

1. Select the first frame of the main Timeline, and open the Actions panel.

2. Declare an int variable named i, and initialize it to 0.

   The names i, j, k, and so forth are often used as loop counter variables.

3. On the next line, enter while, then a set of parentheses and a set of curly braces.

4. In the parentheses, enter i < 361 (**Figure 9.51**).

   This expression acts as a condition, like the condition of an if statement. As long as the condition works out to true, the actions in the curly braces of the loop will repeat, but once it's false, the Flash Player will stop looping.

5. Assign any actions that you want to run while the condition remains true (while i is less than 361).

   In this example, a Shape method is created to draw an ellipse and put it on the display list. The ellipse is rotated according to the counter variable (**Figure 9.52**).

   Continues on next page

6. On the next line, enter i += 10 or the equivalent statement i = i + 10.

Each time the loop runs, the variable i will increase by an increment of 10. When it exceeds 361, the condition that the while statement checks at each pass will become false, and Flash will end the loop (**Figure 9.53**).

The do while statement

The do while statement is similar to the while statement except that the condition is checked at the end of the loop rather than the beginning. This means the actions in the loop are always executed at least once. The script in the preceding task can be written with the do while statement, as shown in **Figure 9.54**.

```
var i:int = 0;
while (i<361) {
    var myShape:Shape = new Shape();
    myShape.graphics.lineStyle(1);
    myShape.graphics.drawEllipse(0,0,200,90);
    addChild(myShape);
    myShape.x=200;
    myShape.y=200;
    myShape.rotation =i;
    i+=10;
}
```

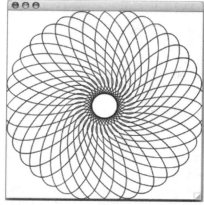

Figure 9.53 At the end of each loop, the variable i increases by 10. This loop will run 37 times. The pattern is formed by the combination of the myShape objects drawn one at a time in the loop.

```
var i:int = 0;
do {
    var myShape:Shape = new Shape();
    myShape.graphics.lineStyle(1);
    myShape.graphics.drawEllipse(0,0,200,90);
    addChild(myShape);
    myShape.x=200;
    myShape.y=200;
    myShape.rotation =i;
    i+=10;
} while (i<361);
```

Figure 9.54 The equivalent do while statement.

The for statement

The for statement provides built-in places to define a counter variable, condition, and operation to increment or decrement the counter, so you don't have to write separate statements. The three statements that go in the parentheses of the for statement are init, where you can initialize a counter variable; condition, which is the expression that is tested before each iteration of the loop; and next, which defines a statement to increment or decrement the counter variable. The preceding task's script can be written with a for loop, as shown in **Figure 9.55**.

✔ Tips

■ Don't use looping statements to build continuous routines to check a certain condition over time. Real-time testing should be done using an if statement in an Event.ENTER_FRAME event handler or from a TIMER event. When Flash executes looping statements, the display remains frozen, and no mouse or keyboard events can be detected.

■ With the while and do while statements, make sure the statement that modifies the variable checked in the condition is inside the curly braces. If it isn't, the condition will never be met, and Flash will be stuck executing the loop infinitely. Fortunately, Flash warns you about this problem when it detects a problem in your script that causes it to stall (**Figure 9.56**).

■ Note that the statements within the parentheses of the for statement are separated by semicolons, *not* by commas.

```
for (var i:int = 0; i < 361; i += 10) {
    var myShape:Shape = new Shape();
    myShape.graphics.lineStyle(1);
    myShape.graphics.drawEllipse(0,0,200,90);
    addChild(myShape);
    myShape.x=200;
    myShape.y=200;
    myShape.rotation = i;
}
```

Figure 9.55 The equivalent for loop. You can read the statements in the parentheses this way: Start my counter at 0; before each loop, check the condition, and as long as it's smaller than 361, perform the loop actions; after each loop, add 10 to my counter and repeat. The for loop is the most efficient way of making loops.

Error: Error #1502: A script has executed for longer than the default timeout perio
    at dowhile_fla::MainTimeline/dowhile_fla::frame1()

Figure 9.56 This warning dialog box appears when you inadvertently cause an infinite loop.

The for..in loop and for each..in loop

Two other kinds of loops, called the `for..in` loop and the `for each..in` loop, are used specifically to look through the properties of an object or elements of an array and to look through the values of those properties or elements. You don't need to use a counter variable as you do for the other kinds of loops. Instead, you use a variable called an *iterator*, which is assigned a new value each time the loop repeats.

The built-in properties for objects (the ones that come with the preexisting classes) are hidden from the `for..in` and the `for each..in` loop—only properties that you define or elements of an `Array` are available.

To use the for..in loop to reference properties of an object:

◆ In the Script pane of the Actions panel, enter the code as follows:

```
for (var iterator:String in
→ myObject){
// do something with iterator
trace (iterator);
}
```

You can name the iterator variable anything you want and target any object you want. Flash goes through each property or element inside the object (here, called `myObject`) and returns the name of that property in your iterator variable. So, if `myObject` contained the properties `name` and `age`, the trace statement above would return `name` and `age`. You can also put the iterator in square brackets for dynamic property access.

To use the for each..in loop to reference values of an object:

◆ In the Script pane of the Actions panel, enter the code as follows:

```
for each (var iterator:String in
→ myObject){
// do something with iterator
trace (iterator);
}
```

You can name the iterator variable anything you want and target any object you want. In the `for each..in` loop, the iterator can be typed to any data type, not just a `String` (for example, if you are looping through an array and you know you've only added int variables to the array, you can type the iterator as int). Flash goes through each property or element inside the object (here, called `myObject`) and returns the *value* of that property in your iterator variable. This loop is useful to automatically go through the elements of an `Array` object or of an `XML` object to access the data.

10

Controlling Text

You know that Flash lets you create visually engaging text elements—such as titles, labels, and descriptions—to accompany your graphics, animation, and sound. But did you know that you can do more with text than just set the style, color, and size? Flash text can be *live*, meaning that your viewers can enter text in the Flash movie as it plays, as well as select and edit the text. And Flash text can be dynamic, so it can update during playback. A text field in which viewers can enter text is called an *input text field*, and a text field that you can update during playback is called a *dynamic text field*. Both input and dynamic text fields are controlled in ActionScript using the `TextField` class. Input and dynamic text fields provide a way to receive complex information from the viewer and tailor your Flash movie by using that information.

During authortime, you use the Text tool and the Property inspector to create your text fields. But you can also create text fields at runtime, dynamically defining their properties (such as background color) or formatting (such as font size and style, set with the `TextFormat` class). This control of text fields' content and appearance lets you animate text purely through ActionScript, making it responsive to the viewer and to different events.

You can also analyze and manipulate the text or the placement of the insertion point within the text. You'll learn to compare text with certain patterns of characters, called *regular expressions*. Using regular expressions provides a way to check if text input by a user matches the correct form of an e-mail or a phone number, for example. Or you can search a piece of text and replace only portions of it based on a particular pattern.

This chapter explores some of the many possibilities of dynamic and input text, and introduces the tools you can use to integrate text and control the information exchange between your Flash movie and your audience.

Input Text

You can build your Flash project to gather information directly from the viewer—information such as a login name and password, personal information for a survey, answers to quiz questions, requests for an online purchase, or responses in an Internet chat room. The text a user inputs into a text field is assigned to the `text` property of the text field. You can retrieve it from that property and pass it along to other parts of the Flash movie for further processing.

The following task demonstrates how you can incorporate user-input text to let your user control the parameters of other methods. In this case, you'll accept information from the viewer in an input text field and use that information to load a Web site.

To use user input to request a URL:

1. Choose the Text tool in the Tools panel, and drag out a text field on the Stage (**Figure 10.1**).

2. In the Property inspector, choose Input Text from the pull-down menu.

   Your selected text field becomes an input text field, allowing text entry during playback.

Figure 10.1 A text field is created with the Text tool. You can resize the text field with any of its handles (the black and white squares around its edges).

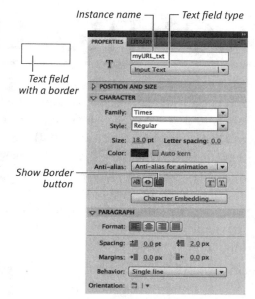

Instance name — Text field type

Text field with a border

Show Border button

Figure 10.2 The Property inspector defines the text field's type as input text. The instance name is `myURL_txt`, and the Show Border button is selected. A text field without a border appears on your Stage in authoring mode with a dotted border, whereas a text field with a border appears with a solid black border and a white background.

```
myURL_txt.addEventListener(KeyboardEvent.KEY_DOWN, gotowebsite);
function gotowebsite(myevent:KeyboardEvent):void {
    if (myevent.keyCode==Keyboard.ENTER) {

    }
}
```

Figure 10.3 This event handler detects when the Enter key is pressed within the text field called `myURL_txt`.

```
myURL_txt.addEventListener(KeyboardEvent.KEY_DOWN, gotowebsite);
function gotowebsite(myevent:KeyboardEvent):void {
    if (myevent.keyCode==Keyboard.ENTER) {
        navigateToURL(new URLRequest(myURL_txt.text));
    }
}
```

Figure 10.4 The contents of the text field `myURL_txt` are used to create the `URLRequest` object and passed to the `navigateToURL()` method.

INPUT TEXT

3. In the Instance Name field of the Property inspector, enter the name for your text field. Use the suffix _txt to identify it as a text field (optional).

4. Click the Show Border button in the Property inspector.

   Your text field is drawn with a black border and a white background so you can see where it is on the Stage (**Figure 10.2**).

5. Select the first frame of the main Timeline, and open the Actions panel.

6. On the first line of the Script pane, add a listener to detect a KeyboardEvent. KEY_DOWN event on your input text field.

7. On the next line, add the function that responds to the KeyboardEvent.KEY_DOWN event. Within the curly braces of the function, add an if statement to check if the key that is pressed is the Enter key (**Figure 10.3**).

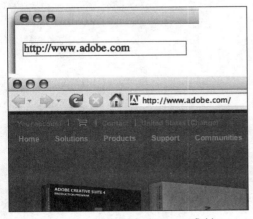

Figure 10.5 The contents of the input text field are used as the URL to open a Web site. Note that the user must include the protocol http:// in the input text field.

8. As the consequence of the if statement, call the navigateToURL() method, and for its parameter, pass a new URLRequest object with the text property of your input text field, like so (**Figure 10.4**):

   ```
   navigateToURL(new URLRequest
   → (myURL_txt.text));
   ```

   The text property of the input text field is used to create a new URLRequest object, which is passed to the navigateToURL() method. This calls up the Web address.

9. Test your movie.

   When the user enters a URL in the text field, the URL is put into the text property of the text field. Then, when the user presses the Enter key, Flash opens a new browser window and loads the specified Web site (**Figure 10.5**).

✔ Tips

■ You can put initial text in an input text field to instruct viewers what to enter. Put Enter Web site address here in your text field, for example, so that users know to replace that text with their Web site address. Or, start them off by putting http:// in the text field.

■ You can also *concatenate*, or connect, pieces of text with other variables and text to work in more flexible ways. For example, by concatenating the contents of the input text myURL_txt in the expression "http://" + myURL_txt.text, you eliminate the requirement that your viewer type the Internet protocol scheme before the Web site address.

INPUT TEXT

Dynamic Text

For text that you control—such as scores in an arcade game, the display of a calculator, or the percentage-of-download progress of your Flash movie—take advantage of Flash's dynamic text option. Whereas input text fields accept information from the viewer, dynamic text fields output information to the viewer. As with input text, the contents of the text field are assigned to its `text` property.

In the following task, you'll create an input text field and a dynamic text field. When viewers enter the temperature in Celsius in the input text field and press the Enter key, Flash will convert the value to Fahrenheit and display it in the dynamic text field.

To use dynamic text to output expressions:

1. Choose the Text tool in the Tools panel, and drag out a text field onto the Stage.

2. In the Property inspector, choose Input Text from the pull-down menu.

3. In the Instance Name field, enter the name of your input text field. Use the suffix `_txt` to identify it as a text field (optional) (**Figure 10.6**).

   Your selected text field becomes an input text field, allowing text entry during playback.

4. Again, choose the Text tool, and drag out another text field on the Stage.

5. In the Property inspector, this time choose Dynamic Text from the pull-down menu.

   Your selected text field becomes a dynamic text field, allowing you to display and update text in that field.

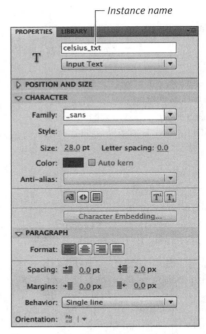

Instance name

Figure 10.6 The instance name for this input field is `celsius_txt`.

Instance name

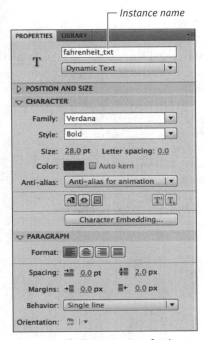

Figure 10.7 The instance name for the dynamic text field is `fahrenheit_txt`.

6. In the Instance Name field of the Property inspector, enter the name for the dynamic text field (**Figure 10.7**).

7. Select the first frame of the main Timeline, and open the Actions panel.

8. On the first line of the Script pane, add a listener to detect a `KeyboardEvent`. `KEY_DOWN` event on your input text field.

9. On the next line, add the function that responds to the `KeyboardEvent.KEY_DOWN` event. Within the curly braces of the function, add an `if` statement to check if the key that is pressed is the Enter key (**Figure 10.8**).

10. As the consequence of the `if` statement, perform calculations on the contents of the input text box (Celsius), and assign the result to a variable that holds `Number` data, as in the following:

```
var conversion:Number = (9 / 5) *
→ Number(celsius_txt.text) + 32;
```

Notice that you must explicitly convert the contents of the text field to a number when doing calculations.

Continues on next page

```
celsius_txt.addEventListener(KeyboardEvent.KEY_DOWN, doConversion);
function doConversion(myevent:KeyboardEvent):void {
    if (myevent.keyCode==Keyboard.ENTER) {

    }
}
```

Figure 10.8 This event handler detects when the Enter key is pressed within the text field called `celsius_txt`.

DYNAMIC TEXT

11. Next, convert the result to a String and assign it to the contents of the dynamic text field, as in the following (**Figure 10.9**):

```
fahrenheit_txt.text =
→ String(conversion);
```

12. Test your movie.

When the user enters a number in the first input text field and presses the Enter key, Flash takes the contents and converts them into a Fahrenheit number. It then puts that number in the contents of the dynamic text field to be displayed (**Figure 10.10**).

✔ Tip

■ Use dynamic text as a debugging tool to show the contents of expressions and variables. If you're developing a complicated Flash movie involving multiple variables, you can create a dynamic text field to display the variables' current values so you know how Flash is processing the information. In Chapter 12, "Managing Content and Troubleshooting," you'll learn other approaches to tracking variables, but this way you can integrate the display of variables into your movie.

```
celsius_txt.addEventListener(KeyboardEvent.KEY_DOWN, doConversion);
function doConversion(myevent:KeyboardEvent):void {
    if (myevent.keyCode==Keyboard.ENTER) {
        var conversion:Number = (9 / 5) * Number(celsius_txt.text) + 32;
        fahrenheit_txt.text = String(conversion);
    }
}
```

Figure 10.9 The contents of the dynamic text field (`fahrenheit_txt.text`) are assigned the correct value from the input text (`celsius_txt.text`) when the Enter key is pressed. Use `Number()` and `String()` to convert the data to numbers or text.

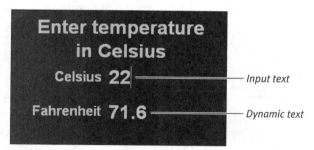

Figure 10.10 The user can convert Celsius to Fahrenheit.

Selecting Text Field Options

The Property inspector offers many options for an input (**Figure 10.11**) or dynamic text field (**Figure 10.12**). The most important field to fill is Instance Name. The Instance Name field contains the instance name of your text field, which you use in ActionScript to refer to the text field to modify its properties and call its methods. The other options let you modify the way text appears.

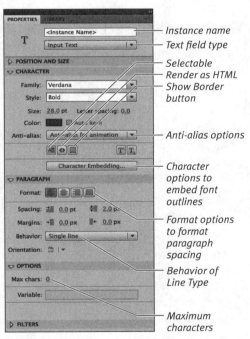

Instance name
Text field type

Selectable
Render as HTML
Show Border button

Anti-alias options

Character options to embed font outlines

Format options to format paragraph spacing

Behavior of Line Type

Maximum characters

Figure 10.11 The options in the Property inspector for input text.

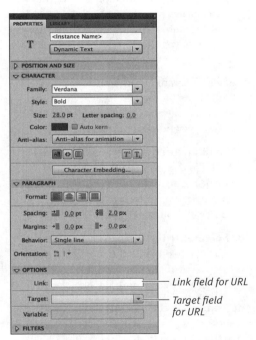

Link field for URL

Target field for URL

Figure 10.12 The options in the Property inspector for dynamic text are nearly identical to input text except for a few in the Options section.

The Character section

The **Anti-alias pull-down menu** allows you to choose the style of anti-aliasing (edge smoothing) to apply to your text. You can choose to have anti-aliasing that is optimized for readability or for animation:

◆ For very small font sizes, choose "Bitmap text (no anti-alias)" to create crisp and legible text optimized for small size representation.

◆ If the text will be animated to move, choose "Anti-alias for animation." The text won't be as smooth looking in general, but it will remain more readable while moving. However, the file size of the final SWF will be larger as a result.

◆ If ease of reading is the priority, choose "Anti-alias for readability," which makes small to medium-sized text look more attractive and easier to read.

◆ For ultimate control, choose "Custom anti-alias," which opens the Custom Anti-Aliasing dialog box, allowing you to specify thickness and sharpness values for your text.

The **Selectable button** allows your viewers to select the text inside the text field. (This button isn't available for input text because input text is—by nature—always selectable.)

The **Render as HTML button** allows text to preserve rich formatting using a few basic HTML tags, including `<a href>`, `<b>`, `<br>`, `<font color>`, `<font face>`, `<font size>`, `<img>`, `<i>`, `<li>`, `<p>`, and `<u>`.

The **Show Border button** draws your text field with a black border and white background.

Deselect this option to leave the text field invisible, but be sure to draw your own background or border if you want your viewers to find your text field on the Stage.

The **Character Embedding button** brings up the Character Embedding dialog box, where you can choose to embed font outlines with your exported SWF so that your text field displays anti-aliased type in the font of your choice. Keep in mind that this option increases your file size. You need to embed fonts if you mask, tween, or make any scaling or rotation transformations on your dynamic or input text fields.

The Paragraph section

The **Format buttons** provide options for paragraph alignment.

The **Behavior pull-down menu** defines how text fits into the text field:

◆ **Single Line** forces entered text to stay on one row in the text field. If text goes beyond the limits of the text field, the text begins to scroll horizontally.

◆ **Multiline** automatically causes the text to wrap when it reaches the edge of the text field.

◆ **Multiline No Wrap** allows entered text to appear on more than one row in the text field if the viewer presses the Enter (Windows) or Return key (Mac) for a carriage return.

◆ **Password** (Input Text only) disguises the letters entered in the text field with asterisks. Use this option to hide sensitive information such as a password from people looking over your viewer's shoulder.

The Options section

The **Maximum Characters field** (Input Text only) puts a limit on the amount of text your viewers can enter. If you want viewers to enter their home state by using only the two-digit abbreviation, for example, enter 2 in this field.

The **Link and Target field** (Static and Dynamic Text only) enables you to make the text hyperlink to a Web address.

✔ Tip

■ Unfortunately, dynamic and input text fields don't support vertical text. Vertical text is allowed only for static text.

Embedding Fonts and Device Fonts

Embedding font outlines via the Character Options dialog box ensures that the font you use in the authoring environment is the same one your audience sees during playback. This operation is done by default for static text, but you must choose the option when you create input text or dynamic text. When you don't embed fonts in your movie, Flash uses the closest font available on your viewer's computer and displays it as aliased text.

Why wouldn't you choose to embed font outlines all the time? Embedding fonts dramatically increases the size of your exported SWF file, because the information needed to render the fonts is included. You can keep the file size down by embedding only the characters your viewers use in the text field. If you ask viewers to enter numeric information in an input text field, for example, you can embed just the numbers of the font outline. All the numbers are available during movie playback; the other characters are disabled and won't display.

Another way to maintain small file sizes and eliminate the problem caused by viewers not having the matching font is to use *device fonts*. Device fonts are grouped in your Font Style pull-down menu. The three device fonts are _sans, _serif, and _typewriter. This option finds the fonts on a viewer's system that most closely resemble the specified device font. The following are the corresponding fonts for the device fonts.

On the Mac:

◆ _sans maps to Helvetica.

◆ _serif maps to Times.

◆ _typewriter maps to Courier.

In Windows:

◆ _sans maps to Arial.

◆ _serif maps to Times New Roman.

◆ _typewriter maps to Courier New.

When you use device fonts, you can be assured that your viewer sees text that is very similar to the text you see in the authoring environment. However, device fonts do have limitations; motion tweening of device fonts is not fully supported. For example, transformations such as scaling and rotation do not work in motion tweens of device fonts.

Displaying HTML

Flash can display HTML formatted text in dynamic text fields. To do so, select the Render as HTML option in the Property inspector and use the `htmlText` property of a text field. When you mark up text with HTML tags and assign the text to a dynamic text field, Flash interprets the tags and preserves the formatting. This means you can integrate HTML content inside your Flash movie, maintaining the styles and links.

The following common HTML tags are supported by text fields:

◆ `<a>`: Anchor tag to create hot links with `href`, `target`, and `event` attributes

◆ `<b>`: Bold style

◆ `<br>`: Line break

◆ `<font>`: Font style with `color`, `face`, and `size` attributes

◆ `<img>`: Image tag with `src`, `width`, `height`, `align`, `hspace`, `vspace`, `id`, and `checkPolicyFile` attributes

◆ `<i>`: Italics style

◆ `<Li>`: List item style

◆ `<p>`: Paragraph style with `left`, `right`, `center`, and `justify` attributes

◆ `<span>`: For use with CSS text styles

◆ `<textformat>`: For use with Flash's `TextFormat` class

◆ `<u>`: Underline style

A useful combination is to load HTML-formatted text from an external document into dynamic text fields with the `URLLoader` class. By changing the HTML that resides outside the Flash file, you can update the information that displays during playback of your movie. This feature can be convenient because you don't have to open the Flash file to make periodic edits, and a server-side script (or even a user unfamiliar with Flash) can make the necessary updates.

To load and display HTML in a dynamic text field:

1. Open a text-editing application or a WYSIWYG HTML editor, and create your HTML document (**Figure 10.13**).

2. Save the file in the same directory where you'll create your Flash document.

3. In Flash, choose the Text tool, and drag out a large text field that nearly covers the Stage.

4. In the Property inspector, choose Dynamic Text and Multiline, and click the Render as HTML button.

    The Render as HTML button lets Flash know to treat the contents of the text field as HTML-formatted text.

```
<html><body><p><b>This is an HTML page</b></p><p>This contains
<i>simple</i> HTML 1.0 tags that <font face="Arial">Flash</
font> can understand. Flash will display HTML formatted text
when the HTML option is selected in Dynamic Text in the
Property Inspector.</p><p><font face="Courier">a href</font>
will also work to create links to Web sites! For example, if
you <font color="#0000FF"><u><a href="http://www.adobe.com">
click here</a></u></font>, you will be sent to Adobe's Web
site.</p>You can also insert images, just like in normal HTML,
like this <img src="logo.jpg"></body></html>
```

Figure 10.13 The HTML text is saved as a separate document.

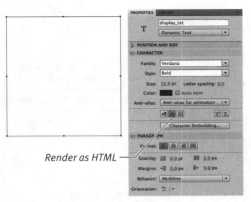

Render as HTML ——

Figure 10.14 Enter `display_txt` as the instance name for your dynamic text field, and click the Render as HTML button.

```
var myURLLoader:URLLoader = new URLLoader();
var myURLRequest:URLRequest = new URLRequest("mypage.html");
myURLLoader.load(myURLRequest);
myURLLoader.addEventListener(Event.COMPLETE, dataOK);
function dataOK(myevent:Event):void {

}
```

Figure 10.15 The external HTML document is automatically loaded. When the load is complete, the function called `dataOK` will get triggered.

```
var myURLLoader:URLLoader = new URLLoader();
var myURLRequest:URLRequest = new URLRequest("mypage.html");
myURLLoader.load(myURLRequest);
myURLLoader.addEventListener(Event.COMPLETE, dataOK);
function dataOK(myevent:Event):void {
    display_txt.htmlText=myURLLoader.data;
}
```

Figure 10.16 The `data` property of the `myURLLoader` object, which contains the HTML text, is assigned to the `htmlText` property of the `display_txt` text field.

5. Give the text field an instance name (**Figure 10.14**).

6. Select the first frame of the main Timeline, and open the Actions panel.

7. Create a new `URLLoader` and a new `URLRequest` object and provide the path to the HTML page, like so:

```
var myURLLoader:URLLoader = new
➝ URLLoader();
var myURLRequest:URLRequest = new
➝ URLRequest("mypage.html");
```

If your HTML page is in the same folder as your Flash movie, you can just enter the filename, as in this example. You can either load a local file or one that's on the Internet.

8. On the next available line, call the `load()` method for your `URLLoader` object with the `URLRequest` object as its parameter.

9. On the next lines, create an `Event.COMPLETE` event handler to detect the completion of the loading process (**Figure 10.15**).

10. In between the curly braces of the event handler function, assign the `data` property of your `URLLoader` object to the `htmlText` property of the dynamic text field (**Figure 10.16**):

```
display_txt.htmlText=myURLLoader.
➝ data
```

When the load is complete, the contents of the text file are assigned to the dynamic text field. The `htmlText` property displays HTML-tagged text correctly, as would a browser.

Continues on next page

DISPLAYING HTML

11. Test your movie.

The text in the external text file is loaded into the `data` property of the `URLLoader` object. When the file has completely loaded, Flash assigns the information to the `htmlText` property of the dynamic text. The dynamic text field displays the information, preserving all the style and format tags (**Figure 10.17**).

✔ Tips

■ Because only a limited number of HTML tags are supported by dynamic text, you should do a fair amount of testing to see how the information displays. When Flash doesn't understand a tag, it ignores it.

■ The anchor tag (`<a>`) normally appears underlined and in a different color in browser environments. In Flash, however, the hot link is indicated only by the pointer changing to a finger. To create the underline and color style for hot links manually, apply the underline tag (`<u>`) and the font-color tag (`<font color="#0000FF">`).

■ The HTML tags override any style settings you assign in the Property inspector for your dynamic text. If you choose red for your dynamic text, when you display HTML text in the field, the `<font color>` tag will modify the text to a different color.

■ The `<img src>` tag supports PNG, JPEG, GIF, and SWF files. So, you can even load in an external Flash movie to play within a dynamic text field!

⌐ Dynamic text field

This is an HTML page

This contains *simple* HTML 1.0 tags that Flash can understand. Flash will display HTML formatted text when the HTML option is selected in Dynamic Text in the Property Inspector.
`a href` will also work to create links to Web sites! For example, if you click here, you will be sent to Adobe's Web site.
You can also insert images, just like in normal HTML, like this

Figure 10.17 The dynamic text field displays the HTML-formatted text, including hyperlinks and embedded images.

To display HTML directly in a dynamic text field:

1. In Flash, choose the Text tool, and drag out a large text field that nearly covers the Stage.

2. In the Property inspector, choose Dynamic Text and Multiline, and click the Render as HTML button.

   The Render as HTML button lets Flash know to treat the contents of the text field as HTML-formatted text.

3. Give the text field an instance name.

4. Enter HTML text within the dynamic text field (**Figure 10.18**).

5. Select the first frame of the main Timeline, and open the Actions panel.

6. Assign the current contents of the dynamic text field (the text property) to its htmlText property as in the following:

   `myText.htmlText=myText.text;`

   When you test your movie, the current contents of your text field will be rendered as HTML-formatted text (**Figure 10.19**).

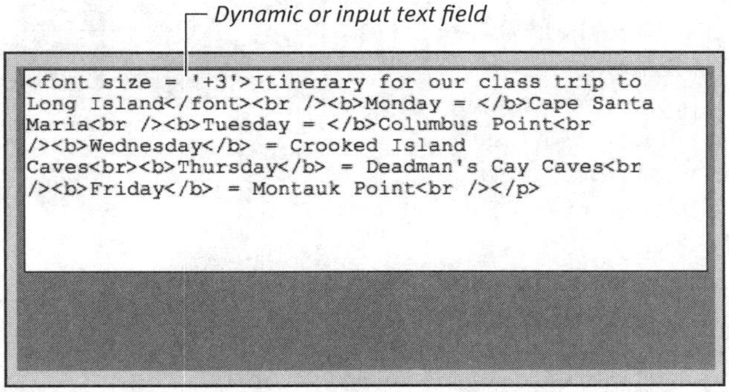

— Dynamic or input text field

```
<font size = '+3'>Itinerary for our class trip to
Long Island</font><br /><b>Monday = </b>Cape Santa
Maria<br /><b>Tuesday = </b>Columbus Point<br
/><b>Wednesday</b> = Crooked Island
Caves<br><b>Thursday</b> = Deadman's Cay Caves<br
/><b>Friday</b> = Montauk Point<br /></p>
```

Figure 10.18 Enter HTML code directly in a dynamic or input text field.

```
Itinerary for our class trip to Long Island
Monday = Cape Santa Maria
Tuesday = Columbus Point
Wednesday = Crooked Island Caves
Thursday = Deadman's Cay Caves
Friday = Montauk Point
```

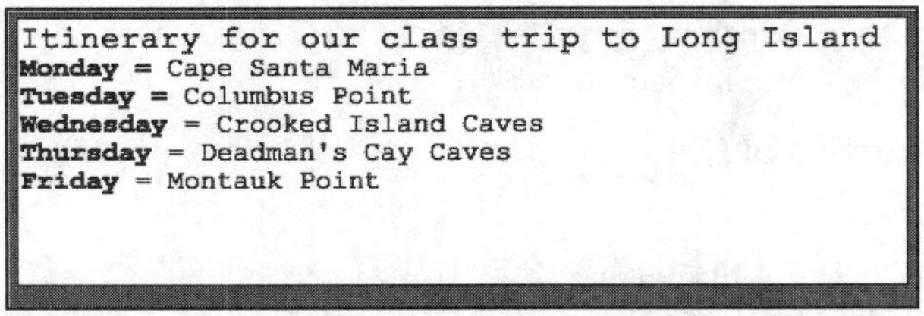

Figure 10.19 At runtime, Flash correctly displays all the HTML code in the text field.

DISPLAYING HTML

TextField Properties

When you drag an input or dynamic text field on the Stage with the Text tool, you're creating an instance of the `TextField` class. Before you can access its methods and properties, however, you must name your text field in the Property inspector so that you can identify it with ActionScript.

The instance name identifies the text field for targeting purposes. When you can target the text field, you can evaluate or modify its many properties. These properties determine the kind and display of the text field. You've already used the `text` property to get and set the contents of text fields and the `htmlText` property to assign HTML-formatted text. There are many other properties, including `type`, which defines an input or dynamic text field, and `border`, which determines whether the text field has one. In addition, since the `TextField` class is a subclass of the `DisplayObject` class, it has all the same properties to control its appearance, such as `rotation`, `alpha`, `x`, `y`, `z`, `scaleX`, `scaleY`, `scaleZ`, and so on.

Table 10.1 summarizes many of the properties of the `TextField` class. Most of them are identical to the properties you can set in authoring mode in the Property inspector.

To modify the properties of the text field:

1. Select the Text tool in the Tools panel, and drag out a text field on the Stage. Enter some sample text inside the field.

2. In the Property inspector, select Dynamic Text, give the text field an instance name, and leave all other options at their default settings (**Figure 10.20**).

Continues on page 401

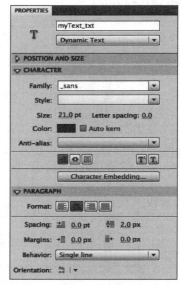

Figure 10.20 The dynamic text field is called myText_txt.

Table 10.1

TextField Properties

PROPERTY	VALUE	DESCRIPTION
alwaysShowSelection	true or false	Keeps a selection highlighted in gray even when the text field is not in focus.
antiAliasType	AntiAliasType.NORMAL or AntiAliasType.ADVANCED	Indicates type of anti-aliasing.
autoSize	TextFieldAutoSize.NONE, TextFieldAutoSize.LEFT, TextFieldAutoSize.CENTER, TextFieldAutoSize.RIGHT	Controls automatic alignment and sizing so that a text field shrinks or grows to accommodate text.
background	true or false	Specifies whether the text field has a background fill.
backgroundColor	A hex code	Specifies the color of the background.
border	true or false	Specifies whether the text field has a border.
borderColor	A hex code	Specifies the color of the border.
bottomScrollV	An integer	Indicates the bottommost line that is currently visible in a text field.
caretIndex	An integer	The index of the insertion point.
textColor	A hex code	Specifies the color of the text.
styleSheet	A StyleSheet object	Defines style rules to be applied to the text field.
sharpness	A number, -400 to 400	Specifies the level of sharpness to apply to character edges.
thickness	A number, -200 to 200	Specifies the thickness to be applied to character edges.
gridFitType	GridFitType.NONE, GridFitType.PIXEL, GridFitType.SUBPIXEL	Indicates whether character lines are fit to exact pixels, or subpixels (fractional pixels on an LCD monitor), or not fit to any grid.
textWidth	A number, in pixels	Specifies the width of the text (read-only).
textHeight	A number, in pixels	Specifies the height of the text (read-only).
length	A number	Specifies the number of characters in a text field (read-only).
scrollV	A number	Specifies the top line visible in the text field.
scrollH	A number, in pixels	Specifies the horizontal scrolling position of a text field. 0 defines the position where there is no scrolling.
maxscrollV	A number	Specifies the maximum value for the scrollV property (read-only).
maxscrollH	A number	Specifies the maximum value for the scrollH property (read-only).
mouseWheelEnabled	true or false	Specifies whether the user's mouse wheel can scroll multiline text fields.

Continues on next page

Table 10.1 *(continued)*

TextField Properties

PROPERTY	VALUE	DESCRIPTION
restrict	A string	Specifies the allowable characters in the text field.
maxChars	A number	Specifies the maximum number of characters allowable.
embedFonts	true or false	Specifies whether fonts are embedded. You must create a font symbol and export it for ActionScript in its Linkage properties.
htmlText	A string	Specifies HTML contents of the text field.
condenseWhite	true or false	Specifies whether extra white space in an HTML text field should be removed.
multiline	true or false	Specifies whether the text field can display more than one line.
wordWrap	true or false	Specifies whether the text field breaks lines automatically.
selectionBeginIndex	A number	Specifies the index position of the first character in a selection (read-only).
selectionEndIndex	A number	Specifies the index position of the last character in a selection (read-only).
selectable	true or false	Specifies whether the contents of the text field are selectable.
text	A string	Specifies the contents of a text field.
displayAsPassword	true or false	Specifies whether input text is disguised.
numLines	A number	Indicates the number of text lines (read-only).
defaultTextFormat	A TextFormat object	Indicates the format for newly inserted text.
type	TypeFieldType.DYNAMIC or TypeFieldType.INPUT	The type of the text field.
useRichTextClipboard	true or false	Specifies whether to copy and paste text formatting along with contents.

```
myText_txt.textColor=0xff0000;
```

Figure 10.21 Change the property `textColor` for the text field named `myText_txt`. In this example, the `textColor` property of the text field `myText_txt` is set to red.

```
myText_txt.textColor=0xff0000;
myText_txt.background=true;
myText_txt.backgroundColor=0x225566;
myText_txt.border=true;
myText_txt.borderColor=0x99ff77;
myText_txt.rotationY=45
```

Figure 10.22 The script modifies many properties of the text field `myTextField_txt`, resulting in the text below. Note that text can be affected by properties for transformations in 3D space. The text was already in the text field on the Stage at authortime.

3. Select the first frame of the main Timeline, and open the Actions panel.

4. In the Script pane, enter the instance name of your text field followed by a period, and then enter a property. For this example, choose `textColor`, and enter an equals sign.

5. After the equals sign, enter `0xff0000`. The completed statement changes the color of the text to red (**Figure 10.21**).

6. Repeat steps 5 and 6, choosing different properties and values to modify your text field (**Figure 10.22**).

✔ Tips

- To modify the font, font size, and other characteristics of the text, you must use the `TextFormat` class, which is discussed later in this chapter.

- If you modify the properties `alpha` and `rotation`, you must embed the font outlines for your text field. If you don't, the text won't be modified correctly.

- The properties x and y refer to the top-left corner of the text field.

- The properties `width` and `height` change the pixel dimensions of the text field but don't change the size of the text inside the text field. The properties `scaleX`, `scaleY`, and `scaleZ`, on the other hand, scale the text.

TEXTFIELD PROPERTIES

401

Controlling text field scrolling

If a text field is too small to display its text content, you can use the TextField properties scrollV, scrollH, maxScrollV, and maxScrollH, all of which give information about the position of the text within the text field.

When the information in a multiline text field exceeds its defined boundaries, Flash displays only the current text (unless you set the autoSize property to fit the information). Text that can't fit within the text field is hidden from view but is still accessible if the viewer clicks inside the text field and drags up or down. You can display different portions of the hidden text dynamically by defining the properties scrollV and scrollH.

Think of the text field as being a window that shows only a portion of a larger piece of text. Each row of text has an index value. The top row is 1, the second row is 2, and so on. The scrollV property refers to the topmost visible row. The maxScrollV property refers to the bottommost visible row. The visible portion of a text field is the rows from scrollV to maxScrollV, and as new lines of text scroll up or down, those properties change (**Figure 10.23**).

If a line of text exceeds the width of its text field, you can use scrollH to display different portions of its horizontal scrolling. The point on the right edge of the text field where the initial text is visible has a scrollH value of 0. The value of scrollH is measured in pixels; as scrollH increases, the text scrolls to reveal more text (**Figure 10.24**).

You can retrieve the values of scrollV and scrollH so you know exactly which portion of the text your viewer is currently looking at, or you can modify their values to force your viewer to look at a particular portion. It's common to provide interface controls so that viewers can control the scrolling of text, just as they control the scroll bars in a Web browser or any window on the computer screen. In the following task, you'll create interface controls of this kind.

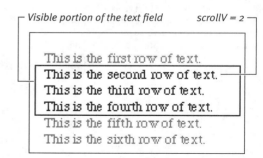

Figure 10.23 The scrollV property is the first visible row of text within a text field.

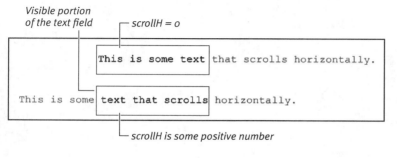

Figure 10.24 The scrollH property is relative to the point at which there is no scrolling. The value of scrollH increases as horizontal scrolling occurs.

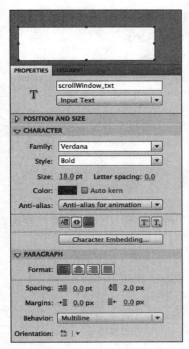

Figure 10.25 Enter `scrollWindow_txt` as the instance name of your text field.

Input text field — *First button instance* —

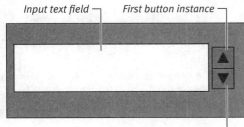

Second button instance —

Figure 10.26 Place two buttons next to the input text field.

```
upButton_btn.addEventListener(MouseEvent.CLICK, scrollup);
function scrollup(myevent:MouseEvent):void{
    scrollWindow_txt.scrollV-- ;
}
```

Figure 10.27 Clicking the `upButton_btn` button subtracts 1 from the property `scrollV`.

To create a vertical scrolling text field:

1. Select the Text tool in the Tools panel, and drag out a text field onto the Stage.

2. In the Property inspector, choose Input Text, enter an instance name, choose Multiline from the pull-down menu, and click the Show Border button (**Figure 10.25**).

3. Create a button symbol of an arrow pointing up, place an instance of the button on the Stage, and give it a name in the Property inspector.

4. Place a second instance of the button on the Stage, choose Modify > Transform > Flip Vertical to make the second button point down, and give the down arrow button a name in the Property inspector.

5. Align both buttons vertically next to the input text field (**Figure 10.26**).

6. Select the first frame of the main Timeline, and open the Actions panel.

7. Create a `MouseEvent.CLICK` event handler for the up arrow button.

8. In between the curly braces of the event handler function, enter the following:

   `scrollWindow_txt.scrollV--`

   When the up button is clicked, the `scrollV` property decreases by 1, which scrolls the text by displaying the previous hidden line of text (**Figure 10.27**).

9. Create a `MouseEvent.CLICK` event handler for the down arrow button.

Continues on next page

TEXTFIELD PROPERTIES

10. In between the curly braces of the event handler function for the down button, enter the following:

```
scrollWindow_txt.scrollV++
```

When the down button is clicked, the `scrollV` property increases by 1, which scrolls the text by displaying the next line of text (**Figure 10.28**).

11. Test your movie. Begin by typing in the input text field several lines of text so only a few lines of the total content are visible. When you click the up or down button, you can scroll to see the different lines of text (**Figure 10.29**).

✔ Tips

■ The buttons that control scrolling are good candidates for a continuous-feedback button. When you press and hold down on the buttons, you want the scrolling to continue. Refer back to Chapter 9, "Controlling Information Flow," to see how to create a continuous-feedback button.

■ You can detect whenever a scroll occurs by listening for the `Event.SCROLL` event.

```
downButton_btn.addEventListener(MouseEvent.CLICK, scrolldown);
function scrolldown(myevent:MouseEvent):void{
    scrollWindow_txt.scrollV++;
}
```

Figure 10.28 Clicking the `downButton_btn` button adds 1 to the property `scrollV`.

Figure 10.29 The buttons on the right increase or decrease the value of the `scrollV` property of the input text field.

Determining the maximum scrolling position

Whereas the `scrollV` property defines the first visible text row in a text field, the `maxScrollV` property defines the maximum allowable value for `scrollV` in that text field. This row appears at the top of the text field when the last line of text is visible (**Figure 10.30**). You can't change the value of `maxScrollV`, because it's defined by the amount of text and the size of the text field, but you can read its value. Assign the value of `maxScrollv` to `scrollV`, and you can make the text jump to the bottom of the text field automatically. Or you can calculate the value of `scrollV` proportionally to `maxScrollV` and build a draggable scroll bar that reflects and controls the text's position within the text field.

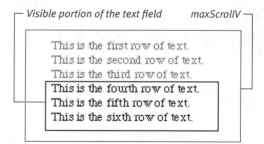

Visible portion of the text field   *maxScrollV*

This is the first row of text.
This is the second row of text.
This is the third row of text.
This is the fourth row of text.
This is the fifth row of text.
This is the sixth row of text.

Figure 10.30 The `maxScrollV` property refers to the maximum value of the `scrollV` property. This value is the value of `scrollV` when the last line of text is visible. In this example, `maxScrollV` is 4.

```
end_btn.addEventListener(MouseEvent.CLICK, end)
function end(myevent:MouseEvent):void{
    scrollWindow_txt.scrollV=scrollWindow_txt.maxScrollV
}
```

Figure 10.31 A portion of the Script pane shows the event handler for a button end_btn. The property maxScrollV is assigned to the scrollV property of scrollwindow_txt.

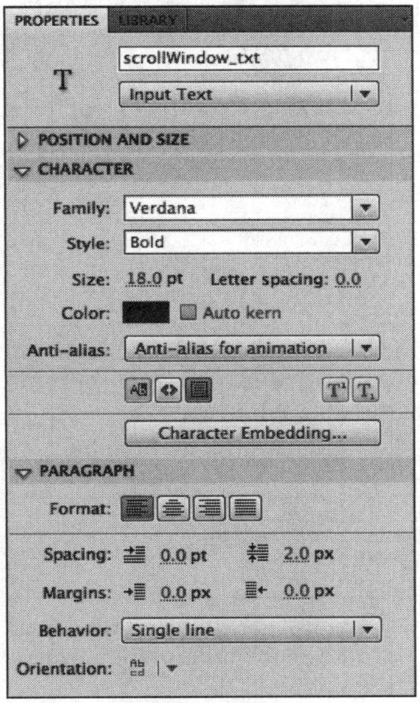

Figure 10.32 Enter scrollWindow_txt as the instance name of your input text field.

To scroll to the end of a text field:

1. Continuing with the preceding task, create a new button symbol, drag an instance of it to the Stage, and give it a name in the Property inspector.

2. Select the first frame of the main Timeline, and open the Actions panel.

3. Create a MouseEvent.CLICK event handler for the new button.

4. In between the curly braces of the event handler function for the new button, enter the following:

   scrollWindow_txt.scrollV=
   → scrollWindow_txt.maxScrollV

   When the new button is clicked, the scrollV property is set to the maxScrollV property, which scrolls the text down so the last line is visible (**Figure 10.31**).

To create a horizontal scrolling text field:

1. Select the Text tool in the Tools panel, and drag out a text field onto the Stage.

2. In the Property inspector, choose Input Text, enter an instance name, choose Single Line from the pull-down menu, and click the Show Border button (**Figure 10.32**).

3. Create a button symbol of a right-pointing arrow, place an instance of the button on the Stage, and give it a name in the Property inspector.

4. Place a second instance of the button on the Stage, choose Modify > Transform > Flip Horizontal to make the second button point left, and give the left arrow button a name in the Property inspector.

Continues on next page

TextField Properties

5. Align both buttons horizontally above the input text field (**Figure 10.33**).

6. Select the first frame of the main Timeline, and open the Actions panel.

7. Create a MouseEvent.CLICK event handler for the right arrow button.

8. In between the curly braces of the event handler function, enter the following:

scrollWindow_txt.scrollH+=10

When the right button is clicked, the scrollH property increase by 10 pixels, which scrolls the text to the right (**Figure 10.34**).

9. Create a MouseEvent.CLICK event handler for the left arrow button.

10. In between the curly braces of the event handler function for the left button, enter the following:

scrollWindow_txt.scrollV-=10

When the left button is clicked, the scrollH property decreases by 10, which scrolls the text to the left (**Figure 10.35**).

11. Test your movie. Begin by typing in the input text field until the window can no longer accommodate all the text. When you click the left or right button, you can scroll left or right to see the text (**Figure 10.36**).

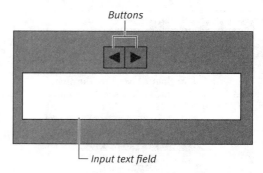

Buttons

Input text field

Figure 10.33 Align two buttons above your input text field.

```
rightButton_btn.addEventListener(MouseEvent.CLICK, scrollright);
function scrollright(myevent:MouseEvent):void{
    scrollWindow_txt.scrollH+=10;
}
```

Figure 10.34 The actions assigned to the rightButton_btn handler add 10 to the value of the scrollH property of scrollwindow_txt.

```
leftButton_btn.addEventListener(MouseEvent.CLICK, scrollleft);
function scrollleft(myevent:MouseEvent):void{
    scrollWindow_txt.scrollH-=10;
}
```

Figure 10.35 The actions assigned to the leftButton_btn handler subtract 10 from the value of the scrollH property of scrollwindow_txt.

ıter text here and use the but

Figure 10.36 The buttons control both the left and right horizontal scrolling of text inside the text field.

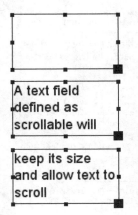

Figure 10.37 When you define a text field as scrollable in authoring mode, the resizing handle turns black (top). You can enter text in authoring mode, but the size of the text field remains constant, hiding text that can't fit and allowing scrolling (bottom).

Constraining text field height in authoring mode

Sometimes, in authoring mode, you'll want to restrict the size of your text field so that its contents are scrollable. By defining your text field as scrollable, you can keep much of the text it contains hidden from view.

To define a scrollable text field in authoring mode:

1. Select the Text tool in the Tools panel, and drag out a text field on the Stage.

2. Choose Text > Scrollable from the main menu.

   The resizing handle at the bottom-right corner of your text field fills in with black, indicating that the text field is scrollable. Although your text field remains resizable, any text that doesn't fit in the text field will begin to scroll (**Figure 10.37**).

   or

   Shift-double-click the resizing handle of the text field.

   The handle turns black, and the text field becomes scrollable.

Generating Text Fields Dynamically

If you need to have text appear in your movie based on a viewer's interaction, you must be able to create a text field during runtime. You can generate text fields dynamically with the TextField class's constructor function, like so:

```
var myTextField:TextField=new
→ TextField()
```

This statement creates a new TextField instance that you can now fill with text. You can also change the appearance of the text field and add it to the display list to make it visible to the viewer. To assign contents to your new TextField object, assign a string to its text property, as in myTextField.text="Hello". Make the text visible by calling the addChild() method as in:

```
stage.addChild(myTextField)
```

To create a text field on the main Stage:

1. Select the first frame of the main Timeline, and open the Actions panel.

2. Declare a variable using the var statement, and assign it the data type TextField. Enter an equals sign and then new TextField(). Don't pass any parameters to the constructor (**Figure 10.38**).

   Your statement looks something like var myText:TextField=new TextField();

3. On the next lines, add content to your TextField object by assigning a string to its text property (**Figure 10.39**).

4. Finally, add the TextField object to the display list (**Figure 10.40**).

   A text field is created and displayed (**Figure 10.41**).

```
var myTextField:TextField = new TextField();
```

Figure 10.38 This code creates a new instance from the TextField class. An object called myTextField is created.

```
var myTextField:TextField = new TextField();
myTextField.text = "Welcome to Flash!";
```

Figure 10.39 New contents are put into the text field.

```
var myTextField:TextField = new TextField();
myTextField.text = "Welcome to Flash!";
stage.addChild(myTextField);
```

Figure 10.40 The dynamically generated text field is put on the display list to make it visible.

Figure 10.41 The dynamically generated text field is positioned at the registration point of its parent, here shown at the top-left corner of the Stage. The default format for a dynamically created text field is black 12-point Times New Roman (Windows) or Times (Mac).

✔ Tip

■ The default size of a dynamically generated TextField object is 100 pixels wide by 100 pixels tall.

The Default Text Field Appearance

When you create a text field dynamically, it has the following default properties:

```
type = dynamic
selectable = true
embedFonts = false
multiline = false
restrict = null
displayAsPassword = false
maxChars = null
wordWrap = false
background = false
autoSize = none
border = false
alwaysShowSelection=false
autoSize=none
antiAliasType="normal"
```

The text field also has the following default format properties (which you can change with a `TextFormat` object):

```
font  = Times New Roman (Windows)
font = Times (Mac)
leftMargin = 0
rightMargin = 0
size = 12
indent = 0
textColor = 0x000000
leading = 0
bold = false
url = ""
target = ""
italic = false
underline = false
bullet = false
align = "left"
```

To remove a text field:

◆ Call the `removeChild()` method and use the text field as its parameter, as in:

`removeChild(myTextField);`

The `TextField` object is removed from the display list and disappears from the Stage or from its `DisplayObjectContainer`.

✔ Tip

■ You can use `removeChild()` to take away a text field generated dynamically or one that was created at authortime with the Text tool.

GENERATING TEXT FIELDS DYNAMICALLY

Modifying Text in Text Fields

Although the properties of a text field can define the way text behaves and the way the text field appears, the properties don't control the formatting of the text the text field contains. For that task, you need to use the TextFormat class. The TextFormat class controls character and paragraph formatting, which are also options available in authoring mode in the Property inspector. The Property inspector is divided into sections of options that are controlled by the TextField class and those that are controlled by the TextFormat class (**Figure 10.42**). **Table 10.2** summarizes the properties of the TextFormat class.

To change the formatting of text in a text field, first create a new instance of the TextFormat class, like so:

```
var myTF:TextFormat = new TextFormat();
```

Then assign values to the properties of your TextFormat object:

```
myTF.size = 48;
```

Finally, call the setTextFormat() method for your text field. This method is a method of the TextField class, not of the TextFormat class:

```
myTextField_txt.setTextFormat (myTF);
```

This statement applies the formatting in the TextFormat object to the text in the text field. In this example, it changes the size of the text in the text field myTextField_txt to 48 points.

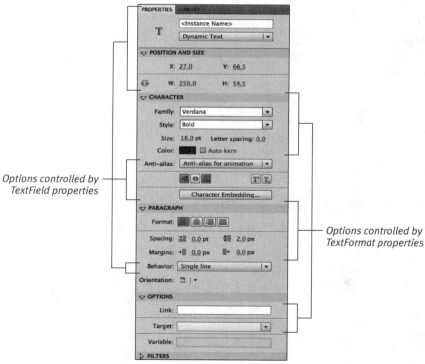

Options controlled by TextField properties

Options controlled by TextFormat properties

Figure 10.42 The Property inspector can be divided into sections of options controlled by TextFormat properties and options controlled by TextField properties.

Table 10.2

TextFormat Properties		
PROPERTY	VALUE	DESCRIPTION
size	A number	Specifies the point size of the text.
font	A string	Specifies the font of the text. You must create a font symbol and choose Export for ActionScript in its Linkage properties. Use the font name from the Property inspector for this property. Works only when embedFonts = true.
color	A hex number	Specifies the color of the text.
underline	true or false	Specifies whether the text is underlined.
italic	true or false	Specifies whether the text is italicized.
bold	true or false	Specifies whether the text is bold.
bullet	true or false	Specifies whether text is in a bulleted list.
align	TextFormatAlign.CENTER, TextFormatAlign.RIGHT, or TextFormatAlign.LEFT	Specifies the alignment of text within the text field.
leading	A number in pixels	Specifies the space between lines.
kerning	true or false	Indicates whether kerning is enabled.
letterSpacing	A number	Specifies the space between characters.
indent	A number	Specifies the indentation of the first line of paragraphs, in points.
blockIndent	A number	Specifies the indentation of the entire text, in points.
rightMargin	A number	Specifies the space between the text and the right edge, in points.
leftMargin	A number	Specifies the space between the text and the left edge, in points.
tabStops	An array of numbers	Specifies the placement (in pixels) of custom tab stops.
url	A string	Specifies the URL that the text links to.
target	A string	Specifies the target window where the hyperlink opens.

MODIFYING TEXT IN TEXT FIELDS

To modify the text formatting of a text field:

1. Create a text field, either by generating one with ActionScript or by selecting the Text tool, dragging out a text field on the Stage, and naming it in the Property inspector.

   In this example, you'll create a text field dynamically (**Figure 10.43**).

2. Assign some text to the text property of your text field (**Figure 10.44**).

3. Declare a TextFormat object using the var statement followed by an equals sign and then the constructor function new TextFormat().

   A new TextFormat object is created.

4. On the next lines, enter the name of your TextFormat object, followed by a period, then a property name, an equals sign, and a value. For example:

   myTF.size=48;

   myTF.color=0xFF0000;

   myTF.italic=true;

   These three statements assign new values for the size, color, and the italics style (**Figure 10.45**).

5. On a new line, enter the name of your text field followed by a period. Then call the setTextFormat() method and pass your TextFormat object as the parameter (**Figure 10.46**).

   The TextFormat object provides the information about all the formatting of the text, and the setTextFormat() method applies those changes.

```
var myTextField:TextField = new TextField();
```

Figure 10.43 Create a new text field from the TextField class.

```
var myTextField:TextField = new TextField();
myTextField.text = "Welcome to Flash!";
```

Figure 10.44 Add text to your text field.

```
var myTextField:TextField = new TextField();
myTextField.text = "Welcome to Flash!";

var myTF:TextFormat=new TextFormat();
myTF.size=48;
myTF.color=0xFF0000;
myTF.italic=true;
```

Figure 10.45 Instantiate a TextFormat object called myTF, and assign new values for its size, color, and italics style.

```
var myTextField:TextField = new TextField();
myTextField.text = "Welcome to Flash!";

var myTF:TextFormat=new TextFormat()
myTF.size=48;
myTF.color=0xFF0000;
myTF.italic=true;

myTextField.setTextFormat(myTF);
```

Figure 10.46 Call the setTextFormat() method and pass the TextFormat object to make the formatting changes.

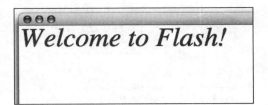

Figure 10.47 The new formatting applies to the entire text field.

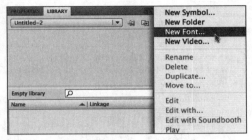

Figure 10.48 Choose New Font from the Library Options menu.

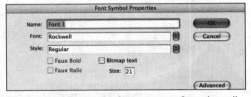

Figure 10.49 Choose the font you want from the pull-down menu and give it a name, which will appear in your Library.

6. If you've dynamically generated the text field, call the `addChild()` method to add it to the display list to make it visible. Also, be sure to change the `width` and `height` properties of the text field to accommodate the text.

7. Test your movie.

   Flash creates a `TextFormat` object. The properties of the object are passed through the `setTextFormat()` method and modify the existing contents of the text field (**Figure 10.47**).

✔ Tip

- The `setTextFormat()` method changes the formatting of existing text only, so you should already have text in your text field to see the changes. If you add more text after `setTextFormat()` is called, that text will have its original formatting.

Embedding and applying fonts

When you want to format a text field with a particular font, you use the `font` property of the `TextFormat` object to provide the name of the font. However, you must do two additional things: First, you must set the `embedFonts` property of the text field to `true`. Second, you must make the font available to the exported SWF by putting it in the Library and marking it in the Linkage options of the Symbol Properties dialog box.

To modify the font of a text field:

1. In the Library, choose New Font from the Options menu (**Figure 10.48**).

   The Font Symbol Properties dialog box appears.

2. In the Font Symbol Properties dialog box, choose a font from the pull-down menu, and give the font a name that will appear in your Library (**Figure 10.49**).

Continues on next page

3. Click the Advanced button.

The Linkage section appears.

4. Select Export for ActionScript, and enter a class name for the font symbol. Leave the base class as `flash.text.Font`. Click OK (**Figure 10.50**).

5. Select the first frame of the Timeline, and open the Actions panel.

6. On the first line of the Script pane, create a new `TextField` object.

7. On the next line, assign some text to the `text` property of your `TextField` object.

8. On the following line, assign the value `true` to the `embedFonts` property of your `TextField` object (**Figure 10.51**).

9. On the next line, create a new `TextFormat` object.

10. On the following line, enter the name of your `TextFormat` object, a period, the property `font`, an equals sign, and then the name of your font as it appears in your Property inspector. Make sure you put quotation marks around the font name.

Note that the `font` property takes a string value. This is not the name of your font symbol in the Library, nor is it the class name in the Linkage properties. It is the name of the font that appears in the Font field of the Font Symbol Properties dialog box, which is identical to the one that appears in the pull-down menu of fonts in the Property inspector (**Figure 10.52**).

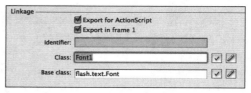

Figure 10.50 The Linkage section of the Font Symbol Properties dialog box. Select the Export for ActionScript box and leave the Base class as `flash.text.Font`.

```
var myTextField:TextField = new TextField();
myTextField.text = "New fonts!";
myTextField.embedFonts=true;
```

Figure 10.51 The property `embedFonts` must be true if you want to embed fonts for a dynamically generated text field.

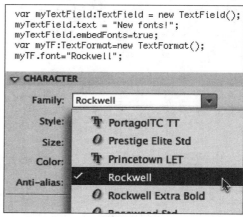

```
var myTextField:TextField = new TextField();
myTextField.text = "New fonts!";
myTextField.embedFonts=true;
var myTF:TextFormat=new TextFormat();
myTF.font="Rockwell";
```

Figure 10.52 Assign the new font to the `font` property of your `TextFormat` object. The font is the name that appears in the pull-down menu in your Property inspector; here it's called "Rockwell". Be sure to use quotation marks around your font name.

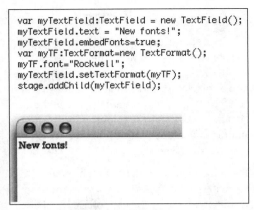

```
var myTextField:TextField = new TextField();
myTextField.text = "New fonts!";
myTextField.embedFonts=true;
var myTF:TextFormat=new TextFormat();
myTF.font="Rockwell";
myTextField.setTextFormat(myTF);
stage.addChild(myTextField);
```

New fonts!

Figure 10.53 The text is displayed in Rockwell font.

11. On a new line, enter the name of your text field and a dot, and then call the `setTextFormat()` method and pass the `TextFormat` object as the parameter.

12. If you've dynamically generated the text field (as you've done in this example), call the `addChild()` method to add it to the display list to make it visible.

13. Test your movie.

The font symbol in your Library is marked for export into your SWF and is available to be referenced by ActionScript. Flash creates a `TextFormat` object and assigns the font outline to its `font` property. When the `setTextFormat()` method is called, the font is applied to the text field (**Figure 10.53**).

Formatting segments of text

The `setTextFormat()` method enables you to format the entire text field, a single character, or a span of characters. To do so, you must specify the portion of the text that you want to format. The position of any given character in a `String` (such as the `text` property of a text field) is known as the character's *index*. The index of the first character is 0, the index of the second character is 1, and so on. If you use an index as the second parameter of the `setTextFormat()` method, only that single character is affected. If you use a beginning index and an ending index as the second and third parameters, the span of characters between the two indexes, including the beginning character, is affected.

To modify the text formatting of a single character:

◆ Call the setTextFormat() method and pass two parameters: The first is the TextFormat object and the second is the index number identifying which character you want the formatting to be applied to:

setTextFormat(myTF, 0);

This statement applies the formatting defined in the TextFormat object myTF to the very first character, which is index number zero.

To modify the text formatting of a span of characters:

◆ Call the setTextFormat() method and pass three parameters: The first is the TextFormat object, the second is the index number identifying the first character, and the third parameter is the index number identifying the first character outside the range of affected characters.

setTextFormat(myTF, 12, 24);

This statement applies the formatting defined in the TextFormat object myTF to 12 characters (index 12 through 24 but not including 24) (**Figure 10.54**).

Text field anti-aliasing

Putting text on a computer screen involves two key things—you want the text to look good, to have smooth edges and not look jagged or pixelated, and you also want the text to be easy to read. *Anti-aliasing* is a technique that is used to make text look smooth and to maintain readability by modifying the edges of the characters.

Flash includes anti-aliasing technology known as FlashType that provides industry-leading text-rendering capabilities: It yields smooth-looking text that's also easy to read on the computer screen. In ActionScript, you can turn on FlashType text rendering for your text field by setting its antiAliasType property to "advanced" or the equivalent constant AntiAliasType.ADVANCED. To use advanced anti-aliasing, you must embed the font outlines for text fields placed on the Stage during authoring. For text fields that are created dynamically, you must create a font symbol in the Library and set the embedFonts property of your TextField object to true.

With FlashType turned on, the quality of the text in your text field will probably improve, but depending on the font and size you're using, you may want to make small adjustments to how Flash displays your text. Two additional properties of the TextField class, sharpness and thickness, give you precise control over the anti-aliasing of your text so you can adjust it to match your needs.

Index 12 ⌐   Index 24 ⌐

Figure 10.54 The statement myTextField. setTextFormat(myTF, 12, 24) formats just the specified characters. The characters beginning at index 12 and up to, but not including, index 24 will change formats. The rest of the text stays the same.

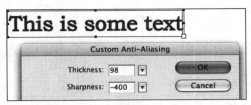

Figure 10.55 The Custom Anti-Aliasing dialog box allows you to experiment to find the best values to use for the thickness and sharpness properties of your text field.

```
var myTF:TextField = new TextField();
myTF.text = "Anti-aliasing";
myTF.embedFonts = true;
```

Figure 10.56 A new text field is created, assigned text, and set to use an embedded font.

How do you know what values to use for sharpness and thickness? To avoid tedious trial and error, experiment in the Flash authoring tool. With a text field selected on the Stage, choose Custom anti-alias in the Anti-alias pull-down menu. In the dialog box, adjust the Thickness and Sharpness values. As you do so, you can see a real-time preview of your text on the Stage, allowing you to easily find values that suit your text (**Figure 10.55**).

To set anti-aliasing for a text field:

1. As described in previous tasks, choose a font and add it to the Library as a font symbol. Be sure to choose Export for ActionScript and give it a class identifier.

2. Select the first keyframe, and open the Actions panel.

3. In the Script pane, enter code to create a new TextField object.

4. Enter code to add text to your TextField object by assigning a value to its text property.

5. Add a statement to set the embedFonts property of your TextField object to true. The text field is created and is ready to be formatted (**Figure 10.56**).

6. On a new line, declare and instantiate a new TextFormat object.

7. Enter a statement to set the TextFormat object's font property to the name of your font.

8. Enter additional statements to set other formatting properties for your TextFormat object and properties for your text field as desired.

Continues on next page

9. On a new line, assign the `TextFormat` object to the text field by calling the `setTextFormat()` method on the text field (**Figure 10.57**).

Remember to use your `TextFormat` object as the parameter of the `setTextFormat()` method.

```
var myTF:TextField = new TextField();
myTF.text = "Anti-aliasing";
myTF.embedFonts = true;
var myFormat_fmt:TextFormat = new TextFormat();
myFormat_fmt.font = "Cooper Black";
myFormat_fmt.size = 12;

myTF.setTextFormat(myFormat_fmt);
```

Figure 10.57 This example creates a `TextFormat` object called `myFormat_fmt`, sets its font property to the Library font Cooper Black, sets the `size` to 12 point, and changes the text field named `myTF`.

10. On the next line, enter the name of your text field followed by a period. Then enter the property `antiAliasType`, an equals sign, and `"advanced"` (in quotes); alternatively, you can use the constant `AntiAliasType.ADVANCED`.

This statement sets the `antiAliasType` property to advanced anti-aliasing.

11. If desired, add statements to set the thickness and sharpness properties of the `TextField` object to alter the anti-aliasing of the text (**Figure 10.58**).

```
var myTF:TextField = new TextField()
myTF.text = "Anti-aliasing";
myTF.embedFonts = true;
var myFormat_fmt:TextFormat = new TextFormat();
myFormat_fmt.font = "Cooper Black";
myFormat_fmt.size = 12;

myTF.setTextFormat(myFormat_fmt);

myTF.antiAliasType = AntiAliasType.ADVANCED;
myTF.sharpness = -200;
```

Figure 10.58 The text field's `antiAliasType` is set to `AntiAliasType.ADVANCED`, enabling FlashType anti-aliasing, and its `sharpness` is set at -200.

12. Add the text field to the display list with `addChild()` and test your movie.

The text field appears on the Stage, is formatted according to the settings you gave, and is rendered using the advanced anti-aliasing technology (**Figure 10.59**).

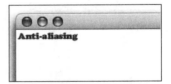

Figure 10.59 The custom anti-aliasing shows up on the Stage.

Formatting Text Fields from an External Style Sheet

External Cascading Style Sheets (CSS) help designers and developers maintain consistency across multiple HTML documents. Flash also allows you to tap into this resource to help maintain the same formatting rules—such as font size, color, and other formatting styles—across all associated dynamic or input text fields. You can even apply styles defined by the style sheet to a text field that contains text structured as HTML or XML.

The most common method of working with a CSS document is to keep it separate from your Flash file. In a text-editing application like Dreamweaver, create your CSS file. Next, in Flash, load the CSS file as you would normally load external data using the `URLLoader` class (see Chapter 9, "Controlling Information Flow"). Then create a new style sheet object from the `StyleSheet` class, just like all other objects:

```
var myStyle:StyleSheet =
→ new StyleSheet();
```

Next, call the `StyleSheet` class's `parseCSS()` method and pass the `URLLoader`'s `data` property as the parameter to decode the CSS information:

```
myStyle.parseCSS(myURLLoader.data)
```

Finally, apply those styles to your text field by assigning your `StyleSheet` object to the text field's `styleSheet` property:

```
myTextField_txt.styleSheet = myStyle;
```

The following common CSS tags are supported by text fields:

◆ `font-family` specifies the font to be used.

◆ `font-size` sets the size of the font.

◆ `font-weight` sets the weight of the font.

◆ `font-style` sets the style of the font (normal, italic, or oblique).

◆ `text-align` aligns the text.

◆ `text-indent` indents the first line of text in a text field.

◆ `color` specifies the color to be used.

◆ `display` specifies the way in which text is displayed.

◆ `kerning` sets the spacing between letters; it only works with embedded fonts that support kerning and on Windows.

◆ `letter-spacing` sets the spacing between letters.

◆ `margin-left` sets the left margin.

◆ `margin-right` sets the right margin.

◆ `text-decoration` sets the text as underlined or not.

By assigning a `StyleSheet` object to the `styleSheet` property of the text field object (containing HTML-formatted text), you can control its format options through an external CSS document. This feature can be very convenient; you don't have to open the Flash file to make text style changes because it can all be done inside one CSS document. In addition, the CSS document applies the same styles to both your HTML pages and your Flash movies.

To display HTML text with CSS formatting:

1. Open a text-editing application or a WYSIWYG HTML editor, and create your CSS document.

2. Save the text file (**Figure 10.60**).

   For external Cascading Style Sheet files, use a .css extension.

3. In Flash, choose the Text tool, and drag out a large text field.

4. In the Property inspector, choose Dynamic Text and enter an instance name (**Figure 10.61**).

5. Select the first keyframe in the main Timeline, and open the Actions panel.

6. On the first line, create the URLLoader and the URLRequest objects. The URLRequest object should provide the information to point to your external CSS file (**Figure 10.62**).

7. On the next line, enter the name of your URLLoader object and a dot, and then call the load() method. Pass the URLRequest object as the parameter.

   The external CSS begins loading into the URLLoader object.

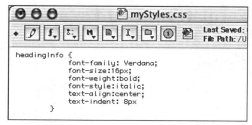

Figure 10.60 In an external Cascading Style Sheet, a selector is defined with the name of headingInfo. This CSS document is separate from your Flash movie.

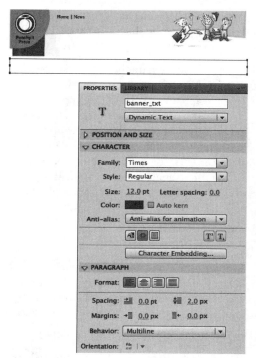

Figure 10.61 A dynamic text field is defined with the instance name banner_txt.

```
var myURLLoader:URLLoader = new URLLoader();
var myURLRequest:URLRequest = new URLRequest("mystyles.css");
```

Figure 10.62 Load the external style sheet document called mystyles.css into a new URLLoader object. The URLRequest object provides the file path information. The mystyles.css document in this example resides in the same folder as the Flash movie.

```
var myURLLoader:URLLoader = new URLLoader();
var myURLRequest:URLRequest = new URLRequest("mystyles.css");
myURLLoader.load(myURLRequest);
myURLLoader.addEventListener(Event.COMPLETE, dataOK);
function dataOK(myevent:Event):void {

}
```

Figure 10.63 As with all loading processes, make sure you detect when the load is complete before you do anything with the external data. The event handler function called *dataOK* will be triggered when the load is complete.

```
var myURLLoader:URLLoader = new URLLoader();
var myURLRequest:URLRequest = new URLRequest("mystyles.css");
myURLLoader.load(myURLRequest);
myURLLoader.addEventListener(Event.COMPLETE, dataOK);
function dataOK(myevent:Event):void {
    var myStyle:StyleSheet = new StyleSheet();
    myStyle.parseCSS(myURLLoader.data);

}
```

Figure 10.64 Create the myStyle StyleSheet object and call its parseCSS() method to decode the loaded data.

```
var myURLLoader:URLLoader = new URLLoader();
var myURLRequest:URLRequest = new URLRequest("mystyles.css");
myURLLoader.load(myURLRequest);
myURLLoader.addEventListener(Event.COMPLETE, dataOK);
function dataOK(myevent:Event):void {
    var myStyle:StyleSheet = new StyleSheet();
    myStyle.parseCSS(myURLLoader.data);
    banner_txt.styleSheet = myStyle;
    banner_txt.htmlText = "<headingInfo>Welcome to the Peachpit Press
Newsletter</headingInfo>";
}
```

Figure 10.65 The full code. After parsing the data, assign the myStyle StyleSheet to the styleSheet property of your text field. You must apply the style before you assign HTML-formatted text to the text field, as is done here in the last line of the function.

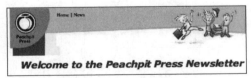

Welcome to the Peachpit Press Newsletter

Figure 10.66 The text displays in the style defined in the external CSS.

8. On the next line, create the event handler to detect the completion of the loading process (**Figure 10.63**).

Make sure the file loads completely before you attempt to do anything with the CSS data.

9. Between the curly braces of the Event. COMPLETE event handler function, create a StyleSheet object.

10. On the next line but still between the curly braces of the function, call the parseCSS() method of the StyleSheet object, passing the URLLoader object's data property as a parameter (**Figure 10.64**). The CSS information is decoded.

11. On the following line but still between the curly braces of the function, assign the StyleSheet object to the text field's styleSheet property.

12. Finally, on the next line but still between the curly braces of the function, assign HTML-formatted text to the text field's htmlText property (**Figure 10.65**).

13. Test your movie.

Flash loads and applies the style defined in the external CSS to the HTML-formatted text in your dynamic text (**Figure 10.66**).

✔ Tips

- To utilize the formatting created in the external CSS, you must begin and end your XML-formatted text with an element (tag) whose name matches the selector name that was used in the style sheet. In this example, the selector name is headingInfo.

- CSS can only be applied to text fields that contain HTML-formatted text.

- The HTML text must be applied after the CSS is applied for any of the formatting to take effect.

Detecting the Focus of Text Fields

When you have multiple input text fields on the Stage, you may want to know in which text field your user is currently entering information. For example, you could provide additional hints that are customized to each text field. As your user moves from text field to text field, the hints change to provide relevant help. You can detect when a text field is *focused*, or active, by listening for the FocusEvent.FOCUS_IN event. There can only be one focused object, whether it is a text field or a button or other interactive object on the Stage. The focus is changed when the user presses the Tab key to move to the next interactive object, or if the user uses the mouse to click on another interactive object. You can detect when the user moves away from a text field with the event FocusEvent.FOCUS_OUT.

You can also detect a change in focus and differentiate whether the change was due to the viewer using the mouse or the Tab key. The FocusEvent.KEY_FOCUS_CHANGE event occurs when there is a change in focus because of a keypress. The FocusEvent.MOUSE_FOCUS_CHANGE event occurs when there is a change in focus because of a mouse click.

In this example, you'll create three input text fields and one dynamic text field. As the user moves from one text field to another, you display information relevant to the user's current text field. You accomplish this by listening to the FocusEvent.FOCUS_IN event and responding.

To detect the focus of a text field:

1. Select the Text tool, and drag out a text field on the Stage.

2. In the Property inspector, choose Input Text and Single Line from the pull-down menus, select the Show Border option, and enter an instance name for this input text field.

   The user will enter a name in this input text field.

3. Select the Text tool, drag out two more similar input text fields, place them below the first one, and name them in the Property inspector.

   The user will enter an address and telephone number in these input text fields.

4. Select the Text tool, drag out one more text field, and place it below the other three text fields.

5. In the Property inspector, choose Dynamic Text and Single Line from the pull-down menus, and enter an instance name for this dynamic text field.

   You'll display information in this dynamic text field. You should have three input text fields and one dynamic text field on the Stage at this point (**Figure 10.67**).

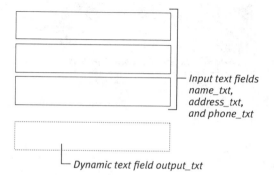

Input text fields
name_txt,
address_txt,
and phone_txt

Dynamic text field output_txt

Figure 10.67 Create three input text fields (top) and one dynamic text field (bottom).

```
name_txt.addEventListener(FocusEvent.FOCUS_IN, namefunction);
```

Figure 10.68 Listen for the FocusEvent.FOCUS_IN event on the name_txt text field.

```
name_txt.addEventListener(FocusEvent.FOCUS_IN, namefunction);
function namefunction(myevent:FocusEvent):void {
    output_txt.text="Please type your name"
}
```

Figure 10.69 When the input text field name_txt is focused, the bottom dynamic text field is assigned new text that tells viewers to enter their name.

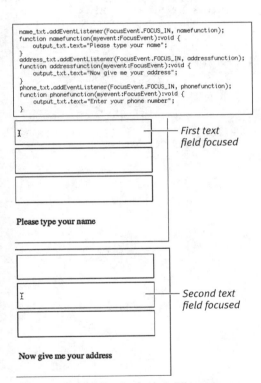

First text field focused

Please type your name

Second text field focused

Now give me your address

Figure 10.70 The full script (top). A different message appears for each focused input text field (bottom).

6. Select the first frame of the Timeline, and open the Actions panel.

7. Enter the name of your first input text field, then a dot, and then call the addEventListener() method to detect the FocusEvent.FOCUS_IN event (**Figure 10.68**).

8. On the next line, create the function that will be triggered by the FocusEvent.FOCUS_IN event. In between the curly braces of the function, assign appropriate text to the text property of the dynamic text field (**Figure 10.69**).

   Flash detects when the first input text field receives focus, and when it does, displays a message in the dynamic text field.

9. Create two similar event handlers for the two other input text fields and respond by displaying different messages in the dynamic text field.

10. Test your movie (**Figure 10.70**).

   As your user moves from one text field to the other, the focus changes and a new message is displayed in the dynamic text field that is relevant to the currently focused text field.

DETECTING THE FOCUS OF TEXT FIELDS

Controlling the Focus and Selection within Text Fields

Not only can you detect when the user moves focus from one text field to another, but you can also control the focus entirely with ActionScript. You control the focus of a text field (and for any interactive object, in fact) with the `stage.focus` property. The Stage can have only one focused object, so if you assign an object to the `stage.focus` property, the currently focused object loses its focus.

When you have a focused text field, you can then control the selection or insertion-point position inside it. This technique lets you direct your viewers' attention to particular characters or words they've entered, perhaps to point out errors or misspellings. It also lets you keep track of the insertion-point position, much as the `mouseX` and `mouseY` properties let you keep track of the location of the viewer's mouse pointer. You can also select certain parts of the text field and replace just those portions with different text. Controlling the insertion and selection within a text field depends on the `TextField` class method `setSelection()`.

You use the `setSelection()` method by providing two parameters: the index number that identifies the start of the selection and then the index number that identifies the end (not inclusive). Recall that each character in a text field is numbered to keep track of its position, as you've learned with the `setTextFormat()` method. The first character in the text field is assigned the index of 0, the second character is 1, and so on. If the two parameters of the `setSelection()` method are identical, no characters are selected, but the position of the cursor (called the *caret*) is placed at that position.

To change the selection in a text field:

1. Select the Text tool in the Tools panel, and drag out a text field on the Stage.

2. Enter the sample text, "Carrots are good to eat".

3. In the Property inspector, choose Input Text and enter an instance name (**Figure 10.71**).

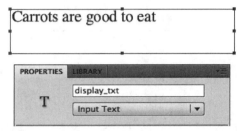

Figure 10.71 This text field is called `display_txt` and has some text already entered into it.

```
stage.focus=display_txt;
display_txt.setSelection(0,7);
```

Figure 10.72 Focus the text field first, and then set the selection inside the text field.

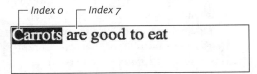

Figure 10.73 The selected characters (including index 0 through index 6) are highlighted.

4. Select the first frame of the main Timeline, and open the Actions panel.

5. On the first line, assign the text field to the `stage.focus` property.

The text field will receive focus.

6. On the next line, enter the name of the text field, then a dot, and then call the `setSelection()` method.

7. For the parameters of the `setSelection()` method, enter 0 followed by a comma and then 7 (**Figure 10.72**).

The `setSelection()` method selects all the characters between the indexes of its first parameter and its second parameter, including the character whose index is the first parameter. This `setSelection()` statement selects the first seven characters (index 0 to index 6) of the text field.

8. Test your movie.

The text field becomes focused, allowing you to set the selection of its contents. The `setSelection()` method then selects the word "Carrots" by highlighting the characters (**Figure 10.73**).

To identify the position of the insertion point in a text field:

◆ Read the value of the `TextField` property `caretIndex`. The property contains the index value of the current position of the insertion point. If the text field is not focused, the value of `caretIndex` is what it would be if the text field were focused (typically, where the insertion point most recently was positioned).

Analyzing Text

When you define a text field as an input text field, you give your viewers the freedom to enter and edit information. Often, however, you need to analyze the text entered by the viewer before using it. You may want to tease out certain words or identify the location of a particular character or sequence of characters. If you require viewers to enter an e-mail address in an input field, for example, you can check to see whether that address is in the correct format. Or you can check a customer's telephone number, find out the area code based on the first three digits, and personalize a directory or news listing with local interests.

This kind of parsing, manipulation, and control of the information within text fields is done with the `String` class and the `RegExp` class. The `String` class is a data type that represents any sequence of characters. You can create a string simply by passing the piece of text in quotation marks to the constructor function, or more simply, by just assigning the text to a variable. The following statements are equivalent:

```
var myString:String=new String("hello");
```

```
var myString:String="hello";
```

The `String` class provides tools to search, analyze, and replace pieces of text, and compare them to patterns that you might be interested in, which are called *regular expressions*. Regular expressions (from the `RegExp` class) are patterns that you create to identify certain combinations of letters. For example, you may want to search input text for a particular person's name, or a sequence of specific numbers, or any number of character combinations. Regular expressions can be quite simple, as in `/hello/`, which matches the word "hello". But they can also be quite complex and difficult to create, and even more difficult to interpret, as in `/^\d{5}(-\d{4})?$/`, which matches a five-digit zip code with an optional dash and four-digit extension. Learning and mastering regular expressions is not an easy task. Entire books are devoted to regular expressions, but if you're willing to put in the time and effort, you'll have a powerful tool for analyzing text. This section covers regular expressions only at a basic level and looks at how Flash can detect and respond to them.

Matching text patterns with regular expressions

The first step in checking a piece of text for a matching pattern is to create the regular expression. You can do this in one of two ways. You can either use the constructor function of the RegExp class to define the regular expression, or you can simply declare a RegExp variable and assign the regular expression between two forward slashes (/). In the first approach, you provide the regular expression (in quotation marks) and a flag that modifies the regular expression. For example:

```
var myMatch:RegExp=new
→ RegExp("hello","i");
```

This statement creates a regular expression that matches the word "hello", and the second parameter (the flag) is the modifier that indicates that case should be ignored, so either uppercase or lowercase letters would match.

The second way of creating a regular expression is to simply assign it to a variable, like so:

```
var myMatch:RegExp=/hello/i;
```

In this statement, the regular expression is in between two forward slashes, and the flag immediately follows.

You learned in Chapter 3, "Getting a Handle on ActionScript," that you include special characters in a string by using the backslash (\). The backslash marks an escape sequence inside a string, so if you want to include quotation marks around the pattern "hello", you would write:

```
var myMatch:RegExp=new
→ RegExp("\"hello\"", "i");
```

or simply,

```
var myMatch:RegExp=/"hello"/i
```

Regular expressions use special codes to search for multiple characters and combinations. For example, \d is the code to use to search for any digit. To incorporate that code into your regular expression, you would write:

```
var myMatch:RegExp=new
→ RegExp("\\d", "g");
```

or simply,

```
var myMatch:RegExp=/\d/g;
```

The g flag in the previous statements is the global modifier that looks for the regular expression throughout the text, not just the first occurrence. Notice that creating regular expressions with strings and the constructor function (the first approach) is a little cumbersome because you have to use *two* backslashes—the first to escape the character and the second to indicate the code to search for any digit. For more complex regular expressions, it becomes difficult to read. For this reason, creating regular expressions by entering them in between two forward slashes is the preferred method.

Table 10.3 shows you some common codes that are used to construct patterns for regular expressions. **Table 10.4** lists the various flags that you can use to modify your regular expressions.

Table 10.3

Common Codes for Regular Expressions

Code	Description	Example
?	Matches the previous character or group zero or one time (character is optional).	/ab?c/ matches abc or ac.
*	Matches the previous character or group zero or more times.	/ab*c/ matches abc or ac or abbbc, with b any number of times.
+	Matches the previous character or group one or more times.	/ab+c/ matches abc or abbbc, with b any number of times.
.	Matches any one character (except newline (\n) unless the dotall flag is set).	/a.c/ matches aac, abc, a4c, and other combinations with any middle character.
|	Or	/hi|hello/ matches hi or hello.
()	Groups the regular expression to confine scope.	/h(i|ey)/ matches hi or hey.
[ ]	Groups possible characters. A dash (-) indicates a range of characters.	/[0-9]/ matches a number from 0 to 9, /[123]/ matches 1, 2, or 3.
{n}	Matches the previous character or group exactly n times.	/a{3}bc/ matches aaabc.
{n,}	Matches the previous character or group at least n times.	/a{3,}bc/ matches aaabc, aaaabc, and other combinations where a is repeated.
{n, m}	Matches the previous character or group at least n times but no more than m times.	/a{3,4}bc/ matches aaabc and aaaabc.
\d	Matches any number.	/a\dc/ matches a1c or a2c, or other combinations where the middle character is a number.
\D	Matches any character other than a number.	/a\Dc/ matches abc but not a2c. Middle character must not be a number.
\s	Matches a whitespace character (space, tab, etc.).	/a\sc / matches a c where the middle character is a whitespace character.
\S	Matches any character other than a whitespace character.	/a\Sc/ matches abc but not a c. Middle character must not be a whitespace character.
\w	Matches any word character.	/a\wc/ matches abc but not a&c. Middle character must be a word character.
\W	Matches any character other than a word character.	/a\Wc/ matches a&c but not abc. Middle character must not be a word character.

Table 10.4

Flags for Regular Expressions

Flag	Description
g	Global flag, matches more than one match.
i	Ignore case flag; ignores uppercase or lowercase.
m	Multiline flag.
d	The dotall flag. A dot (.) can match the new line character (\n).
x	Extended flag; allows spaces to be ignored for user readability.

```
var myMatch:RegExp=/(\w|[_.\-])+@((\w|-)+\.)+\w{2,4}+/ig;
```

Figure 10.74 This regular expression matches a correctly formed e-mail address, with the global and the ignore case flags set.

```
var myMatch:RegExp=/Flash\s?\d+/ig;
```

Figure 10.75 This regular expression matches the word "Flash" and any number of digits, with an optional space in between. The global and ignore case flags are set.

To create a regular expression:

1. Select the first frame of the Timeline, and open the Actions panel.

2. Enter var, the name of your regular expression, a colon, the RegExp data type, an equals sign, a forward slash, your regular expression, and finally another forward slash. Include any of the flag modifiers after the last forward slash (**Figure 10.74**).

   Your regular expression is defined.

Searching text to match a regular expression

You search text to match a regular expression with several methods. The String method search() uses a regular expression as its parameter to scan the piece of text and returns the index of the first occurrence of the matching text. The index is the position of each character in a string. If the search() method doesn't find a match, Flash returns a value of –1.

The String method match() also uses a regular expression as its parameter to scan the piece of text, but it returns an Array object containing all the occurrences of the actual matching text. If the match() method doesn't find a match, Flash returns a value of null.

To find the position of a pattern match in a piece of text:

1. Select the first frame of the Timeline, and open the Actions panel.

2. Create a regular expression as described in the previous task (**Figure 10.75**).

   In this example, the regular expression /Flash\s?\d+/ig matches the word "Flash" followed by any series of numbers with an optional space in between. The flags ignore case and will search globally.

Continues on next page

3. On the next line, obtain the text that you want to search. This could be text you assign to a String variable, text that you load in from an external document, or text from an input text field.

In this example, just assign a simple piece of text to a String variable (**Figure 10.76**).

4. On the next line, enter your String variable, then a dot. Then call the method search() and pass the regular expression as its parameter. Assign the results to the trace() method (**Figure 10.77**).

The search() method looks through the text to find a match. It returns the position of the match in the display window in testing mode.

5. Test your movie.

To find the pattern matches in a piece of text:

1. Select the first frame of the Timeline, and open the Actions panel.

2. Create a regular expression as described in the previous task.

In this example, the regular expression /Flash\s?\d+/ig matches the word "Flash" followed by any series of numbers with an optional space in between. The flags ignore case and will search globally.

3. On the next line, obtain the text that you want to search. This could be text that you assign to a String variable, text that you load in from an external document, or text from an input text field.

In this example, just assign a simple piece of text to a String variable.

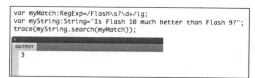

```
var myMatch:RegExp=/Flash\s?\d+/ig;
var myString:String="Is Flash 10 much better than Flash 9?";
```

Figure 10.76 Create a sample string to test your regular expression.

```
var myMatch:RegExp=/Flash\s?\d+/ig;
var myString:String="Is Flash 10 much better than Flash 9?";
trace(myString.search(myMatch));
```

OUTPUT
```
3
```

Figure 10.77 The search() method matches the regular expression with your string and returns the index position of the match. The word "Flash 10" matched and was located at index 3.

ANALYZING TEXT

```
var myMatch:RegExp=/Flash\s?\d+/ig;
var myString:String="Is Flash 10 much better than Flash 9?";
var myArray:Array=myString.match(myMatch);
```

Figure 10.78 The match() method matches the regular expression with your string and returns an Array object containing the matched substrings.

```
var myMatch:RegExp=/Flash\s?\d+/ig;
var myString:String="Is Flash 10 much better than Flash 9?";
var myArray:Array=myString.match(myMatch);
trace(myArray[0]);
trace(myArray[1]);
```

```
OUTPUT
  Flash 10
  Flash 9
```

Figure 10.79 To see the matched terms, display the elements in the Array to the Output panel. Here, you see that two matches were found, "Flash 10" and "Flash 9".

4. On the next line, enter your String variable, then a dot. Then call the method match() and pass the regular expression as its parameter. Assign the results to an Array object (**Figure 10.78**).

The match() method looks through the text to find a match. It returns an Array object that contains all the occurrences of the match.

5. On the next line, enter the trace() method to display the elements of the Array object. Test your movie (**Figure 10.79**).

The matches are displayed in the display window in testing mode.

Greedy and Lazy Patterns

Sometimes when you search for particular patterns with character repetitions (using *, +, or {} sequences), Flash will grab more than you actually want. For example, suppose you look for a sequence of characters that begin with "www." and end with ".com", with any number of characters in the middle using the code .+ (match any character multiple times). If you searched the following string, "My favorite Web sites are www.adobe.com as well as www.peachpit.com.", the resulting match would be "www.adobe.com as well as www.peachpit.com" because Flash first matches "www.", then marches all the way through the string because of the .+ instructions. When it reaches the end, it backtracks and finds the ".com" match and stops. This is called a *greedy* pattern. To fix this problem, you need to tell Flash to match the fewest number of characters as possible. You can do so by adding the *lazy* pattern, which is indicated by a question mark (?). If you use the code .+? instead of just .+, Flash will match the minimum number of characters until it finds the next match.

Searching and replacing text

When you find matches for your regular expression in a piece of text, you can replace the matches with another string, much like the search and replace function in a word processing application. You use the `String` class method `replace()`, which takes two parameters: one for the regular expression and another for the replacement string.

The replacement string can also include codes in it to allow parts of the pattern to be used as the replacement. **Table 10.5** lists the replacement codes. This is a powerful way to replace text. For example, you could search a text document with Web site addresses that begin with "www." and end in ".com". Once identified, you can strip them out and put them back in with HTML anchor tags around them, such as `<a href></a>`.

To replace the pattern matches in a piece of text:

1. Select the first frame of the Timeline, and open the Actions panel.

2. Create a regular expression as described in the previous task (**Figure 10.80**).

   In this example, the regular expression `/www\..+?\.com/ig` matches any sequence of text that begins with "www." and ends with ".com". The question mark is a code to identify a lazy pattern so multiple sequences of Web sites can be identified (see the sidebar "Greedy and Lazy Patterns").

```
var myMatch:RegExp=/www\..+?\.com/ig;
```

Figure 10.80 This regular expression is a simple check for a Web address beginning with "www." and ending with ".com".

Table 10.5

Replacement Codes	
CODE	**DESCRIPTION**
$&	The matched substring.
$`	The text that precedes the match. Note that the code uses the backtick key found on the same key as the tilde (the key to the left of the number 1 key).
$'	The text that follows the match. Note that the code uses the single quote character, which is found to the left of the Enter key.
$n	The nth group match.
x	Extended flag; allows spaces to be ignored for user readability.

3. On the next line, obtain the text that you want to search. This could be text that you assign to a `String` variable, text that you load in from an external document, or text from an input text field.

In this example, just assign a simple piece of text to a `String` variable (**Figure 10.81**).

4. On the next line, enter your `String` variable, then a dot. Then call the method `replace()` and pass the regular expression as its first parameter. For its second parameter, enter (**Figure 10.82**):

`"<a href=\"http://$&\">$&</a>"`

The replacement string includes quotation marks that are escaped as well as replacement codes ($&) that insert the matched text at those specified points.

5. On the next line, create a new text field and display the results of the replaced string in the text field (**Figure 10.83**).

The Web site names are stripped out and put back in with HTML anchor tags around them to make them clickable in the newly generated text field (**Figure 10.84**).

✔ Tip

■ The `String` class methods that you've learned in the preceding section, `search()`, `match()`, and `replace()`, don't necessarily have to always use regular expressions as parameters. You can also use these methods just with normal strings. Make sure you pass string parameters with quotation marks.

```
var myMatch:RegExp=/www\..+?\.com/ig;
var myString:String="Visit Adobe at www.adobe.com or my website at www.RussellChun.com";
```

Figure 10.81 Create a sample string with a few Web site addresses.

```
var myMatch:RegExp=/www\..+?\.com/ig;
var myString:String="Visit Adobe at www.adobe.com or my website at www.RussellChun.com";
var myResult:String=myString.replace(myMatch, "<a href=\"http://$&\">$&</a>");
```

Figure 10.82 The `replace()` method can replace the matched terms with new text. Here, it will replace the matches with anchor tags in front, then put in the matched substrings, and anchor tags behind, to automatically format it as HTML.

```
var myMatch:RegExp=/www\..+?\.com/ig;
var myString:String="Visit Adobe at www.adobe.com or my website at www.RussellChun.com";
var myResult:String=myString.replace(myMatch, "<a href=\"http://$&\">$&</a>");

var myTextField:TextField=new TextField();
myTextField.width=500;
myTextField.multiline=true;
myTextField.htmlText=myResult;
addChild(myTextField);
```

Figure 10.83 The full script.

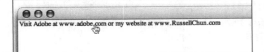

Figure 10.84 When the `replace()` method has done its work and the results are displayed in a text field, the Web links are now active.

Searching for a simple string

When you don't need to find patterns with regular expressions, you can rely on simpler methods to search for a piece of text. The methods discussed previously, the `search()`, `match()`, and `replace()` methods, can take regular strings as their parameters. Instead of searching for a pattern match, Flash searches for an exact match of the string. A few other methods work using simple strings as the search term. The `String` method `indexOf()` searches text for a character or a sequence of characters and returns the index position of its first occurrence.

To identify the position of a character or characters:

1. In the Actions panel, enter the `String` you want to search, then a dot; then call the `indexOf()` method.

2. For the parameters of the `indexOf()` method, enter a character or sequence of characters within quotation marks, a comma, and then an optional index number.

   The `indexOf()` method takes two parameters: `searchString` and `fromIndex`. The parameter `searchString` is the specific character or characters you want to identify in the `String`. The parameter `fromIndex`, which is optional, is a `Number` representing the starting position for the search within the `String`.

   Flash searches the contents of the `String` for the specified character and returns the index position of the character (**Figure 10.85**).

✔Tips

- The opposite of the method `indexOf()` is `charAt()`. This method returns the character that occupies the index position you specify for a string.

- If the character you search for with `indexOf()` occurs more than once in the string, Flash returns the index of only the first occurrence. Use the method `lastIndexOf()` to retrieve the last occurrence of the character.

- If Flash searches a `String` with the `indexOf()` or `lastIndexOf()` method and doesn't find the specified character, it returns a value of –1. You can use this fact to check for missing characters within a string. For example, if `indexOf("%") == -1`, you know that the percent symbol is missing from the string.

Determining a String's size

The `String` class has one property, `length`, that tells you the number of characters in the `String`. This is a read-only property that is useful for checking the relative positions of characters. Since you know the value of `length`, you can always target the last character of a `String`, which would have the index position of `length-1`.

One way you can use the `length` property is to make sure that the `length` of an input text field isn't 0 (meaning that the viewer hasn't entered anything). If it is 0, you can send an error message or further instructions for the viewer. The following task demonstrates this application.

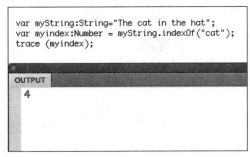

Figure 10.85 The `indexOf()` method returns the first occurrence of the simple string search term. The word "cat" appears at index 4.

ANALYZING TEXT

```
input_txt.addEventListener(KeyboardEvent.KEY_DOWN, enterkey);
function enterkey(myevent:KeyboardEvent):void {
    if (myevent.keyCode==Keyboard.ENTER) {

    }
}
```

Figure 10.86 This event handler detects when the user presses the Enter key while the text field called input_txt has focus.

```
input_txt.addEventListener(KeyboardEvent.KEY_DOWN, enterkey);
function enterkey(myevent:KeyboardEvent):void {
    if (myevent.keyCode==Keyboard.ENTER) {
        if (input_txt.length==0) {
            input_txt.text="Please enter your name!";
        }
    }
}
```

Figure 10.87 The conditional statement (highlighted) inside the event handler function checks if the length of the text field's contents is 0, which means no information has been entered.

Please enter your name!

Figure 10.88 If the user presses Enter without any text in the text field, this message is displayed.

To check the length of a String:

1. Select the Text tool in the Tools panel, and drag out a text field on the Stage.

2. In the Property inspector, choose Input Text, select the Show Border option, and enter an instance name.

3. Select the first frame of the main Timeline, and open the Actions panel.

4. On the first line, assign an event handler to detect the KeyboardEvent.KEY_DOWN event in the text field.

5. Inside the event handler function, enter a conditional statement with the if statement as follows (**Figure 10.86**):

   ```
   if (myevent.keyCode==Keyboard.ENTER){
       }
   ```

   Flash checks to see if the key that is pressed is Enter.

6. Inside the if statement's curly braces, create another conditional statement that checks if the length property of the text field is 0. As the consequence, assign some text to the text property of the input text field as follows (**Figure 10.87**):

   ```
   if (input_txt.length==0) {
   input_txt.text="Please enter your
   → name!";
   }
   ```

   Flash checks the length property of the input text field. If there is no content, the value of length is 0, and Flash can respond with an appropriate message.

7. Test your movie (**Figure 10.88**).

Modifying Text

After you've analyzed your text using regular expressions or other methods of the `TextField` and `String` classes, you can modify it to suit your needs. You can select a portion of the `String` (called a *substring*) and put it in a new variable, join two substrings together, split a `String` into individual ortions based on a delimiter, or even

change the case of a `String`. Flash provides many methods to perform these tasks, which are summarized in **Table 10.6**. This section demonstrates a few of these methods for you to see how you can use a combination of these methods along with properties and methods of the `TextField` class to control the information that flows from input text fields into the rest of your Flash movie and back out into dynamic text fields.

Table 10.6

Some String Methods

METHOD OR PROPERTY	DESCRIPTION
`indexOf(searchString, fromIndex)`	Searches the `String` and returns the index of the first occurrence of a substring specified in the parameter `searchString`. The optional `fromIndex` parameter sets the starting position of the search.
`lastIndexOf(searchString, fromIndex)`	Searches the `String` and returns the index of the last occurrence of a substring specified in the parameter `searchString`. The optional `fromIndex` parameter sets the starting position of the search.
`charAt(index)`	Returns the character at the specified index position.
`substring(indexA, indexB)`	Returns a `String` that is the portion of the original `String` between positions `indexA` and `indexB`.
`substr(start, length)`	Returns a `String` containing the portion of the original `String` with the specified length from the start index.
`concat(string1,...,stringN)`	Concatenates the specified `Strings`.
`toLowerCase()`	Returns a copy of the original `String` that contains all lowercase characters.
`toUpperCase()`	Returns a copy of the original `String` that contains all uppercase characters.
`match(pattern)`	Returns an `Array` of strings that matches the regular expression.
`replace(pattern, replacement)`	Matches the regular expression against the string and replaces matches, returning a new `String`.
`search(pattern)`	Returns the index of first occurrence of the match.
`slice(startIndex, endIndex)`	Returns a String between the `startIndex` and `endIndex`, inclusive of the `startIndex`.
`split(delimiter, limit)`	Returns an `Array` containing substrings that were divided using the delimiter.

To get selected portions of Strings:

1. Select the Text tool, and drag out a text field on the Stage.

2. In the Property inspector, choose Input Text and Multiline from the pull-down menus, and enter an instance name for this input text field.

3. Drag out another text field on the Stage.

4. In the Property inspector, choose Dynamic Text and Multiline from the pull-down menus, and enter an instance name for this dynamic text field.

5. Create a button symbol, place an instance of it on the Stage between the input text field and the dynamic text field, and give it an instance name.

   You should have an input text field on the top, a button in the middle, and a dynamic text field on the bottom (**Figure 10.89**).

6. Select the first keyframe on the root Timeline, and open the Actions panel.

7. Enter the name of your input text field, a dot, the property `alwaysShowSelection`, and an equals sign followed by `true`.

   Flash will always show the selection within the input text field, even when it doesn't have focus.

8. On the next line, create an event handler for a mouse click over the button.

9. In between the curly braces of the event handler function, retrieve the `selectionBeginIndex` property of your input text field and assign it to a `Number` variable (**Figure 10.90**).

   The position of the start of the selection is assigned to this variable.

10. On the next line, but still between the curly braces of the event handler function, retrieve the `selectionEndIndex` property of your input text field and assign it to another `Number` variable (**Figure 10.91**).

    The index position of the end of the selection is assigned to this variable.

Continues on next page

Figure 10.89 On the Stage, there is an input text field, a button, and a dynamic text field.

```
inputBox_txt.alwaysShowSelection=true;

copyPaste_btn.addEventListener(MouseEvent.CLICK, makepaste);
function makepaste(myevent:MouseEvent):void {
    var mystart:Number=inputBox_txt.selectionBeginIndex;
}
```

Figure 10.90 When the button is clicked, Flash stores the index number of the beginning of the selection in the variable called `mystart`.

```
inputBox_txt.alwaysShowSelection=true;

copyPaste_btn.addEventListener(MouseEvent.CLICK, makepaste);
function makepaste(myevent:MouseEvent):void {
    var mystart:Number=inputBox_txt.selectionBeginIndex;
    var myend:Number=inputBox_txt.selectionEndIndex;
}
```

Figure 10.91 In the next line, Flash stores the index number of the end of the selection in the variable called myend.

11. On the next line, but still between the curly braces of the event handler function, call the `substring()` method on the input text field's `text` property and assign it to a `String` variable.

The `substring()` method takes two parameters: `indexA` and `indexB`. `indexA` defines the start of the sequence of characters you want to grab, and `indexB` defines the end of the sequence.

12. Between the parentheses of the `substring()` method, enter the name of your first `Number` variable (the starting index of the selection) and then the second `Number` variable (the ending index of the selection), separated by commas (**Figure 10.92**).

13. On the next line, but still between the curly braces of the event handler function, assign the `String` variable to the `text` property of the dynamic text field.

14. Test your movie.

The user can enter information in the input text field and select portions of the text. When the user clicks the button that you created, Flash captures the position of the selection and puts the substring into another variable, and it appears in the dynamic text field (**Figure 10.93**).

```
inputBox_txt.alwaysShowSelection=true;

copyPaste_btn.addEventListener(MouseEvent.CLICK, makepaste);
function makepaste(myevent:MouseEvent):void {
    var mystart:Number=inputBox_txt.selectionBeginIndex;
    var myend:Number=inputBox_txt.selectionEndIndex;
    var copiedtext:String=inputBox_txt.text.substring(mystart, myend);
}
```

Figure 10.92 The `substring()` method creates a smaller segment of text using the beginning and end of the selection.

```
inputBox_txt.alwaysShowSelection=true;

copyPaste_btn.addEventListener(MouseEvent.CLICK, makepaste);
function makepaste(myevent:MouseEvent):void {
    var mystart:Number=inputBox_txt.selectionBeginIndex;
    var myend:Number=inputBox_txt.selectionEndIndex;
    var copiedtext:String=inputBox_txt.text.substring(mystart, myend);
    outputBox_txt.text=copiedtext;
}
```

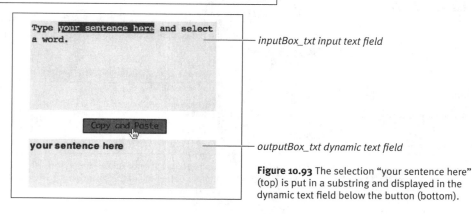

inputBox_txt input text field

outputBox_txt dynamic text field

Figure 10.93 The selection "your sentence here" (top) is put in a substring and displayed in the dynamic text field below the button (bottom).

MANIPULATING INFORMATION

11

The information that you store in variables, modify in expressions, and test with conditional statements often needs to be processed and manipulated by mathematical functions such as square roots, sines, cosines, and exponents. Flash can perform these calculations with the Math class, which lets you create formulas for complicated interactions between the objects in your movie and your viewer or for sophisticated physics in your motion. You can also turn to the Point class for help in geometry. Imagine modeling the correct trajectory of colliding objects to create a game of pool, simulating the effects of gravity for a physics tutorial, calculating probabilities for a card game, or generating random numbers to add unpredictable elements to your movie. All of those scenarios are possible with the Math and Point classes. Much of the information you manipulate sometimes needs to be stored in a structured manner to give you better control of your data and a more efficient way to retrieve it. You can use the Array class to keep track of ordered sets of data such as shopping lists, color tables, and scorecards.

When the information you need depends on the time or the date, you can use the Date class to retrieve the current year, month, or even millisecond. You can build clocks and timers to use inside your Flash movie, or send the time information (along with a viewer's profile) to a server-side script.

This chapter explores the variety of ways you can manipulate information with added complexity and shows you how to integrate many of the predefined classes you've learned about in previous chapters.

Making Calculations with the Math Class

The Math class lets you access trigonometric functions such as sine, cosine, and tangent; logarithmic functions; rounding functions; and mathematical constants such as pi and *e*. **Table 11.1** summarizes the methods and properties of the Math class. The Math class has *static* methods and properties, which means you don't need to create an instance of the Math class to access them. Instead, you precede the method or property with the class name, Math. To calculate the square root of 10, for example, you write:

```
var myAnswer:Number = Math.sqrt(10);
```

The calculated value is put in the variable myAnswer.

All the Math class's properties are read-only values that are written in all uppercase letters. To use a constant, use syntax like this:

```
var myCircum:Number=Math.PI*2*
→ myRadius;
```

The mathematical constant *pi* is multiplied by 2 and the variable myRadius, and the result is put into the variable myCircum.

Table 11.1

Methods and Properties of the Math Class	
abs(number)	Calculates the absolute value. Math.abs(-4) returns 4.
acos(number)	Calculates the arc cosine.
asin(number)	Calculates the arc sine.
atan(number)	Calculates the arc tangent.
atan2(y, x)	Calculates the angle (in radians) from the x-axis to a point on the y-axis.
ceil(number)	Rounds the number up to the nearest integer. Math.ceil(2.34) returns 3.
cos(number)	Calculates the cosine of an angle, in radians.
exp(number)	Calculates the exponent of the constant e.
floor(number)	Rounds the number down to the nearest integer. Math.floor(2.34) returns 2.
log(number)	Calculates the natural logarithm.
max(x, y)	Returns the larger of two values. Math.max(2, 7) returns 7.
min(x, y)	Returns the smaller of two values. Math.min(2, 7) returns 2.
pow(base, exponent)	Calculates the exponent of a number.
random()	Returns a random number between 0 and 1 (including 0 but not including 1).
round(number)	Rounds the number to the nearest integer. Math.round(2.34) returns 2.
sin(number)	Calculates the sine of an angle, in radians.
sqrt(number)	Calculates the square root.
tan(number)	Calculates the tangent of an angle, in radians.
E	Euler's constant e; the base of natural logarithms.
LN2	The natural logarithm of 2.
LOG2E	The base-2 logarithm of e.
LN10	The natural logarithm of 10.
LOG10E	The base-10 logarithm of e.
PI	The circumference of a circle divided by its diameter.
SQRT1_2	The square root of $\frac{1}{2}$.
SQRT2	The square root of 2.

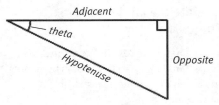

Sin theta = opposite/hypotenuse
Cos theta = adjacent/hypotenuse
Tan theta = opposite/adjacent

Figure 11.1 The angle, theta, of a right triangle is defined by sin, cos, and tan and by the length of the three sides.

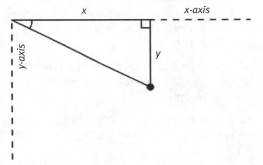

Figure 11.2 A point on the Stage makes a right triangle with x (adjacent side) and y (opposite side).

Calculating Angles

The angle that an object makes relative to the Stage or to another object is useful information for creating many game interactions, as well as for creating dynamic animations and interfaces based purely in ActionScript. To create a dial that controls the sound volume, for example, compute the angle at which your viewer drags the dial relative to the horizontal or vertical axis, and then change the dial's rotation and the sound volume accordingly. Calculating the angle also requires that you brush up on some of your high school trigonometry, so a review of some basic principles related to sine, cosine, and tangent is in order.

The mnemonic device *SOH CAH TOA* can help you keep the trigonometric functions straight. This acronym stands for Sine = Opposite over Hypotenuse, Cosine = Adjacent over Hypotenuse, and Tangent = Opposite over Adjacent (**Figure 11.1**). Knowing the length of any two sides of a right triangle is enough information to calculate the other two angles. You'll most likely know the lengths of the opposite and adjacent sides of the triangle because they represent the y- and x-coordinates of a point (**Figure 11.2**). When you have the x- and y-coordinates, you can calculate the angle (theta) by using the following mathematical formulas:

```
tan theta = opposite/adjacent
```

or

```
tan theta = y / x
```

or

```
theta = arctan(y / x)
```

In Flash, you can write this expression by using the Math class this way:

```
var myTheta:Number =
→ Math.atan(this.y/this.x)
```

Continues on next page

Alternatively, Flash provides an even easier method that lets you define the y and x positions without having to do the division. The Math.atan2() method accepts the y and x positions as two parameters, so you can write the equivalent statement:

```
var myTheta:Number =
→ Math.atan2(this.y,this.x)
```

Unfortunately, the trigonometric methods of the Math class require and return angle values in radians, which describe angles in terms of the constant pi—easier mathematically, but not so convenient if you want to use the values to modify the rotation property of an object. You can convert an angle from radians to degrees, and vice versa, by using the following formulas:

```
radians = Math.PI/180 * degrees
```

```
degrees = radians * 180/Math.PI
```

The following tasks calculate the angle of the mouse pointer relative to the Stage and display the angle (in degrees) in a dynamic text field.

To calculate the angle relative to the Stage:

1. Create a dynamic text field on the Stage, choose Single Line in the Property inspector, and give the dynamic text field an instance name.

    In this example, the text field is called myDegrees_txt.

2. Select the first frame of the main Timeline, and open the Actions panel.

3. Create a new instance of the Shape class.

    You will dynamically draw a line segment from the top-left corner of the Stage to the current position of your mouse pointer to visualize the angle.

4. On the next line, add an event listener to the Stage to detect the Event.ENTER_FRAME event.

5. On the next line, create the function that responds to the Event.ENTER_FRAME event (**Figure 11.3**).

```
var myShape:Shape=new Shape();
stage.addEventListener(Event.ENTER_FRAME, displayangle);
function displayangle(myevent:Event):void {

}
```

Figure 11.3 The ENTER_FRAME event happens continuously.

```
var myShape:Shape=new Shape();
stage.addEventListener(Event.ENTER_FRAME, displayangle);
function displayangle(myevent:Event):void {
    var myRadians:Number = Math.atan2(mouseY, mouseX);
    var myDegrees:Number = myRadians * 180 / Math.PI;
    myDegrees_txt.text =  String(myDegrees) + " degrees";
}
```

Figure 11.4 The Math.atan2() method calculates the angle that the mouse pointer makes with the origin (top-left corner of the Stage). The results are converted into degrees, converted into a string, and displayed in the text field called myDegrees_txt.

6. Within the curly braces of the function, enter this statement:

```
var myRadians:Number =
→ Math.atan2(mouseY, mouseX);
```

The current mouse position is used to calculate the angle (in radians) it makes with the top of the Stage.

7. On the next line, still within the function, enter the statement:

```
var myDegrees:Number = myRadians *
→ 180 / Math.PI
```

The angle is converted from radians to degrees and then assigned to the variable called myDegrees.

8. On the next line, still within the function, convert myDegrees to a string and assign the string to the text property of your dynamic text field. Concatenate the string " degrees" to the end of the text field (**Figure 11.4**).

The angle (now in degrees) is displayed in the text field.

9. On the next line, still within the function, call the clear() method of the graphics property of your Shape object.

10. Next, assign a line style and a fill style to the graphics property of your Shape object.

11. Next, call the moveTo() method to move the drawing location to 0, 0; call the lineTo() method to the mouseX and mouseY position; and call another lineTo() method to the mouseX and 0 position.

The dynamic drawing methods draw line segments from the corner of the Stage to the mouse pointer and up to the top edge of the Stage, creating the triangle whose sides are used to calculate the angle.

12. Add the Shape object to the display list with the addChild() method (**Figure 11.5**).

Continues on next page

```
var myShape:Shape=new Shape();
stage.addEventListener(Event.ENTER_FRAME, displayangle);
function displayangle(myevent:Event):void {
    var myRadians:Number = Math.atan2(mouseY, mouseX);
    var myDegrees:Number = myRadians * 180 / Math.PI;
    myDegrees_txt.text =  String(myDegrees) + " degrees";
    //
    // draw lines to show triangle
    //
    myShape.graphics.clear();
    myShape.graphics.lineStyle(1, 0x000000, 1);
    myShape.graphics.beginFill(0xff0000, .5);
    myShape.graphics.moveTo(0, 0);
    myShape.graphics.lineTo(mouseX, mouseY);
    myShape.graphics.lineTo(mouseX, 0);
    addChild(myShape);
}
```

Figure 11.5 The lines are drawn dynamically to show the triangle whose angle is being measured.

13. Test your movie.

As the viewer moves the pointer around the Stage, Flash calculates the angle that the mouse pointer makes with the x-axis of the root Timeline and displays the angle (in degrees) in the dynamic text field. The triangle is also drawn between the top-left corner of the Stage, the mouse pointer, and the x-axis (**Figure 11.6**).

Rounding off decimals

So far, the returned values for your angles have had many decimal places. Often, you need to round those values to the nearest whole number (or integer) so that you can use the values as parameters in methods and properties. Use Math.round() to round values to the nearest integer, Math.ceil() to round up to the closest integer greater than or equal to the value, and Math.floor() to round down to the closest integer less than or equal to the value.

To round a number to an integer:

1. Continuing with the file you used in the preceding task, select the first frame of the main Timeline and open the Actions panel.

2. Select the statement that converts the angle from radians to degrees.

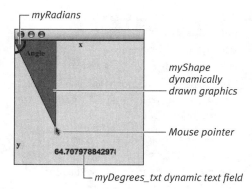

Figure 11.6 The line between the top-left corner of the Stage and the mouse pointer makes an angle of approximately 65 degrees below the x-axis.

```
var myShape:Shape=new Shape();
stage.addEventListener(Event.ENTER_FRAME, displayangle);
function displayangle(myevent:Event):void {
    var myRadians:Number = Math.atan2(mouseY, mouseX);
    var myDegrees:Number = Math.round(myRadians * 180 / Math.PI);
    myDegrees_txt.text =  String(myDegrees) + " degrees";
    //
    // draw lines to show triangle
    //
    myShape.graphics.clear();
    myShape.graphics.lineStyle(1, 0x000000, 1);
    myShape.graphics.beginFill(0xff0000, .5);
    myShape.graphics.moveTo(0, 0);
    myShape.graphics.lineTo(mouseX, mouseY);
    myShape.graphics.lineTo(mouseX, 0);
    addChild(myShape);
}
```

Figure 11.7 The expression within the parentheses (in the highlighted statement) is rounded to the nearest integer using Math.round() and displayed in the dynamic text field myDegrees_txt.

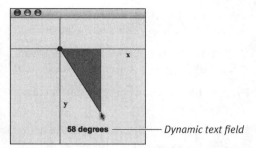

————— *Dynamic text field*

Figure 11.8 The dynamic text field displays the angle rounded to the nearest whole number.

Figure 11.9 Place a circular movie clip called myDial_mc on the Stage.

3. Place your pointer in front of the expression, and enter the method `Math.round()` (**Figure 11.7**).

Flash converts the angle from radians to degrees and then applies the method `Math.round()` to that value, returning an integer (**Figure 11.8**).

Putting it together: Creating a rotating dial

You can apply the methods that calculate angles and round values to create a draggable rotating dial. The approach is to calculate the angle of the mouse's position relative to the center point of the dial and then set the `rotation` property of the dial to that angle.

To create a rotating dial:

1. Create a movie clip symbol of a dial, place an instance of it on the Stage, and give it a name in the Property inspector.

In this example, the name is `myDial_mc` (**Figure 11.9**).

2. Select the first frame of the main Timeline, and open the Actions panel.

3. Declare a `Boolean` variable named `pressing` followed by an equals sign and the value `false`.

This variable keeps track of whether your viewer is pressing or not pressing this movie clip.

Continues on next page

4. On the next line, create the listener that detects the `MouseEvent.MOUSE_DOWN` event over your movie clip and create the function that responds to the event.

5. Within the `MouseEvent.MOUSE_DOWN` event handler function, enter `pressing` followed by an equals sign and then the `Boolean` value of `true` (**Figure 11.10**).

   The variable named `pressing` is set to true whenever you click on your movie clip.

6. On the next line, create the listener that detects the `MouseEvent.MOUSE_UP` event over the Stage and create the function that responds to the event.

7. Within the `MouseEvent.MOUSE_UP` event handler function, enter `pressing` followed by an equals sign and then the `Boolean` value of `false` (**Figure 11.11**).

   The variable named `pressing` is set to false whenever you release your mouse button.

8. On a new line, create an event handler that detects the `MouseEvent.MOUSE_MOVE` event.

9. Within the `MouseEvent.MOUSE_MOVE` event handler function, enter an `if` statement.

10. For the condition of the `if` statement, enter `pressing == true`.

11. Between the curly braces of the `if` statement, declare a new `Number` variable followed by an equals sign.

    This variable will be assigned the angle between the mouse pointer and the center of the movie clip, in radians.

12. After the equals sign, enter the following expression so the full statement reads:

    ```
    var myRadians:Number =
     → Math.atan2((mouseY - myDial_mc.y),
     → (mouseX - myDial_mc.x));
    ```

    Flash calculates the angle between the mouse pointer and the center of the movie clip (**Figure 11.12**).

```
var pressing:Boolean = false;
myDial_mc.addEventListener(MouseEvent.MOUSE_DOWN, pressdown);
function pressdown(myevent:MouseEvent):void {
    pressing=true;
}
```

Figure 11.10 Set `pressing` to true when the movie clip is pressed.

```
stage.addEventListener(MouseEvent.MOUSE_UP, released);
function released(myevent:MouseEvent):void {
    pressing=false;
}
```

Figure 11.11 Set `pressing` to false when the movie clip is released.

```
stage.addEventListener(MouseEvent.MOUSE_MOVE, movedial);
function movedial(myevent:MouseEvent):void {
    if (pressing==true) {
        var myRadians:Number = Math.atan2((mouseY - myDial_mc.y), (mouseX - myDial_mc.x));

    }
}
```

Figure 11.12 The variable `myRadians` contains the calculated angle between the pointer and the movie clip.

CALCULATING ANGLES

13. On the next line, declare a new `Number` variable followed by an equals sign.

This variable will be assigned the angle value converted to degrees.

14. After the equals sign, enter an expression to convert radians to degrees, so the full statement reads as follows:

```
var myDegrees:Number = myRadians
→ * 180 / Math.PI;
```

15. On the next line, enter `myDial_mc.rotation`, an equals sign, the variable that holds the angle in degrees, a plus sign, and `90`.

The rotation of the movie clip is assigned to the calculated angle. The 90 degrees are added to compensate for the difference between the calculated angle and the movie-clip `rotation` property. A value of 0 for `rotation` corresponds to the 12 o'clock position of an object, but a calculated arctangent angle value of 0 corresponds to the 3 o'clock position; adding 90 equalizes them (**Figure 11.13**).

16. Test your movie.

When users press the movie clip in the dial, they can rotate it by dragging it around its center point. When they release the mouse button, the dial stops rotating.

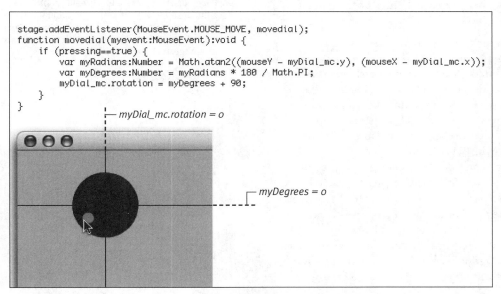

Figure 11.13 The angle is converted from radians to degrees and assigned to the variable `myDegrees`. The final statement within the `if` block modifies the rotation of the `myDial_mc` movie clip. The rotation of `myDial_mc` is set at `myDegrees + 90` to account for the difference between the reference point of the trigonometric functions and Flash's `rotation` property.

CALCULATING ANGLES

Creating Directional Movement

To control how far an object on the Stage travels based on its angle, you need to use a method of the Point class called Point.polar(). The Point class is a class that simply helps you with geometric manipulations by representing a location with an x- and y-coordinate. The Point.polar() method is a static method, which means it is available from the class named Point, not from a particular instance. The Point.polar() method converts polar coordinates, which track position in terms of an angle and its distance from another point, to regular (Cartesian) coordinates that you're familiar with, which track position in terms of x and y.

Suppose that you want to create a racing game featuring a car that your viewer moves around a track. The car travels at a certain speed, and it moves according to where the front of the car is pointed. If you know the angle of the car and the distance that it would travel at each time interval, you can use the Point.polar() method to calculate its x and y position relative to its previous position. The Point.polar() method takes two parameters: the first is the distance of the point from the reference point, and the second is the angle, in radians. The triangle that the polar coordinates form determines the x- and y-coordinates that the method returns as a new Point object (**Figure 11.14**).

In the following task, you'll create a movie clip whose rotation can be controlled by the viewer. The movie clip has a constant velocity, so it will travel in the direction in which it's pointed, just as a car moves according to where it's steered.

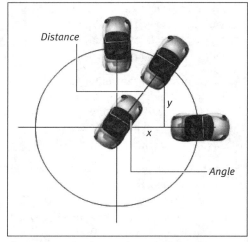

Figure 11.14 Polar coordinates describe position with angle and distance, whereas Cartesian coordinates describe position with an x- and y-coordinate. The method Point.polar() takes polar coordinates and converts them into a Point object with the matching x and y properties.

To create a controllable object with directional movement:

1. Create a movie clip symbol, place an instance of it on the Stage, and name it in the Property inspector.

   In this example, the name is car_mc.

2. Select the first frame of the main Timeline, and open the Actions panel.

3. Create an event handler assigned to the Stage that detects the KeyboardEvent.KEY_DOWN event.

4. Within the KeyboardEvent.KEY_DOWN event handler function, enter an if statement that determines whether the right arrow key is pressed. If so, add 10 degrees to the current rotation property of the movie clip (**Figure 11.15**).

Whenever you press the right arrow key on the keyboard, the movie clip rotates clockwise.

5. Within the KeyboardEvent.KEY_DOWN event handler function, enter another if statement that determines whether the left arrow key is pressed. If so, subtract 10 degrees to the current rotation property of the movie clip (**Figure 11.16**).

   Whenever you press the left arrow key on the keyboard, the movie clip rotates counterclockwise.

6. On a new line, create a new event handler assigned to the Stage that detects the Event.ENTER_FRAME event.

Continues on next page

```
stage.addEventListener(KeyboardEvent.KEY_DOWN, rotatecar);
function rotatecar(myevent:KeyboardEvent):void {
    if (myevent.keyCode==Keyboard.RIGHT) {
        car_mc.rotation+=10;
    }
}
```

Figure 11.15 The car_mc movie clip rotates 10 degrees clockwise when the right arrow key is pressed.

```
stage.addEventListener(KeyboardEvent.KEY_DOWN, rotatecar);
function rotatecar(myevent:KeyboardEvent):void {
    if (myevent.keyCode==Keyboard.RIGHT) {
        car_mc.rotation+=10;
    }
    if (myevent.keyCode==Keyboard.LEFT) {
        car_mc.rotation-=10;
    }
}
```

Figure 11.16 The car_mc movie clip rotates 10 degrees counterclockwise when the left arrow key is pressed.

CREATING DIRECTIONAL MOVEMENT

7. Within the Event.ENTER_FRAME event handler function, enter the following statement:

```
var radians:Number = Math.PI/180
→ * (car_mc.rotation-90);
```

This expression converts the angle of the movie clip to radians. Notice that you have to subtract 90 degrees from the value of rotation to get the equivalent angle for polar coordinates (**Figure 11.17**).

8. On the next line, still within the Event. ENTER_FRAME event handler function, enter the following expression:

```
var newSpot:Point=Point.
→ polar(5,radians);
```

The Point.polar() method takes the distance that the car travels (in this case, 5 pixels) and its angle (in the variable called radians), and returns a new Point object that contains the equivalent x- and y-coordinates. The x- and y-coordinates can be represented with the properties newSpot.x and newSpot.y.

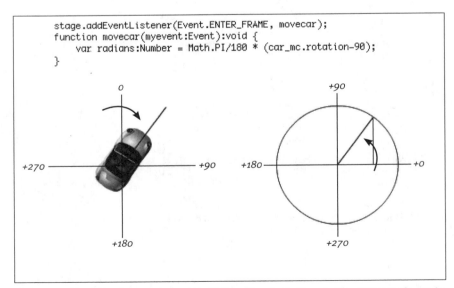

Figure 11.17 The angle of the car is converted into radians (top). The rotation property of a movie clip begins from the vertical axis and increases in the clockwise direction (left). Values for radian angles begin from the horizontal axis and increase in the counterclockwise direction (right).

9. On the next line, still within the `Event.ENTER_FRAME` event handler function, add the new x- and y-coordinates to the current coordinates of the movie clip, as follows (**Figure 11.18**):

    `car_mc.x+=newSpot.x;`

    `car_mc.y+=newSpot.y;`

10. Test your movie.

    When the user presses the left or right arrow key, the rotation of the movie clip changes. The x and y positions change continuously as well and are calculated from the angle of the movie clip and the constant distance it travels using the `Point.polar()` method. The movie clip moves according to where the nose of the car is pointed (**Figure 11.19**).

```
stage.addEventListener(Event.ENTER_FRAME, movecar);
function movecar(myevent:Event):void {
    var radians:Number = Math.PI/180 * (car_mc.rotation-90);
    var newSpot:Point=Point.polar(5, radians);
    car_mc.x+=newSpot.x;
    car_mc.y+=newSpot.y;
}
```

Figure 11.18 The x- and y-coordinates of the resulting `Point` object called newSpot are added to the existing position of the car_mc movie clip to make it move in the right direction and by the appropriate amount.

Figure 11.19 The car moves according to where its nose is pointing.

451

Calculating Distances

The Point class can also be used to calculate the distance between two objects. This technique can be useful for creating novel interactions among interface elements—graphics, buttons, or sounds—whose reactions depend on their distance from the viewer's pointer, for example. You can also create games that involve interactions based on the distance between objects and the player. A game in which the player uses a net to catch goldfish in an aquarium, for example, can use the distance between the goldfish and the net to model the behavior of the goldfish. Perhaps the closer the net comes to a goldfish, the quicker the goldfish swims away.

The distance between any two points is calculated by the Point.distance() method, which takes two parameters: the first Point object and a second Point object. It returns a number representing the distance between the two points.

Because the Point.distance() method requires Point objects as its parameters, you can't just plug in x- and y-coordinates. You must create Point objects for the coordinates between which you want to find the distance.

In this example, you'll calculate the distance between the mouse pointer and another movie clip, and display the distance in a dynamic text field.

To calculate the distance between the mouse pointer and another point:

1. Create a movie clip, place an instance of it on the Stage, and give it a name in the Property inspector.

   In this example, the name is center_mc.

2. Select the first frame of the main Timeline, and open the Actions panel.

3. Create an event handler to listen for the MouseEvent.MOUSE_MOVE event on the Stage.

4. Within the MouseEvent.MOUSE_MOVE event handler function, create a new Point object with the mouseX and mouseY properties as its x and y properties, like so (**Figure 11.20**):

   ```
   var mousePt:Point = new
   → Point(mouseX, mouseY);
   ```

5. On the next line, still within the function, create another Point object with the x and y properties of the movie clip as the x and y properties of the Point object, as follows (**Figure 11.21**):

   ```
   var centerPt:Point = new
   → Point(center_mc.x, center_mc.y);
   ```

```
stage.addEventListener(MouseEvent.MOUSE_MOVE, showdistance);
function showdistance(myevent:MouseEvent):void {
    var mousePt:Point = new Point(mouseX, mouseY);
}
```

Figure 11.20 Create a new Point object whose x and y properties are the same as the mouse pointer's x and y properties.

```
stage.addEventListener(MouseEvent.MOUSE_MOVE, showdistance);
function showdistance(myevent:MouseEvent):void {
    var mousePt:Point = new Point(mouseX, mouseY);
    var centerPt:Point = new Point(center_mc.x, center_mc.y);
}
```

Figure 11.21 Create a second Point object whose x and y properties are the same as the movie clip's x and y properties.

6. On a new line, still within the function, call the `Point.distance()` method and pass the two `Point` objects as parameters. Assign the result to a `Number` variable, like so:

```
var myDistance:Number =
  Point.distance(mousePt, centerPt);
```

The distance between the `Point` object called `mousePt` and the `Point` object called `centerPt` is assigned to the variable `myDistance` (**Figure 11.22**).

Continues on next page

```
stage.addEventListener(MouseEvent.MOUSE_MOVE, showdistance);
function showdistance(myevent:MouseEvent):void {
    var mousePt:Point = new Point(mouseX, mouseY);
    var centerPt:Point = new Point(center_mc.x, center_mc.y);
    var myDistance:Number = Point.distance(mousePt, centerPt);
}
```

Figure 11.22 The distance between the two points is calculated from the method `Point.distance()`.

Calculating Distances and Angles in 3D

With the brand-new support for 3D in Flash CS4, you may need to know distances and angles of objects in 3D space. You can do so with another class in the Flash geometry package called the `Vector3D` class. An object of the `Vector3D` class takes three parameters: the x position, the y position, and the z position, and an optional fourth parameter, which can hold information about its orientation in space. Define two `Vector3D` objects as in the following:

```
var myvector1:Vector3D = new Vector3D
  (myObject1_mc.x, myObject1_mc.y,
  myObject1_mc.z);
```

```
var myvector2:Vector3D = new Vector3D
  (myObject2_mc.x, myObject2_mc.y,
  myObject2_mc.z);
```

You can calculate the distance between the two objects with the static `distance()` method, like so:

```
var mydistance:Number =
  Vector3D.distance(myvector1,
  myvector2);
```

Similarly, you can use the `angleBetween()` method to calculate the angle between two `Vector3D` positions. The result is the angle in radians.

7. On the next line still within the function, round the value of myDistance and then convert it to a string with String(Math.round(myDistance)). Assign the result to the text property of a dynamic text field.

8. On the Stage, create a dynamic text field and give it an instance name, the same name that is referenced in your ActionScript in step 7.

9. Test your movie.

As the pointer moves around the movie clip, Flash calculates the distance between points in pixels (**Figure 11.23**).

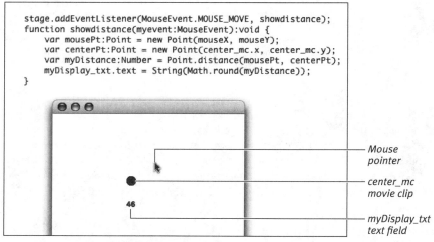

```
stage.addEventListener(MouseEvent.MOUSE_MOVE, showdistance);
function showdistance(myevent:MouseEvent):void {
    var mousePt:Point = new Point(mouseX, mouseY);
    var centerPt:Point = new Point(center_mc.x, center_mc.y);
    var myDistance:Number = Point.distance(mousePt, centerPt);
    myDisplay_txt.text = String(Math.round(myDistance));
}
```

Mouse pointer

center_mc movie clip

myDisplay_txt text field

Figure 11.23 The full script is shown at the top. The dynamic text field myDisplay_txt displays an integer of myDistance.

CALCULATING DISTANCES

Generating Random Numbers

When you need to incorporate random elements into your Flash movie, either for a design effect or for game play, you can use the Math class's Math.random() method. The Math.random() method generates random numbers between 0 and 1 (including 0 but *not* including 1). Typical return values are

0.242343544598273

0.043628738493829

0.7567833408654

You can modify the random number by multiplying it or adding to it to get the span of numbers you need. If you need random numbers between 1 and 10, for example, multiply the return value of Math.random() by 9 and then add 1, as in the following statement:

Math.random() * 9 + 1

You always multiply Math.random() by a number to get your desired range and then add or subtract a number to change the minimum and maximum values of that range.

It's important that you understand that Math.random() generates random numbers between 0 and 1, but it will never produce 1. So, if you need an integer, apply the Math.round() method to round the number down to the nearest integer, like the following statement:

Math.round(Math.random()*9+1)

To generate a random integer:

1. In the Actions panel, enter var, then a variable name, and strictly type it to an integer data type.

2. On the same line, enter an equals sign and then the Math.round() method.

   The Math.round() method rounds any decimal number to the nearest whole number.

3. Inside the parentheses of the Math.round() method, enter the Math.random() method, multiply it by 1 less than the range of numbers you desire, and add 1, as follows:

   ```
   var myResult:int =
   → Math.round(Math.random()*9+1);
   ```

   The resulting number will be a random number between 1 and 10 (**Figure 11.24**).

✔ Tip

■ Be aware of when you can use decimals and when you must use integers. For example, many properties, such as the x and y of a movie clip, can take decimal values. However, the gotoAndStop() method, which moves the playhead to a specific frame on the Timeline, must use an integer. Use the Math.round() method (or, alternatively, the Math.floor() or Math.ceil() method) to convert a decimal number to an integer before using it as a parameter in the gotoAndStop() method.

```
var myResult:int = Math.round(Math.random()*9+1);
```

Figure 11.24 A random number between 1 and 10 is assigned to the variable called myResult.

Ordering Information with Arrays

When you want to store many pieces of related information as a group, you can use the Array class to help arrange them. Arrays are containers that hold data, just as variables do, except that arrays hold multiple pieces of data in a specific sequence. The position of each piece of data is called its index. Indexes are numbered sequentially, beginning at 0, so that each piece of data corresponds to an index, as in a two-column table (**Figure 11.25**). Because each piece of data is ordered numerically, you can retrieve and modify the information easily—and, most important, automatically—by referencing its index. Suppose you're building an address book of a list of your important contacts. You can store names in an Array so that index 0 holds your first contact, index 1 holds your second contact, and so on. By using a looping statement, you can check every entry in the Array automatically.

An *element* (individual item) can be accessed using the Array object's name followed by the element's index in square brackets, like this:

myArray[4]

The square brackets are known as array access operators. The previous statement accesses the data in index 4 of the array called myArray. The number of elements is known as the length of the Array; for example, the length of the Array in Figure 11.25 is 6.

It's useful to think of an Array as a set of ordered variables. You can convert the variables myScores0, myScores1, myScores2, and myScores3 to a single Array called myScores of length 4 with indexes from 0 to 3. Because you have to handle only one Array object instead of four separate variables, using Arrays makes information easier to manage.

Index	Value
0	"monitor"
1	"mouse"
2	"keyboard"
3	"CPU"
4	"modem"
5	"speakers"

Figure 11.25 An Array is like a two-column table with an Index column and a corresponding Value column.

```
var myScores:Array = new Array();
```

Figure 11.26 A new `Array` called `myScores` is instantiated.

In ActionScript, the type of data that `Arrays` hold can be mixed. You can have a `Number` in index 0, a `String` in index 1, and a `Boolean` value in index 2. You can change the data in any index in an `Array` at any time. The length of `Arrays` isn't fixed, either, so they can grow or shrink to accommodate new information as needed.

Creating an `Array` involves two steps. The first is to declare an `Array` variable and use the `Array` class's constructor function to instantiate a new `Array` instance, as in this example:

```
var myArray:Array = new Array();
```

The second step is to fill, or *populate,* your `Array` with data. One way to populate your `Array` is to assign the data to each index in separate statements, like this:

```
myArray[0] = "Adam";
myArray[1] = "Betty";
myArray[2] = "Zeke";
```

Another way to assign the data is to put the information as parameters within the constructor function:

```
var myArray:Array = new Array ("Adam",
→ "Betty", "Zeke");
```

The latter is a more compact way of populating your `Array`, but you're restricted to entering the data in sequence.

To create an Array:

1. Select the first frame of the Timeline, and open the Actions panel.

2. Declare your `Array` by entering `var`, the object's name, and then `:Array`. On the same line, enter an equals sign and then the constructor `new Array()`.

   Flash instantiates a new `Array` (**Figure 11.26**).

Continues on next page

3. On the next line, enter the name of your new Array, an index number between square brackets, and then an equals sign.

4. Enter the data you want to store in the Array at that index position.

5. Continue to assign more data to the Array (**Figure 11.27**).

```
var myScores:Array = new Array();
myScores[0] = 2;
myScores[1] = 3;
myScores[2] = 6;
myScores[3] = 4;
```

Figure 11.27 This Array contains four elements.

Two-dimensional Arrays

An Array has been compared to a two-column table in which the index is in one column and its contents are in a second column. But what if you need to keep track of information stored in more than one row in a table, as in a traditional spreadsheet? The solution is to nest an Array inside another one to create what's known as a *two-dimensional Array*. This type of Array creates two indexes for every piece of information. To keep track of a checker piece on a checkerboard, for example, you can use a two-dimensional Array to reference its rows and its columns (**Figure 11.28**).

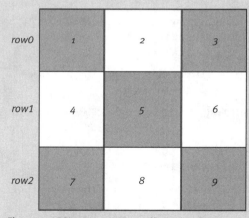

Figure 11.28 You can use a two-dimensional Array to map a checkerboard and keep track of what's inside individual squares. Each row is an Array. The rows are put inside another Array.

For the three rows, create three separate Arrays and populate them with numbers:

```
var row0:Array = new Array(1,2,3);
var row1:Array = new Array(4,5,6);
var row2:Array = new Array(7,8,9);
```

Now you can put those three Arrays inside another Array, like so:

```
var gameBoard:Array = new Array();
gameBoard[0] = row0;

gameBoard[1] = row1;

gameBoard[2] = row2;
```

To access or modify the information of a checkerboard square, first use one set of square brackets that references the row. The statement gameBoard[2] references the Array row2. Then, by using another set of square brackets, you can reference the column within that row. The statement gameBoard[2][0] accesses the number 7.

```
var myScores:Array = new Array();
myScores[0] = 2;
myScores[1] = 3;
myScores[2] = 6;
myScores[3] = 4;
```

Figure 11.29 This Array called myScores contains four elements.

Automating Array operations with loops

Because the elements of an Array are indexed numerically, they lend themselves nicely to looping actions. By using looping statements such as while, do while, and for, you can have Flash go through each index and retrieve or assign new data quickly and automatically. To average the scores of many players in an Array without a looping statement, for example, you have to total all their scores and divide by the number of players, like this:

```
mySum = myScores[0] + myScores[1] +
→ myScores[2] + ...

myAverage = mySum / myScores.length;
```

(The property length defines the number of entries in the Array.)

Using a looping statement, however, you can calculate the mySum value quickly this way:

```
for (var i:int=0; i<myScores.length;
→ i++) {
    mySum = mySum + myScores[i];
}

myAverage = mySum / myScores.length;
```

Flash starts at index 0 and adds each indexed entry in the Array to the variable mySum until it reaches the end of the Array. Then it divides the sum by the number of elements to calculate the average.

To loop through an Array:

1. Select the first keyframe of the Timeline, and open the Actions panel.

2. Declare and instantiate a new Array called myScores.

3. Populate the myScores Array with numbers representing scores (**Figure 11.29**).

4. On the next line, declare an int variable called mySum and initialize it to 0.

Continues on next page

5. On the next line, enter a `for` statement.

6. In between the parentheses of the `for` statement, enter the following:

```
var i:int = 0;
→ i<myScores.length; i++
```

Flash begins with the counter variable i set at the value 0. It increases the variable by increments of 1 until the variable reaches the length of myScores (**Figure 11.30**).

7. Between the curly braces of the `for` loop, enter mySum followed by an equals sign.

8. On the same line, enter mySum + myScores[i] (**Figure 11.31**).

Rather than using an explicit index, the value of the variable i will define the index (and, consequently, which element's value is retrieved and added to mySum).

Flash loops through the myScores's elements in turn, adding the value in each element of the Array to mySum. When the value of i reaches the value of myScores.length, Flash jumps out of the for loop and stops retrieving values. Therefore, the last element accessed is myScores[myScores.length - 1], which is the last element of the Array.

9. On a new line after the ending curly brace of the for statement, enter myAverage_txt.text = String(mySum / myScores_array.length) (**Figure 11.32**).

10. Create a dynamic text field on the Stage with the instance name myAverage_txt.

11. Test your movie.

Flash loops through the myScores Array to add the values in all the elements, and then it divides the total by the number of elements. The average is displayed in the dynamic text field on the Stage (**Figure 11.33**).

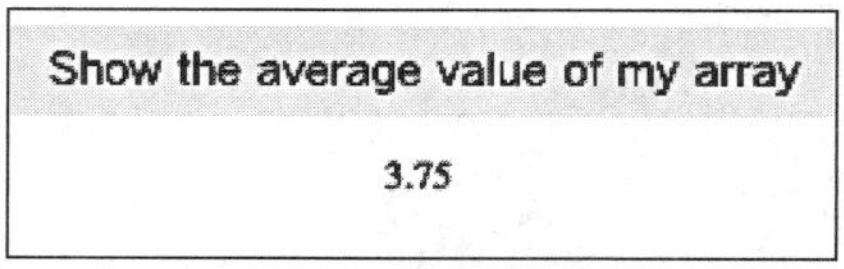

```
var myScores:Array = new Array();
myScores[0] = 2;
myScores[1] = 3;
myScores[2] = 6;
myScores[3] = 4;
var mySum:int = 0;
for (var i:int = 0; i < myScores.length; i++) {
}
```

Figure 11.30 This `for` statement loops the same number of times as there are elements in the Array myScore.

```
var myScores:Array = new Array();
myScores[0] = 2;
myScores[1] = 3;
myScores[2] = 6;
myScores[3] = 4;
var mySum:int = 0;
for (var i:int = 0; i < myScores.length; i++) {
        mySum = mySum + myScores[i];
}
```

Figure 11.31 The value of each element in the Array is added to the variable mySum.

```
var myScores:Array = new Array();
myScores[0] = 2;
myScores[1] = 3;
myScores[2] = 6;
myScores[3] = 4;
var mySum:int = 0;
for (var i:int = 0; i < myScores.length; i++) {
    mySum = mySum + myScores[i];
}
myAverage_txt.text = String(mySum / myScores.length);
```

Figure 11.32 After the `for` loop, the average value of the elements in the Array is calculated and displayed in the text field myAverage_txt.

> **Show the average value of my array**
>
> 3.75

Figure 11.33 The final result (3.75) is displayed in the dynamic text field on the Stage.

The Array class's methods

The methods of the Array class let you sort, delete, add, and manipulate the data in an Array. **Table 11.2** summarizes some methods of the Array class. It's convenient to think of the methods in pairs: shift() and unshift(), for example, both modify the beginning of an Array; push() and pop() both modify the end of an Array; and slice() and splice() both modify the middle of an Array.

Table 11.3 gives examples of how some of the methods in Table 11.2 operate.

Table 11.2

Methods of the Array Object

METHOD	DESCRIPTION
concat(array1,...,arrayN)	Concatenates the specified Array objects, and returns a new Array.
join(separator)	Concatenates the elements of the Array, inserts the String separator between the elements, and returns a String. The default separator is a comma.
pop()	Removes the last element in the Array, and returns the value of that element.
push(value)	Adds a new element value to the end of the Array, and returns the new length.
shift()	Removes the first element in the Array, and returns the value of that element.
unshift(value)	Adds a new element value to the beginning of the Array, and returns the new length.
slice(indexA, indexB)	Returns a new Array beginning with element indexA and ending with element (indexB - 1).
splice(index, count, elem1,..., elemN)	Inserts or deletes elements. Set count to 0 to insert specified values starting at index. Set count > 0 to delete the number of elements starting at and including index.
reverse()	Reverses the order of elements in the Array.
sort()	Sorts the elements of the Array. Numbers are sorted in ascending order, and strings are sorted alphabetically.
sortOn(fieldName)	Sorts an Array of objects based on the value in each element's fieldName (a String) property.
toString()	Returns a String with every element concatenated and separated by a comma.
indexOf(searchterm, startindex)	Searches the Array for the searchterm starting at the startindex and returns the first index position of the match. Returns –1 if the searchterm is not found.
lastIndexof(searchterm, startindex)	Searches the Array for the searchterm starting at the startindex and returns the last index position of the match. Returns -1 if the searchterm is not found.

✔ Tips

■ It's important to note which methods of the Array class modify the original Array and which ones return a new Array. The methods concat(), join(), slice(), and toString() return a new Array or String and don't alter the original Array. The expression var newArray:Array = originalArray.concat(8), for example, puts 8 at the end of originalArray and assigns the resulting Array to newArray. originalArray isn't affected. Also note that some methods modify the Array as well as return a specific value. These two things aren't the same. The statement myArray.pop(), for example, modifies myArray by removing the last element and also returns the value of that last element. At the end of this example, the value of myResult is 8, and the value of myArray is 2, 4, 6:

```
var myArray:Array=new Array
→ (2, 4, 6, 8);

myResult = myArray.pop();
```

■ An easy way to remember the duties of some of these methods is to think of the elements of your Array as being components of a stack. (In fact, *stack* is a programming term for a type of array where the last element added is the first element retrieved.) You can think of an Array object as being like a stack of books or a stack of cafeteria trays on a spring-loaded holder. The bottom of the stack is the first element in an Array. When you call the Array's push() method, imagine that you literally push a new tray on top of the stack to add a new element. When you call the pop() method, you pop, or remove, the top tray from the stack (the last element). When you shift an Array, you take out the bottom tray (the first element) so that all the other trays shift down into new positions.

Table 11.3

Examples of Array Methods	
STATEMENT	VALUE OF myArray
var myArray:Array = new Array(2, 4, 6, 8)	2, 4, 6, 8
myArray.pop()	2, 4, 6
myArray.push(1, 3)	2, 4, 6, 1, 3
myArray.shift()	4, 6, 1, 3
myArray.unshift(5, 7)	5, 7, 4, 6, 1, 3
myArray.splice(2, 0, 8, 9)	5, 7, 8, 9, 4, 6, 1, 3
myArray.splice(3, 2)	5, 7, 8, 6, 1, 3
myArray.reverse()	3, 1, 6, 8, 7, 5
myArray.sort()	1, 3, 5, 6, 7, 8

Keeping Track of Objects with Arrays

Sometimes, you have to deal with multiple objects on the Stage at the same time. Keeping track of them all and performing actions to modify, test, or evaluate each one can be a nightmare unless you use Arrays to help manage them. Imagine that you're creating a game in which the viewer has to avoid rocks falling from the sky. You can use the hitTestObject() method to see whether each falling-rock object intersects with the viewer. But if there are 10 rocks on the Stage, that potentially means 10 separate hitTestObject() statements. How do you manage these multiple operations? The answer is to put them in an Array. Doing so allows you to perform the hitTestObject() in a loop on the elements in the Array instead of in many separate statements.

Put an object into an Array just as you put any other data into the Array, using an assignment statement:

```
rockArray[0]=fallingRock0_mc;

rockArray[1]=fallingRock1_mc;

rockArray[2]=fallingRock2_mc;
```

These statements put the movie clip fallingRock0_mc in element 0 of the Array rockArray, the movie clip fallingRock1_mc in element 1, and the movie clip fallingRock2_mc in element 2. Now you can reference the movie clips through the Array. This statement changes the rotation of the movie clip called fallingRock2_mc:

```
rockArray[2].rotation = 45;
```

You can even call methods this way:

```
rockArray[2].hitTestPoint(mouseX,
→ mouseY, true);
```

This statement checks to see whether the fallingRock2_mc movie clip intersects with the mouse pointer.

The following tasks use looping statements to populate an Array with dynamically drawn Sprites. When the Array is full of objects, you can perform the same action, such as modifying a property or calling hitTestObject(), on all the Sprites by referencing the Array.

To populate an Array with objects:

1. In the Actions panel, instantiate a new Array object.

   In this example, the instance name is blockArray.

2. On the next line, create a for statement.

3. With your pointer between the parentheses, enter var i:int = 0; i < 15; i++ (**Figure 11.34**).

   This loop will occur 15 times, starting with i equal to 0 and ending after i equals 14.

4. Inside the curly braces of the for statement, create a new Sprite object.

   In this example, the instance name for your new Sprite object is block.

5. On the next line, still within the for statement, call the lineStyle(), beginFill(), and drawRect() methods on the graphics property of your Sprite object (**Figure 11.35**).

   Flash draws a rectangle.

```
var blockArray:Array=new Array();
for (var i:int = 0; i < 15; i++) {
}
```

Figure 11.34 A new Array called blockArray is instantiated and a for loop created. This loop uses a counter that begins at 0 and ends at 14, increasing by 1 with each loop.

```
var blockArray:Array=new Array();
for (var i:int = 0; i < 15; i++) {
    var block:Sprite = new Sprite();
    block.graphics.lineStyle(1);
    block.graphics.beginFill(0x000000);
    block.graphics.drawRect(0,0,30,30);
}
```

Figure 11.35 The Sprite called block is created and a rectangle is drawn with it.

```
var blockArray:Array=new Array();
for (var i:int = 0; i < 15; i++) {
    var block:Sprite = new Sprite();
    block.graphics.lineStyle(1);
    block.graphics.beginFill(0x000000);
    block.graphics.drawRect(0,0,30,30);
    block.x=Math.random()*400;
    block.y=Math.random()*400;
    addChild(block);
}
```

Figure 11.36 The Sprite is randomly positioned on the Stage and then added to the display list to make it visible.

```
var blockArray:Array=new Array();
for (var i:int = 0; i < 15; i++) {
    var block:Sprite = new Sprite();
    block.graphics.lineStyle(1);
    block.graphics.beginFill(0x000000);
    block.graphics.drawRect(0,0,30,30);
    block.x=Math.random()*400;
    block.y=Math.random()*400;
    addChild(block);

    block.name="block"+i;
    blockArray[i] = this.getChildByName("block"+i);
}
```

Figure 11.37 The newly created Sprite is put in the blockArray.

6. On the next line, still within the for statement, change the x and y positions of the Sprite object with a random number.

7. On the next line, still within the for statement, call the addChild() method to add the Sprite to the display list to make it visible (**Figure 11.36**).

8. On the next line, still within the for statement, enter the name of the Array object, then the variable i in square brackets, followed by an equals sign. After the equals sign enter block.. Each newly named Sprite object is put inside a different element of the Array (**Figure 11.37**).

Accessing movie clips in an Array

Now that your Array is populated with Sprites, you can reference them easily with just the Array's index value to change their properties or call their methods.

In the next task, you'll check to see whether the viewer's pointer touches any of the Sprite objects displayed randomly on the Stage. Instead of checking each Sprite with a separate hitTestPoint() method, you'll loop through the Array and check all the Sprites with only a few lines of ActionScript.

To reference objects inside an Array:

1. Continuing with the file you used in the preceding task, select the main Timeline and open the Actions panel.

2. On a new line after the for statement, create an Event.ENTER_FRAME event handler.

3. Inside the function for the Event.ENTER_FRAME event handler, create another for statement.

4. With your pointer between the parentheses of the for statement, enter var i:Number = 0; i < 15; i++ (**Figure 11.38**).

   Your second for statement will have the same number of loops as your first for statement.

5. Inside the for statement, enter the conditional statement, if.

6. For the condition, enter the name of your array followed by [i] to reference each Sprite inside the Array.

7. On the same line, call the hitTestPoint() method with the parameters mouseX, mouseY, and true (**Figure 11.39**).

```
stage.addEventListener(Event.ENTER_FRAME, checkhit);
function checkhit(myevent:Event):void {
    for (var i:int = 0; i < 15; i++) {

    }
}
```

Figure 11.38 Enter the same loop statements for the for loop that you did for the first loop that generated the Sprites.

```
stage.addEventListener(Event.ENTER_FRAME, checkhit);
function checkhit(myevent:Event):void {
    for (var i:int = 0; i < 15; i++) {
        if (blockArray[i].hitTestPoint(mouseX, mouseY, true)) {

        }
    }
}
```

Figure 11.39 Flash checks every Sprite inside blockArray to see whether the objects intersect with the mouse pointer.

8. Choose actions to perform when the mouse pointer intersects a `Sprite` object, and enter them in the curly braces of the `if` statement.

   For example, enter this expression: `blockArray[i].alpha = .3` (**Figure 11.40**).

9. Test your movie.

   When the `for` loop is performed, all the `Sprites` inside the `Array` are tested to see whether they intersect with the pointer. Because the `for` loop is within an `Event. ENTER_FRAME` event handler, this check is done continuously. If an intersection occurs, that particular movie clip turns 30 percent opaque (**Figure 11.41**).

```
stage.addEventListener(Event.ENTER_FRAME, checkhit);
function checkhit(myevent:Event):void {
    for (var i:int = 0; i < 15; i++) {
        if (blockArray[i].hitTestPoint(mouseX, mouseY, true)) {
            blockArray[i].alpha=.3;
        }
    }
}
```

Figure 11.40 If Flash detects an intersection between a `Sprite` and the pointer, that particular `Sprite`'s transparency changes.

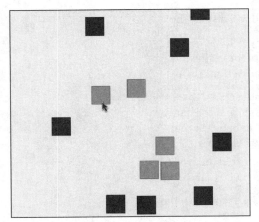

Figure 11.41 The pointer has passed over many of the `Sprites`, which have turned semitransparent. Use this technique to manage multiple objects that must be tested and controlled similarly.

Using the Date and Time

The Date class lets you retrieve the local or universal (UTC) date and time information from the clock in your viewer's computer system. Using a Date object, you can retrieve the year, month, day of the month, day of the week, hour, minute, second, and even millisecond. Use a Date object and its methods to create accurate clocks in your movie or to find information about certain days and dates in the past. You can create a Date object for your birthday, for example, by specifying the month, day, and year. Using methods of the Date class, you can retrieve the day of the week for your Date object that tells you what day you were born.

You first need to instantiate a Date object with the constructor function new Date(). Then you can call on its methods to retrieve specific time information. **Table 11.4** summarizes the common methods for retrieving the date and time information.

To create a clock:

1. Create a dynamic text field on the Stage, and give it an instance name in the Property inspector.

   The dynamic text field will display the time.

2. Select the first frame of the main Timeline, and open the Actions panel.

3. Enter var, then a name, a colon, the Timer data type, an equals sign, and the constructor new Timer(). In between the parentheses, enter 1000.

   A new Timer object is created that will trigger a TimerEvent every 1,000 milliseconds.

4. On the next line, call the start() method of your Timer (**Figure 11.42**).

   Your Timer will start to count.

Table 11.4

Methods of the Date Class

METHOD	DESCRIPTION
getFullYear()	Returns the year as a four-digit number
getMonth()	Returns the month as a number from 0 (January) to 11 (December)
getDate()	Returns the day of the month as a number from 1 to 31
getDay()	Returns the day of the week as a number from 0 (Sunday) to 6 (Saturday)
getHours()	Returns the hour of the day as a number from 0 to 23
getMinutes()	Returns the minutes as a number from 0 to 59
getSeconds()	Returns the seconds as a number from 0 to 59
getMilliseconds()	Returns the milliseconds

```
var myTimer:Timer=new Timer(1000);
myTimer.start();
```

Figure 11.42 The Timer object is instantiated and started to fire every 1,000 milliseconds.

5. On the next line, create an event handler to detect the `TimerEvent.TIMER` event.

6. Within the `TimerEvent.TIMER` event handler function, use the `var` statement to declare a `Date` object, followed by an equals sign, then the constructor `new Date()`. The `Date` object is instantiated (**Figure 11.43**). If you don't specify any parameters in the constructor, the `Date` object is populated with the current date and time information. You can also specify parameters in the constructor to create an object that references a specific date and time.

7. On a new line, call the `getHours()` method of your `Date` object and assign the result to a new `Number` variable (**Figure 11.44**). Flash retrieves the current hour and puts it in the variable `currentHour`.

8. Repeat step 7 to retrieve the current minute with the `getMinutes()` method and the current second with the `getSeconds()` method, and assign the returned values to variables (**Figure 11.45**).

9. On a new line, enter the conditional statement, `if`.

Continues on next page

```
var myTimer:Timer=new Timer(1000);
myTimer.start();

myTimer.addEventListener(TimerEvent.TIMER, showtime);
function showtime(myevent:Event) {
    var myDate:Date = new Date();
}
```

Figure 11.43 The `Date` object is instantiated.

```
var myTimer:Timer=new Timer(1000);
myTimer.start();

myTimer.addEventListener(TimerEvent.TIMER, showtime);
function showtime(myevent:Event) {
    var myDate:Date = new Date();
    var currentHour:Number = myDate.getHours();
}
```

Figure 11.44 The current hour is assigned to the variable currentHour.

```
var myTimer:Timer=new Timer(1000);
myTimer.start();

myTimer.addEventListener(TimerEvent.TIMER, showtime);
function showtime(myevent:Event) {
    var myDate:Date = new Date();
    var currentHour:Number = myDate.getHours();
    var currentMinute:Number = myDate.getMinutes();
    var currentSecond:Number = myDate.getSeconds();
}
```

Figure 11.45 The current hour, minute, and second are retrieved from the computer's clock and assigned to different variables.

USING THE DATE AND TIME

10. For the condition, enter `currentHour > 12`.

11. On the next line inside the `if` statement, enter `currentHour = currentHour – 12` (**Figure 11.46**).

12. Place your pointer after the closing curly brace for the `if` statement, and enter the statement `else if`.

13. For the condition of the `else if` statement, enter `currentHour == 0`.

14. Inside the `else if` block, enter `currentHour = 12` (**Figure 11.47**).

15. On a new line after the closing curly brace of your `else if` statement, enter the name of your text field, followed by a period, the `text` property, and an equals sign.

```
var myTimer:Timer=new Timer(1000);
myTimer.start();

myTimer.addEventListener(TimerEvent.TIMER, showtime);
function showtime(myevent:Event) {
    var myDate:Date = new Date();
    var currentHour:Number = myDate.getHours();
    var currentMinute:Number = myDate.getMinutes();
    var currentSecond:Number = myDate.getSeconds();
    if (currentHour > 12) {
        currentHour = currentHour - 12;
    }
}
```

Figure 11.46 The returned value for the method `getHours()` is a number from 0 to 23. To convert the hour to the standard 12-hour cycle, subtract 12 for hours greater than 12.

```
var myTimer:Timer=new Timer(1000);
myTimer.start();

myTimer.addEventListener(TimerEvent.TIMER, showtime);
function showtime(myevent:Event) {
    var myDate:Date = new Date();
    var currentHour:Number = myDate.getHours();
    var currentMinute:Number = myDate.getMinutes();
    var currentSecond:Number = myDate.getSeconds();
    if (currentHour > 12) {
        currentHour = currentHour - 12;
    } else if (currentHour == 0) {
        currentHour = 12;
    }
}
```

Figure 11.47 Because there is no 0 on a clock, have Flash assign 12 to any hour that has the value 0.

16. After the equals sign, create an expression that concatenates the variable names for the hour, the minute, and the second with appropriate spacers between them (**Figure 11.48**).

17. Test your movie.

The `Timer` object dispatches a `TimerEvent.TIMER` event every second, and the event handler detects each time it happens. As a response, the current hour, minute, and second in the 12-hour format are displayed in a dynamic text field.

✔ Tip

■ Note that minutes and seconds that are less than 10 display as single digits, such as 1 and 2, rather than as 01 and 02. Refine your clock by adding conditional statements to check the value of the current minutes and seconds and add the appropriate 0 digit.

```
var myTimer:Timer=new Timer(1000);
myTimer.start();

myTimer.addEventListener(TimerEvent.TIMER, showtime);
function showtime(myevent:Event) {
    var myDate:Date = new Date();
    var currentHour:Number = myDate.getHours();
    var currentMinute:Number = myDate.getMinutes();
    var currentSecond:Number = myDate.getSeconds();
    if (currentHour > 12) {
        currentHour = currentHour - 12;
    } else if (currentHour == 0) {
        currentHour = 12;
    }
    myDisplay_txt.text = "The time is now: \n" + currentHour + ":" + currentMinute + ":" + currentSecond;
}
```

The time is now:
9:36:43 ———— myDisplay_txt dynamic text field

Figure 11.48 The dynamic text field displays the concatenated values for the hour, minute, and second.

Date numbers and names

The values returned by the getMonth()
and getDay() methods of a Date object are
numbers instead of string data types. The
getMonth() method returns values from 0
to 11 (0 = January), and the getDay() method
returns values from 0 to 6 (0 = Sunday). To
correlate these numeric values with the names
of the months or days of the week, you need
to create Arrays that contain this information.
You can create an Array that contains the
days of the week with the following statements:

```
var dayNames:Array = new Array();

dayNames[0] = "Sunday";

dayNames[1] = "Monday";

dayNames[2] = "Tuesday";

dayNames[3] = "Wednesday";

dayNames[4] = "Thursday";

dayNames[5] = "Friday";

dayNames[6] = "Saturday";
```

To create a calendar:

1. Create a dynamic text field on the Stage,
   and give it an instance name in the
   Property inspector.
   The dynamic text field will display the date.

2. Select the first keyframe of the Timeline,
   and open the Actions panel.

3. Declare an Array object that will hold the
   days of the week followed by an equals sign.

4. Enter the constructor function new Array().

5. In a series of statements, assign Strings
   representing the names of the days of
   the week as elements of your Array
   (**Figure 11.49**).

6. On a new line, declare a second new Array
   followed by an equals sign.

7. Enter the constructor function new Array().
   This Array will hold the months of the year.

8. In a series of statements, assign Strings
   representing the names of the months of
   the year to the elements of this Array
   (**Figure 11.50**).

```
var monthNames:Array = new Array();
monthNames[0] = "January";
monthNames[1] = "February";
monthNames[2] = "March";
monthNames[3] = "April";
monthNames[4] = "May";
monthNames[5] = "June";
monthNames[6] = "July";
monthNames[7] = "August";
monthNames[8] = "September";
monthNames[9] = "October";
monthNames[10] = "November";
monthNames[11] = "December";
```

Figure 11.50 The Array monthNames contains
Strings of all the months.

```
var dayNames:Array = new Array();
dayNames[0] = "Sunday";
dayNames[1] = "Monday";
dayNames[2] = "Tuesday";
dayNames[3] = "Wednesday";
dayNames[4] = "Thursday";
dayNames[5] = "Friday";
dayNames[6] = "Saturday";
```

Figure 11.49 The Array dayNames contains
Strings of all the days of the week.

9. On a new line, declare a new `Date` object followed by an equals sign.

10. Enter the constructor function `new Date()` without any parameters.

11. In a series of statements, call the `getFullYear()`, `getMonth()`, `getDate()`, and `getDay()` methods, and assign their values to new `Number` variables (**Figure 11.51**).

12. Enter the name of your dynamic text field, followed by a period, the `text` property, and an equals sign.

13. Enter the name of the `Array` that contains the days of the week. As its index, put in the variable containing the value returned by the `getDay()` method.

    The value of this variable is a number from 0 to 6. This number is used to retrieve the correct string in the `Array` corresponding to the current day.

14. Concatenate the `Array` that contains the days of the month, and as its index put the variable containing the value returned by the `getMonth()` method call.

15. Concatenate the other variables that hold the current date and year (**Figure 11.52**).

16. Test your movie.

    Flash gets the day, month, date, and year from the system clock. The names of the specific day and month are retrieved from the `Array` objects, and the information is displayed in the dynamic text field.

```
var myDate:Date = new Date();
var currentYear:Number = myDate.getFullYear();
var currentMonth:Number = myDate.getMonth();
var currentDate:Number = myDate.getDate();
var currentDay:Number = myDate.getDay();
```

Figure 11.51 The current year, month, date, and day are retrieved from the computer's clock and assigned to new variables.

```
myDisplay_txt.text = "Today is \n" + dayNames[currentDay] + ", " +
monthNames[currentMonth] + " " + currentDate + ", " + currentYear;
```

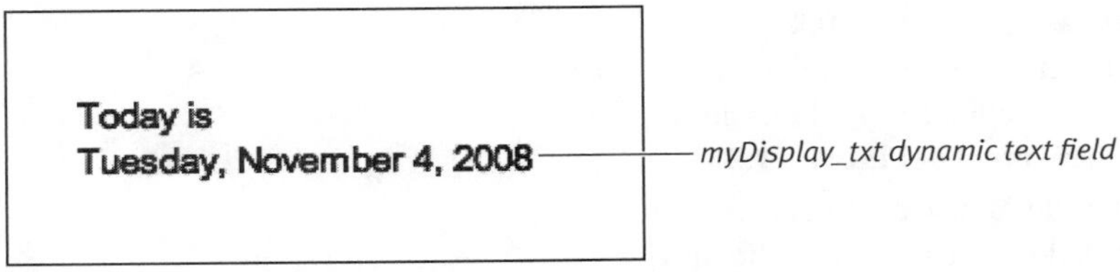

**Today is
Tuesday, November 4, 2008** ———— *myDisplay_txt dynamic text field*

Figure 11.52 The day, month, date, and year information is concatenated and displayed in the `myDisplay_txt` text field.

Tracking elapsed time

Another way to provide time information to your viewer is to use the Flash function getTimer(). This function returns the number of milliseconds that have elapsed since the Flash movie started playing. You can compare the returned value of getTimer() at one instant with the returned value of it at another instant, and the difference gives you the elapsed time between those two instants. Use the elapsed time to create timers for games and activities in your Flash movie. You can time how long it takes for your viewer to answer questions correctly in a test or give your viewer only a certain amount of time to complete the test. Or, award more points in a game if the player successfully completes a mission within an allotted time.

Because getTimer() is a built-in function and not a method of an object, you call it by using the function name.

To create a timer:

1. Create a dynamic text field on the Stage, and give it an instance name in the Property inspector.

2. Select the first frame of the main Timeline, and open the Actions panel.

3. Declare a Number variable named startTime, and assign it an initial value of 0.

4. Create an event handler to detect the MouseEvent.CLICK event.

5. Within the MouseEvent.CLICK event handler function, enter startTime, followed by an equals sign, then the function getTimer() (**Figure 11.53**). Whenever the mouse button is pressed, the time that has passed since the movie started playing is assigned to the variable startTime.

```
var startTime:Number= 0;
stage.addEventListener(MouseEvent.CLICK, reset);
function reset(myevent:MouseEvent):void {
    startTime = getTimer();
}
```

Figure 11.53 When the viewer clicks the mouse button, the getTimer() function retrieves the time elapsed since the start of the Flash movie. That time is put in the variable startTime.

6. On a new line, enter another event handler to detect the `Event.ENTER_FRAME` event.

7. Within the `Event.ENTER_FRAME` event handler function, declare a `Number` variable named `currentTime`, followed by an equals sign, and then the function `getTimer()` (**Figure 11.54**).

   Flash continuously retrieves the time that has passed since the movie started and puts that information in the variable called `currentTime`.

8. On the next line still within the function, declare a `Number` variable named `elapsedTime` followed by an equals sign.

9. Enter `(currentTime - startTime) / 1000`.

   Flash calculates the difference between the current timer and the timer at the instant the mouse was clicked. The result is divided by 1,000 to convert it to seconds (**Figure 11.55**).

   Continues on next page

```
stage.addEventListener(Event.ENTER_FRAME, showTime);
function showTime(myevent:Event):void {
    var currentTime:Number = getTimer();
}
```

Figure 11.54 On an ongoing basis, the `getTimer()` function retrieves the time elapsed since the start of the Flash movie. That time is put in the variable `currentTime`.

```
stage.addEventListener(Event.ENTER_FRAME, showTime);
function showTime(myevent:Event):void {
    var currentTime:Number = getTimer();
    var elapsedTime:Number = (currentTime - startTime) / 1000;
}
```

Figure 11.55 The variable `elapsedTime` is assigned the difference between the two instances of time recorded in the variables `startTime` and `currentTime`.

USING THE DATE AND TIME

475

10. On a new line, convert the value of elapsedTime to a string and assign the result to the text property of your dynamic text field (**Figure 11.56**).

11. Test your movie.

Flash displays the time elapsed since the last instant the viewer pressed the mouse button.

✔ Tip

■ Experiment with different event handlers to build a stopwatch with Start, Stop, and Lap buttons.

```
var startTime:Number= 0;
stage.addEventListener(MouseEvent.CLICK, reset);
function reset(myevent:MouseEvent):void {
    startTime = getTimer();
}

stage.addEventListener(Event.ENTER_FRAME, showTime);
function showTime(myevent:Event):void {
    var currentTime:Number = getTimer();
    var elapsedTime:Number = (currentTime - startTime) / 1000;
    myDisplay_txt.text = String(elapsedTime);
}
```

Figure 11.56 The value of elapsedTime is converted into a string and then displayed in the text field myDisplay_txt.

Managing Content and Troubleshooting

12

As the complexity of your Flash movie increases with the addition of bitmaps, videos, sounds, and animations, as well as the ActionScript that integrates them, you need to keep close track of all the elements so you can make necessary revisions and bug fixes. After all, the most elaborate Flash movie is useless if you can't pinpoint the one variable that's keeping the whole thing from working. Fortunately, Flash provides several tools for troubleshooting and managing Library symbols and code.

This chapter shows you how to create shared Library symbols that supply common elements to a team of Flash developers working on a project. This chapter delves into the Movie Explorer, the Find and Replace, and the Output panels, which offer information about the organization and status of your movie. The Movie Explorer and the Find and Replace panels provide an overview of all the elements of your movie and can quickly track the objects that interest you. The Output panel can output values and custom messages while your movie plays, helping you isolate troublesome variables or behaviors of your objects.

Finally, you'll learn some strategies for making your Flash movie leaner and faster—optimizing graphics and code, organizing your work environment, and avoiding some common mistakes—guidelines to help you become a better Flash author and developer.

Sharing Library Symbols

Flash makes it possible for teams of animators and developers to share common Library symbols for a complex project. Each animator might be working on a separate movie that uses the same symbol—the main character in an animated comic book, for example. An identical symbol of this main character needs to reside in the Library of each movie; if the art director decides to change this character's face, a new symbol has to be copied to all the Libraries—that is, unless you create a shared Library symbol. There are two kinds of shared symbols: runtime shared symbols and authortime shared symbols.

Runtime sharing of symbols

In runtime sharing, one movie provides a symbol for multiple movies to use during runtime. This simplifies the editing process and ensures consistency throughout a Flash project (**Figure 12.1**).

Your viewers also benefit from the shared symbols because they have to download them only once. For example, a main character would be downloaded just once, for the first movie, and all subsequent movies will use that character.

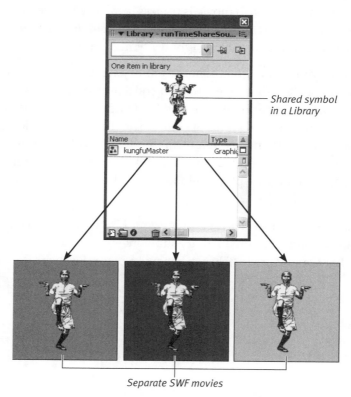

Shared symbol in a Library

Separate SWF movies

Figure 12.1 A runtime shared symbol in the Library in one SWF (top) can be used by multiple SWF files.

To create a runtime shared Library symbol, mark the symbol for "Export for runtime sharing" in the Advanced section of the Symbol Properties dialog box and give the symbol a class name so you can call on it. When you export the SWF file, the symbol will be available to other SWF movies.

Figure 12.2 Choose Properties from the Library panel's Options menu.

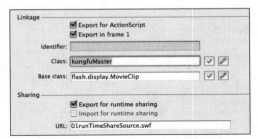

Figure 12.3 To mark a symbol as a shared symbol, select it for export in the Sharing section, and give a URL where it can be found. In the Linkage section, give it a name in the Class field. This shared symbol is located in the same folder as the movies that will share it. The shared symbol extends the properties and methods of the MovieClip class.

Once you create a movie that shares a Library symbol, you can create other movies that use it. You do this by opening a new Flash document and creating a symbol. In the Advanced section of the Symbol Properties dialog box, mark the symbol to "Import for runtime sharing" and enter the name and location of the source symbol as it appears in the Class field of its own Symbol Properties dialog box. At runtime, your new movie finds, imports, and uses the source symbol.

To create a runtime shared symbol:

1. In a new Flash document, create or import a symbol you want to share.

   The symbol can be a button, movie clip, font symbol, sound, or bitmap.

2. In the Library panel, select your symbol. From the Library panel's Options menu, choose Properties (**Figure 12.2**).

   The Symbol Properties dialog box appears.

3. Click the Advanced button.

   The Symbol Properties dialog box expands, showing the Linkage and Sharing sections.

4. In the Sharing section, select the "Export for runtime sharing" option. In the URL field, enter the relative or absolute path to where the SWF file will be posted. In the Class field, enter a unique name for your symbol. Leave the Base class field as is. Keep the "Export in frame 1" check box selected. Click OK (**Figure 12.3**).

   Your selected symbol is now marked for export and available to be shared by other movies.

5. Export your Flash movie as a SWF file with the name and in the location you specified in the URL field of the Symbol Properties dialog box.

   This is your source movie that shares its symbol.

SHARING LIBRARY SYMBOLS

To use a runtime shared symbol:

1. Open a new Flash document, and create a new symbol of the kind that the source document is sharing.

   For example, if your source document is sharing a bitmap symbol, in the destination document import another bitmap symbol. The contents of your destination symbol will be replaced by the shared symbol from the source document at runtime. The symbol in your destination movie is simply a placeholder.

2. In the Library panel, select your symbol. From the Options menu, choose Properties.

   The Symbol Properties dialog box appears.

3. If the Symbol Properties dialog box is not already expanded, click the Advanced button.

   The Symbol Properties dialog box expands, showing the Linkage and Sharing sections.

4. From the Sharing section, select the "Import for runtime sharing" option. In the URL field, enter the path to the source movie. In the Class field, enter the name for the shared symbol in the source movie (as it appears in the Class field of its own Symbol Properties dialog box). Click OK (**Figure 12.4**).

   Your selected symbol is now marked to find the shared symbol in the source movie and import it.

   or

1. Open a new Flash document, and choose File > Import > Open External Library (**Figure 12.5**). Choose the Flash file that contains the shared Library symbol.

   The Library of the Flash file that contains the shared Library symbol appears.

2. Drag the shared Library symbol into your new document's Library.

   The shared symbol appears in your destination document's Library. The symbol will automatically be marked to be imported for runtime sharing with the correct Class name and URL.

   After completing either steps 1–4 or 1–2 above, proceed with step 3.

3. In your destination movie, drag an instance of the symbol onto the Stage, and use it in your movie.

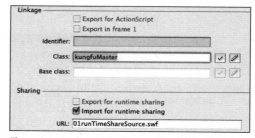

Figure 12.4 In the Symbol Properties dialog box, select the "Import for runtime sharing" check box, and enter the same Class name and location of the shared symbol you want to use.

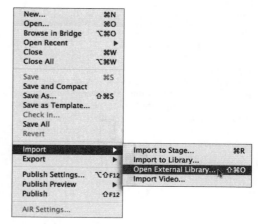

Figure 12.5 Choose File > Import > Open External Library to open the Library of the source movie that shares its symbol.

4. Export your Flash movie as a SWF file, and place it in a location where it can find the source movie.

   When you play the SWF file, it imports the shared symbol from the source movie. The shared symbol appears on the Stage (**Figure 12.6**).

   When you make changes and revisions to the shared symbol in the source movie, all the destination movies that use the shared symbol are automatically updated to reflect the change.

Continues on next page

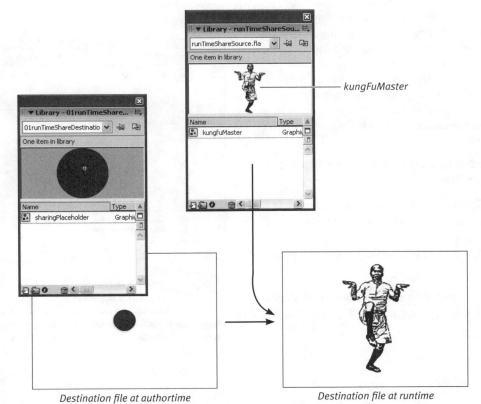

kungFuMaster

Destination file at authortime

Destination file at runtime

Figure 12.6 The destination SWF imports the shared symbol from the source SWF. The URL fields in Figures 12.3 and 12.4 specify where the source SWF is located relative to the destination SWF. The black circle symbol in the destination movie (left) imports the kungFuMaster shared symbol from the source SWF at runtime. As a result, the shared symbol appears in the destination SWF file (right).

SHARING LIBRARY SYMBOLS

✔ Tip

- If you have many symbols in the source movie that you want to share, choose Shared Library Properties from the Library Options menu (**Figure 12.7**). Enter the URL of the source movie's location to set the URL for all the shared symbols in the Library.

Authortime sharing of symbols

When you want to share symbols among FLA files instead of SWF files, turn to authortime sharing. Authortime sharing lets you choose a source symbol in a particular FLA file so that another FLA file can reference it and keep its symbol up to date. You have to worry about modifying only one FLA file containing the source symbol instead of multiple FLA files that contain the same symbol. Each movie stores its own copy of the common symbol. You can update the symbol to the source symbol whenever you want, or even make automatic updates before you publish a SWF file.

To update a symbol from a different Flash file:

1. Select the symbol you want to update in the Library panel. From the Options menu, choose Properties.

   The Symbol Properties dialog box appears.

2. Click Advanced.

   The Symbol Properties dialog box expands to display more options (**Figure 12.8**).

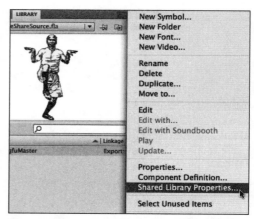

Figure 12.7 Choose Shared Library Properties from the Library Options menu to set the URL path of the shared symbols.

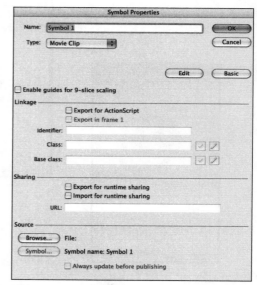

Figure 12.8 The Advanced button expands the Symbol Properties dialog box and displays more options.

Figure 12.9 Select the source symbol for authortime sharing.

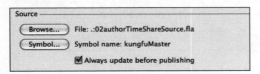

Figure 12.10 The Source section of the Symbol Properties dialog box displays the path to the authortime source symbol and the name of the source symbol.

3. In the Source section of the dialog box, click Browse. Select the Flash file that contains the symbol you want to use to update your currently selected symbol. Click OK (Windows) or Open (Mac).

   The Select Source Symbol dialog box appears, showing a list of all the symbols in the selected Flash file's Library.

4. Select a symbol, and click OK (**Figure 12.9**).

   The Select Source Symbol dialog box closes.

5. In the Symbol Properties dialog box that is still open, note the new source for your symbol (**Figure 12.10**). Click OK.

   The Symbol Properties dialog box closes, and your symbol is updated with the symbol you just chose for its new source. Your symbol retains its name, but its content is updated to the source symbol.

To make automatic updates to a symbol:

◆ In the Symbol Properties dialog box, select the "Always update before publishing" check box.

   Whenever you export a SWF file from your Flash file, whether by publishing it or by using the Test Movie command (Control > Test Movie), Flash will locate the source symbol and update your symbol.

Runtime Sharing or Authortime Sharing?

Although they may seem similar, runtime and authortime sharing are two very different ways to work with symbols. Each approach is better suited for different types of projects and workflows. Runtime sharing is useful when multiple SWF movies can share common assets, thus decreasing symbol redundancy, file size, and download times. You publish a single SWF file holding all the common symbols that multiple SWF files can access. Authortime sharing, on the other hand, is useful for organizing your workflow *before* you publish your SWF movie. You can use authortime sharing to keep different symbols in separate FLA files. A master FLA file can reference all the symbols in the separate files and compile them into a single SWF. Working this way, you can have different members of a Flash development team work on different symbols and rely on authortime sharing to ensure that the final published movie will contain the updated symbols. Compare these two ways of sharing Library symbols in **Figure 12.11**.

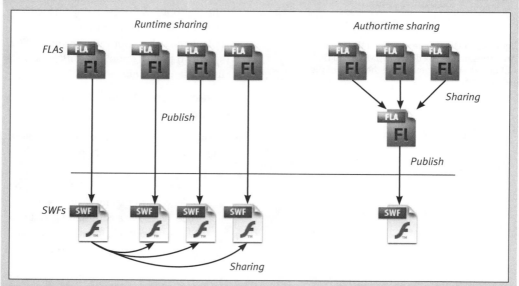

Figure 12.11 During runtime sharing (left), multiple SWF files can share symbols from a single common SWF file after publication. During authortime sharing (right), multiple FLA files can provide updated symbols to a single FLA file before publication. The single FLA file publishes a SWF file to play during runtime.

SHARING LIBRARY SYMBOLS

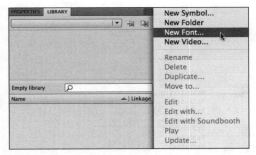

Figure 12.12 Choose New Font from the Library panel's Options menu.

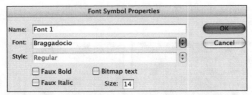

Figure 12.13 Create a font symbol by choosing a font and giving it a name in the Font Symbol Properties dialog box.

Sharing Fonts

Just as you can create symbols to share between movies, you can create font symbols and share them. After creating a font symbol, you identify it to be exported using the Class identifier in the Symbol Properties dialog box, a process similar to the one used to create runtime shared symbols. You use shared fonts to reduce the need to embed the same font outline for multiple movies. When multiple movies share a common font, the font has to be downloaded only once for the first movie, thus reducing file size and download times for the subsequent movies.

To create a font symbol to share:

1. Open the Library panel. From its Options menu, choose New Font (**Figure 12.12**). The Font Symbol Properties dialog box appears.

2. Enter a name for your new font symbol in the Name field. From the Font pull-down menu, select the font you want to include in your Library as a font symbol. Select the optional check boxes for Style (**Figure 12.13**).

Continues on next page

3. Click the Advanced button.

The Font Symbol Properties dialog box expands.

4. From the Linkage section, select the "Export for runtime sharing" option. In the URL field, enter the path where this SWF file will be placed. In the Class field, enter a unique name for your symbol. Leave the Base class as is. Click OK (**Figure 12.14**).

Your selected font symbol is now marked for export and available to be shared by other movies.

5. Export your Flash movie as a SWF file with the name and in the location you specified in the URL field of the Linkage section of the Font Symbol Properties dialog box.

Your selected font symbol resides in the SWF file. This SWF file provides the shared font to other movies.

To use a shared font symbol:

1. Open a new Flash file (the destination file) where you want to use a shared font symbol.

2. Open the Library of the source file that contains your shared font symbol by choosing File > Import > Open External Library. Drag the shared font symbol from its Library to the Library of the destination Flash file.

The font symbol appears in the Library of the destination Flash file. The font symbol is automatically marked as "Import for runtime sharing" (**Figure 12.15**).

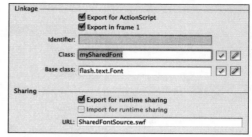

Figure 12.14 In the Linkage section, export your symbol font for runtime sharing, specify the location where this source SWF will be placed, and give it a Class name. If the destination and source file will reside in the same directory, enter the name of the source file in the URL field, as shown here.

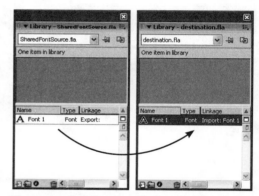

Figure 12.15 Drag the shared font symbol from the source Library (left) to the destination Library (right).

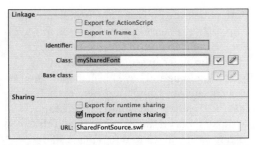

Figure 12.16 The Linkage section for the font symbol in the destination file. This font symbol will import the font called mySharedFont from the file SharedFontSource.swf.

Figure 12.17 Shared fonts are available in the Property inspector and are distinguished by an asterisk after their names.

3. In the destination Flash file, select the font symbol in the Library panel. From the Options menu, choose Properties.

The Font Symbol Properties dialog box appears.

4. Confirm that "Import for runtime sharing" is selected, that the Class field contains the name of the shared font symbol in the source movie, and that the URL field contains the path to the source movie (**Figure 12.16**). Click OK.

Your font symbol in the destination movie is now set to share the font symbol in the source movie.

5. Select the Text tool in the Tools panel. In the Property inspector, choose the shared font symbol from the pull-down list of available fonts (**Figure 12.17**).

Create input text or dynamic text, and be sure to embed all the font outlines in the Character Options.

6. Publish the destination SWF file and the source SWF file.

The source SWF shares its font with the destination SWF. The destination SWF displays the shared font correctly and with anti-aliasing, but its file size remains small (**Figure 12.18**).

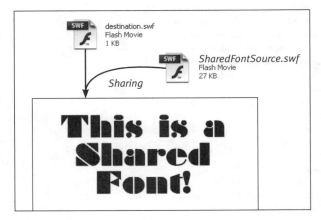

Figure 12.18 The destination SWF file displays the shared font correctly because the font is supplied by the source SWF file. Notice the difference in file size between destination.swf (1 KB) and SharedFontSource.swf (27 KB).

Tracking, Finding, and Managing Flash Elements

To manage the myriad Flash elements in your movie—symbols, text, bitmaps, ActionScript code, and so on—you can turn to the Movie Explorer panel or the Find and Replace panel. The Movie Explorer panel (Alt-F3 for Windows, Option-F3 for Mac) gives you a bird's-eye view of your Flash movie and presents its various elements in a hierarchical display. From the hierarchical display, you can quickly go to individual elements to edit them. The Movie Explorer even updates itself in real time, so as you're authoring a Flash movie, the panel displays the latest modifications. The Find and Replace panel (Ctrl-F for Windows, Cmd-F for Mac), on the other hand, lets you search your entire Flash movie for different elements, edit individual search results, and even replace multiple elements at once.

Both panels are powerful and useful tools to help you make sense of complex Flash movies. For example, to find all the instances of a movie clip, you can search for them in the Movie Explorer and have Flash display the exact scene, layer, and frame where each instance resides. You can then quickly go to those spots on the Timeline to edit the instances. If you wanted to replace all the text in your movie with a different font, you can use the Find and Replace panel to find all text of a certain font and replace that font with a new font.

The Movie Explorer panel

Use the Movie Explorer panel to provide a visual display of all your Flash elements on the Stage and on the Timeline (**Figure 12.19**).

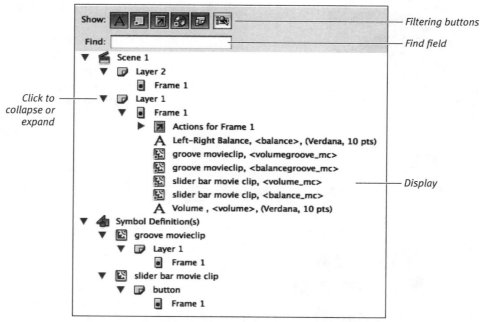

Figure 12.19 A typical display in the Movie Explorer shows various elements of the movie in an expandable hierarchy.

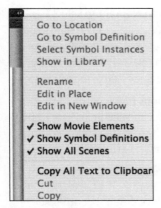

Figure 12.20 The Options menu of the Movie Explorer panel.

To display different categories of elements:

◆ From the Options menu at the right of the Movie Explorer panel, select one or more of the following (**Figure 12.20**):

Show Movie Elements displays all the elements in your movie and organizes them by scene. Only the current scene is displayed.

Show Symbol Definitions displays all the elements associated with symbol instances that are on the Stage.

Show All Scenes displays all the elements in your movie in all scenes.

To filter the categories of elements that are displayed:

◆ From the row of filtering buttons at the top of the panel, select one or more to add categories of elements to display (**Figure 12.21**):

Show Text displays the actual string in a text selection, the font name and font size, and the instance name and variable name for input and dynamic text.

Continues on next page

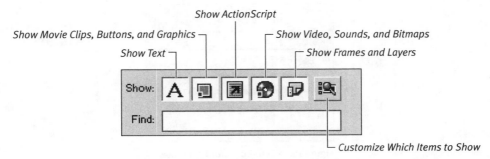

Figure 12.21 The filtering buttons let you selectively display elements.

Show Movie Clips, Buttons, and Graphics displays the symbol names of buttons, movie clips, and graphics on the Stage, as well as the instance names of movie clips and buttons.

Show ActionScript displays the ActionScript code assigned to frames (and to buttons or movie clips, if authoring in ActionScript 2.0 or earlier).

Show Video, Sounds, and Bitmaps displays the symbol names of imported video, sounds, and bitmaps on the Stage.

Show Frames and Layers displays the names of layers, keyframes, and frame labels in the movie.

Customize Which Items to Show displays a dialog box from which you can choose individual elements to display.

To find and edit elements in the display:

1. In the Find field at the top of the Movie Explorer panel, enter the name of the element you want to find (**Figure 12.22**).

All the elements of the movie that contain that name appear in the display list automatically as you type in the field.

2. Click the desired element to select it.

The element is also selected on the Timeline and on the Stage. If a scene or keyframe is selected, Flash takes you to that scene or keyframe.

3. From the Options menu of the Movie Explorer panel, choose Edit in Place or Edit in New Window to go to symbol editing mode for a selected symbol.

or

Choose Rename from the Options menu.

The name of the element becomes selectable so that you can edit it.

or

Double-click the desired element to modify it. Flash makes the element editable or opens an appropriate window, depending on what type of element it is:

Double-clicking a symbol (except for sound, video, and bitmaps) opens symbol editing mode.

Double-clicking ActionScript opens the script in the Actions panel.

Double-clicking a scene or layer lets you rename it.

Double-clicking a text selection lets you edit its contents.

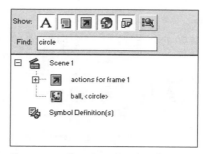

Figure 12.22 Entering a word or phrase in the Find field displays all occurrences of that word or phrase in the Display window. Here, the instance named circle of the movie clip symbol ball has been found.

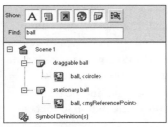

Figure 12.23 Entering the symbol name ball in the Find field displays all the instances of the ball symbol. There are two instances listed: one called circle in the draggable ball layer and another called myReferencePoint in the stationary ball layer.

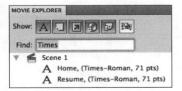

Figure 12.24 All the occurrences of the Times font appear in the Display window.

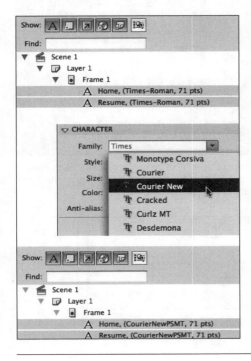

To find all instances of a symbol:

◆ In the Find field of the Movie Explorer panel, enter the name of the symbol whose instances you want to find.

All instances of that symbol appear in the display (**Figure 12.23**).

To replace all occurrences of a particular font:

1. In the Find field of the Movie Explorer panel, enter the name of the font you want to replace.

   All occurrences of that font appear in the display (**Figure 12.24**).

2. Select all the text elements, using Shift-click to make multiple selections.

3. In the Property inspector, choose a different font and style for all text elements.

   All the selected text elements change according to your choices in the Property inspector (**Figure 12.25**).

Figure 12.25 With the Times text elements selected, choose a different font, such as Courier New (top) from the Property inspector. Flash changes those text elements from Times to Courier New (bottom).

TRACKING, FINDING, MANAGING FLASH ELEMENTS

The Find and Replace panel

Use the Find and Replace panel Edit > Find and Replace, Cmd-F for Mac, Ctrl-F for Windows) to search your whole Flash movie for various elements (text string, a font, a color, a symbol, a sound file, a video file, or an imported bitmap) and replace them with another. You can find and replace individual search results or replace all of them at once. The Find and Replace panel is particularly powerful with its text searching capabilities and options.

To find and replace text:

1. In the For pull-down menu, select Text.

2. In the Text box, enter the text that you want to find.

3. In the Replace with Text box, enter the replacement text.

4. Select the options for text searching (**Figure 12.26**):

   Whole Word searches for the entire word only and won't return results if the text is part of a larger text string.

   Match Case searches for the text that exactly matches uppercase and lowercase characters.

   Regular Expressions searches for text that matches a pattern specified by a regular expression (see Chapter 10).

   Text Field Contents searches for the text in text fields.

Frames/Layers/Parameters searches for the text in frame labels, layer names, scene names, and component parameters.

Strings in ActionScript searches for the text in strings in ActionScript code.

ActionScript searches for the text throughout the entire ActionScript code.

5. Click Find All or Find Next.

   All occurrences of that text appear in the display at the bottom if you click Find All, or just the first occurrence if you click Find Next (**Figure 12.27**).

   Double-click the search result to immediately go to particular text to edit.

   or

   Click Replace All or Replace.

   All occurrences of that text are replaced with the replacement text if you click Replace All, or just the first occurrence if you click Find Next.

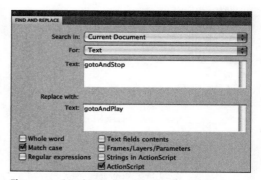

Figure 12.26 In this Find and Replace panel, the text gotoAndPlay will replace gotoAndStop in all the ActionScript code throughout the movie.

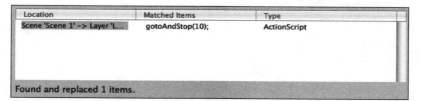

Figure 12.27 One instance of the searched text was found and replaced with the new text. The results are displayed in the bottom window.

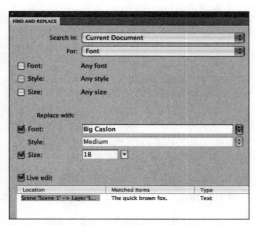

Figure 12.28 Find all text in your movie by keeping the search options to Any font, Any style, and Any size. Replace the text with a particular font by specifying the Replace with options.

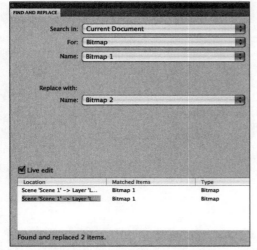

Figure 12.29 Find and replace colors, bitmaps, symbols, sounds, or videos. In this example, all the bitmaps in the movie named Bitmap 1 were replaced by the bitmap named Bitmap 2.

To find and replace fonts:

1. In the For pull-down menu, select Font.

2. In the Search options, select Font, Style, or Size to search for particular fonts or particular styles, or to search a range of font sizes. Leave all options deselected to search for all fonts in your Flash movie.

3. In the Replace options, select Font, Style, or Size to replace all the found text with a new font, a new style, or a different font size.

4. Click Replace All.

   All occurrences of the particular font, size, or style are replaced by the selected replacement font, size, or style. The results are also listed in the display at the bottom of the dialog box (**Figure 12.28**).

To find and replace a symbol, sound, video, or bitmap:

1. In the For pull-down menu, select the type of element that you want to find.

2. In the Name pull-down menu, select the name of the symbol, sound, video, or bitmap. The name should be the name in the Library.

3. In the Replace with pull-down menu, select the name of a different symbol, sound, video, or bitmap.

4. Click Replace All.

   All occurrences of the particular symbol, sound, video, or bitmap are replaced by the selected replacement. The results are also listed in the display at the bottom of the dialog box (**Figure 12.29**).

✔ Tip

■ You can only find and replace elements of the same kind. For example, you can replace one bitmap with another bitmap, but you can't replace one bitmap with a symbol.

Tracing Variables in the Output Panel

Sometimes you need to know the status of a variable or expression at a particular point during the playback of your movie. For example, imagine that you've created a game of Pong in which a movie clip of a ball bounces between two other movie clips of paddles. You want to find out, for testing purposes, the position of the paddle at the instant of a collision with the ball. To find out the value of a variable or an expression at any given moment, you use the action trace. You can place trace at any point in the movie to have Flash send a custom message to the Output panel during testing mode. The custom message is an expression you create that gives you tailored information at just the right moment. In the Pong example, you use the trace action as follows:

```
trace("x is " + myPaddle_mc.x);

trace("y is " + myPaddle_mc.y);
```

Place these two trace statements in the if statement that detects the collision. At the moment of collision, Flash sends the Output panel a message that looks something like this:

```
x is 25

y is 89
```

You can also use trace to monitor the condition of an expression so you can understand the circumstances that change its value. For example, in the following task, you'll create a simple draggable movie clip and another movie clip that remains stationary. You'll assign a trace action to display the value of the draggable movie clip's hitTestObject() method, letting you see when and where the value becomes true or false.

To display an expression in the Output panel:

1. Create a movie clip symbol, place an instance of it on the Stage, and name the instance myMovieClip_mc.

2. Create another movie clip symbol, place an instance of it on the Stage, and name the instance rock_mc.

3. Select the first frame of the main Timeline, and open the Actions panel.

4. Create an Event.ENTER_FRAME event handler on the stage.

5. Within the Event.ENTER_FRAME event handler function, enter myMovieClip_mc, followed by a period.

```
stage.addEventListener(Event.ENTER_FRAME, drag);
function drag(myevent:Event):void {
    myMovieClip_mc.startDrag(true);
}
```

Figure 12.30 The startDrag() method will make the movie clip myMovieClip_mc follow the pointer.

```
stage.addEventListener(Event.ENTER_FRAME, drag);
function drag(myevent:Event):void {
    myMovieClip_mc.startDrag(true);
    trace(myMovieClip_mc.hitTestObject(rock_mc));
}
```

Figure 12.31 The trace action evaluates the expression within its parentheses and displays the value in the Output panel.

6. On the same line, call the method startDrag(). Enter true for the method's parameter (**Figure 12.30**).

7. On the next line, enter trace().

8. Between the parentheses, enter the following expression (**Figure 12.31**):

   myMovieClip_mc.hitTestObject(rock_mc)

   Flash evaluates the hitTestObject() method to determine whether the draggable movie clip collides with the movie clip rock_mc. The returned value is displayed in the Output panel in testing mode.

9. Test your movie.

   The Output panel opens, displaying the result of the trace action (**Figure 12.32**).

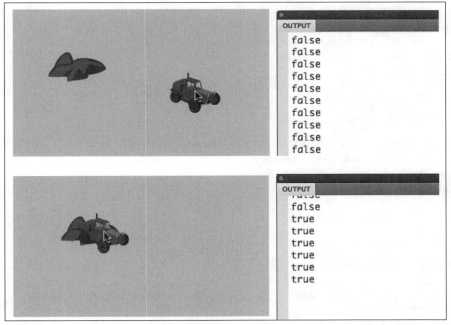

Figure 12.32 The Output panel displays false when myMovieClip_mc is clear of the rock_mc movie clip (top). It displays true when there is a collision (bottom).

TRACING VARIABLES IN THE OUTPUT PANEL

Determining a Variable's Data Type

You can use the `is` and the `as` operators in conjunction with the `trace` action to display a variable's data type. This information is useful for checking and converting data types at runtime to prevent runtime type mismatch errors. The `is` operator determines whether the variable on the left is the same data type as the object on the right, and returns either true or false. For example, the following statements return a value of false that is displayed in the Output panel:

```
var myName:String="Russell";

trace(myName is Number);
```

The `as` operator works similarly, but it returns the value of the first expression if the data types are the same. If not, it returns the value of null. For example, the following statements would display the word "Russell" in the Output window:

```
var myName:String="Russell";

trace(myName as String);
```

Using the `as` operator can help you make sure that the data type of a variable is compatible before passing its value on to other parts of your program for processing.

To check the data type of a variable:

1. Select the first frame on the Timeline, and open the Actions panel.

2. Create a new variable, specify its data type, and assign a value (**Figure 12.33**).

3. On the next line, enter the `if` statement.

4. In between the `if` statement's parentheses, enter the name of your variable, the word `is`, and then a data type that you want to check your variable against (**Figure 12.34**).

   The `is` operator checks the data type equivalence of the two objects on either side of it.

5. Between the curly braces of the `if` statement, enter any response or consequences when the variable and data type are the same.

```
var myName:String="Russell";
```

Figure 12.33 The data type of the variable called myName is a String, and its value is "Russell".

```
var myName:String="Russell";
if (myName is String){
    //verify datatype of myName
}
```

Figure 12.34 You can verify the data type of variables and expressions with the operator is.

Optimizing Your Movie

Understanding the tools you use to create graphics, animation, sound, and ActionScript is important, but it's equally important to know how best to use them to create streamlined Flash movies. After all, the best-laid designs and animations won't be appreciated if poor construction and clunky code make them too large to download or too inefficient to play easily. To streamline a Flash movie, use optimizations that keep the file size small, the animations smooth, and the revisions simple. Many factors affect the file size and performance of the final exported SWF file. Bitmaps, sounds, complicated shapes, color gradients, alpha transparencies, filters, and embedded fonts all increase the Flash file size and slow the movie's performance.

Only you can weigh the trade-offs between the quality and quantity of Flash content and the size and performance of the movie. Keep in mind the audience to whom you're delivering your Flash movies. Are you delivering content to mobile devices or to desktop computers with broadband Internet access? What is the resolution of your audience's computer screen? Knowing the answers to these questions can help you make more informed choices about what to include in your movie and how to build it.

The following strategies can help you work more efficiently and create smaller, more manageable, better-performing Flash movies.

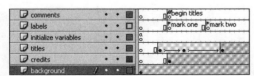

Figure 12.35 Well-organized layers like these are easy to understand and change.

Optimizing your authoring environment

◆ Use layers to separate and organize your content. For example, place all your ActionScript on one layer, all your frame labels on another layer, and all your sounds in still another layer. By using layers, you'll be able to understand and change different elements of your movie quickly (**Figure 12.35**). Having many layers doesn't increase the size of the final exported SWF file. Lock or hide individual layers to isolate just the elements you want to work on. This will prevent you from accidentally moving or deleting other objects in the way. Use comments in keyframes as well to explain the different parts of the Timeline.

◆ Organize the layers on your Timeline and the symbols in your Library with folders. Just as folders on your desktop can help you group related items, folders for layers and folders for symbols will reduce clutter and make your Flash authoring environment a more manageable workspace.

◆ Use the trace action to observe variables in your movie. The trace action let you display expressions and variables at any point during the execution of your ActionScript code.

◆ Avoid using scenes in your movie. Although scenes are a good organizational feature for simple movies, Timelines that contain scenes are more difficult to navigate. In addition, movie clip instances aren't continuous between scenes, so they are reset from one scene to another. Instead, use labels to mark different areas of the Timeline, use movie clips to hold different parts of your animation, or load external assets as they are needed.

Optimizing bitmaps and sounds for playback performance

◆ Avoid animating large bitmaps. Keep bitmaps as static background elements if they're large, or make them small for tweening.

◆ Place streaming sounds on the main Timeline instead of within a movie clip. A movie clip needs to be downloaded in its entirety before playing. A streaming sound on the root Timeline, however, begins playing as the frames download. Better yet, keep your sound as an external asset and use ActionScript to dynamically load it.

◆ Use the maximum amount of compression tolerable for bitmaps and sounds. You can adjust the JPEG quality level for your exported SWF file in Publish Settings. You can also adjust the compression settings for the stream sync and event sync sounds separately, so you can keep a higher-quality streaming sound for music and narration and a lower-quality event sound for button clicks (**Figure 12.36**).

◆ Avoid using the Trace Bitmap command to create an overly complex vector image of an imported bitmap. The complexity of a traced bitmap can make the file size larger and the performance significantly slower than if you use the bitmap itself.

◆ Import bitmaps and sounds at the exact size or length that you want to use them in Flash. Although editing within Flash is possible, you want to import just the information you need to keep the file size small. For example, don't import a bitmap and then reduce it 50 percent to use in your movie. Instead, reduce the bitmap 50 percent first and then import it into Flash.

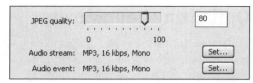

Figure 12.36 The JPEG quality and audio-compression options in the Publish Settings dialog box.

Figure 12.37 A symbol defined as separate groups (top left) contains more information (top middle) and can produce undesirable transparency effects (top right). A symbol defined as a shape (bottom left) contains less information (bottom middle) and becomes transparent as one unit (bottom right).

Optimizing graphics, text, and tweening for playback performance

◆ Use tweening wherever you can instead of frame-by-frame animation. In an animation, Flash only has to remember the keyframes, making tweening a far less memory-intensive task.

◆ Avoid creating animations that have multiple objects moving at the same time or that have large areas of change. These kinds of animations tax a computer's CPU and slow the movie's performance.

◆ If you have a large vector graphic that isn't animated (such as a background), select the "Use runtime bitmap caching" option in the Property inspector for the instance. This option instructs the Flash Player to not redraw the graphic's content every frame, reducing the playback computer's workload.

◆ Break apart groups within symbols to simplify them. Once you're satisfied with an illustration in a symbol, break the groups into shapes to flatten the illustration. Flash will have fewer curves to remember and thus will have an easier time tweening the symbol instance. Alpha effects on the instance also affect the symbol as a whole instead of the individual groups within the symbol (**Figure 12.37**).

Continues on next page

◆ Use color gradients and alpha transparencies sparingly.

◆ Avoid setting filters on High quality.

◆ Use the Property inspector to change the color, tint, and brightness of instances instead of creating separate symbols of different colors.

◆ Optimize curves by avoiding special line styles (such as dotted lines), by using the Pencil tool rather than the Brush tool, and by reducing the complexity of curves with Modify > Shape > Optimize or by pressing Ctrl-Alt-Shift-C for Windows or Cmd-Shift-Option-C for Mac (**Figure 12.38**).

◆ Use fewer font styles, and embed only the essential font outlines.

Optimizing ActionScript code

◆ Keep all your code in one place—preferably on the main Timeline—and keep code in just one layer.

◆ Use a consistent naming convention for variables, objects, and other elements that need to be identified. A consistent, simple name makes the job the variable performs more apparent.

◆ Use comments within your ActionScript to explain the code to yourself and to other developers who may look at your Flash document for future revisions.

◆ Think about *modularity*. Use smaller, separate components to build your interactivity. For example, use functions to define frequently accessed tasks and keep large or common assets outside your movie but available through shared symbols and Loader objects. You'll reduce redundancy, save memory, and make revisions easier.

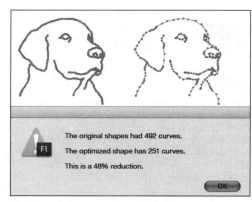

Figure 12.38 Complex curves and shapes can be simplified without losing their detail.

Avoiding Common Mistakes

When you're troubleshooting your Flash movie, there are a few obvious places you should look first to locate common mistakes. These problems usually involve simple but critical elements, such as overlooking quotation marks or a relative path term or forgetting to name an instance. Pay close attention to the following warning list to ensure that all your Flash movies are free of bugs:

◆ Be mindful of uppercase and lowercase letters. ActionScript 3.0 is case-sensitive, so make sure the names of your variables and objects exactly match. Flash keywords must also match in case. For example, `keyCode` isn't the same as `keycode`.

◆ Double-check the data types of your values. Review the Script pane to make sure quotation marks appear only around string data types. Target paths and the keyword `this` should not be within quotation marks.

◆ Double-check the target paths for your variables and objects.

◆ Remember to name your movie clip, button, and text field instances in the Property inspector. Be sure your names adhere to the naming rules explained in Chapter 3, "Getting a Handle on ActionScript."

◆ Check to see whether ActionScript statements are within the correct parentheses or curly braces in the Script pane. For example, verify that statements belonging to an `if` statement or to a function statement are contained within their curly braces. Every opening parenthesis or curly brace needs a closing parenthesis or curly brace.

Continues on next page

- Don't forget to add any dynamically generated object to the display list to make it visible. The addChild() method is commonly left out, especially for those users used to previous versions of ActionScript.

- Place a stop() action in the first keyframe of a movie clip to prevent it from playing automatically and looping.

- To test simple actions and simple buttons, choose Enable Simple Frame Actions and Enable Simple Buttons from the Control menu. For more complex button events, you must choose Test Movie from the Control menu.

- Remember that the default setting for your Flash movie in the testing mode is to loop.

For additional help and advice about debugging your movie, check out the vast Flash resources on the Web. Begin your search at Adobe's Web site, which provides a searchable archive of tech notes, documentation, tutorials, case studies, and more. You'll also find links to other Web sites with articles, FLA source files, bulletin boards, blogs, and mailing lists. Check out the companion Web site that accompanies this book at www. peachpit.com/flashcs4visualquickpro for more Flash links and resources.

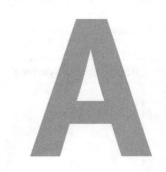

KEYBOARD KEY CODES

Letters

LETTER KEY	KEY CODE
A	65
B	66
C	67
D	68
E	69
F	70
G	71
H	72
I	73
J	74
K	75
L	76
M	77
N	78
O	79
P	80
Q	81
R	82
S	83
T	84
U	85
V	86
W	87
X	88
Y	89
Z	90

Function Keys

FUNCTION KEY	KEY CODE	KEYBOARD CLASS PROPERTY
F1	112	F1
F2	113	F2
F3	114	F3
F4	115	F4
F5	116	F5
F6	117	F6
F7	118	F7
F8	119	F8
F9	120	F9
F10	121	F10
F11	122	F11
F12	123	F12
F13	124	F13
F14	125	F14
F15	126	F15

Numbers and Symbols

KEY	KEY CODE	KEYBOARD CLASS PROPERTY
0	48	
1	49	
2	50	
3	51	
4	52	
5	53	
6	54	
7	55	
8	56	
9	57	
Numpad 0	96	NUMPAD_0
Numpad 1	97	NUMPAD_1
Numpad 2	98	NUMPAD_2
Numpad 3	99	NUMPAD_3
Numpad 4	100	NUMPAD_4
Numpad 5	101	NUMPAD_5
Numpad 6	102	NUMPAD_6
Numpad 7	103	NUMPAD_7
Numpad 8	104	NUMPAD_8
Numpad 9	105	NUMPAD_9
Numpad *	106	NUMPAD_MULTIPLY
Numpad +	107	NUMPAD_ADD
Numpad Enter	108	NUMPAD_ENTER
Numpad –	109	NUMPAD_SUBTRACT
Numpad .	110	NUMPAD_DECIMAL
Numpad /	111	NUMPAD_DIVIDE
Backspace	8	BACKSPACE
Tab	9	TAB
Clear	12	
Enter	13	ENTER
Shift	16	SHIFT
Control	17	CONTROL
Alt	18	
Caps Lock	20	CAPS_LOCK
Esc	20	ESCAPE
Spacebar	32	SPACE
Page Up	33	PAGE_UP
Page Down	34	PAGE_DOWN
End	35	END
Home	36	HOME
Left arrow	37	LEFT

Numbers and Symbols *(continued)*

KEY	KEY CODE	KEYBOARD CLASS PROPERTY
Up arrow	38	UP
Right arrow	39	RIGHT
Down arrow	40	DOWN
Insert	45	INSERT
Delete	46	DELETE
Help	47	
Num Lock	144	
;:	186	
=+	187	
-_	189	
/?	191	
`~	192	
[{	219	
|	220	
]}	221	
'"	222	

504

INDEX

S